The Morals
of Monster Stories

The Morals of Monster Stories

Essays on Children's Picture Book Messages

EDITED BY LESLIE ORMANDY

McFarland & Company, Inc., Publishers
Jefferson, North Carolina

LIBRARY OF CONGRESS CATALOGUING-IN-PUBLICATION DATA

Names: Ormandy, Leslie, editor.
Title: The morals of monster stories : essays on children's picture book messages / edited by Leslie Ormandy.
Description: Jefferson, North Carolina : McFarland & Company, Inc., Publishers, 2017 | Includes bibliographical references and index.
Identifiers: LCCN 2017031380 | ISBN 9781476664842 (softcover : acid free paper) ∞
Subjects: LCSH: Children's literature—Moral and ethical aspects. | Picture books for children—History. | Literature and morals. | Monsters in literature.
Classification: LCC PN1009.5.M67 M67 2017 | DDC 809/.89282—dc23
LC record available at https://lccn.loc.gov/2017031380

BRITISH LIBRARY CATALOGUING DATA ARE AVAILABLE

ISBN (print) 978-1-4766-6484-2
ISBN (ebook) 978-1-4766-2769-4

© 2017 Leslie Ormandy. All rights reserved

No part of this book may be reproduced or transmitted in any form or by any means, electronic or mechanical, including photocopying or recording, or by any information storage and retrieval system, without permission in writing from the publisher.

Front cover image © 2017 egal/iStock

Printed in the United States of America

McFarland & Company, Inc., Publishers
  Box 611, Jefferson, North Carolina 28640
  www.mcfarlandpub.com

Acknowledgments

This book traveled a rather circuitous path from conversations to conception to draft to the finished product you now hold in your hands. I owe thanks to a great many terrific people for steering this text to completion. My daughter, Althea Infante, has put up with my fascination with vampires for many years now—including the casket in the dining room; her tolerance is much appreciated. My sister, Sandra Ormandy, and her husband, Brian Marrone, have done nothing but encourage me as I muttered over half-framed ideas about good and evil. We have had many long drives conversing about whether the idea of evil is still necessary. My friend Simon Bellamy has challenged me to think more clearly and more cohesively, demonstrating great forbearance as the questions raised, and answers found, morphed over time. Carol Burnell has been my formatting guru for all the odd questions which fall well outside my norm as a teacher of freshman composition. Simon Bacon has taken time not only to write an excellent essay about vampires for this edited collection, but he has also shared his knowledge of the expectations and minutiae of publishing such a work. I owe thanks to many other folks, for instance the friends in my vampire book club: Rebecca Pimley, Deborah Riefstahl, Elise Cannon, Jeffrey Takehashi, and Becky Gannon. Their intelligent discussions of the books we read kept me moving forward. And of course I owe a large debt of gratitude to all of the contributors who have given generously of their own time to join the first discussion seeking to examine directly not just the morals which are lying in wait on the page, but "how" those morals are offered. Thank you all!

Table of Contents

Acknowledgments v
Preface 1
Introduction 3

Part 1: Monstrous Instructors

My Monster ABCs: What Can *A*(bominable Snowmen) to *Z*(ombies) Teach Our Kids?
    Carla Kungl   15

Green Legs and Hands: *The Lorax* as a Medievalist Morality Tale
    Corwin R. Baden   32

Monsters in the Closet: Narrative Therapy and Fairy Tales
    Lisa LeBlanc *and* Carla B. Morrissey   50

Part 2: Normalization of the "Other"

"Let the wild rumpus start!" Adventures in Acceptance and Understanding—Picture Books and the Other
    Kelly F. Franklin   64

"You can't get rid of the Babadook": The Supertextual Supernatural
    Lloyd Isaac Vayo   78

Monsters Like Us
    Gerald Raymond Gordon   93

Part 3: Fostering Heteronormativity, Agency and Racial Superiority

The Scars of Dracula: Dracula and the Undead Meaning in Children's Early Readers
    Simon Bacon   110

viii   Table of Contents

Misogyny, Monsters and Malice: Dismantling Troy Cummings'
The Notebook of Doom Series
    HOLLY A. WHEELER   126

Part 4: Evolving Monsters

Ogress, Fairy, Sorceress, Witch: Supernatural Surrogates and
the Monstrous Mother in Variants of "Rapunzel"
    MELISSA MULLINS   142

Swimming with Serpents: Dismantling Boundaries in Sea
Monsters Picture Books
    REBECCA A. BROWN   158

Part 5: Monstrous Monsters

The House That Drac Built: Faith-Based Qualms About
Halloween Picture Books
    CORWIN R. BADEN   175

Wicked "Others": Christian Conservatism and the Rejection
of the Supernatural
    BRENDA S. GARDENOUR WALTER   195

Part 6: Moral Agencies

The Fantastic in the Everyday: Growing Up with *The Mysteries
of Harris Burdick*
    MARIAELENA DIBENIGNO   209

Crossing the Threshold: Ghosts and Haunted Houses as Moral
Messengers
    BRENDA S. GARDENOUR WALTER   226

About the Contributors   241
Index   243

Preface

As a new mother I was told, as most parents are, to model the behaviors I wanted my child to replicate. Swearing, treating others badly, lying, and many other behaviors frowned upon by the moral constructs holding our society together should never be done in front of my daughter. Basically I was to teach her how to function in our culture. It made—and makes—sense. Inasmuch as I wanted my daughter to learn to enjoy books as much as I did, I modeled reading—a lot. Visits to the library were a weekly (and inexpensive) introduction to literacy. I never really thought about the relationship between "teachable moments" and "acculturation" (introduction to our spoken and unspoken cultural agreements) and "agenda" and "indoctrination." I paid no attention to the incredible drive felt by my child to please me by correctly matching the apple on the page to the fruit sitting in the bowl in the kitchen. I was, perhaps from her perspective, sharing the key to the hidden world inside both words and society—and adulthood—all without having any real idea that I was doing so. To me, I was just sharing enjoyable time and a love of reading with my daughter. I was blithely oblivious to the undercurrents present in the picture books.

Fast forward a couple of decades and throw my education and my literature specialization (vampires and other monsters) into the mix, and a whole new picture emerges when I look at those same picture books. Now when I look at those illustrated narratives, the social picture emerging is complex, multifaceted, and enlightening. It is also, in many ways, powerful and frightening. I now know to ask what the relationships are between "teachable moments," "acculturation," "agenda," and "indoctrination." I now know to ask, always, what the moral of the story is. Through the fourteen essays of this text, I argue that there is *always* a moral. There are always behaviors being modeled at the intersection of settings, actors, and narrative.

This text is about supernatural characters and social norms as they intersect on the pages offered to, held by, and read by a child. The overriding question I asked contributors was what morals the supernatural characters illustrated on the pages presented to readers. For just as ideas of morals are, arguably, social constructs, monsters too are social constructs; they are "born," according to Jeffrey Jerome Cohen, "as an embodiment of a certain cultural moment—of a time, a feeling, and a place" (4). How many twelve-foot-tall trolls does any reader know? As I have worked on this text, it has been interesting to see these monsters through other eyes—for my own are, by their very nature, limited by my own life experience. In very many ways, the contributors to this text are "reading" to me as I read to my daughter all those years ago. And in a very personal way, it is pretty darn cool.

Works Cited

Cohen, Jeffrey Jerome. "Monster Culture (Seven Theses)." *Monster Theory: Reading Culture*, ed. Jeffrey Jerome Cohen. Minneapolis: University of Minnesota Press, 1996. 3–25. Print.

Introduction

This is a text about monsters: supernatural monsters, not human monsters; about picture books and their child readers; and perhaps most importantly about morals.[1] The overriding premise of this text is that the picture books offered to the youngest members of our culture carry messages through the use of supernatural characters, such as witches, ghosts, vampires, sea serpents, and so on, creatures neither accepted, nor integrated, within "normal" society, yet utilized to tell readers about ourselves, about our relationships, and about our society; basically, to tell them how they are to behave in the culture in which they find themselves living. For several centuries this initiation by book was so accepted that it was bluntly stated with Aesop's traditional "The moral of this story is...."

The power of the medium impacting our children has not altered from those earlier days, only, arguably, societal perception regarding the seemingly simple picture books which are now seen primarily as a tool to teach the alphabet or to entertain. I argue that the socialization of children via messages embedded in picture books has not magically vanished in the 20th or 21st centuries, and positive or negative messages about behaviors are either introduced, or strengthened, through the physical medium of the book itself as well as through the child-parent/adult relationship which urges the child to learn to "read" (to interpret the represented sign or symbol and assign a meaning to it) in order to more fully become a member of a more adult society.

Educators working in classrooms refer to picture books as offering "character development"[2] in small, "educable moments," in which interest and opportunity combine to allow adults to promote certain accepted standards of behavior to children. The teachable moment allows "children [to] develop moral and ethical perspectives and values from the books they read or that are read to them," for "a good story can help reader[s] make connections to their own experiences and the experiences of others" (Bock 95). I suggest that it is in the blending together of those reflected illustrated experiences and the emotions lurking within the presented experience—as well as the behavioral outcomes which are seen—that moral conditioning occurs. For both political sides—along with all reaches of the religio-political spectrum—would agree that children are taught something through the roles assigned to the characters within the books with which the children interact. Few people disagree that "developing moral and ethical perspectives" (Bock 95) are positive outcomes. The flaw, for many adults, is that it is so easy for "character development" to become, in some ways, "indoctrination" (teaching an adult or child to agree to an idea or behavior without any critical thought on his or her own part regarding its worth). In many ways, in insurance company parlance, picture books are an attractive nuisance: beautiful, educational, and fun, while containing potentially seductive and powerful (or hazardous—depending upon one's religio-political stance) moral imperatives often with little adult supervision.

This collection is meant to examine the role assigned to supernatural characters as children learn to "read" and interpret the values in the interplay of illustrations, words, and authority. However, in order to begin the process of unpacking the "morals of the stories" offered by, and carried in, the picture books, it is necessary to take a look at how picture books function as meaning-making tools.[3] In hopes of presenting a more coherent reading experience, instead of including a plethora of influential authors in each part of this Introduction, I have chosen to provide a jumping-in point of seminal authors in the Notes section.

How Picture Books Work

Picture books are, by their very nature, multi-disciplinary; they ask for a great deal of interpretation and interaction from the child-reader. The complexity of picture books begins with the physical form of the text in which each choice is thoughtfully made by the publisher, illustrator, and author to enhance the narrative and evoke a certain unconscious response from the reader. The complexity is furthered at the moment of meaning-making when the words and illustrations on the pages collide in the reader's mind to create a coherent whole narrative regarding presented behaviors and their likely outcomes. The complexity deepens as the parents offer a picture book—for the parents have chosen that particular book, suggesting that interaction with the book will likely win approval. All interaction which is to be done with the book includes (either explicitly or implicitly) the idea that one should learn to read the book without the parents' direct interaction. The child, on an instinctual level, often believes that when he or she learns to read, he or she becomes a "big boy" or "big girl," with a wider understanding of the world outside the house, and how to behave[4] outside the house. Growing up begins when a child picks up a picture book.

The Power of the Physical

While the parents might choose what book to purchase and present to the child, and the child chooses which book to continue interacting with, the physical form of the text is decided upon by the publisher, illustrator, and author. According to Perry Nodelman in his seminal discussion of the intricacies of the picture book's physical structures, "Aspects [of the book] focus [our] expectations even before [we] explore the pictures closely enough to notice the relationships between the details; [the details] imply an overall mood or atmosphere that controls our understanding of the [book]" (42). The basic influential details of the physical packaging of the picture book include the book's size, the colors chosen for the cover and the illustrations, the way the illustrations are spread over the page and are drawn, and the type of paper on which the book is printed,

The physical size of the book matters to a small child who might think that bigger is better, for what child doesn't want a bigger cookie? According to Nodelman, a physically large book not only offers more space for illustrations and textual interactions, but it also causes the child to "expect energetic rambunctiousness—and to find it even if it is not there" (44). And yet while a physically small picture book holds less space for illustrations and words, anticipation of what is to occur is raised by a physically small book as well. It creates an "expect[ation of] charm and delicacy" (Nodelman 44) in the reading child, who will, again, "find [the charm and delicacy] even if it is not there" (Nodelman 44). The expectation aroused simply through the size of the book allows the words/picture blend to attain an almost subliminal tone in the understanding of the reader who "hears" the words through the filters of "rambunctious" or "delicate" or "charming," allowing the characters to become more active, more real—and thus allowing the depicted (or suggested) positive or negative outcomes of the characters' behaviors to be more readily interpreted and reinforced.

I will not belabor the use of color as an influence over moods. Most adult readers are aware of the way colors are coded to specific meanings within society—although the color coding will vary from culture to culture. In Western society, red represents warmth (passion); yellow represents happiness. The use of these coded colors in a picture book cover or illustration can strengthen the message which is coded in the image since, according to Nodelman, children respond to color on the same level as the adult, for "picture books ... often fill in the details of emotion and of setting that their words leave out and that color seems most suited to convey" (69). Picture, for instance, a man with a cherry-red face; we infer the that the man is angry even as we read the words "the red-cheeked man," internalizing the words as "the angry man" even if the words themselves do not say "angry." Color is an integral part of the narrative which the child is interpreting.

As important as color is, the choice of the medium made by the illustrator to render the illustration, chalk, pencil, ink, etc., is equally important. The lightness or heaviness of the lines, the size of the images, the completeness of the images, and the placement of the illustration on the page[5] all raise reader expectations. Nodelman states that "a frame around a picture makes it seem tidier, less energetic" (50). In the child's developing understanding, a frame might equate to the borders he or she has experienced which limit his or her activities, such as the sides of a playpen. An illustration rendered in soft lines might equate to a restful moment a character is experiencing or a character with a gentle personality while hard and bold lines might lead the reader to interpret the strength of character or forcefulness of an action. The child certainly has experience of hard and soft voices, and gentle and rough events, from which to interpret the ulterior meanings and to infer the outcomes of the pictured behaviors.

Even something so basic as the type of paper the book is printed on, whether glossy or matte or textured, carries a message to the reader. Roughly textured paper begs to be touched, whereas glossy paper will allow the image to be very bright against the page (Nodelman 48). So even the paper choice made by the author, illustrator, and publisher imbue some sort of preset meaning into the text.

The physical choices made therefore can influence the reception of the narrative message contained within the pages even before the picture book is read. The complexity of interpretation for the child continues beyond holding the book in his or her hand and judging its size, seeing the colors and illustrations, and feeling the paper those illustrations are printed upon, although by then the child has already begun creating a personal understanding of the ideas and feelings presented through the page.

Semiotics and Synergy

Once beyond the basic physical form of the book, the narrative influence becomes more important. The illustrated characters' interactions with each other and with their environments depict actions which may be rather simplistically interpreted by a child as good or bad behaviors, and often the illustrations also show the consequences of the interactions of the depicted characters. The illustrations are powerful tools. Nodelman suggests that in picture books, "the words usually stick to telling us about what happens, and we expect the pictures to add something the words do not tell" (71). Thus the illustrations and the words have a synergistic relationship. A synergistic relationship is one in which two pieces of information, while making sense individually, combine to create an enhanced whole. As the child reads the words which are enhanced when combined with the illustrated characters, he or she gets a different storyline than he or she would get with either only words, or only pictures. Lawrence Sipe suggests that in picture books, "the total effect depends not only on the union of the text and illustrations, but on the *perceived* interactions or transactions between these two" ("How Picture Books" 99; italics mine). It is in the perception of the child—in the reading into the narrative—that the real magic of meaning-making occurs. Kirstiva utilizes the term "intertextuality" to describe the way a picture book reader "utilizes the illustrations and text to discover a meaning, but also utilizes the 'text' of [his or her] own life, as a collection of various overlapping social and personal experiences" (qts. in Sipes, "Gingerbread House" 74). "Intertextuality"/"synergy" can be seen in the way words, illustrations, and experiences interact, allowing the child to come to a greater meaning than is shown in either illustration or text alone. An example of synergy can be seen in the children's picture book *Hampire!* (Bardhan-Quallen), which is an amusing romp featuring what the child is led to presume is a vampiric pig. Without the illustration, the word on the cover, "Hampire!" can have little meaning to the child. It is just a word; just a collection of sounds. It is only through the illustration of a pig with fangs wearing a long Dracula-esque cape that the child understands that the pig, the "Ham," is a vampire. The child understands that a normal pig—whom he has seen perhaps on a farm or on multiple pictures—does not have fangs nor wear a cape. The child, if he or she has had even one Halloween experience, associates the cape and fangs with a vampire. The collision of the three distinct meaning-making markers sparks a deeper understanding in the reader; this is a pig which is a vampire: the word pig within the illustration and the prior knowledge of a vampire combine to create a new meaning. The three then have a symbiotic relationship, a synergy, in which each part benefits through the presence of the others. It is through the synergistic relations that the meaning-making moral of *Hampire!* is offered.

The Child Translator

The combination of the physical form of the text, and the synergistic relationship of the illustration to the words, cannot be understated in their roles as meaning-making tools, for children have fewer experiences to draw from while interpreting the illustrated characters on the page. They have only their own extended families from which to connect the visually human characters—for instance, the illustration of a boy with brown hair connects to the brown-haired boy in daycare with whom the child is familiar, making the character on the page acquire a distinct personality based on the known real-world child. If this process has been used so successfully by the child to interpret information, why would he or she not use the same process when the character illustrated is a sea serpent or Sendak's "Wild Things"? Does the child reader grasp that these creatures are not real? According to the 2013 study by Martinianili and Mast regarding how children's previous experience impacts their reading of fantasy figures such as fairies and trolls, "Children, unlike adults, show a tendency to err by judging [supernatural] entities as real" (141). Arguably, then, to the child the supernatural character illustrated on the page is no more "Other" than any other person who is outside the child's limited acquaintance-ship. Reverse that, and the florid freckle face of the new postman can provide the same "Other-ness" as the Wild Things. The interpretation of the characters perhaps comes from some pre-existing emotion somewhere between fear, interest, and acceptance when the reader is confronted with an unfamiliar character, and the behaviors of the "Other" depicted on the page either reinforces, or counters, that instinctual emotional response. I suggest that it is at this point that the mature understanding of the adult steps in to offer an interpretation of the "Other." If the supernatural figure is treated as bad, evil, or to be feared, then the child will internalize that interpretation, whereas if the supernatural character is treated as though it is just another person who is not fear-inducing, the child internalizes some amount of acceptance of the representational character. Thus the adult becomes integral to the moral meaning-making.

The Organization of This Collection

This collection discusses many different supernatural characters—"monsters" from all over the world, and all periods of history. The contributors utilize a wide variety of critical approaches from gender to historicism, ecocriticism to post-colonialism, Structuralism to Lacanianism. There are six parts in the book, each containing a small number of essays for a total of fourteen distributed among the parts. This organizational pattern reflects my choice to take the widest possible critical look at how supernatural characters are used as vehicles to present moral imperatives to child readers. My hope is that this collection begins a conversation, and as an introductory collection and the first to attempt a blending of quite so many disciplines or to examine this many "monsters." *Values in Selected Children's Books of Fiction and Fantasy* is only other book examining "values" in children books. Published in 1982,[6] it has a comprehensive listing of various types of values, and the books they are promoted within, but what the supernatural "monsters" might be offering of "value" is not discussed.

The first part, "Monstrous Instructors," includes three essays which discuss the ways in which supernatural characters are used to teach children very specific lessons: multi-culturalism and environmentalism. Carla Kungl's "My Monster ABCs: What Can a—Zombies Teach Our Kids?" examines the way a simple A to Z alphabet book can be utilized to teach pre-reading skills, and then be repositioned from teaching basic letter-to-word recognition into a tool to teach very young children about other cultures by learning about the monsters of those varying cultures. Kungl suggests, using Structuralist and Lacanian tools, that by demystifying the cultures the monsters derive from, the "Other" is also made a bit more familiar, and that understanding the other culture assists the child in gaining a bit more control over his or her understanding of the world. Corwin R. Baden's "Green Legs and Hands: *The Lorax* as a Medievalist Morality Tale" takes a very popular Dr. Seuss picture book as his "text," and posits that the Lorax is used as a tool to call children to action on environmental issues, suggesting that many of these environmental issues are caused by capitalistic motives and rampant, thoughtless consumerism. He utilizes a variety of critical perspectives to discuss the impact of the behavioral changes the Lorax asks of its child-readers. Baden's connection of the "morality tale" offered in church pageants in the Middle Ages to Seuss' *Lorax* is subtle, and speaks to the reality that every book is built upon the cultural understanding of what has occurred before. Lisa LeBlanc and Carla B. Morrissey's coauthored essay, "Monsters in the Closet: Narrative Therapy and Fairy Tales," introduces readers to the idea that the monster *as* monster can be utilized by children undergoing psychological therapy as a tool to combat various behavioral issues. In this form of therapy the behavioral change sought for the child, as well as the criteria for successful attainment of that behavioral change, is agreed upon by all participants before the therapy begins. Therapist, parents, and child all agree that the child will be capable of heroically winning a battle against the monstrous behavior. In narrative therapy, the monster is of necessity a representative of characteristics which are bad behaviors and the monsters is thus "bad."

The second part, "Normalization of the 'Other,'" includes three essays which progressively question what acceptance into human society costs the "Others." Kelly F. Franklin uses post-colonialism and critical race theory in "'Let the wild rumpus start!' Adventures in Acceptance and Understanding— Picture Books and the Other" to uncover the several possible morals encountered when working toward acceptance of a friendly "Other." Franklin's argument is that by demonstrating friendly, or occasionally inept monsters, the field of monster picture books moves to a position of no longer using "monstrous" creatures to frighten children; instead they make the monsters seem more similar to normal, everyday acquaintances as well as readily conquerable creatures. Lloyd Isaac Vayo, in "'You can't get rid of the Babadook': The Supertextual

Supernatural," examines the picture book, *The Babadook*, which is the prime plot mover within the film *The Babadook*. It would be an understatement to say that this is a friendly monster. Vayo suggests that this picture book—a pop-up picture book—not only introduces the supernatural "Other" into the household *as* a monster, this picture book presents a prime example in which the monstrous "Other" remains "Other" even after being accepted and to some degree "tamed" or acculturated; the "Other" is always going to be a somewhat dangerous "Other." Gerald Raymond Gordon's "Monsters Like Us" translates from the original Japanese story of "The Red Oni" in order to discuss from the Oni's perspective what it feels like to be an outsider who wants to belong to the dominant society. In order to gain acceptance, the Red Oni must forsake friendship with his own kind and embrace the only role offered: protector. The overall message for the child seems to encourage empathy and an enlarged role assignment. Gordon suggests that there is a high price to be paid by the "Other" in order to be accepted within human society—he or she can only be accepted if they forsake their own cultural identity.

In order to provide the widest possible view for examination of monsters and morals and children, the third part, "Fostering Heteronormativity, Agency and Racial Superiority," includes two essays, both interacting with books offered to slightly older readers: early reader books (ages 5–9), short books which include more words, but still include illustrations of important points. These are often chosen by adults as proper read-aloud choices. Both of these essays discuss the idea of acceptance, or lack thereof, of not only supernatural characters, but humans who are not accepted within a specific setting. Simon Bacon suggests, in "The Scars of Dracula: Dracula and the Undead Meaning in Children's Early Readers," that memories of vampires in previous media representations haunt the reader's interpretation of the vampire character. Bacon tracks Dracula from his appearance in Bram Stoker's seminal novel *Dracula* though the varying semiotic meanings implicit in the character's varying refigurations. As Bacon tracks the vampiric figure, the trail leads him to suspect that rather than promoting an acceptance of diversity, the books are instead promoting heteronormativity and white male sexual and racial superiority. Holly A. Wheeler's "Misogyny, Monsters and Malice: Dismantling Troy Cummings' *The Notebook of Doom* Series" examines the moral education offered in that series' pages. Wheeler maintains that this series demonstrates to children that adults are either unwilling, or incapable, of recognizing or destroying monsters, and thus children must acquire agency to defend themselves. She notes that the series offers few positive or non-problematic feminine examples—Nikki, the female protagonist of the threesome, is a full member of the monster-hunting group, is revealed to be a "Jampire," a monster who has altered her species' entry in the inclusive

Monster text. She has inscribed the character of the "Jampire" into a good monster, not an evil one, therefore making the authority of books suspect to the readers.

"Evolving Monsters," the fourth part, contains two essays which focus on picture books, both utilizing a historical approach examining how the monstrous representation has shifted to match the time period in which it appears. Melissa Mullins' "Ogress, Fairy, Sorceress, Witch: Supernatural Surrogates and the Monstrous Mother in Variants of 'Rapunzel'" follows the shifting female monster "sorceress"/"enchantress"/"witch" from its inception in fairy tales to our modern *Rupunzel* representations. Mullins demonstrates that the message offered child readers via illustrations and words regarding the supernatural-mother-surrogate, was, and is, unremittingly negative although, mostly, the mother offers little direct harm to her foster-child Rapunzel. Rebecca A. Brown's "Swimming with Serpents: Dismantling Boundaries in Sea Monsters Picture Books" problematizes the human to monster relationship. She does this by tracing the changing relationship of humans to sea serpents. Brown posits that since sea serpents first appeared as a warning on maps, they have often functioned as a monster-hero, thus providing children with a social model which breaks down social boundaries between a child and the "Other." If the behavior of monsters makes them helpful, and the outcome of that behavior is positive, then the "Others" must be seen as non-monstrous.

The fifth part, "Monstrous Monsters," contains two essays examining the "moral of the story" presented when "Othered" characters are read through religious lenses, offering a very brief look at the socio-political division regarding character development versus indoctrination. Both essays cite historical interpretations of the root causes for the behavioral messages embedded in the stories. Corwin R. Baden's "The House That Drac Built: Faith-Based Qualms About Halloween Picture Books" explores the reasons for conservative readers' qualms regarding supernatural monsters and the increasing intrusion of the supernatural in its guise of the haunted house and the ghosts which live in them. Baden speaks to the religious community's issue with normalizing supernatural spaces and demystifying supernatural creatures, thus allowing the supernatural to encroach on the boundary of home, family, and religiously sound thoughts and behaviors. Brenda S. Gardenour Walter's "Wicked 'Others': Christian Conservatism and the Rejection of the Supernatural" juxtaposes the liberal values depicted in many picture books to those she posits are shown in conservative Christian stories. Gardenour Walter's examination of picture books such as the 2005 title *Help! Mom! There Are Liberals Under My Bed!* leads her to posit that these picture books lead to a narrowing of acceptance of differing viewpoints, and an increasing distrust of all "Others" from outside that particular community.

The final part, "Moral Agencies," includes two essays engaging with the idea that the supernatural creatures offer children windows into the possible similarities of their own behaviors with those of the monsters, thus possibly influencing their own attributions of meaning. Both essays note the importance of the teaching aspects of the books, and add that the child is the ultimate decision maker over what morals he or she will eventually embrace. Mariaelena DiBenigno utilizes a post-modern critical approach in "The Fantastic in the Everyday: Growing Up with *The Mysteries of Harris Burdick*." Her examination of this post-modern picture book argues that its lack of sequential narrative structure forces a child to create for themselves the traditional narrative continuity important to most readers. DiBenigno posits that a post-modern picture book such as this, with its fragmented pieces requiring interactive organizing on the child's part, offers the child the opportunity to come to his or her own conclusions instead of being led to them by the picture book itself or through the adult mediator. Brenda S. Gardenour Walter, through "Crossing the Threshold: Ghosts and Haunted Houses as Moral Messengers," discusses the way the supernatural character of the ghost can raise questions in readers regarding life, death, and souls when they bump into ghosts in their picture books. Gardenour Walter expresses the perspective that the negotiation of "The moral of the story…" when performed in tandem via the pictorial texts read to, and by, the child, allow the child to come to his or her own conclusion regarding a central question of humanity—"What follows death?"—while perhaps also allowing the reader to create a belief system of his or her own regarding the existence of the human soul.

The supernatural characters, the non-human "Others" of children's picture books, present the author/illustrator/publisher triad an opportunity to present a message to its child readers regarding the personality, attributes, and extra powers which the supernatural character might possess—through the synergy of words and illustrations, and through the intertextuality of personal life and created character, for, as Jeremy Cohen suggests, "[monsters] ask us to reevaluate our cultural assumptions about gender, sexuality, our perception of difference…. They ask us why we have created them" (20). The essays that follow attempt to answer the "Why?" question by positing that through them we expose our children to the core beliefs of our society.

Notes

1. *Morals*: For this text, I am defining morals rather loosely as the internal personal decision concerning the goodness or badness of any given behavior. Adults, through media and personal connections, offer children concrete positioning concerning what is considered good or bad behaviors and responses to stimuli which they should accept as normal, and learn to emulate if they wish to be accepted members of our society.

2. *Character development*: To learn more about character development, begin with Lori Ann Prior, Angeli Willson and Miriam Martinez, "Picture This: Visual Literacy as a Pathway to Character Understanding," *The Reading Teacher* 66 (2012): 195–206, and L.R. Sipe, "Look-

ing Closely at the Characters: How Illustrations Support Children's Understanding of Character through Picturebook Illustrations," in N. Roser and M. Marinez, eds., *What a Character! Character Study as a Guide to Literacy Learning Making in Grades K–8* (Newark, DE: International Reading Association, 2005), 134–53.

    3. *Meaning-making*: This can be loosely defined in picture books lexicon as the process the child uses to assign a concept to a word or idea so that it has an actual, real meaning for them. It includes all aspects of the media in which they find the word or idea, and their own—or someone who intercedes—preexisting experience with the word or idea.

    4. Lawrence Sipe, "Revisiting the Relationships Between Text and Pictures," *Children's Literature in Education* 43 (2012): 2–21, provides a short, but comprehensive, breakdown of picture book terminology describing the action of blending text and illustration as well as providing a comprehensive glossary of basic terminology used by illustrators, authors, and picture book publishers.

    5. For a fuller discussion of the various ways authors impact children through the medium of picture books, please see Perry Nodelman's *Words About Pictures: The Narrative Art of Children's Picture Books* (Athens: University of Georgia Press, 1988). See also Lawrence Sipe, "Revisiting the Relationships Between Text and Pictures," *Children's Literature in Education* 43 (2012): 2–21.

    6. Carolyn W. Field and Jaqueline Shachter Weiss, *Values in Selected Children's Books of Fiction and Fantasy* (Hamden, CT: Library Professional Publications, 1982).

Works Cited

Bardhan-Quallen, Sudipta. *Hampire!* Illus. Howard Fine. New York: Harper, 2011. Print.
Bock, Lee. "Moral and Ethical Concepts." *School Library Journal* 49 (Feb. 2013): 95–98. EBSCOhost.
Cohen, Jeffrey Jerome. "Seven Thesis." *Monster Theory: Reading Culture*, ed. Jeffrey Jerome Cohen. Minneapolis: University of Minnesota Press, 1996. Print.
Field, Carolyn W., and Jaqueline Shachter Weiss. *Values in Selected Children's Books of Fiction and Fantasy.* Hamden, CT: Library Professional Publications, 1982.
Lintner, Timothy. "Using 'Exceptional' Children's Literature to Promote Character Education in Elementary Social Studies Classrooms." *The Social Studies* (2011): 200–03. EBSCOhost.
Martinianili, Corinna, and Fred W. Mast. "Is It Real or Is It Fiction? Children's Bias Toward Reality." *Journal of Cognition and Development* 14.1: 141–53. EBSCOhost. Web.
Nodelman, Perry. *Words About Pictures: The Narrative Art of Children's Picture Books*. Athens: University of Georgia Press, 1988. Print.
Sipe, Lawrence. "How Picture Books Work: A Semiotically Framed Theory of Text-Picture Relationships." *Children's Literature in Education* 29.2 (1998): 4–21. EBSCOhost. Web. 1 Feb. 2014.
_____. "Learning the Language of Picture Books" *Journal of Children's Literature* 24.2 (Fall 1998). Print.
_____. "'Those two gingerbread boys could be brothers': How Children Use Intertextual Connections During Storybook Readalouds." *Children's Literature in Education* 31.2 (2000). Print.

PART 1: MONSTROUS INSTRUCTORS

My Monster ABCs
What Can A(bominable Snowmen) to Z(ombies) Teach Our Kids?

CARLA KUNGL

> Do monsters really exist? Surely they must, for if they did not, how could we?—*Jeffrey Jerome Cohen*

My boys love monsters. They are captivated by the varieties of monsters they meet throughout the days in various ways—in readers, activity books, videogames, and other media. Last Christmas, my youngest son received Michael Spradlin's *The Monster Alphabet* when he was three years old. Reading this book both started this current fascination of mine—monster ABC books in general—and solidified my younger sons' fascination with the monster panoply. My sons quickly memorized each of the twenty-six monsters presented A to Z, and over the next two days, asked me to act out the text and pictures of what that monster was pictured doing. When we mentally flipped the page to the next monster (because we didn't need the physical book after those two days), I had to remind them of the monster's home country and its location, and then I had to recite with them the couplet accompanying the picture, describing what the monster might do. I felt more than a little silly leaping through the air and shrieking like a banshee, but it is what the text—and my children—required. I was astounded that the kids not only quickly learned many new monsters, since the A to Z format served as an effective mnemonic device, but that they loved learning about them.

These activities raised several questions for me: Why was this so fun for my kids? Since they pretty much already knew the alphabet, what were they actually learning? And (I thought with alarm) isn't three a little too young to want to learn details about the flesh-eating proclivities of a Redcap demon? It was with these questions in mind that I approached this essay, examining alphabet books that use "real" monsters from various cultures as their organizing principle: "A" does not stand for Apple, in other words, but for Abominable Snowman; the letter "B" does not feature Barney playing ball but a Basilisk. And as I've also learned from my kids, the books that hold their attention most are those with realistic and frightening imagery and simple but informative text.

How popular are monster books these days? Lauren Oliver noted in a recent *NY Metro* blog post that her search for "children" and "monsters" elicited eight million Google hits. The Barnes & Noble online site has its own section for children's monster books. And this isn't even touching the adult audience for monster material. So yes, they are popular—but I am quite sure that previous generations of children were taught to fear creatures of the night. How is it that they have become so popular as to star in a burgeoning field of monster alphabet books? And are these alphabet books really the educational tool that parents seem to approach them as? Everything from Scholastic Books to the Department of Education advises parents to read alphabet books to their children to help them learn to read. But my own conclusion is that monster ABC books do *not* help small children gain the phonemic awareness that one school of thought suggests is a pre-cursor to successful reading. Evers, Lang, and Smith write that "*traditionally*, authors crafted the alphabet book to support the development of phonemic awareness through alliteration and assonance in emergent and beginning readers" (462; emphasis mine). But this tradition has not come down intact to us today. Most monster ABC books specifically, as part of what might be called the "genre" type of alphabet books, seem to presuppose a preexisting knowledge of the alphabet.

And yet, monster ABC books are nonetheless a perfect match for small children. The first part of this chapter lays the groundwork for understanding what function ABC books in general might have in helping children develop pre-reading skills, followed by a closer examination of a few monster ABC books. The final section looks at how the monster ABC book specifically meet more fundamental aspects of growth beyond learning to read, drawing from mythological and structuralist understandings of development.

The Traditional Role of Alphabet Books

As a typical reader and parent, I have several types of alphabet books in the house, as well as magnetic letters, blocks with letters—all those items we usually assume are "helping our children learn to read," in a leap of metonymic logic that somehow presumes the connection. This school of thought is one promulgated officially by the U.S. Department of Education, which notes matter-of-factly that "sharing the alphabet with children helps them learn letter names and shapes, and link the letters to the sounds of oral language"

("Helping Your Preschool Child"). But research is not consistent concerning the relationship between alphabet books and their role in helping small children learn phonemic awareness—the ability to distinguish and manipulate individual sounds—which is typically considered a necessary pre-reading step. Again, this is contested territory, which accounts for my otherwise slippery language. But I wondered if, and how, learning that the letter "z" makes a "zzzz" sound, combined with seeing a picture of a zombie, could eventually help my children learn to read.

Two prominent researchers bear witness to the mixed results of trying to track what many feel is a "natural" purpose of ABC books as a means of developing pre-reading skills. David B. Yaden, whose research centers on literacy acquisition in young children, found that children are far more interested in the narrative—the story and the accompanying illustrations that help create the story—than in any more "formal aspects" of books like the letters themselves or the page formats, despite their parents' consistent attempts to draw attention to those types of "reading" skills (44). Yaden describes a study indicating that a child's letter recognition did not necessarily translate into either phonemic awareness or into an understanding of the sound-symbol relationship.[1] In one example, a father and daughter were looking at the page for the letter "O"; though the child knew the letter "O," she looked at the picture for help determining what "O" might stand for. She said, "O is for mouse," because the opossum looked to her like a mouse. She did not know what an opossum was and had never seen one. When she got to the letters "W" and "Y," and again had no context for the animals pictured, she had no idea what to say to her father's prompting, even though she knew the letters "W" and "Y." Yaden writes:

> In both cases, however, the child responds "I don't know" more as a result of being unfamiliar with walruses and yaks as opposed to not recognizing the letter shape. In the child's view, it is the pictured referent of the sign which is unclear, not the sign itself. And even when Miriam's father supplies the name of the animal, as in the case of "Walrus," the child is surprised, making the letter association at the semantic level, not the language level [53].

In this case, the illustration was the cue for the child, rather than the shape of the letter, knowledge of the letter itself, or the beginning sound of the letter, and letters were "indiscriminately" associated with objects pictured (43).

Murray, Stahl and Ivey also point to contradictory findings concerning the role of alphabet books in the reading process, saying in guarded language that their research "suggests strongly that alphabet book reading *might be* an important factor in the development of phoneme awareness" (318; emphasis mine). They do note that alphabet books which feature large letters designed to attract attention are more successful than other picture books in getting children to discuss print aspects of text (309). In addition, they broach the problems of reading alphabet books to children that "feature language poorly adapted to the linguistic capabilities of young children" (310) and refer to research that suggests alphabet books should use language that is familiar to the child. Finally, they suggest that there should be a basic phonemic awareness already extant if children are to make what is in fact an arbitrary connection between the sound of a letter and the picture of the letter itself, much less a connection to the picture which might be accompanying the letter. Since the signs are truly arbitrary, the connections children make are both arbitrary and unreliable as well—the T for toad might just as easily be a frog, and why not?

Other research suggests that certain types of alphabet books are better than others in developing children's ability to create associations between letters and sounds. A study by Barbara Bradley and Jennifer Jones suggests that both a teacher's reading style and the type of alphabet book will influence what children might learn from an alphabet book that is read to them. Books that show letters as characters in a book or as part of a story will likely lead to discussion of the story itself, whereas texts with alliteration will encourage more discussion of the sounds of letters (457). A strong "letter-picture correspondence" can "provide teachers with the opportunity to discuss the multiple sounds of letters" and can teach children "to think flexibly about the alphabet" (457). A genre book, on the other hand, which focuses "on a theme by presenting specific concepts or words in alphabetical order," will more likely lead the teacher to discuss content rather than the letters themselves or the sounds those letters make (459). My monster alphabet books, then, as theme-based genre books, fall into this category.

Finally, the images that go along with the text also matter greatly. Yaden's work with storybooks suggests that children see images in books as "snapshots" of their lives. This explains the myriad of traditional alphabet books that feature the "b is for ball" types of text and illustration. For children to make a connection between an object, the letter it starts with, and the sound that both the object and the letter make, it helps to feature an image of an object with which the child is already familiar. Children attribute meaning "first to the pictures, then to the oral narrative and, finally, com[e] to understand some of the conventional knowledge regarding the reading process" including, with their parents' prodding, to understand "the oral referents of letters" (Yaden 44). The shape of the letter "B" means nothing without context; children make first a visual and then aural connection in figuring out what that letter might mean or do.

Looking at the illustrations in alphabet books specifically, Ted McGee believes that interesting and appealing artwork is of primary importance. It is vital, he writes, that the artwork "engages the interest of children" because it "suggests a complex network of connections fundamental to reading and writing" (31). The art in alphabet books can "stir up and sustain the interest of children by providing pleasure too. To the extent that they do that, they become useful tools for those teaching literacy" (31). But if the art doesn't engage interest, the letters by themselves certainly won't.

The roles of illustrations in children's books are many.[2] George Bodmer writes that illustrations serve to "expand, explain, interpret, or decorate a written text" ("Approaching..." 72). Zhihui Fang notes that pictures can develop characters and plot, determine mood, and establish setting; they can provide textual coherence or a different viewpoint, and they can reinforce the story. More pointedly, Fang discusses how illustrations help children, not just the story they illustrate. He notes that they can "entice children to read and interact with text," they can "serve as an effective tool to stimulate and promote children's creativity," and they "facilitate their [children's] understanding of the written text" by acting as "mental scaffolds" for young readers (138). All of these researchers, in other words, note that illustrations are immeasurably important in alphabet books.

So how do we relate all of this knowledge of reading and letters and pictures to monster ABC books? Following the format suggested earlier by the research, we might say that children will first look at the pictures of monsters, then notice the letter, and then, depending on their abilities, any accompanying text. But because children will often have little familiarity with the imagery and names of monsters, and because the text used to describe them (sometimes easy couplets, sometimes paragraphs) is usually way beyond a 4-year-old's comprehension, the reverse might occur instead: children's knowledge of the alphabet might serve as a device for teaching them about monsters. Evers, Lang, and Smith, in their recap of using of alphabet books as a writing tool for older children, note that "alphabet texts generally follow a consistent and predictable organizational pattern rendering them user-friendly and effective to serve as mentor texts for writers of all ages and stages" (462). As "mentor texts," they inspire habits of mind and foster ideas about reading that are supported in school. In other words, alphabet books have uses beyond what is considered the conventional one: teaching children letters.

What Have Monsters Got to Do with the Alphabet?

So to recap briefly, to have the most success in teaching children phoneme awareness (which I am going to assume is a goal of most parents, like myself, who read alphabet books to their children), the print needs to be salient; the language needs to be linguistically at the child's level; and, since children tend to see pictures as "snapshots" of their daily lives, the illustrations should feature items already in a child's vocabulary.

Let's look at a few monster ABC books in more detail to see how they fare. I'll start with Michael Spradlin's *The Monster Alphabet,* since that text started my family off on this adventure. This book introduces a young boy, Morgan Marvin Marshall, who asks children to go exploring with him, "finding monsters, A to Z!" (1). Each page of the book features a monster, sometimes having scary features, sometimes harmless features; and below each picture is a couplet, providing a location where the monster might be found and describing briefly a major feature of the monster. Included in the picture are other objects that start with that letter. For instance, the letter G's squatting **g**argoyle on top of the Notre Dame Cathedral is holding an electric **g**uitar and wearing Ray-Ban sun **g**lasses. The images work together to tell a story of sorts because the other objects in the picture support the possibly new monster word; in this case, we've got a rocker gargoyle checking out the city below him. By including perhaps already-familiar objects that start with the featured letter, the text consciously tries to connect "new information" (the monster being introduced) with items already part of the child's consciousness or vocabulary.

But the story isn't seamless. For some reason, a King Kong–like gorilla is in the distance hanging from the Eiffel Tower, a flock of geese is flying overhead, and a gumball machine is sitting on the ledge next to the gargoyle. Other words that begin with g—, for instance, can be found in the picture, some more fitting than others, with the gumball machine the most egregiously out of place. This disconnect, however, far from confusing children, can actually further help them make the phonemic connection. Drawing on his analysis of two alphabet books, Ted McGee argues that including objects in a picture that do not fit the story told in the picture is "crucial": "the incompatibility of the [object] helps a child reader to focus on that thing and say the word in which the relevant letter appears" (28). A combination of design elements like foregrounding, color contrast, and textural differences means that a scene that appears cohesive at first glance may not be. In our monster alphabet example, then, children are forced to ask, "Why is there gum sitting there?" They say gum, they say gargoyle, and the connection is solidified.

Connecting the image to a letter and to a sound, however, is not clear-cut for small children, and this book shows that strain in places; we see the mixed results of relying on an alphabet book to help make those connections. In "K is for Kraken," for example, a verb is included as part of the picture, and the sound awareness is linked to an action, a much more difficult connection. The poem accompanying the Kraken reads: "The kraken is from the ocean, where the cold water makes us gasp. / This mighty beast is strong and big; we must escape its grasp." Our boy hero, Morgan, is in a diving suit, and lines showing motion allow us to see that he is "**k**icking" one of the kraken's giant legs. Elsewhere, a "**k**iller whale" and the "**K**ing" of the mermaids look on. In addition, making the letter-sound connection even more confusing, one of the kraken's arms is tied in a "knot."

Using Yaden's research on phonemic knowledge as a blueprint, we can imagine children looking at this picture and getting nearly every name wrong, except the main one of the kraken, and that is because it was told to them and written down below the big letter K. My own experience was one of straining to figure out why an orca and a mermaid were in the picture. It was humbling, in fact—I had to try to think of what things making the "k-" sound were present. Oh, they mean *killer* whale, not orca. That's not just any mermaid—he's wearing a crown so he must be the *king* of mermaids. And what is the name of that fish hanging out next to Morgan? Must be something that starts with a k. A koi? It looks like a koi, but do they live in the ocean? Surely parents would have to point out that the kraken is getting kicked, since the connection between an action verb as an image with the phonemic sound is less tangible than it would be for a noun. And then there is that problem of "knot," which begins with a k but doesn't make the hard "k" sound.[3]

I don't mean to imply flaws in the way *The Monster Alphabet* presents its information; it meets several parameters of a "good" alphabet book. First, each letter is presented on a single page and every page is formatted in the same way. The featured letter is large and black against a light brown background in the side margin, and the name of the monster is printed in black directly underneath. A square picture with a white-bordered frame, designed to look like an old snapshot taken with a camera, shows both the monster and several other items starting with that letter, as I've described. Finally, the couplet about the monster has a pleasing sing-song rhythm, and while a parent is most likely reading this rhyme to a child, the rhyme is easy enough and short enough for the child not to lose interest.

Two other monster alphabet books do not necessarily seem to be as concerned with presenting a minimal amount of text, perhaps with the assumption that a small child learning the alphabet would not be reading it without help. The audience for this type is more clearly adults who are reading the book to a child. Lynn Hunter's *A Little Book of Monsters* is set up similarly to Spradlin's: there is one large letter in black on each page with the image separated out and emphasized; in this case, the monster is drawn inside a white circle that takes up a portion of the page. But in place of a simple couplet setting the groundwork, Hunter's poems are all three quatrains long, consisting of language far beyond what an alphabet-learning child would use or understand. "I for Imp" begins:

> A trickster; spawn of demons,
> an imp's desire most dear
> is corruption of a human,
> with anger, greed, and fear.

And two more quatrains follow. In other words, though increasing vocabulary is a laudable goal, these poems are not necessarily linguistically or emotionally suitable for children, contradicting Murray's suggestion that alphabet books should use language that meets a child's linguistic capability. A second disconnect in this book comes from the juxtaposition of the sophisticated, sometimes gruesome text that describes the monster with the unthreatening large-eyed—indeed, childish—monster drawn within the circle. Is this a book for children after all, with these eye-lashed and wide-eyed colorful creatures? Most likely not. My own children personally don't seem to be as taken with this one. It could be the book's physically small size—it is not much more than 5" × 5" inches—or it could be the sameness and style of the drawings, which are closer to cartoons than to what might be considered an actual depiction of a monster.

M Is for Monster: A Fantastic Creatures Alphabet by Patrick Lewis seems to straddle the line in understanding its dual audiences, parents and children. Its large 12" × 14" format means that illustrations (by Gerald Kelly) take center stage, and nearly every letter-monster combo has a full double-page spread. The monsters are elaborately, carefully, and often scarily drawn in watercolor-like imagery, the soft lines of which perhaps emphasize the ethereal nature of the monster. Again, an initial large black letter and easy-to-read couplet accompany the picture of the monster. But in the far margins on a solid color background, Lewis provides a several-paragraph description of the creature, its cultural significance, and its other features. In this case a child who can read may just read the couplet and look at the pictures; a parent reading to a child would probably do the same, but an older child or an interested adult can read the descriptions on the side for more information. The publisher, Sleeping Bear Press, apparently does not intend these for children to learn the alphabet. A search at their website for an alphabet book appropriate for ages 0 to 4 under the Language Arts category elicits only (and very surprisingly) *Z Is for Zamboni*. Clicking on the "ages 5 to 7" button gives us 10 choices for the letter A (*A Is for Aloha* or *Abraham* or *Algonquin*). *M Is for Monster* is one of about 12 choices for the letter M at the suggested reading level of grade 4, ages 7 to 10. As genre books, these texts most likely help kids mnemonically learn items associated with something (*M Is for Michigan*, for instance, helps us learn lots about Michigan, but not about letters).

For whom, then, are these alphabet books meant? This question could be posed about most books designed for small children. As Jacquelyn Ardam notes, writing about Gertrude Stein's *To Do: A Book of Alphabets and Birthdays*, children's books are marketed to parents or others who buy books for children; "the ultimate consumer of children's literature does not have buying power" (579). In most cases, small children do not choose or purchase texts. But regardless of who makes the actual purchase, to suggest that alphabet books are "meant" for children—especially those alphabet books with very complex rhymes and text—ignores a stark disconnect, argues Ardam: "If a child can already read the text of an alphabet book, it's unlikely that she needs the alphabet book for any didactic purpose. There is thus an inherent temporal problem in the genre; the alphabet book constitutes its audience retroactively" (589). Why, if a child can already read, would she pick up such a book?

However, as I noted above, the point of these genre-type books is rarely to teach the alphabet. Does it matter, then, if the audience for some of these books is parents if they are cross-marketed to adult audiences? Spradlin and the illustrator Jeff Weigel, for instance, collaborated on three zombie books, most recently *Jack and Jill Went Up to Kill: A Book of Zombie Nursery Rhymes*, before they wrote *The Monster Alphabet* (which, however, is the only monster book in the children's section of Spradlin's web page). And *M Is for Monster*, as I noted, is part of a sustained series by Sleeping Bear Press aimed at anyone but children who need to learn their letters.

Perhaps we expect too much from an alphabet book. George Bodmer suggests that authors have long used the format of the alphabet book for tasks other than teaching children the alphabet; it "looks like a teaching tool for children, but its entertainment value has always lain in the stretching of its borders" (115). Seeing the alphabet book as entertainment, rather than as a moral, didactic tool, is one example of that stretch. Examining post-modern techniques in alphabet books by Dr. Seuss and Edward Gorey, Bodmer suggests that 20th-century writers of the alphabet book were affected by a postmodern zeitgeist of sorts that allowed them to move beyond the rigidity of traditional modes, reminding us that "from its overly didactic beginning, the alphabet book has always reflected the time and culture from which it springs" (115).[4] And there is no doubt that our own culture is fascinated with monsters.

So, perhaps we should expect more. The monster alphabet book might not teach my kid the plosive "p" sound, but monster books that are meant for small children meet their developmental needs on several other levels, which can be examined through both structuralist and Lacanian psychoanalytic theoretical constructs. In fact, despite the fact that most children already know their ABC's when they look at these books, I posit that scary monsters and the alphabet make a perfect combination.

Moving Beyond the Book

Let's set aside the research on reading for a bit. One other basic function of the monster ABC book, bringing me back to the beginning of this project, is to teach kids about monsters and therefore other cultures and eras. My children, remember, made me tell them the country of each monster and when it "lived" while we were reciting a to z (in fact, we had to move to different rooms of the house as we traveled to a new country). All of these monster ABC books include monsters from many different lands and times and cultures—there just aren't many monsters that start with "x" and "q" in the English language; nor are there many monsters in American culture to draw upon. These texts, though driven to multiculturalism by necessity, nonetheless allow parents to introduce other cultures' monsters to their children.

Darren J. Gendron is one such writer who deliberately searched for "unusual" monsters to include in his *Monster Alphabet* board book which he wrote when he became a father. It features bright colorful illustrations; verses in iambic heptameter, "as the gentle rhythm will help lull young-ones to sleep" (Kickstarter); and monsters from many cultures, which he says he hopes will lead parents to find out more about other cultures and their myths. It also features a pronunciation guide to help "parents tell [their] little ones about the Xiuhcoatl or the Jörmungandr" and some "fun facts about the respective legends" (Kickstarter). But Gendron's book is unusual, and he had to create this book himself, using a Kickstarter campaign to fund his project; there was no monster alphabet board book already out there designed for very small children. And he says he truly hopes that the book can develop his child's vocabulary, teaching him that "B stands for Basilisk" (in addition to the more pedestrian "ball").

By helping children understand their place in the world, geographically and temporally, monster books can help children deal with their own monsters. Like with most "unknowns," they become less threatening when we learn about them. The diversity of monsters and monster archetypes allows children to understand the role of monsters in every culture, which can therefore demystify the monster. Furthermore, if children are being read to, they are getting this information from a trusted source, perhaps in a comfortable place, which might help overcome any accompanying anxiety. Monsters can scare our kids, and from a developmental standpoint, learning to face a fear is vital. R. L. Stine, creator of the Goosebumps series, was initially surprised when he asked children why they liked his books: "Every single time the kid would say: 'I like to be scared!' I thought about it a lot and now I think we all like to be scared, if we know we're also safe at the same time. Kids can have these adventures, and have these creepy things happen to them, and know that they're safe in their rooms reading" (in Kirkland n. pag.). Judging from the immense popularity of the Goosebumps series (and so many others with monstrous beings as main characters), such texts not only can teach kids about their place in a larger world and help them face fears, but they can also foster a sustained love for reading—not a bad side effect.

Thus, even if most monster ABC books are not designed to teach the alphabet (with a very few exceptions like Genrdon's), they can nonetheless teach children about monsters. They can help children diffuse their own set of monsters, knowing that every culture across time has had a set of monsters with which they have grappled. For children, learning about monsters can be an ideal way of confronting fear and progressing emotionally. But a book about monsters that is tied to language, tied to the alphabet, engages children differently, even more deeply.

Monsters have much to do with how we define ourselves, whether we see them as fragmented parts of our psyche, remnants of nightmares, or as external symbolic representations of battles we need to fight. Philosophy professor Stephen Asma, in trying to account for why "monsters are on the rise" (61), writes that "monsters can stand as symbols of human vulnerability and crisis, and as such they play imaginative foils for thinking about our own responses to menace"; the monster concept is "a permanent player in the moral imagination because human vulnerability is permanent" (62, 66). The monster as "Other," whether symbolic or formed, has existed as a key character in imaginations, in mythologies, and in oral narratives long before humans had the capacity to record their nefarious deeds on paper, much less write about them in alphabet books.

But language, too, helps to define us: it is an integral part of our growth, our humanity, our indoctrination into our culture, and our understanding of our place in the world, not to mention the means by which we express our place. Its importance to us undoubtedly accounts for so much of the controversy in trying to determine how we acquire it, whether spoken or written. Placing the monstrous "Other" and language acquisition beside each other, as innate and intrinsic parts of our humanity, opens rich avenues of exploration.

We can begin to see why a monster ABC book is such an ideal text for small children using a structuralist lens. Structuralism, though in literary theory circles is limited to the study of language, began as a theory to try to uncover what all cultures might have in common, a structure upon which to study all human behavior (language being one of those aspects). Using monsters to guide children to the building blocks of language combines these fundamental elements of our human selves.

David Williams, whose heady treatise *Deformed Discourse* examines the language of monstrosity in medieval Christian symbolism, is one such theorist who explores what he sees as an inherent connection between monsters and language, saying that their association is "a profound, longstanding one" (61). Pointing to the many Tower of Babel types of mythologies in human history, for example, he notes that the emergence of monstrosity became linked with the multiplicity of languages that proceeded from the fall of the Tower. Previous to this episode of human history, language betokened "a kind of remnant of an original unity of being" (61), but after the fall of the Tower of Babel, language divided us and prevented us from being whole.

But children can't talk about monsters on a theoretical level; they have a more visceral relationship to them. For children, who inhabit their imaginations much more vividly (and not coincidentally, who are just learning perhaps to "order" their experience through writing), monsters can be terrifyingly real. Sharon and Woolley address children's belief in the verity of monsters in their article, "Do Monsters Dream?" They write of the difficulty children have deciding whether a fantastical creature was real, noting that when children have to reconcile the "contradictory properties" (307) that a creature might possess—for instance if it has a physical human property like recognizable facial features but also a non-human physical property, like inhabiting several places at one time—children tended to assign it to the "not sure" category. The researchers suggest that for children: "Inferring the correct category [real or fantasy] when given contradictory property information was especially difficult. Yet this is precisely the challenge that fantastical entities raise" (307). A belief that a fantastical creature could possess even one non-human quality was enough to make preschoolers question whether it was "real" or "not real."

Thus, even preschoolers know that monsters are messy and that they don't have to conform to human rules. Jeffrey Cohen writes that monsters refuse to participate in the "order of things"; they are "disturbing hybrids whose externally incoherent bodies resist attempts to include them in any systematic structuration" (6). Paul Goetsch states, "As liminal characters, monsters offer resistance to attempts to pin them down, or allegorize them, as conservative or subversive, or as the id or other components of the self" (1). But what if children *could* find a way to pin them down? What if they found a tool that helped provide order to the chaos of the monster world? Enter the alphabet book. If monsters inhabit the borders of society, having a monster alphabet book to bring them to heel gives children a modicum of control. How might this occur?

Even the very young children studied by Yaden and Murray often bring letter name knowledge to the task of reading; to restate Yaden: "In the child's view, it is the pictured referent of the sign which is unclear, not the sign itself" (53). They might recognize a shape of a letter and perhaps the sound it makes, but more specifically, children have to learn the connection between the arbitrary sign of a letter attached to the sound and its connection to an image in an alphabet book. So what happens when we assign the sign /w/ a monster as the pictured referent? Small children examining books will most likely first examine the picture, then perhaps the "salient" letter, followed by linguistically appropriate text. In looking at a monster ABC book then, what the children first pay attention to is the monster—a werewolf, a witch, a wendigo—which possibly frightens them and which they very possibly do not know. What they see next is the letter, a W, but that they can know; that they often do know.

If children need monsters to be pinned down, categorized so that they can comprehend and overcome their fear of them, then linking a monster to an alphabet letter is a perfect vehicle for taming. They have been given a way to defeat it, to place it in some order. In other words, despite the fact that monsters "resist classification built on hierarchy or a merely binary opposition" (Cohen 7), an alphabet book that does give order to this class—gives it a letter name—can be a potent savior for a child straddling the worlds between the real and unreal, the us and the not-us.

David Williams makes an even more potent argument: that it is *because* monsters tend towards chaos that order is possible. Specifically connecting monstrosity with language, he writes:

> While the taxonomy of the entire range of monstrous forms may be viewed ... as the contradiction of our effort to order and categorize our experience of the world, in the larger perspective it must also be seen in the first instance as providing the very possibility of that ordering function, and in the second, as providing the possibility of transcending it to understand "order" itself.... [T]he identification of the monster with disorder makes it also the potential for order [82–83].

Thus the force of the binary opposition model can provide the safety of order, the shackling of fear. Patricia Crain, who traces the history of the alphabet book in America, calls the "A is for apple" type of textual construction in alphabet books the "alphabet array" or the "worldly alphabet" (91; qtd. in Ardam 586), which "emphasizes the alphabet's function of ordering" objects in the world. She writes: "This alphabet represents, in words or images, the world at large, arrayed through the arbitrary but powerful order of the ABCs, forcefully producing a world that is knowable, graspable" (qtd. in Ardam 586). By tying down a monster to a letter, monsters can be made known; they can be tamed. Again, for children with vivid imaginations, the force of the alphabet may be just what they need to help them sleep at night.

This argument isn't without problems, certainly. Because monsters inhabit the fringes and tend to defy categorization, one could also argue that the monster ABC undermines the binary oppositions on which structuralism rests. If, as structuralists would contend, language is a system of arbitrary signs nonetheless comprised of unchanging patterns—an /a/ is an /a/ only because it is /not-a/—it can only be defined in contrast to something else. But again, monsters are messy; they move beyond our simple system of classification. Cohen writes: "The horizon where the monsters dwell might well be imagined as the visible edge of the hermeneutic circle itself; the monstrous offers an escape from its hermetic path, an invitation to explore new spirals, new and interconnected methods of perceiving the world" (7). If monsters represent the edges of knowing, how children imagine or perceive the world presented in a monster book will ultimately be unstable.

Compounding this instability is that fact that the drawn images in these books are necessarily conceptual referents as opposed to concrete referents (such as photographs).[5] Thus, the methods these texts use to present monsters, despite their link to a letter, are even less structured. "Y for yeti" might be comforting—I know this letter; I can handle this monster—but ultimately there are only conceptions of the yeti, not a single dominant "correct" image. This fluidity is especially apparent when children have exposure to several monster books and see several depictions; they must mediate between images to find the one that resonates with them. Though children might develop a body of knowledge about a monster, which can help them categorize it, the pictured sign of the referent will always be unique, based on the artist.

I don't see this instability—the solidity of a letter on the one hand and the fluidity of image on the other—as a problem. The indeterminate nature of monsters, as evidenced through various artists' depictions and verified by children's own imaginations, means that children have to take charge of the image and of the monster, with the letter to help show them the way. The monster alphabet can help children make meaning and therefore make sense of the world of language into which they are being inculcated as members of their culture. For Karen Coats, opening up what the alphabet can portray, in part through presenting the letters in non-conventional ways, can ease children into that new and complicated world. She aligns the traditional alphabet book with the patriarchal Lacanian view of development, in which children leave the "wholeness" of the more body-focused imaginary order for the language-based and representational symbolic order. However, Coats notes that "pictures and images offer a more immediately available form of representation, since they operate on a less abstract, more sensual principle of expression" (88). Analyzing the "alphabet's usurpation of the image" (93), she looks to books that play with language, "perform" the alphabet, contribute unsettling or unconventional imagery, and undermine the supposed simplicity of "a is for—" paradigm. For Coats, "true literacy is a negotiation between image and the alphabet" (96).

The monster ABC book could serve as another example of the type of expansion she hopes for. Again, monsters pre-date written language. They have been a part of our culture and have inhabited our imaginations long before we had the ability to assign them to an arbitrary system of signification. In looking at monster ABC books, children must negotiate between images, between image and letter, between their imaginations and the reality of the outside world, before they can adopt a certain referent for a sign. It seems to me entirely fitting that the ultimate symbol of the cultural "Other," monsters, help usher children into the symbolic order through alphabet books.

These theoretical discussions move far beyond what children can begin to understand from looking through monster ABC books; their appeal is multi-faceted. But in addition to entertaining, to stimulating curiosity, to expanding cultural horizons, monster ABC books can give children a way to order an unordered world and provide a sense of control over ever-growing knowledge. And while children may not "learn to read" from them, ABC books can help develop children's pre-reading skills and vocabulary development, though the vocabulary might be a little off the beaten path.

Perhaps the popularity of monster ABC books in the early 21st century can also be linked to the greater variety of monsters to which children are exposed, since they are bombarded with visual stimuli. I, for one, never dreamed that I would play Plants vs. Zombies apocalypse games with my children, acting out portions of a video game while looking through a "tips for playing" book to find the best strategy to defeat the bucket-head zombie (and frankly, pretending to be the plants that fight the zombies is even stranger). But I have decided that the monster ABC book is an ideal teacher; I have a great image in my head of a freaky creature holding my child's hand and pulling back the curtain of knowledge with one of its other three. While I find my children's love of scary creatures both strange and strangely satisfying, I wouldn't have it any other way.

NOTES

1. Another article in this vein, which examines the way parents and children interact when looking through alphabet books, is Bronwen J. Davis, Mary Ann Evans, and Kailey Pearl Reynolds, "Child Miscues and Parental Feedback During Shared Alphabet Book Reading and Relations With Child Literacy Skills," *Scientific Studies of Reading* 14.4 (2010): 341–64. To read more about the debate among researchers about phoneme awareness and reading, a good place to start is National Institute of Child Health and Human Development, *Report of the National Reading Panel. Teaching Children to Read: An Evidence-Based Assessment of the Scientific Research Literature on Reading and Its Implications for Reading Instruction: Report of the Subgroups* (NIH Publication No. 00-4754) (Washington, D.C.: U.S. Government Printing Office, 2000).

2. If illustrations in children's books interests you, a good place to begin is Lawrence R. Sipe, "Revisiting the Relationships Between Text and Pictures," *Children's Literature in Education* 43.1 (2012): 4–21; and Perry Nordelman, *Words About Pictures: The Narrative Art of Children's Picture Books* (Athens: University of Georgia Press, 1988).

3. Bradley and Jones would argue that although these kinds of correspondences create "potentially confusing situations," they "can be opportunities to teach children to think flexibly about the alphabet" (459).

4. One of my favorite examples is the anti-slavery alphabet from the 1850s, discussed in Martha L. Sledge: "A Is for Abolitionist: *The Anti-Slavery Alphabet* and the Politics of Literacy," in Monica Elbert, ed., *Enterprising Youth: Social Values and Acculturation in Nineteenth-Century American Children's Literature* (New York: Routledge, 2008).

5. Kummerling-Meibauer and Meibauer use this language in "Early-Concept Books: Acquiring Nominal and Verbal Concepts," in Bettina Kümmerling-Meibauer, ed., *Emergent*

30   Part 1: Monstrous Instructors

Literacy: Children's Books from 0 to 3. Studies in Written Language and Literature (Philadelphia: John Benjamins, 2011): 91–114.

ADDITIONAL READING

Brooks, Mikey. *ABC Adventures: Magical Creatures*. Children are led through cartoonish drawings by Dr. Vontriponmybottom.

Froyd, K.D. *The Monster ABC Book*. Gives just the name and one realistically drawn monster.

Knox, Charlie. *A Small Book of Monsters A–Z*. Featuring Knox's unique drawing style, from "alligators to zombies."

McRae, Andrew. *S Is for Sasquatch: The Cryptozoological ABC's*. Takes children through an unusual "zoo" of cartoonish drawings

Phillips, Dee. *The Alphabet Book of Monsters: A Kids Book with an Alphabetical List of Monsters*. Lists 5–6 monsters for each letter; has a drawing of one of them.

WORKS CITED

Ahrens, Kathleen. "Picturebooks: Where Literature Appreciation Begins." *Emergent Literacy: Children's Books from 0 to 3* 13 (2011): 77–90. Web.

Ardam, Jacquelyn. "'Too old for children and too young for grown-ups': Gertrude Stein's *To Do: A Book of Alphabets and Birthdays*." *Modernism/modernity* 18.3 (2011): 575–95. Web.

Asma, Stephen. "Monsters and the Moral Imagination." *Monsters*, ed. Andrew J. Hoffman. Bedford Spotlight Series. Boston: Bedford St. Martins, 2016. 61–67. Print.

Bodmer, George R. "Approaching the Illustrated Text." *Teaching Children's Literature: Issues, Pedagogy, Resources*, ed. G. E. Sadler. New York: MLA, 1992. 72–79. Print.

_____. "The Post-Modern Alphabet: Extending the Limits of the Contemporary Alphabet Book, from Seuss to Gorey." *Children's Literature Association Quarterly* 14.3 (1989): 115–17. Web.

Bradley, Barbara, and Jennifer Jones. "Sharing Alphabet Books in Early Childhood Classrooms." *The Reading Teacher* 60.5 (Feb. 2007): 452–63. Print.

Coats, Karen. "P Is for Patriarchy: Re-Imaging the Alphabet." *Children's Literature Association Quarterly* 25.2 (Summer 2000): 88–97. Project Muse.

Cohen, Jeffrey Jerome. "Monster Culture (Seven Theses)." *Monster Theory: Reading Culture*, ed. Jeffrey Jerome Cohen. Minneapolis: University of Minnesota Press, 1996. Print.

Evers, Amy J., Lisa F. Lang, and Sharon V. Smith. "An ABC Literacy Journey: Anchoring in Texts, Bridging Language, and Creating Stories." *The Reading Teacher* 62.6: 461–70.

Fang, Zhihui. "Illustrations, Text, and the Child Reader: What Are Pictures in Children's Storybooks For?" *Reading Horizons* 37 (Nov./Dec. 1996): n. pag. Web.

Gendron, Darren J. *The Monster Alphabet Board Book*. Self-published, 2013.

Goetsch, Paul. *Monsters in English Literature: From the Romantic Age to the First World War*. Frankfurt Am Main: Peter Lang, 2002. Print.

"Helping Your Preschool Child. " *U.S. Department of Education*, 16 Sept. 2008. Web. 15 Apr. 2016.

Hunter, Llyn. *A Little Book of Monsters*. Atascadero, CA: Bobcat, 2007. Print.

Kickstarter. *The Monster Alphabet Board Book*, Darren J. Gendron. Kickstarter, 2016. Web. 9 Aug. 2015.

Kirkland, Bruce. "'Goosebumps' Author R. L. Stine Knows Why Kids Like to Be Scared." *Toronto Sun* 14 Oct. 2014. Web. 2 Nov. 2015.

Lewis, J. Patrick. *M Is for Monster: A Fantastic Creatures Alphabet*. Sleeping Bear Press, 2014. Print.

McGee, Ted. "ABCs of ABCs: Two Canadian Exemplars." *Canadian Children's Literature* 71.1 (1993): 26–32. Web.

Murray, Bruce A., Steven A. Stahl, and M. Gay Ivey. "Developing Phoneme Awareness through Alphabet Books." *Reading and Writing* 8.4 (1996): 307–22. Web.

Oliver, Lauren. "Why Do Children Like Books About Monsters?" *NYMetroParents Staff* 27 Nov. 2012. Web.

Sharon, Tanya, and Jacqueline D. Woolley. "Do Monsters Dream? Young Children's Understanding of the Fantasy/Reality Distinction." *British Journal of Developmental Psychology* 22 (2004): 293–310. EBSCOhost. Web. 13 May 2016.
Sleeping Bear Press. sleepingbearpress.com, 2016. Web. 21 Sept. 2015.
Spradlin, Michael P., and Jeff Weigel. *The Monster Alphabet*. New York: Price Stern Sloan, 2012. Print.
Williams, David. *Deformed Discourse: The Function of the Monster in Mediaeval Thought and Literature*. Montreal: McGill-Queen's University Press, 1996. Print.
Yaden, David, Laura Smolkin, and Laurie MacGillivray. "A Psychogenic Perspective on Children's Understanding About Letter Associations During Alphabet Book Readings." *Journal of Reading Behavior* 25.1 (1993): 43–68. Web.

Green Legs and Hands
The Lorax *as a Medievalist Morality Tale*

CORWIN R. BADEN

"It's not easy being green," sings Kermit the Frog of *Sesame Street* fame. Echoing this sentiment, Dr. Seuss' *The Lorax* is a ballad about green-ness and the trials such a color entails. Now more than three decades old, the story of *The Lorax*—which is also the story of a monstrous creature named "The Once-ler"—has captivated children across the years. It is also a story which conjures comparisons with medieval morality tales in its imagery, dissociated narration, and longing for what has been lost.

The Lorax tells the story of an Edenic land that has been robbed of its innocence. A pioneering pair of hands and legs (for this is all we ever see) arrives, takes command of the region's resources, drives out the local inhabitants (all exotic creatures in Seussian fashion), and degrades the environment, apparently past the point of no return. The Once-ler has extracted the precious "Truffula" trees from a pristine paradise and has colonized a land previously at liberty.

On Imperialism and Individuation

By centering on loss and corruption, *The Lorax* picks up a medieval gauntlet in order to tell a very different type of morality tale. It is an ethical quest that is presented to young readers as an opportunity, not as a didactic sermon.

The story is introduced as a present-tense pilgrimage predicated on the conditional. From its opening qualifier ("*If* you look *deep* enough") to its concluding reminder ("*UNLESS* someone like you cares a whole awful lot") (Seuss, n. pag.; italics mine), the tale is distinctly moral and interactive, especially when compared to the rest of Seuss' lighthearted fare. It is a morality tale which has its literary antecedents in the Middle Ages. Following the archetypal romantic quest pattern, *The Lorax* coaxes us into its narrative space with an ambivalent "some people say," leading readers hesitantly toward a holy relic within a sacred site: the crumbling stone launching pad of the raptured Lorax. The narrative voice is hardly omniscient. It is the voice of ballads past, the vacillating and uncertain tale of a historiographer who remains uncertain of the way things have come to such a pass ... and in the dark as to how it will all turn out. There is no happy ending within the book's pages, and no turn for the better in the conventional, Tolkienesque sense.[1]

Psychoanalytical critic Bruno Bettelheim has theorized that children require fairy tales. Using medievalist J.R.R. Tolkien's framework from his seminal lecture "On Fairy-stories," Bettelheim has shown that traditional "happy endings" and unambiguous binaries can help children cope with real life.[2] In addition, Alison Lurie has speculated that writers of children's literature "in some essential way are children themselves" (*Boys*, ix). Yet the ecological catastrophe and postcolonial scars that frame *The Lorax* are global and thus insurmountable for individuals, and perhaps unfathomable for children. As philosopher and pedagogue, Seuss is transparent in his leanings. His tale, on its surface, lends itself to ecocritical and postcolonial interpretations. Yet it is because of its medievalist echoes that archetypal critics are able to find in this story a pilgrimage for Jungian individuation, a means by which Seuss—and his readers—access unconscious imagery by igniting imagination and achieving a personal emotional and psychological reconciliation.

Using conceptual scholarly maps provided by medievalist critics Tison Pugh and Angela Jane Weisl in *Medievalisms: Making the Past in the Present* and Kathleen Biddick in her entire body of work, readers are able to examine aspects of the medieval, such as the influence and echoes of traditional tales in Seuss, that necessarily intersect with social and emotional development and which are simultaneously adjacent to postcolonial and ecocritical concerns. At heart, though, *The Lorax* is the tale of a young person—a dim reflection of the child that Seuss has always been—and that child's search for a reconstitution of identity in the face of global and personal dissociation. Each of these critical perspectives (ecocritical, postcolonial, and medievalist/archetypal) can provide a unique vantage from which to understand the tale's impact and the dynamics of its reception.

While the story is simple, the framing narrative voice of the tale is fragmented. As with Dickens' Scrooge, three otherworldly apparitions are visiting young readers: the green Once-ler, the wooly-bully Lorax, and an altogether disembodied and nameless narrative voice that points to humanity's collective grave yet also allows for hope. It is this last voice which introduces and frames the tale in mythical time and space at the outskirts of possibility. DeLoughrey and Handley provide for us an almost fantastical lens through which to gaze on the world—and history—as today's imaginative child might see it: "[T]he landscape (and seascape) [is] *a participant* in this historical process rather than a bystander to human experience. Engaging nonhuman agency creates an additional challenge because nature's own processes of regeneration and change often contribute to the burial of postcolonial histories" (4; emphasis mine). In other words, the landscape itself has come alive and is telling the story, providing yet another "narrator," one that requires a "speaker for the trees," the Lorax himself, to translate.

Three Green Ghosts

By analyzing the different voices of these varied "speakers," readers can consider the complexity of environmental concerns and the consequences of complicity for beings and organizations that fail to respond to changing circumstances. Once-ler is an obvious case-in-point. Not only has he capitalized on the fabricated needs of others, but he has also drawn others into a tangled web of destruction by inviting his whole green clan to colonize this unnamed Truffula land. Even more, the complicit consumers portrayed in this book—to whom the Youth is heir—are not visibly monstrous. They are wholly human, and it is they who linger on, squeezing the sponge of a spent land in perpetuity. They are both the haunters and the haunted.

Within this simple children's story, medieval precedents dialogue intertextually with modern tales to provide novel insights regarding ethical and meaning-making systems. To explore these possibilities I will consider each of the story's three characters in turn: the guilt-ridden Once-ler, the hand-wringing Lorax, and a naïve "eco-knight," the uninitiated young Everyman.

The image of the "green ghost"—an oxymoron which presents bodies as simultaneously living and dead—captures emblematically the hope for a resurrection "turn" from death to life. Whether found in the wound of the Arthurian Fisher King or Eliot's "Waste Land," there remains a dim hope that restoration will come to a desperate space. This fantasy is a "medievalism," not to be confused with the "medieval." Both terms—"medieval" and "medievalism"—are unstable signifiers. The first term implies an "authentic" historical recovery, while the second is essentially a copy of a copy. Medievalism is sometimes viewed as "hyper-reality," by which a constructed, "historically inspired" element appears even more "medieval" than the original, such as a Disney tug at the "Sword in the Stone" or a utensil-free dinner in Medieval times. Within the tradition of medievalism, the advance of the modern world has damaged pastoral nature. It is this pastoral tradition of a "protected past" that ecocritic Greg Garrard places in context: "We can set out [...] orientations of pastoral in terms of time: the *elegy* looks back to a vanished past with a sense of nostalgia" (42). *The Lorax* falls within the elegiac mood: it looks back with longing at what has been lost while viewing the future with dread. Yet there is also hope and potential in the action that lies between past and future. This medieval liminality, the "everytime in-between-ness" of the "Middle" Ages (represented in literature and art both as a time of decay *and* an Edenic age) fires the imaginations of authors of all ages and is supremely *productive*. Pugh and Weisl write that "liminal spaces open up the possibility of magic, of rules and expectations turned upside down" (52). From Tolkien to HBO's *Game of Thrones*, this medieval liminality has spawned an unpredictable proliferation of magical, anachronistic, and even anarchical rule-breaking.

The three characters encountered in Seuss' *The Lorax* can all be considered "green," tapping the endless associations of that word. The Once-ler is literally green, the Lorax is a "green" advocate, and the Nameless Youth is a greenhorn, playing the gendered role of mere receptacle for the Lorax's story as told by the Once-ler. Significantly, the youngest of these has no voice within the confines of Seuss' narrative and, as a pre-pubescent, he is the closest thing to female in the entire chain of narration. Perhaps this is Seuss' effort at portraying what he perceives the feminine to be: passive and voiceless. Yet the Youth alone, as the "feminine," is "fertile" ground, the only one who can make things grow again. In fact, all three of the book's characters—Once-ler, Lorax, and Youth—are assuming roles they may not be fully equipped to perform. They are ghosts, inhabiting a haunted world that somehow produces power or flame enough to light its darkened windows.

The Once-ler: The Green Machine

To begin with, the primary character associated with this book is most likely "the Once-ler," a figure who is always only half-discerned. Yellow eyes. Green arms. This is all we ever see of Once-ler; and his visual dismemberment reminds us of medieval horrors from a London dungeon. This is the proverbial "man" without a face. His green fingers poke through gapped boards on the book's introductory end pages, and when his arms emerge from those same gaps several pages later, they are a strange reflection of the drooping, pale-green cactus that perches on the balcony of his leaning dwelling, his "Lerkim." These arms are wrinkled and reptilian, signifying both age and utility as they bend and contort to collect the Youth's payment for Once-ler's story. We later see these same arms and hands grabbing greedily at Truffula tufts and then emptying a Conestoga wagon of the tools of his trade. In the strokes of Seuss' brush that shoot out from the back of that wagon, readers perceive streaks of green, lines of frenetic industry and motion, as if those arms are shedding their scales onto an already green landscape. Of course, Once-ler's green is a sorry, faux replacement for the real article.

Thus, like the haunted Mariner at Coleridge's medievalist wedding feast in "The Rime of the Ancient Mariner," Once-ler's narrative is unstable and unreliable. We cannot take his story at face value, just as we cannot trust Seuss' *Grinch* when that other monstrous messenger explains to Cindy Lou Who that he merely intends to repair the tree he is forcing up the chimney. Even Once-ler's green color ambiguously signifies both nature itself and the economic greed of ownership lust which so often annihilates nature. Like the Mariner of old, Once-ler is sentimental in a manipulative sense. He only tells his story for a fee. Moreover, both Mariner and Once-ler tell their tales within a "closeted" confessional narrative. Readers are told neither where Once-ler has come from nor what his intentions are.

We, with the story's nameless dark-haired Youth, seek the green goblin's counsel in no man's land and are led through gothic ruins, tumbled like tombstones along "The Street of the Lifted Lorax." We arrive suddenly at Once-ler's Lerkim, a secluded structure that is detached from a community of people painted into the pages' hinterlands. While we only see the Youth's world at a distance, the buildings appear sleeker, less jagged, even more spiritualized, since a steepled structure is prominent on the near side of the street on which the Youth walks. There are lighted edges in the windows, yet all among and beyond those "human" buildings is an even gray, without any apparent vegetation. In contrast, Once-ler's Lerkim stands in the midst of skeletal tree trunks and grasses that remind viewers of Chinese brushstrokes in black. It is clear that this Street of the Lifted Lorax has been forgotten, or at least has been isolated irreparably from the existing background community.

Smelling opportunity in the form of this lone Youth, Once-ler lowers his bucket, receives a payment of odds and ends, grotesquely sucks them into his hollow green finger, and then lowers a "Whisper-ma-Phone" through which to tell the Youth exactly why the mysterious "Lorax" has been "lifted" away from this Street of the Lifted Lorax.

Once-ler will only speak for a fee, but once the payment is made, it appears that he has a load to get off his chest. Through a carelessly boarded-up window (which, strangely, floats emblematically in mid-air on the book's end-pages), we can see his eyes, and through his "Whisper-ma-Phone" we can hear his raspy tale. Eyes and voice—along with legs and hands—never appear wholly contrite, lined as they are by Seuss' strokes and words with a duplicitous edge.

Once-ler's story is fairly straightforward. He arrives as a pilgrim-settler, awed by the potential of the region's natural wealth. Readers' eyes, like Once-ler's, are fixed on the tufts of fluorescent pinks, yellows, purples, and oranges—and even one or two greens. Seuss highlights their multi-sensory essence:

"The touch of their tufts was much softer than silk. And they had the sweet smell of fresh butterfly milk." Meanwhile, the pinwheel quality of the tree-tufts makes our own eyes spin, and the trunks follow the zebra-striped black-and-yellow pattern visible in the earlier image of the Youth's mauve clothing, as if humanity is now paying tribute to a lost past by ritually wearing those stripes. Moreover, there are fruits—colored like grapes yet nearly as large as pears—hanging in clusters below the tufts. It is these fruits that sustain the brown "Bar-ba-loots," fuzzy, dog-eared, Teddy-bear beasts that populate the Truffula forests.

Once-ler, dismissing any life-giving aspect of the trees themselves, remains fixated on the "spinning" tufts. Almost immediately, he harvests some and invents a "Thneed," a one-piece outfit created from the tree he has just chopped down. Yet Once-ler's massive knitting needles—eerily reminiscent of the nail given as payment for his story—take the life out of the tufts. The Thneed is oddly misshapen, a fashion abomination, with its sleeve and leg oddly conjoined. It appears to be an "ouroboros" (the image of the snake eating its own tail), an Escher-like impossibility that no one could ever even wear. The tufts are essentially gone, insinuated only by the light fuzz of the pink garment, which is itself pocked with holes—for buttons, head, hands and feet—that remind us of Once-ler's index finger opening oddly to consume. Once-ler's small hut has become a new "Little Shop of Horrors," and we wonder what his ax, protruding from the dismembered stump, will chop up next.

Before readers can blink, a creature—the irascible Lorax—appears from a crack in that stump (thereby displacing the ax) to scold Once-ler for his recklessness. But this is not the only response from the Truffula community. Before readers can blink again, a human-appearing customer appears to exchange a handful of bills and coins for the now needed Thneed. This initial success spurs Once-ler to augment production, call his green-handed relatives in for support, and begin a thorough ransacking of the countryside. The Lorax appears a charm-like three times, but on each occasion is rebuffed until the last Truffula tree is hacked to the ground. The displacement of all the land's creatures (Swomee Swans, fantastical fish, and furry brown Bar-ba-loots) and a subsequent exodus of Once-ler's family members empty the land of life. Finally, in a strange mix of triumph and humiliation, the ineffectual Lorax lifts himself by the seat of the pants into the sky. Only Once-ler remains to meditate—monk-like—on his own handiwork.

Lest readers be hoodwinked, the Once-ler's confession is not a general admission of guilt. It is merely a private one that reinscribes the "Othering" which has cast this narrator as pariah. Like Coleridge's Mariner, a sailor who has recklessly killed a magnificent seabird, Once-ler now has an albatross around his neck. He has violated nature and continues to pay the price. In the case of the old Mariner, the forces of death have lost their game of casting lots for his soul, and he has survived. Still, he appears to be a hollow man. It is this same limbo life that the Once-ler leads in *The Lorax*, having created his own purgatory in which to lurk.

Alternately, the Once-ler might be recognized as a medievalist re-telling of the Arthurian tale of *Sir Gawain and the Green Knight*. In that medieval tale, a giant all-green messenger comes to Camelot to engage Arthur's court in Yuletide play. To the surprise of Arthur, Guinevere, and the whole Grail Gang, the visiting Green Knight offers his neck for one of the knights to take a swing at. His insults become insufferable, and the honorable Gawain steps up to the plate to defend his lord's honor. In one stroke, the Green Knight's head is severed. It is then that readers realize that the game is not over. The Green Knight uncannily picks up his own head and reminds Gawain and all hearers that Gawain must now receive his own decapitating blow one year from that very day. In *The Lorax*, Once-ler's arrogance and his imagined impunity can be compared to Gawain's confidence in his own abilities. Both are subsequently marked in a green that reminds all they meet of their greatest failures.

Seuss most certainly saw a parallel between medieval tales and the moral of his own story. The animated television special inspired by Seuss' *Lorax* actually uses narrator Eddie Albert as a tale-telling troubadour, intoning the introduction in *jongleur* style. Like Gawain, Once-ler has broken faith. While Gawain is tempted both by physical pleasure and by an ever-present fear of an unpleasant end, Once-ler is overtaken by his own entrepreneurial passion. He seeks to turn beautiful things—Truffula tufts—into beautiful cash.[3] The key resemblance between the green Once-ler and the green-girdled Gawain is that neither of them is truly green: they are copies of the "green" they have displaced, only wearing a green "skin" to remind everyone of their breach of faith.

For the Once-ler, his "green-ness" has been a signifier from the beginning, yet interpreting his color through the lens of race troubles our view of him. It is possible to see in Once-ler a demonized, scapegoated "Other" who has been "marked" to pay for the sins of society at large. We must recognize that Once-ler's green-ness, and that of his entire family, can be taken as semiotic boundary drawing that exonerates the rest of society, those who still burn precious resources through the lighted windows of Seuss' backdrop landscape, whose feet but not faces have been seen speeding off with the Thneed that ultimately leads to ecological collapse. In fact, Once-ler is depicted as disembodied hands (and feet, if we also consider the 1972 television special produced by Fritz Freleng and over which Seuss exercised considerable control).[4] Yet there is no denying Once-ler his agency in all of this. Even in confession, as much as readers would like to believe that Once-ler has changed, he remains a reluctant messiah. After all, he has had the story-turning seed for some time but hasn't made a move to plant it himself, nor has he gone out of his way to recruit someone to help him plant it. And yet he is always "worrying." Readers realize that Seuss doesn't trust Once-ler either. This green ghost reflects "adult society"—from the midst of which Seuss recuses himself—as active, or at least complicit, in the capitalist colonization of the environment.

At the same time, leaders find themselves always under the Once-ler's panoptic gaze, and especially at story's end do readers feel implicated in the trauma of the tale. His eyes—at once both moralizing and predatory—follow us, and we suddenly realize that food is scarce—non-existent, really—in this barren place left behind by the Bar-ba-loots when their fruits were exhausted. What, exactly, does Once-ler eat? In medievalist terms, Once-ler is the cannibal witch, the marginalized and disciplined figure that Kathleen Biddick surveys in her book *The Shock of Medievalism*: "Witches are cannibals—their practice of devouring their children [...] sets them apart from humans, although there is a space for the wolf inside this strong frame" (222). In essence, the exiled witch-figure serves as a distraction from the wolves that still prowl within the fence. For the reality is that all adults "eat their young" through their collective (if not personal) modeling of moral failure. Seuss is not about to let anyone off the hook here.

Once-ler's collection of payment, and the specific ingredients involved ("fifteen cents and a nail and the shell of a [...] snail"), remind us of the "eye of newt and tongue of dog and wing of bat" so caricatured in depictions of Loony Toon witchcraft. Yet there is significance even here. The coarse items collected as payment by Once-ler seem to have symbolic purchase. Apart from the money, the nail can be seen as a medieval relic (i.e., from the cross of Christ) while the snail represents an odd tradition in illuminated manuscripts, with which Seuss was clearly familiar, pictures in which knights are depicted riding on the backs of snails. In these simple—yet odd—objects we might be able to view Once-ler as *both* ecological knight and demonic foe. Yet in the blink of an eye, Once-ler scoops snail and nail from the bucket he has lowered to the boy. He then magically *opens his finger* and vacuums the offered objects into his hollow index-finger hose. It is an image that makes one's hair stand on end.

The Lorax: Benevolent Buzzkill

So where, then, does the eponymous Lorax come from? As an emblem, Lorax, too, is "green." He is the "inconvenient truth," the collective conscience and Unconscious (he emerges from below ground) invoked to give Once-ler and his ilk a good tongue-lashing since the trees have no tongues of their own. Physically, his appearance is less-than-dominating. His orange skin, bald head, and bushy whiskers evoke the archetypal Moses, a prophet come down from the mountain only to find his existential purpose under attack. It is also frequently noted that the Lorax's appearance is based on the no-nonsense, environmental-championing visage of Teddy Roosevelt.[5] Yet this rough-riding Lorax is always angry. In addition, his commitment to nature itself appears arbitrary and fleeting. Instead of remaining to mourn its ashes at story's end, he zooms away like a bull moose, lifting himself supernaturally by his own rear end—a literal enactment of American "by-your-own-boot-straps" attitudes. If this is Seuss' tribute to a hero, what could it mean?

Another documented connection between the Rough Rider and Seuss is helpful in determining the Lorax's intentions. Seuss' earliest biographers and close personal friends, Judith and Neil Morgan, tell the following story:

> [A]t the age of fourteen, [Seuss] stood with nine other Scouts [...] to receive an award from Colonel Theodore Roosevelt himself [...] One by one each Scout saluted smartly and marched off-stage. Finally [Seuss] was left alone onstage facing the former president, who was clearly out of medals. "What's this little boy doing here?" Roosevelt bellowed at the scoutmaster, who frowned and scuttled [Seuss] offstage. Within a few years [Seuss'] fear of public platforms bordered on the neurotic and he began devising complex excuses to avoid them [22].

By channeling this bogey from his own past—a President who towered above him, whose first name was the same as his own, and who shook his confidence irrevocably—Seuss gives readers an inkling that the Lorax signifies far more than benevolent pastoral care. This shepherd of the trees doesn't just say "bully." He *is* a bully. Without question Seuss would have seen the implications, or at least the irony. As a supernatural being, then, the Lorax simply doesn't quite fit the bill. He is able to pop out of tree stumps, and perhaps he can be credited with uncanny vision in knowing the ultimate progress of ecological disaster. Nevertheless, he is soft—a "doughboy"—when it comes to confronting the Once-ler. Instead of defending the trees, he merely lets things run their course, moralizes about the demise of all things Truffula, and vanishes.

Despite the Lorax's impotence, there is no denying that Seuss frames him as a messianic figure: come as advocate, rejected as irrelevant, and ascended into the sky, leaving only a memorial of his presence behind: a pedestal that is sacramental and participatory, yet itself crumbling in disuse. Seuss portrays the Lorax as insignificant, and annoying yet wise: the Guru of Green. As far as biblical allusion takes the reader, it is better to say that this Lorax is Elijah running from Jezebel in the midst of impossible drought. The Lorax is both friend and foe. He, too, represents the adult world—the same one which has been complicit in Seuss' perceived destruction of the environment—as well as the fantasy-world of the child's own imaginings. He is the "Lore-ax," a mythical figure who simultaneously embodies myth and allows it to be destroyed. There is a sense that the Lorax, too, has failed to curb the gases in this "greenhouse." Indeed, his coughing signifies that, while he may be supernatural, he is limited. In even stronger terms, there is the intimation that the Lorax has enabled the destruction the Once-ler and his ilk have caused. He is not omnipotent, or even omnipresent, and he can be chased away. He appears three times to appeal to the Once-ler, but with each successive attempt readers realize that he cannot save them. Even eschatologically speaking, his hoped-for return will be a function of responsible living, not of his own power or authority.

The Nameless Youth: Color Blind or Clueless?

And so the seed is passed, baton-like, to the Nameless Youth, whom I shall call "Percival" after the Grail knight who enters the castle of the Fisher King, sees the Grail pass before him three times, and yet does not open his mouth, fearing an impolite and unseemly interruption. Since he does not self-advocate, the opportunity to heal the Wasteland vanishes, along with ladies-in-waiting, King, and castle itself. The Youth depicted by Seuss to receive these narratives is the disciple of three separate narrative masters (if we are to include the disembodied voice that frames the story). His dark hair, tangled and spiky like the tree carcasses which surround him, sets him apart from the colors of the original *Lorax* landscape, yet in his pinkish face and striped mauve shirt and pants (curiously reminiscent of a traditional prison uniform) we see the colors of hope. His wide white eyes are saucers eager to be filled. He, too, is nameless and voiceless, having no lines of dialogue within the book's pages. It is possible that, in withholding the child's voice, Seuss wants to advocate for the "voiceless" child who has, up to this point in time, had no say regarding stewardship of the environment. At the same time Seuss also reminds adult readers of our own deafening silence when confronted with controversy.

In the end, this "Percival" character is given the key to restoring the wasteland, yet he opens not his mouth. I could just as easily refer to the Youth as "Seuss' Youth," an image of the author's own frustrated childhood. "Othered" from birth by his German family background during World War I, Seuss was subsequently rendered "speechless" by a former President. Of course, he found his voice through images and words on paper, and he was active in politics throughout his life, but a case could be made that this is Seuss' own ghost, the specter of his own childhood.

Trauma, particularly during his later years, most certainly complicated the lifelong process of individuation by which Seuss sought to reintegrate his own personality. His eventual drift away from his first wife Helen, particularly since she was suffering from a debilitating chronic illness, eventually resulted in her suicide and most likely heaped guilt upon Seuss' head. Pease delves into Seuss' subsequent frame of mind, a jarring discord that threatened to split him in half. Pease writes that "[a]fter reading Helen's suicide note, [Seuss] reportedly said that he didn't know whether he should kill himself or burn down the house. He titled the first book he published after Helen's death *The Foot Book*. This pre–Beginner Book was about how to put one foot in front of the other. It began 'Left foot Right foot'" (133). Without a doubt, there was a murky darkness behind Seuss' green grass and brilliant Truffulas, and like any public figure Seuss was forced to work through his private problems in public.

Seuss, in fact, had a habit of drawing himself—or at least his alter-egos—into his work. There is evidence from his own illustrations that he identified with both the Grinch and the Cat in the Hat, both created in 1957. Whether or not Seuss intended the nameless Youth to represent himself, his illustrations consistently provide reflections of his own foibles and internal conflicts.[6] As an archetype, the Youth reminds us that *The Lorax* is a children's story and also a plea for a return to innocence. Pugh and Weisl tell us that "as authors of children's literature construct the children necessary for their fictions, both in terms of the readers of the texts and any children depicted therein, so too must authors of 'medieval' children's literature create the Middle Ages that they need for their narratives to unfold" (42). Seuss needs "Percival"—both as a way to communicate with and embody his intended audiences and for his own individuation and re-integrative work.

Zoot Suits and Bar-Ba-Loots: Postcolonial Problems

This Seussian wasteland is a tapestry woven from three strands: medievalism, postcolonialism, and ecocriticism. Yet the threads of this tapestry easily become tangled. While Seuss' conscious motives seem clear enough, we are left to interrogate his work based on his own history as a Euro-American writer emerging from a racist past. This sometimes leads us where we don't want to go, particularly with a beloved children's author.

First, in choosing to use a medievalist filter, Seuss betrays his own distance from his contemporary world. He also demonstrates a tendency to "medievalize" others, whether as monsters or as knights. Pugh and Weisl write that "[t]he medieval past, however it is constructed or defined, is a kind of other, whose differences we putative non-medievals must engage" (53). This engagement is often a mask for conflict or unresolved dissonances.

Furthermore, his position within a multiethnic and multiracial America during the first half of the century shaped his interactions with minority groups in the United States and his perceptions of colonial influences around the globe. The young Seuss and his family were themselves "Othered" by an America at war with Germany. His later position as a propagandist for U.S. Armed Forces during World War II clearly influenced his interactions with groups with whom he came into contact. Of all Seuss' biographers, Cohen is the one who takes the most time to connect some of these dots, relating them directly to Seuss' illustrations and stories. Seuss "pointed out that bad things can happen to good and innocent people, often at the whim of people in positions of power" (Cohen 193). Cohen summarizes these influences with the following poignant assessment: "In [Seuss'] experience, an ex-president of the United States could run out of medals just when he got to you, even though you'd done just as much as the people who received their medals. The government could pass legislation that suddenly made your family's business illegal" (Cohen 193). Nevertheless, Seuss, so aware of personal injuries and injustice, is himself enmeshed in societal and global "Othering." Medievalist Kathleen Biddick writes that our actions and reactions are intertwined with "the historically situated Euroamerican project of producing an experience of scholarship, order, truth, and management based on the textualization of imagining others exterior to Europe who inhabit an imaginary space constructed by Europeans" (91). To extricate himself from such imaginary constructions, Seuss needed a lifetime of cathartic creating—a career of "Sneetches" and "Bitter Butter Battles" to help him overcome previous bigotry and cultural blindness.

"Here we go round the prickly pear"

There is no doubt that Seuss shifted his culturally cued stances on race and ethnicity over the course of his long life. Yet there are ghosts of racial attitudes past that are difficult to dispel. Within *The Lorax*'s unpaginated frames, an element that suggests timelessness, we see brown Bar-ba-loots, Teddy bear–like creatures with "crummies in their tummies" (Seuss, *Lorax*, n. pag.). They are marching off in a line reminiscent of traders marching enslaved Africans along the Barbary Coast. While Seuss is certainly insinuating a new ecoslavery created by colonizing capitalists, the postcolonial picture he creates is one of subalterns, once again at the mercy of a hegemonic West, unable to feed themselves and alternately victimized and patronized by more powerful "Others"—even the Lorax himself—in a vicious cycle of never-ending futility.

There are suspicions, too, that the "contrite" Once-ler, even as he pleads with the story's Percival to re-green the world, is poised to become the "Once-again-ler," eager to reinscribe his hegemonic power if and when the chance arises. His claim that he has "worried and worried" echoes ironically the "biggering and biggering" of which he has so habitually been guilty. His shifting identity denotes regret, but not necessarily his true contrition and change. In the end of the story the "Youth" is tossed the means of production, but a wasteland of postcolonial experience will not be easily "re-greened." Fraud abounds. Still, it would be ungenerous to claim that rehabilitation is impossible. Meanwhile, the postcolonial shadows linger. Once-ler is bourgeois and Lorax is aristocratic, with his head literally in the clouds, and even he has emigrated during the reign of eco-terror. He may return, but recovery does not depend on his return. Readers must remember that nostalgic longing can lead to what critic Abdul JanMohamed has termed "[h]istorical catalepsy or cultural petrifaction" ("JanMohamad").

Within this postcolonial subtext, the rise of capitalism has brought the end of happy feudalism, a rural Arcadian economy that dominated the European Middle Ages and which has been sentimentalized by Western writers at the expense of real members of "pastoral" societies around the world. Without a doubt, *The Lorax* is a cautionary tale, but its message of caution for capitalists is much more utilitarian than we might think. It cautions, "Do not be overconfident that you will win and that your resources will last forever."

This utilitarian message is the true horror of the Once-ler's open finger, the one in which he deposits the Youth's offering for some esoteric future use. The Once-ler is a living vending machine, or perhaps just a slot machine. The startling image of his open finger may just be a feature of the "gruvvulous glove" he apparently wears, but its open mouth appears supernaturally to swallow, as if the being to which that finger is attached is a shapeshifting "blob" that is capable of swallowing the world, given time and opportunity. Despite Once-ler's claims of restoration, he is still a very hollow man. After all, why hasn't he planted the seed himself?

These empty mysteries are the effects of the Once-ler's lonely Lerkim. On the third page of Seuss' story (not counting cover, end pages, or title page), readers' eyes are drawn to the Lerkim's gothic grill-work, spider-like and reminiscent of New Orleans–style decadence. Our eye is then drawn downward from that iron grate to a twisted dripping faucet. Once-ler has, predictably, left the water running. The stone steps below its invisible puddle are rising up as if they have been shrugged off by a disapproving earth. Surrounding this little drama is a leaning, wrinkled mauve structure that appears ready to fall at the slightest provocation. The door is cracked from top to middle, and a doorknob juts out. Strikingly, the keyhole is shaped like a question mark. Once-ler dwells in a cloistered post that has given him tunnel-vision and produced only one cactus, a prickly reminder of lost green that bows submissively toward a darkened eastern sky. Finally, the entire structure is undermined by its architectural extravagances. An arch below the Lerkim-structure's porch—presumably for an unseen creature kept as a pet—weakens that approach and marks it as treacherous.

This is where the book's authoritative speaker—who has arrived from nowhere and lives in limbo—dwells. He is not of this once-Edenic world. In fact, as I looked back at two editions of Seuss' book, it was the transformation of the Once-ler himself that threw me for a loop. In comparing my childhood copy, the old 1971 edition, with a later 1986 re-print that removes a derogatory reference to Lake Erie, I discovered that colors have been altered with the later printing. For the panels depicting the advent of the Lorax in the 1986 edition, the grass is still green, yet the Once-ler is something else entirely. His new hue is an *off*-green. There has been a clear attempt over the years by all hands involved in this book to differentiate Once-ler from the environment he has decimated.

Going Green

The message of the book has struck most adult readers, and probably most young readers, as straightforward, if not heavy-handed. Pease writes that "[a]fter Random House distributed *The Lorax* to bookstores in 1971, *Newsweek* called it a hard-sell ecological allegory" (140). At least on the surface, the moral appears so transparent that it has led to confrontation with the logging industry in northern California. Lurie writes that "[t]he loggers saw it as blatant propaganda and agitated to have it banned from the school's required reading list" ("Cabinet" 158). Yet there is more to the moral than meets those green eyes. A key clue to understanding Seuss' diverse purposes lies in his goal of granting agency to his young readers in influencing the decisions that adults make. It's easy for me to imagine how children might respond to this story because I remember how I responded at that early age. I was afraid. The Once-ler is no green Grinch: his heart never grows three sizes. He remains shut off from the world, lurking in his haunted Lerkim. But I think I was afraid because I, like other children, could learn not to buy and sell ... but I could not control the actions of adults.

Children, fearing the ax, might well avoid killing plants or harming animals. Yet the problem of this unnamed Wasteland is cosmic. It goes deeper than seeds and water. It seems to lie in the lack of sunlight. Certainly, Seuss seeks to teach young people that a small act can lead to larger ones, and the domino effect can travel both directions. He also reminds us that invention, so celebrated in the industrialized West, is not always benign. Rachel Carson has famously married medieval imagery to the ecological crises confronting the world today. In *Silent Spring*, she writes that "[n]o witchcraft, no enemy action had silenced the rebirth of new life in this stricken world. The people had done it themselves" (qtd. in Garrard 2). Carson has served as a kind of spirit guide for more than half a century now, yet many of the same conditions still obtain.

Even Seuss seems to indicate that there must be guidance, that his three-dimensional narrative is a "read-aloud," a story to be shared and explicated by the adults that are conspicuously absent, except as consumers of Thneeds. It is the adults which are key to effecting change, and Seuss signals this with his barely visible adult narrator, "an adult instructing a child in how and what to inherit from the adult's generation. All of these adult figures want to pass something on. They are liminal figures in that they do not belong to a present or a past and they cannot quite be included in the social order of which they are a part" (Pease 137). Seuss, caught between times and stations of the social order, invokes the medieval Green Man to solve problems of modernity.

Green Man of the Greenwood

The archetypal "Green Man" figure is as old as the hills, and Seuss seems aware of this trope as he creates a Scrooge-like figure clad in verdant garb. It is difficult to discern whether Once-ler was born green or whether his green hue has been brought on to teach him a lesson, much as Gawain is required to wear his green sash to remind him of his failure. Green, of course, can signify life and hope, a resilient nature that can't be tamed or understood. Even Seuss' *Lorax* grass is supremely resilient to the end, glowing eerily even after the last Truffula tree is gone. Finally, after all has turned gray, we still see a green beacon shining from a streetlamp within the book's second-to-last image. Green will always be associated with the American Dream in all its many guises.[7]

Interestingly enough, Seuss' story was inspired not by Western industrialization but by a trip he took to Africa. In a 1978 interview for the *Christian Science Monitor*, Seuss responded directly regarding his views of a book which had changed the trajectory and tenor of his career: "His favorite story is *The Lorax* [...] 'The Lorax book was intended to be propaganda [...] I was angry about the ecology problems [...] Going over the Serengeti Plain one afternoon, he looked up and said, 'Look at that tree.' He said, 'They've stolen my trees'" (Frutig 80–81). Pease offers even more details regarding this African genesis:

> His health supported by his wife Audrey, who reinvigorated his palette with softer hues of "mauve, plum purple, and sage green" and who took him on a trip to Africa when he was suffering blocks to his creative process, an epiphany occurred as he

watched elephants pass his hotel. Seuss writes that "I don't know how it happened, but the logjam broke, I had nothing but a laundry list with me, and I grabbed it, I wrote 90% of the book that afternoon" [137].

These changes to Seuss' palette remind us that "sage green" has more than one use. It can represent our own ecocentrism—the green-eyed monster that seeks to turn resources to reward—or the natural life-force of the planet itself. While it is unclear whether the trees or the elephants inspired him more, it is clear that an ecosystem was spread before him and that he was inexorably caught in its web (although, like all the colonial-minded, he lays his own claim to Africa's trees). Perhaps he saw himself in the Once-ler as well, realizing his complicity in the "logjam," and his illness may have led him to consider his own muffled voice. Pease writes that "the Once-ler's vocal eccentricities and apparel—the snergedly hose, the gruvvulous glove, the miff-muffered moof—exemplify symptoms of the ecological disaster he has wrought" (139). Yet eccentricities or no, he must speak as a member of this narrative relay: "The Once-ler now speaks for the Lorax just as the Lorax had formerly spoken on behalf of the trees" (Pease 139). Seuss, too, is speaking for others, in a literary relay that continues a long literary tradition.

In *Dr. Seuss: American Icon*, critic Philip Nel reminds us of Seuss' place within a broader and deeper tradition of word games: "Dr. Seuss is heir to Edward Lear. All nonsense writers invent fantastic animals [...] However, Lear invented more than most [...] Seuss has dreamed up Dike Trees, Beezlenut Trees, Truffula Trees and Stickle-Bush Trees, but Lear takes the prize in nonsense botany" (23). Nevertheless, in the end, it is that sterile, prickly, accusing cactus teetering on the ledge of the Once-ler's Lerkim that gives us pause, and which may leave a lasting impression on children readers after thirty-six framed images, counting the cover. Even the book's final page provides no soft landing—only the seed of the future floating in mid-air.

For me, as a child of five, it was a different image that fixed me, that still transfixes me today: that greedy green hand receiving payment. Each time I saw Once-ler open the tip of his finger, I wondered whether I might somehow be able to do the same. Yet it was perhaps in that very same finger that the Once-ler hid the seed of life for so long. He is a hollow man whose soul seems empty, except for the seed it grudgingly contains. Children's books are seed-baskets, too, subtly sowing reminders of the inequities in the world, the injustices of hegemonic teetering, and the slings and arrows of climatic misfortune combined with our own bad behavior. Seuss has not created this seed, but he *has* passed it on.

There is, perhaps, a silver lining here. It may not be enough, but even the symbolic opening of Once-ler's finger is a faint copy of a plant as it emerges from crusted soil. Perhaps his greenness is merely a suit that he will untie and discard, or perhaps it is the beginning of an "unravelling" of capricious hegemonic forces. After all, the passing of the seed—seen as a post-diluvian rainbow through a pillar of cloud on the book's last page—is a return of the means of production to those from whom they have been usurped, and perhaps green, in the end, means go: not toward the orgiastic future but toward a "going and doing likewise." Seuss models for us Bruno Bettelheim's thesis for healthy individuation and ecological remediation. "Only by going out into the world," Bettelheim writes, "can the fairy-tale hero (child) find himself there" (11). And perhaps that child will also find the courage to lead green-eyed Parents down the "Street of the Lifted Lorax" to plant seeds of their own.

Notes

1. Tolkien's seminal address "On Fairy Stories," delivered at the University of St. Andrews on 8 March 1939, is a foundational theoretical text for fantastic and children's literature.

2. Bettelheim's controversial work was re-issued in 1989 and has remained influential despite being opposed by Alan Dundes in "Bruno Bettelheim's Uses of Enchantment and Abuses of Scholarship," *The Journal of American Folklore* 104.411 (1991): 74–83, among others.

3. Medievalist Bruce Holsinger writes in his *Burnable Books* blog: "Nowhere are these lines of visual influence realized more clearly (and uncannily) than in Seuss' appropriation of the Utrecht Psalter's enchanting trees, which seem to float over the page even while tethered to the parchment by a series of twisted, gnarled trunks often jutting from perilous escarpments. These trees were apparently the direct inspiration for the 'Truffalump tree' [sic] the threatened species inspiring the environmental imagination of *The Lorax*, as well as other imaginative renderings of the semi-forested pastoral scenes abounding in Seuss' oeuvre."

4. During an animated Fritz Freleng-Dr. Seuss *Lorax* television production, it is approximately fifteen minutes into the show that viewers finally see the Once-ler's legs. This viewing is preceded by a barbershop quartet, hats on green chests, singing his praises. Freleng's influences on Seuss can be seen in linked buildings that appear as Once-ler's empire expands ("progress progresses too fast," says the Lorax). These "complexes" are labeled "Ye Once-ler's Arms," "Annex," and "Ye Annex Annex," again demonstrating Seuss' proclivities toward the medieval, as well as the influence of Freleng's Bugs Bunnyesque tendencies in reformatting this narrative for the television special; for comparison, see *Bonanza Bunny* (1959). There is also a fascinating Freudian scene where Once-ler sings of his confrontations with his doppelgänger conscience-superego (mirrored in ghostly animation).

5. While perhaps not generally recognized, the resemblance between Roosevelt and the Lorax is striking. See http://seuss.wikia.com/wiki/The_Lorax_(Character) and http://www.cs.mcgill.ca/~rwest/wikispeedia/wpcd/wp/t/The_Lorax.htm.

6. Charles Cohen gathers an enormous amount of source material in exploring Dr. Seuss' personal relationship to his work. He relates a quote from Seuss' step-daughter explaining that "I always thought the Cat ... was [Seuss] on his good days, and the Grinch was [Seuss] on his bad days." Seuss drew sketches of himself blended with both of these hallmark characters. See Cohen 1; 321; 330–31.

7. The economic implications of the color green are unavoidable. With my family I visited Universal Studios Orlando in the summer of 2015, and I was stunned to discover their World of Dr. Seuss, complete with themed restaurants ("Green Eggs and Ham Café") and mint-colored trash cans bearing the Lorax's image: the irony of such a profit-driven park proclaiming Seuss' green message ... was Once-leresque. Green, of course, signifies the all-powerful greenback.

Works Cited

Bettelheim, Bruno. *The Uses of Enchantment*. New York: Vintage, 1989. Print.
Biddick, Kathleen. *The Shock of Medievalism*. Durham: Duke University Press, 1998. Print.

Chesterton, G.K. "Fairy Stories." SurLaLunefairytales.com. Web. 10 Dec. 2015.
Cohen, Charles D. *The Seuss, the Whole Seuss, and Nothing but the Seuss*. New York: Random House, 2002. Print.
DeLoughrey, Elizabeth, and George B. Handley. "Introduction: Toward an Aesthetics of the Earth." *Postcolonial Ecologies: Literatures of the Environment*, ed. Elizabeth DeLoughrey and George B. Handley. Oxford: Oxford University Press, 2011. 3–39. Print.
Dundes, Alan. "Bruno Bettelheim's Uses of Enchantment and Abuses of Scholarship." *The Journal of American Folklore* 104.411 (1991): 74–83. JSTOR. Web. 20 June 2016.
Eliot, Thomas Stearns. *The Waste Land*. New York: Horace Liveright, 1922. Bartleby.com, 2011. 20 June 2016. Web.
Frutig, Judith. "Dr. Seuss' Green-Eggs-and-Ham World." *Of Sneeches and Whos and the Good Dr. Seuss*, ed. Thomas Fensch. Jefferson, NC: McFarland, 1997. 80–81. Print.
Game of Thrones: The Complete First Season. HBO Studios, 2012. DVD.
Garrard, Greg. *Ecocriticism*, 2d ed. New York: Routledge, 2012. Print.
Holsinger, Bruce. "Dr. Seuss and the Utrecht Psalter." *Burnable Books*, 21 Oct. 2013. Web. 24 July 2015.
How the Grinch Stole Christmas. Writ. Dr. Seuss. Dir. Chuck Jones and Ben Washam. Prod. Chuck Jones and Dr. Seuss. Warner Home Video, 2008. DVD.
"JanMohamad on Chinua Achebe's 'Things Fall Apart.'" Jahangirnagar University, 7 Mar. 2012. Web. 10 Dec. 2015.
The Lorax. Writ. Dr. Seuss. Dir. Hawley Pratt. Ex. Prod. David H. DePatie. Prod. Dr. Seuss and Fritz Freleng. Warner Home Video, 2012. DVD.
Lurie, Alison. *Boys and Girls Forever*. New York: Penguin, 2003. Print.
_____. "The Cabinet of Dr. Seuss." *Of Sneeches and Whos and the Good Dr. Seuss*, ed. Thomas Fensch. Jefferson, NC: McFarland, 1997. 155–64. Print.
Morgan, Judith, and Neil. *Dr. Seuss and Mr. Geisel: A Biography*. New York: Random House, 1995. Print.
Nel, Philip. *Dr. Seuss: American Icon*. New York: Continuum, 2004. Print.
Pease, Donald E. *Theodor Seuss Geisel*. Oxford: Oxford University Press, 2010. Print.
Pugh, Tison, and Angela Jane Weisl. *Medievalisms: Making the Past in the Present*. New York: Routledge, 2013. Kindle.
Seuss, Dr. *The Butter Battle Book*. New York: Random House, 1984. Print.
_____. *The Foot Book*. New York: Random House, 1968. Print.
_____. *The Lorax*. New York: Random House, 1971. Print.
_____. *The Lorax*. New York: Random House, 1986. Print.
_____. *The Sneetches and Other Stories*. New York: Random House, 1961. Print.
Tolkien, J. R. R. "On Fairy Stories." *The Tolkien Reader*. New York: Del Rey, 1986. Print.

Monsters in the Closet
Narrative Therapy and Fairy Tales

LISA LEBLANC and CARLA B. MORRISSEY

> Fairy tales are more than true: not because they tell us that dragons exist, but because they tell us that dragons can be beaten.—Neil Gaiman

From a very young age we have all been enchanted with fairy tales. Their motifs, characters, and plot lines, all told against a surreal landscape, have been around as long as recorded history. Through time and geography they have evolved through oral traditions, myth, troubadours, poetry, music, theatre, ballet, vaudeville, paintings, book illustrations, television sitcoms, and video games; fairy stories have been created by every known human community. According to McAdams, "Our personal myths ... help to create the world we live in, at the same time that it is creating us ... we find meaning and connection within a web of story making and story living" (37). People have counted on stories to explain life circumstances that are difficult to understand. With universal themes of fear, greed, jealousy, death, abandonment, suffering, and loss, a fairy tale fulfills the need for the individual to see his or her own life experiences cast into a fictionalized narrative. They are a description of thoughts, feelings, and actions, expressed remotely and at a distance, to give personal meaning to the constant fluctuations within the emotional self.

From the ancient *Arabian Nights* of Aladdin's lamp revealing a wish granting genie as a short route to wealth, to the Sanskrit Epic *Mahabharata* as life drama for adjustment, to Cinderella's rags becoming a ball gown to allow her to attend the Prince's ball and there to find happiness, fairy tales dramatically demonstrate for the reader the potential for human development through change. The stories imagine other possibilities and awaken intuitive, creative solutions, along the way developing the ideas of strength of will and personal freedom. Fairy tales are neither accepting nor judging; they are framed in hope and desire, announcing what may be with a bit of luck or personal agency. A fairy tale causes the reader to consider the character's past, such as the poverty that led to Jack impulsively climbing a beanstalk for adventure and a chance at betterment. The fairy tales reveal the need to study the immediate present, to ask perhaps how will Jack battle the charging bloodthirsty giant? The fairy tale also shows careful deliberations for the imminent future: What must be done to escape the top of the beanstalk with the golden goose.

Narrative therapy uses fairytales, or monster stories, to help clients deal with personal problems; by retelling the narratives of their lives in a new way, clients can sometimes find ways of dealing with problems. When dealing with children, this new narrative sometimes takes the form of turning a child's problem, such as ADHD, into a monster which may be defeated. Instead of viewing the child perceiving him or herself as misbehaving, the child is encouraged to see the ADHD as a monster taking him or herself over and making him or her misbehave; but it is a monster that can be controlled and defeated.

This approach of objectifying, giving concrete expression to an abstract disorder through the image of a monster, may seem like a strange approach; how might a child feel when told that there is a monster controlling him or her? However, fairy tale theory does support this idea. Many psychologists and critics have looked at fairy tales as lessons that teach children that monsters can be defeated, so when their disorders are objectified in this way, the children already have lessons to follow that show that children can defeat monsters. This suggests to children that they are the heroes or heroines of their own narratives.

Narrative Therapy and Monsters

During the 1980s, personality theorists began to consider seriously the relationship between how an individual makes sense of the world and the telling of his or her autobiographical story. They recognized that, throughout people's development, many different stories are told to them, and about them, that work to explain external actions and observations. A mother tells a child the story of his or her birth, a teacher tells a story of scholarship, religious stories impart a code of ethics, society tells of its mores. All the stories are then dynamically and intrapsychically (a psychological process occurring within the mind) brought together by the individual to understand varied life experiences. In *Young Man Luther: A Study in Psychoanalysis and History*, Eric Erikson defines the self and the narrative understanding:

> The person is able to selectively reconstruct his past in such a way that, step for step, it seems to have planned him, or better, he seems to have planned *it*. In this sense, psychologically we *do* choose our parents, our family history, and the history of our kings, heroes, and gods. By making them our own, we maneuver ourselves into the inner position of proprietors, of creators [111–12; italics Erickson's].

Our reality is constructed by the narratives we choose to embrace and to tell.

Narrative theory provides the foundation of the practice of narrative as family therapy, as it is interpreted by Michael White and David Epston. They built on French philosopher and philologist Michael Foucault's concept of knowledge and power that speaks of modes of objectifying the person as well as the method of isolating the person from himself and others. White and Epston introduced externalization into family therapy as a means to separate the individual from his or her problem. Externalization suggests that by creating a distance from which to explore a life event more effectively, the individual is enabled to separate him or herself from the event. The separation enables collaboration that works to shift the individual's self view and their internal narrative.

For families polarized by the inability to resolve an issue that has them helplessly trapped, narrative therapy recognizes that the parents author a story about the child's struggle. The parents may judge the situation as the child controlling the unwanted behavior and believe the child is making a conscious decision to intentionally act badly. Both parents may view the child as inherently flawed with a corrupt personality. Now that the parents have fabricated a story to explain the child's behavior the child is bad. They act towards the child in accordance with this narrative. Thus, the parents may speak about the child in ways that put down the child and will be negative in terms of the appropriate solution. This can have the effect of reinforcing the problem behavior, creating a relentless tension between child and parent. The parents' shallow evaluation of the problem, that the child is bad, has its only root in the connection between the child's unwanted behavior and in the parental narrative that is created.

The parents' powerful narrative of the problem is clearly made known to the child, both openly and discreetly. The parents' narrative is usually accepted by the child as truth, causing the child to form the belief that he or she is fundamentally bad. Eventually, as the child tries to make sense of him or herself, the belief is internalized by the child, and this truth becomes justifiably entwined in the child's identity. The family's situation only worsens as the child now attempts to live up to the criteria established by his parents' story, that he or she is a bad child. The story not only constructs a way of understanding the issue, it now directs the family's actions, in this case, causing a repeated negative affect experience. Thus, something must happen to the story to significantly change the outcome.

There is a great difference between saying that the child *is* bad and that the child *does* bad things. It is paramount to accept that the child is not the problem; the unwanted behavior is the problem. The transference of the problem to an imaginary monster offers the child impartiality from the unwanted behavior. The child is still held accountable for the misbehavior, but it is now easier for the child to accept control of the problem through the monster. The external monster works to help the child face the problem, encouraging a new story dialogue.

In narrative therapy, the importance of how a problem is framed or reframed and who gets to tell the story cannot be overemphasized. While the parents are reacting to the manifestation of the problem, sometimes by screaming, punishing, and rejecting, the child's relationship with him or herself and with the parents is heavily affected by these negative responses. The child needs to realize that this is not solely his or her problem; the problem arrives with its own storied background. Family, friends, school, culture, social class, economics, and a myriad of other outside forces work to further give meanings to the story.

Narrative therapy encourages the child and his or her parents to assume a new perspective that considers the child and the issue as separate unto themselves. With a collaborative approach, the parent, child, and therapist all agree to respond and conceptualize the issue in a like-manner. This understanding is paramount to the success of narrative therapy because only in the joining together of all people involved to rewrite the story can the child find a new understanding and a different approach to the issue. Furthermore, the mutual cooperation reveals that the child and parents are open to building a different relationship base that will help in the discovery of new ways of acting. Collectively agreeing to clear a space for the exchange of ideas forms a respect for the alternate story about both the child and the problem behavior. Once a specific commitment to action is obtained, it further ensures a positive outcome for psychological growth and development/adaptation for the child.

Externalizing the problem is a critical element of White's therapeutic process of separating the problem from the child. With thoughtful questioning, the therapist enlists the child to help understand why the problem is occurring and to learn the impact of the problem on the child's life. The driving force behind this line of interviewing is to demonstrate to the child that the therapist is dependent upon the child to provide the information that will lead to a solution. In creating a narrative and explaining the problem to the therapist, the child experiences a mastery over the problem enhancing his or her abilities to cope with the problem. In the telling and retelling of the problem, a level of control is discovered, instilling a confidence within the child who develops inner strength. In valuing the child's storytelling, the therapist addresses the fears of inadequacy, inferiority, and apprehension, and the child learns strategies to care for him or herself that are reworked into the child's own story.

In 1984, Michael White published an article in which he showed his success in using externalization in helping a child to deal with the problem of pseudo-encopresis (fecal soiling). White, rather than following the standard theory of the time which simply blamed an overprotective parent as the cause of the child's rebellion as the child fought to attain personal power beyond the parent, thought the dynamics in the families he was counseling did not fit this model. He did, however, acknowledge "a mutual causality," that there are different elements that influence the situation and that these elements can snowball until the initial element isn't even known anymore (152). Perhaps the most important aspect White introduced, however, is that "the soiling is beyond anyone's control" (153). He helped the family change the narrative to move from guilt and blame laid on the child, to solving the problem.

White's next step in helping the child was the introduction of the character of "Sneaky Poo," a treacherous character that is causing the child to soil himself. Together, the therapist and child could then evaluate how much Sneaky Poo controlled the child and how much the child controlled Sneaky Poo. Then the child had to make decisions about what to do; controlling Sneaky Poo is presented as a battle, which sometimes Sneaky Poo will win. Actually carrying out the process of defeating Sneaky Poo took a long time and many strategies. But White has found with time that externalizing the problem and presenting it as a monster to be overcome has been accepted quite willingly by children and their parents, and it has led to many successes in treating children with this disorder.

Since White's time, many narrative therapists have adopted the idea of a monster to be overcome when dealing with problems that children face. Building up a motivating power, a monster, to be strategically understood, challenged, and overcome, encourages the child to look to his or her problem in unique and different ways. The child profits by the objectification of the problem, as he or she can now contribute to a clear understanding of the monsters' actions. It provides a safe place from which to explore possibilities of how best to confront the problem. The child will reflect feelings onto the monster, labeling it with emotions such as angry, afraid, happy, and sad. This change in narrative from the child being at fault to the child being affected by a monster may be a strange way to deal with problems, perhaps even a frightening one for a child, but fairy tale theory actually shows us that such a strategy can work with children.

Fairy Tales, Psychological Criticism and Monsters

Many critics begin the psychological study of fairy tales with Bruno Bettelheim, but, in fact, Bettelheim was influenced by Julius Heuscher and his book, *The Psychiatric Study of Myth and Fairy Tales*. Heuscher's book presents a lot of information about fairy tales and myths, but in certain sections he focuses specifically on the link between psychology and fairy tales. He argues that fairy tales help children to relate to the world around them and to deal with their own psychological development. Furthermore, he argues that "the fairy tale nourishes the child's courage to widen his horizons and to tackle all the challenges successfully" (291). One concern that Heuscher talks about is the damage that modernizations made in order to protect children does to fairy tales and to children. He argues that the violence, the impossible actions, and the vagueness of settings typical in fairy tales is actually beneficial for children; since the stories are therefore more unrealistic, the child does not feel threatened by them. When modernization tempers the violence, reduces the impossible actions and makes the setting more concrete, the child has more trouble distinguishing reality from fiction and therefore is more threatened by the story (293–95).

Several critics, both literary and psychological, have looked at the connection between fairy tales and psychology. Heuscher approaches this from actual therapy sessions as well as theories of child development, whereas Bettelheim shows the Freudian connection in various fairy tales. Zipes, on the other hand, argues for a more socio-political approach to fairy tales, thus studying the psychological impact of the times the stories were written, and Bloch studies the impact fairy tales have on the readers.

The link between fairy tales and therapy is first discussed by Heuscher. He reviews the use of patterns in fairy tales to understand the actions of a client, for example the client used tales such as *Little Red Riding Hood* to reflect the life patterns of a woman who is "carelessly seduced by the splendor of the world and by the cunning wolf, [and who is expecting] again and again to be rescued from the wolf's stomach" (363). Other uses of fairy tales that Heuscher sees tend to reflect Freud's use of associations. Heuscher reviews the tales told by clients who are telling fairy tales from memory and uses the changes that the clients introduce into a story to discover what the clients have left hidden from the therapist, and sometimes even from themselves. Lastly, Heuscher reports on his own experience of a therapist who uses patterns in fairy tales to analyze client dreams. For instance, one of his clients reports of leading a tour group to a temple deep in the woods near a lake. Heuscher points out that the buildings in a forest by a body of water are very common in fairy tales and usually represent the quest for wholeness. In this case, he was able to see how the client is searching for wholeness in his life.

Overall, Heuscher's book explores in depth the impact that fairy tales have on the development of children. He particularly sees their relevance in early childhood, latency and adolescence. His book explores many aspects and themes that run through the fairy tales, arguing that such tales are important in the psychological development of the child.

Bruno Bettelheim continues Heuscher's arguments, although Heuscher is uncredited in Bettelheim's book, *The Uses of Enchantment* (1976). In this work, Bettelheim uses Freudian criticism to argue that fairy tales are essential in the development of psychologically sound children. He saw fairy tales as carrying messages to the conscious, preconscious and unconscious, helping a child to deal with the complexities of growing up in ways the child was not even aware of. Bettelheim traces several Freudian conflicts through different fairy tales, such as the pleasure principle vs. the reality principle in which one must learn to delay what one wants to do until one has done what one needs to do. For instance, in the fairy tale the *Three Little Pigs*, the pigs who build their houses of straw and sticks do so to complete the task quickly so they may return to playing, and this prioritizing of pleasure leads to their destruction. The unifying of the dual nature of lower id impulses and higher ego and superego functions is seen in *Brother and Sister* when the brother is turned into a deer and the sister dies, but both are restored through their loyalty to each other. The Oedipal conflict of seeing the same sex parent as a rival for love is seen in *Rapunzel* when the enchantress locks Rapunzel in a tower to keep her from the prince. Bettelheim argues that these stories are essential to the development of the child, but that it must be the original version of the story, not a modernized version that will remove the psychological reality of the story because the modern authors are concerned about traumatizing children with frightening or violent stories.

In the second part of his book, Bettelheim performs an in-depth Freudian analysis of some of the best known fairy tales, such as *Little Red Riding Hood, Snow White*, and *Cinderella*. When discussing *Little Red Riding Hood*, Bettelheim criticizes Perrault's additions of a moral and having Little Red Riding Hood undress before joining the wolf in bed because he feels that Perrault makes the story too obvious to a child. Instead he focuses on the Grimm version, where he sees the titular character dealing with the reality and pleasure principles (staying on the right path or leaving it to pick flowers) as well as the wolf as an external representation of the internal sexual temptations faced by a pubertal child (which would remain in the preconscious of a younger child hearing the story). Bettelheim's analysis of *Snow White* focuses on the oedipal conflict that arises in the conflict between the stepmother and Snow White over the father. At the end of the story, the prince who takes Snow White away completes the oedipal process by serving as the acceptable male who replaces the father in the oedipal conflict. *Cinderella*, on the other hand, is analyzed as a story of sibling rivalry in which the natural superiority of Cinderella overcomes the temporary feelings of degradation that can accompany such rivalry. Bettelheim continues to analyze other versions of the story in which the social lowering of the main character to a servant occurs not because of jealousy of the stepmother and sisters, but due to incestuous designs of the father. These stories present a version of the oedipal conflict where the desire is projected from the girl onto the father.

Many critics today find Bettelheim's interpretation of the role of fairy tales and the development of children as problematic. Certainly much of Bettelheim's work has come under attack, starting with criticism of his work as a psychoanalyst as abusive. But this criticism has also been applied to his work on fairy tales and psychoanalysis. Jack Zipes presents Bettelheim's theories as "false notions about the original intent of Freudian psychoanalytic theory and about the literary quality of fairy tales ... [and] the manner in which Bettelheim would impose meaning onto child development through the therapeutic use of the fairy tale authoritarian and unscientific" (181). Alan Dundes also criticizes Bettelheim's lack of folkloric background and the fact that his work ignores many psychoanalytic readings of the stories that went before him. Despite these critiques, both authors still recognize that there is still merit to the work. Furthermore, Bettelheim's dismissal of other children's literature as helping in the development of young children is short-sighted. However, Bettelheim does raise ideas about monsters which are still valid and contribute to the ideas used in narrative therapy. He discusses those who have banned fairy tales as too frightening for children.

Those who outlawed traditional folk fairy tales decided that if there were monsters in a story told to children, these must be all friendly—but they missed the monster a child knows best and is most concerned with: the monster he or she feels or fears himself or herself to be, and which also sometimes persecutes him. By keeping this monster within the child unspoken of, hidden in his or her unconscious, adults prevent the child from spinning fantasies around it in the image of the fairy tales he or she knows. Without such fantasies, the child fails to get to know his or her monster better, nor is he or she given suggestions as to how he or she may gain mastery over it (120). Thus fairy tales help children acknowledge the monster within themselves, and to understand that such a monster can be defeated.

Of course, one of the drawbacks to using Bettelheim to study how monsters in fairy tales affect children psychologically is his complete Freudian focus. To Bettelheim, monsters almost always reflect fears of sexuality or obstacles to overcome in sexual development. The animal husband tale, where a woman marries an animal who eventually turns into a man, reflects a child's fear of sexual development, giants represent the father who is the threat in the oedipal conflict, and the witch becomes the oedipal bad mother. But the problems of children go beyond this. In reality giants may not be oedipal, but simply a feeling of powerlessness while growing up. Bettelheim does say that "fairy stories provide reassurance to children that they can eventually get the better of the giant—i.e., they can grow up to be like the giant and acquire the same powers" (28). In this case, Bettelheim is referring to the child seeing the parent as a giant, larger and more powerful, but he later argues that these powers are sexual development. There are many other ways in which children feel powerless in the world, but fairy tales can still show a young hero or heroine overcoming greater forces.

Although Bettelheim's use of Freudian psychology limits his use of fairy tales in ways critics find problematic today, the idea the that monsters in fairy tales can help children to face their difficulties is still valid. In his analysis of *Hansel and Gretel*, Bettelheim argues that the story represents the need to move out of the oral stage and the witch, who wants to eat the children, serves as "a personification of the destructive aspects of orality" (162). While we may wonder why children old enough for fairy tales still have concerns related to the oral stage of development, the idea that the witch represents problems that the children may need to overcome is of particular use in narrative therapy.

Literary critic Jack Zipes is one of the leading critics of Bettelheim's work. In *Breaking the Magic Spell: Radical Theories of Folk and Fairy Tales*, instead of following Bettelheim's Freudian analysis of fairy tales,[1] Zipes looks at such tales from a socio-political background. However, this does not mean that the psychological impact of the stories is irrelevant here. By looking at the socio-political origins of the tales, we can also see the concerns of the time. Zipes does caution the reader to remember that the tales do change over time to reflect different concerns and that they were not always written for children, so the concerns are not always that of children. When discussing the impact of fairy tales during changing social conditions, Zipes mentions that during the rise of capitalism: "The tales took on a compensatory function for children and adults alike who experienced nothing but the frustration of their imaginations in society ... the tales no longer served their original purpose of clarifying social and natural phenomena but became forms of refuge and escape in that they made up for what people could not realize in society" (*Breaking the Magic Spell*, 196). While his book looks at the purpose of fairy tales from a social perspective, it also discusses the impact of fairy tales from a psychological perspective. Fairy tales do offer a way to cope with the social situation an individual is in, and that includes the situation of a child.

The final fairy tale critic to consider is Ernst Bloch. Bloch worked to show the influence of literature on how we view reality around us. One of the specific issues Bloch deals with is how fairy tales can reflect our wish-projections when they don't reflect our reality. As he puts it, "real kings no longer even exist" (163). But he dismisses this concern, arguing that fairy tales, unlike legends, are not locked in time and that the core of the fairy tale is as relevant today as in the fairy tale time. And through fairy tales, we can see our wish-projections mirrored as we face monsters: "Unfortunately, we must equally contend with the smoke of witches and the blows of ogres habitually faced by the fairy-tale hero in the now" (166). The fairy tale, by presenting a hero or heroine who can overcome brutes through cleverness as well as courage, encourages modern readers as well.

Integration

Stories can be incorporated into therapeutic efforts on behalf of the child client to redirect aggressive impulses and resolve seemingly impossible conflicts. In this process the child becomes more open to experience, more openly aware of his or her own feelings. The narrative creates a filter through which the child can feel safe in expressing his or her feelings; thus, children can come closer to what is deep within themselves. A narrative approach views problems as separate from the child and that the solution already exists within the individual. As Heuscher points out, Fairy tales reduce, "The inner distance between understanding and experiential owning that often remains unaffected by mere intellectual insight. It is this experiential owning that leads to basic change or growth" (376). Being told that one can control ones impulses isn't as effective as seeing someone that one identifies with as able to control impulses. Jack successfully ventures outside of his comfort zone and ends up defeating the giant, Rapunzel finds escape from the witch and her locked tower with her long hair as solution, Red Riding Hood learns to think critically in order to save herself from the wolf, and even Cinderella retains a steady kindness as the bad behaviors of her stepmother and stepsisters swirl around her.[2] As Heuscher says, "[F]airy tales can be helpful in recognizing the meaning and potential usefulness of spontaneous productions of the human psyche" (378). By reading fairy tales, a child can sometimes come to a realization about him or herself, either on his or her own or with the help of an adult.

The goal of this process of identifying with the fairy tale hero is to cause the child to be more attentive to his or her inner feelings and more receptive to alternative ideas. He or she needs to trust him or herself to make meaningful decisions with the understanding that the act of being may be enough. That the end goal is not the need to repackage oneself into a new and improved product, but the realization that seeing the process of learning and growth is good enough. The willingness to make meaning through the use of the personal narrative process is the child's accomplishment.

How a child understand the story of his or her actions and consequences shapes new realities, therefore, making new meanings in an individual's life. For example, a child of newly divorced parents manifests his or her internal frustrations by hitting his or her classmates. The child is viewed by the teacher as an annoyance, a trouble maker to be disciplined. The child can use a monster to write a story that explains hidden emotions of distress caused by the divorce. "The monster is mad that Daddy left" expresses feelings of being powerless. "My mom hates the monster" articulates the child's feeling of being unloved. When the child is acting out by hitting classmates, he or she internalizes the teacher's response and understands this as he or she *is* bad and not that his or her actions are bad. Hence, the monster then acts a mechanism that contains the hitting problem, separate from the child's character. At this junction the child can craft stories that disable the monster and that simultaneously work to address his or her inner life.

Narrative therapy can utilize a monster to externalize the bad behavior to better separate the child from the issue. Thus it is not that the child hits because he or she is bad, it's the angry monster that causes him or her to hit. The monster gives a body and meaning to the child's inner problems that otherwise seems difficult and impossible to solve. Rather that the issue of hitting as a core character trait of the child, it is the monster affecting the child's life. This gives the child something outside him or herself to fight, rather than feeling as if he or she was simply bad. The problem is pushed onto the monster. Hence, the monster is the aggressor, the enemy, the mischief-maker, directing the child, or in some way trying to upset or harm the child. This new story can offer a powerful positive influence in the way the child views him or herself, his or her life and his or her capabilities. The monster is now the challenge from which coping skills will arise. In much the same way, Jack Zipes suggests of fairy tales, "the effectiveness of fairy tales and other forms of fantastic literature depends on the innovative manner in which we make the information of the tales relevant for the listeners" (*The Enchanted Screen* 1). In this way, fairy tales operate in the same manner as narrative therapy, offering children narratives that are relevant to the development of problem solving skills.

While fairy tales inform narrative theory, the reverse is also true. Many fairy tales resolve the issues in them through a reframing of the problem. *Beauty and the Beast* is perhaps the best example of this. One of the two main characters, Beast, sees himself, and is seen by others as just that, a beast. It is only when Beauty comes to see him as no longer a beast but an individual who is kind and sincere that the problem of their relationship can be resolved. Once the monster is externalized to the character himself, his real nature shows through. The Beast is made human again, and the characters can live happily ever after.

Conclusion

While telling a child that a monster is controlling his or her behavior may seem intimidating, fairy tale theory supports this approach to dealing with problems the child may be facing. Whether the child sees his or her monster as a giant, witch, ogre or just a generic monster, the fairy tale has told the child repeatedly that even the young child can defeat the monster in the end. The child who has been told many times over that his or her behavior is bad or wrong may not know how to deal with this behavior. But when told that this behavior is not caused by him or herself as a bad child, but is caused instead by a monster that controls him or her, the child may be more ready to fight that behavioral battle.

This is not to say that only fairy tales work in this context. Many other children's stories, such as those by Maurice Sendak, Roald Dahl, Jane Yolen, and Neil Gaiman, present children dealing with monsters, sometimes in human form but always larger and scarier than the child. The young heroes of the modern children's stories also show children that monsters that control them, such as Sendak's Wild Things, Dahl's Trunchbull, Yolen's dragon and Gaiman's others, can be defeated. They can be ignored or driven off in the same way that the child's monster, prompting him or her to misbehavior, can also be ignored or driven off. This chapter only looked at fairy tale theory in this regard because of the widespread knowledge of fairy tales and their history of criticism, not because they are the only tales that work in this context.

Many fields of therapy have used narratives to help individuals to understand themselves better. Freud analyzed the stories of dreams to better understand the individual's needs and conflicts through an examination of subconscious motives. Jung looked to the collective unconscious of innate archetype knowledge that recognized symbols in myths. The primal structures of story telling are contained in a myth, providing a safe space to explore personal identity and the relationship of an individual to his or her environment. Jung contends that the associations an individual makes in connecting feelings to images, shapes what we make of ourselves and how we make it–an exchange of narratives. While Northwestern University researcher Jonathan Adler's interests lie in how a person accounts for his or her life events as they provide clues to their future, he found that when individuals saw themselves as the lead character in their stories, their life situations vastly improved. "'You tell the story first and then you live your way into it,' Adler says. 'There is a certain amount of 'fake it 'til you make it'" (qtd. in Dingfelder). In Sarbins' 1986 foundational volume, *Narrative Psychology,* the narrative and its use in counseling patients became central. Sarbin contends that a story "provides the basis for analogy, and if linguistic translation is necessary, the partial similarity is expressed as metaphor" (6), recognizing that people craft drama from stances in everyday life situations that include unknown elements of the self. By reframing the story, an individual can view the problem in a new and better way, giving the individual new solutions for the problem.

With the child as author, the monster is used to bring forth his feelings, expectations, and the beliefs imposed on him by others. The child tells a tale that brings together threads of ideas, sensations, and thoughts, creating a storyline that contains aspects of the monster along with meaning, significant events, consequences and judgments. Thus the therapist acts as editor in chief, posing delicate, yet intricate, questions that lead the child/author to create alternate narratives that encourage and provide hope to face fears. The therapist/editor firmly influences the child/author to integrate the new story regarding the behavior to the past story and to extend the story into the future.

There may be some debate about the true impact of fairy tales on children, but it is generally agreed that they do have a formative influence on children. In this particular case, it offers a frame of reference for narrative therapy to draw on and a justification for the externalization of problems in therapy. Fairy tales and narrative therapy can work in tandem to help children overcome obstacles which seem insurmountable to them. ADHD, anger issues, encopresis, and other such disorders can leave a child feeling guilt and shame. By externalizing the problem, the child can let go of those feelings of guilt and shame and focus on dealing with the problem and with seeking a solution. By viewing the disorder as a monster, the child can see him or herself as the hero or heroine of the story and can set out to defeat the monster. As many children's tales also include helpers along the way, parents and the therapist can be brought in as the sidekicks, there to help the hero or heroine, and thus the parents move from sources of disapproval and blame to sources of support. And, just as the fairy tale hero or heroine often faces setbacks, times when the child fails to control the problem can be seen as a delay in the story, not the end of the story.

NOTES

1. Zipes devotes an entire chapter of *Breaking the Magic Spell* to explaining the flaws in Bettelheim's works.
2. While we are using specific editions of the fairy tales, the elements we are looking at are the common ones and therefore other editions should contain the same elements.

WORKS CITED

Bettelheim, Bruno. *The Uses of Enchantment: The Meaning and Importance of Fairy Tales.* New York: Knopf, 1976. Print.

Bloch, Ernst. *The Utopian Function of Art and Literature*. Trans. Jack Zipes and Frank Mecklenburg. Cambridge: MIT Press, 1988. Print.
Brett, Jan. *Beauty and the Beast*. New York: Clarion Books, 1989. Print.
Dahl, Roald. *Matilda*. New York: Puffin Books, 1988. Print.
Dingfelder, Sadie. "Our Stories, Ourselves." *APA Monitor* 42.1 (Jan. 2011): 42. Web. 8 Dec. 2015.
Dundes, Alan. "Bruno Betelheim's Uses of Enchantment and Abuses of Scholarship." *The Journal of American Folklore* 104.411 (1991): 74–83.
Erickson, Erik. *Young Man Luther: A Study in Psychoanalysis and History*. New York: W.W. Norton, 1958. Print.
Foucault, Michel "The Subject and Power." *Michael Foucault: Beyond Structuralism and Hermeneutics*, ed. H. Dreyfus and P. Rabinow. Chicago: University of Chicago Press, 1982. 208–28. Print.
Freud, Sigmund. *The Interpretation of Dreams*. Mineola, NY: Dover, 2015. Print.
Gaiman, Neil. *Coraline*. New York: HarperCollins Children's Books, 2002. Print.
Grimm, Jacob, and Wilhelm. *Cinderella*. Trans. and retold Nonny Hogrogian. New York: Greenwillow, 1981. Print.
_____. *Hansel and Gretel: A Grimm's Fairy Tale*. Trans. and retold Susan Jeffers. New York: Dutton Children's Books, 2011.Print.
_____. *Little Red Riding Hood*. Trans. and retold Trina Schart Hyman. New York: Holiday House, 1983. Print.
_____. *Rapunzel*. Trans. and retold Amy Ehrlich. New York: Dial Books, 1989. Print.
Heuscher, Julius E. *A Psychiatric Study of Myths and Fairy Tales: Their Origin, Meaning and Usefulness*, 2d ed. Springfield, IL: Charles C. Thomas, 1974. Print.
Jung, C. G. *The Collected Works of C. G. Jung: Complete Digital Edition*. Princeton: Princeton University Press, 2014. Print.
McAdams, Dan P. *The Stories We Live by: Personal Myths and the Making of the Self*. New York: Guilford Press, 1993. Print.
Nesbit, Edith. *Jack and the Beanstalk*. Cambridge: Candlewick Press, 2006. Print.
Sarbin, Theodore R. "The Narrative as a Root Metaphor for Psychology." *Narrative Psychology: The Storied Nature of Human Conduct*. New York: Praeger, 1986. 3–22.
Sendak, Maurice. *Where the Wild Things Are*. New York: HarperCollins, 1991. Print.
White, Michael. "Pseudo-Encopresis: From Avalanche to Victory, from Vicious to Virtuous Cycles." *The Australian Journal of Family Therapy* 2.2 (1984): 150–60.
_____, and David Epston. *Narrative Means to Therapeutic Ends*. New York: W.W. Norton, 1980. Print.
Yolen, Jane. *Dove Isabeau*. San Diego: Harcourt, Brace, Jovanovich, 1989. Print.
Zipes, Jack. *Breaking the Magic Spell: Radical Theories of Folk and Fairy Tales*. Lexington: University Press of Kentucky, 2002. Print.
_____. *The Enchanted Screen: The Unknown History of Fairy-tale Films*. New York: Routledge, 2011. Print.

PART 2: NORMALIZATION OF THE "OTHER"

"Let the wild rumpus start!" Adventures in Acceptance and Understanding
Picture Books and the Other

KELLY F. FRANKLIN

> There is no such thing as fantasy unrelated to reality.
> —Maurice Sendak

During the 90s Robert Fulgham wrote the book *All I Really Need to Know I Learned in Kindergarten*. His text featured musings on life experiences and ultimately a harkening back to the wisdom that many people learned in their Kindergarten classrooms. Soon, the "All I Ever Needed to Know I Learned in Kindergarten" inspirational posters spun off from the novel and became widespread in popular culture. School teachers proudly displayed the image on their walls, and these witty signs could also be seen circulating outside of schools, often found in businesses, attached to emails, and counselor offices. Fulgham's message, embraced by so many, suggests that people follow these simple rules in order to peacefully coexist and understand one another. Throughout the text Fulgham argues that people should play fair, share everything, clean up their messes, be aware of wonder, refrain from violent behavior, not be afraid to be sorry (as well as say it), and depend on one another (Fulgham 2). Though the book itself delves deeper into the ideas of how the Kindergarten experience shapes adult lives, his simple rules can be easily applied to everyday living. In fact, children's literature (CL) accomplishes the same ideology as Fulgham was preaching. In CL, important life-impacting messages often jump from colorful page to colorful page, lessons are taught with whimsy, being accepting of others is encouraged, and the strong morals are explained in a way that is easily applicable to life (for both children and adults).

Certainly, not every children's tale has an obvious moral, and sometimes finding the moral to the story can be quite the task—most especially when reading original versions of fairy tales. However, many children's texts boast a lesson even if it is not tightly presented in the end of the book in a final "And the moral to the story is..." section. Picture books often deliver a strong moral through images without verbiage. Indeed, it has been argued that children respond to visuals more than they do words, perhaps one of the reasons vibrant imagery is employed in picture books (Brown, Tomlinson, and Short 81–105). Children also respond to animals, most especially cute and cuddly animals, so it is not a surprise that CL embraces the use of animal characters to educate and delight children. The term for this technique is anthropomorphism, loosely defined it means the act of assigning human characteristics and mannerisms to animals (Brown, Tomlinson, and Short 136). CL authors employ this strategy in picture books, creating vibrant animal characters that are used to engage children and adults, as many picture books are delightfully cross-written. CL authors are typically very audience aware and use this knowledge to create pieces that entertain and as well as educate readers about the moral to the story.

Fictional monsters in children's literature are used in much the same way as real animals. However, monsters have a more difficult task—in picture books monsters represent the "Other."[1] Not only are these monsters assigned the role of "Other," an important part in any tale, they are also often given the responsibility of delivering the moral of the story. Certainly, the idea of a moral monster sounds outlandish. However, this has been much the case in monster fiction throughout history, most famously *Frankenstein*. The presence of the "Other" in picture books in monster incarnation is pivotal to how children learn to understand and navigate the real world. These characters, often oversized and quite silly in appearance, provide children the opportunity to begin to have an adventure with someone drastically different than themselves and their own social groups. Ultimately, these monsters teach children that the moral does not always lie in the hands of the familiar majority.

Instruct and Delight—A Tall Order

Academics, most famously Peter Hunt, often wrestle with the agenda that lies within a picture book. Indeed, the vast majority of picture books are "written by adults who have an agenda. Even those writers who claim to be nothing but entertainers have their own ideological stance, their own ideas of what is right and wrong, their own way of seeing the world" ("Peter Hunt" par. 6). Certainly, the plan for any author may solely be one of entertaining children. However, each writer is wrapped up in their own ecology of thought, and sometimes subconsciously include powerful messages in their work that cause readers to think in a way that they may not have prior to having read the story.

Whether the author realizes it, he or she may be employing the notion of "instruct and delight." Certainly, instruct and delight is a mode of educating that can, arguably, be dated back to oral storytelling traditions. Though children's literature has evolved remarkably over time, and most especially during the 18th century, it has always been given the task of teaching children—either about social class, societal rules, or simply to be more imaginative. Then it should be no surprise that children's literature, and those that write it, often offer an agenda of acceptance. Though many adults are not accepting of others in their own lives, many picture book authors imbue their texts with a message of acceptance and understanding—a message very much needed during this current cultural moment. As such, monster texts themselves are most often whimsical and silly but also pack a powerful punch meant to affect both reader and listener.

Though CL typically does not represent them in this way, monsters are historically intended be scary—throughout history monsters have existed to frighten/entertain but to also warn people of danger, so the evolution of the CL monster can be troublesome for some monster fans. Simply ask any dedicated horror movie aficionado or child who is terrified to look underneath their bed and into their closet what they think of monsters, and then be prepared for a dramatic response. Ironically, the term itself is not as frightening as one would think, and can be used positively. The OED boasts several definitions for the word "monster," but the two that best apply to picture books are "a mythical creature which is part animal and part human, or combines elements of two or more animal forms, and is frequently of great size and ferocious appearance ... any imaginary creature that is large, ugly, and frightening" and "something extraordinary or unnatural; an amazing event or occurrence; a prodigy, a marvel" ("monster" n. pag.). Working together, these two definitions describe monsters in picture books—extraordinary combinations of elements, typically appearing over-sized, driving the story in a marvelous direction.

Famous monsters from children's literature range from Sendak's "Wild Things" to Mo Willems' "Dinosaurs"; their behavior is over the top, silly, and sometimes quite sweet. However, traditional monsters like Frankenstein's Monster, Dracula, and the Wolf-man have been used in picture books, though they are typically assigned to seasonal texts (appearing mostly during Halloween). Characters in picture books, most often cautionary tales, are seen frolicking alongside these monsters, plotting with (and sometimes against them), and from time to time end up leaving these monsters behind in order to return home forever changed from their monstrous experience. This can be directly connected to how a child interacts with someone different from them—when children are given the opportunity to have an adventure with different ethnic and cultural groups, the end result can be (and most often is) a positive change in the life of the child, and how he or she envisions the world.

Childhood, and the experiences had during these formative years, affects adulthood. Indeed, children who do not have the experience of meeting people from different cultural groups or ethnic groups during their childhood run the risk of becoming adults who do the same thing, staying within their comfort zones. When people lack the opportunity to get to know other cultures empathy can fail to properly develop. Instead, people who are stunted in their cultural development, can view other cultures as dangerous, wrong, or even ignorant. Introducing children to different cultural groups at a young age, gives them the opportunity to develop a strong sense of empathy which is needed in order to navigate, and live with, people who identify differently them. In 2012 the U.S. Census announced, "Whites now account for under half of the births in the United States. Despite this milestone, there is no guarantee that children from different backgrounds will encounter one another in their neighborhoods, schools or social life" (Slotnik par. 1). Statistics suggest that though the nation is becoming more diverse, people are staying closer to their own ethnic groups. In a personal interview, Lonnie Chester (a freshman student at Southwestern Community College in Creston, Iowa) states:

> Before I came to Creston, I had never seen a white person in real life, just on TV. I had never spoken to a white person, and I thought that all white people were rich and snotty. I'm from the south side of Chicago. I'm from bad neighborhoods. If a white person is knocking on your door, you've done something wrong. When I first came to Iowa I was really nervous because I didn't know how these people would treat me. They were so different from me, at least I thought. And now some of my best friends are white. I never thought I'd be able to say that. Now, I don't know if I should bring them home with me to visit ... because I'll be honest, I don't think they'd be safe there. I mean. I do want them to live. I guess what I've learned the most is that people are always afraid of what they don't understand, and that even applies to me. A kid from the 'bad' side of town [n.pag].

Naturally, Lonnie's experience is his own, and he cannot speak for all children hailing from the Southside of Chicago. However, people from all ethnic groups can experience much the same thing. It can be seen in rural farming communities, German sections of Chicago, and even Chinatown in San Francisco.[2] As such, the "Other" typically represents someone from a culture different than your own—which means the other can then signify many different races and cultural backgrounds.

When viewed through this lens, monsters are powerful literary tools that can be used to educate children from all cultural backgrounds. Texts that feature monsters as characters give children the opportunity to vicariously adventure with someone different than themselves, and in a way that parents may not at first realize. Sadly, racism is alive in well in the 21st century. Arguably, it always will be. Therefore, monsters are able to do what some parents fail to do (sometimes purposefully): teach that "normal" differs for everyone based upon their personal and cultural experiences, and that it is okay to have a friend who looks different than themselves. Different does not equal scary.

Where the Wild Things Are

Maurice Sendak's famous CL classic *Where the Wild Things Are* was published in 1963, and quickly became the favorite story of children and parents. *Where the Wild Things Are* is the story of the naughty child Max who is sent to his room without dinner. Max sails away from his bedroom to a place where the "Wild Things" live, and has many adventures. Eventually he returns home to his bedroom having grown weary of adventuring (Sendak 1–40). Sendak's "Wild Things" are monsters who are oversized, shaggy haired, with sharp pointy teeth. Frequently, the monsters claim that they are going to eat Max up, but Max is never eaten up, nor does he appear frightened by his new friends.

Sendak claims that the "Wild Things," or monsters, found in his book were inspired by his unruly, and sometimes bossy, relatives that would visit his childhood home for Sunday dinners. Sendak was so affected by these visitors because he did not have a lot of contact with other people in the outside world, perhaps offering a reason as to why Max embarks on such a wild adventure to the far, far away. Sendak himself lived a somewhat reclusive childhood due to the fact that his family had been heavily affected by the holocaust. His parents had been Jewish immigrants from Poland, and had lost many relatives during World War II ("This Day in History" par. 1). This experience directly shaped how Sendak envisioned the outside world, and also makes him similar to his fictional Max. He spent many days alone in his room imagining other worlds because his family desired to keep him close and away from harm. According to Sendak, this made for a sad and lonely childhood ("This Day in History" par. 3). The colors used in *Where the Wild Things Are* mimic this feeling of loneliness, steeped in grays and neutral tones, and though quite adventurous the book itself never feels arresting to the eye. Due to the color scheme, the "Wild Things" found in the book never come across to a reader as frightening. However, they are quite different than traditional monsters. These "monsters" have sharp pointy teeth, appear to have no manners, and are desperate for a "wild rumpus." While living with the monsters, Max quickly makes fast friends who look very different than him. Despite their seemingly fun relationship, Max's monsters frequently tell him that they are going to eat him up because they love him so—yet they never do.

The "Wild Things'" threats toward Max could be thought of as self-defense. Max is a boy who has ventured to their land and quickly become King Max; as such, Max can be viewed as a threat to the way of life for the "Wild Things." Thus, their threats toward him appear justified. Certainly, a connection can be made between Max's all white wolf suit and the notion of white power. Read through the lens of post-colonialism and critical race theory, *Where the Wild Things Are* becomes a terrifying story—one where Max is nothing more than a bully. Despite this troubling fact, the "Wild Things" embrace Max (although they do issue him the "eat you up" warning). Together they all have many "wild rumpuses" and adventures; until Max decides it is time to return home (much to the chagrin of the Monsters).

Children reading this book are given the opportunity to see a child, Max, navigate a world very different from that of his own, and do it successfully. Instead of being afraid of those different than him, Max learns to get along with the "Wild Things" as well as become friends with them. Yet, the moral of Sendak's classic story can be hard to discern. Indeed, it has been argued that the moral is to respect others (Lynch-Brown, Tomlinson, and Short 136). Certainly, Max must learn to respect his mother, and even respect the "Wild Things" that he has encountered. However, other morals have been argued to be "Don't be afraid to have an adventure" and "Sometimes monsters are not as scary as you think." Sendak's monsters appear sad, desperate to connect with and have an adventure with someone other than themselves. Though each monster looks dissimilar from the other, they all seek Max's love and attention. In some ways, the monsters are holding the moral in their clawed hands—eager to befriend someone outside of their own cultural group because inclusion is fun. The end of the story does feature Max making the long journey home to his bedroom, appearing quite changed, and exhausted, by his experience. Perhaps a nod to the notion that stepping outside a comfort zone and meeting new people/cultures is exhausting, but it is worth the adventure.

Mo Willems' Kind Hearted Monsters

For many years Dr. Seuss was the darling of children's literature, his fantastical stories not only taught children how to read but also instructed them about important life lessons. Mo Willems can be thought of as the modern day Dr. Seuss. Although Willems' texts typically do not rhyme, they contain much of the same whimsy found in a Seuss story. Known for popular books such as *Don't Let the Pigeon Drive the Bus, Knufflebunny,* and the *Elephant and Piggy* tales, Willems has a signature style recognizable in not only his hand drawn and computer colored artwork, but also in his delightfully cross-written stories. Willems once stated that, "The difference between children and adults is that they're shorter—not dumber." As such, Willems' texts are typically sophisticated and hilarious. Readers must pay close attention in order to figure out the twist in the story, which Willems generally offers. Indeed, Willems leaves foreshadowing clues throughout his texts that savvy readers will pick up on. He is also quite fond of leaving Easter Eggs—his popular Pigeon can be seen making sneaky cameo appearances in many of his books, most recently *Goldilocks and the Three Dinosaurs*. A Mo Willems book is sure to enchant both children and adults, all while teaching important lessons.

When asked about his writing mantra, in regard to writing children's literature, Willems replies, "Always think of your audience, but never think for your audience" (Wrenn par. 1). Certainly, Willems understands how to write for an audience of children and adults. His books feature bold lines and soft colors, witty humor (typically ripe with sarcasm), and words that often escape their confining text boxes in fun and exciting ways. It is clear that he is thinking of children and adults when he creates his beloved texts, leaving clues that pinpoint his featured moral agenda.Perhaps most famous for his cautionary tales, Willems creates stories that teach important life lessons, whimsically using animals and monsters to deliver the moral. His 2013 retelling of the classic Goldilocks, *Goldilocks and the Three Dinosaurs*, gives nod to the modern moral: "If you ever find yourself in the wrong story, leave" (Willems 31). Though dinosaurs are not considered monsters, as there is physical proof of their existence, they do share many of the same characteristics typically relegated to fictional beasts. Willems' choice of dinosaur also speaks to his audience, children who have become used to dinosaurs being friendly sources of entertainment thanks to the movie industry, specifically companies like Dreamworks and Pixar.

Dinosaurs in children's literature are most often kind, they become fast friends with the main character in the story, or simply lead the story altogether. *Goldilocks and the Three Dinosaurs* features these creatures in a monstrous role—they knowingly set a trap to catch a little girl in order to turn her into a chewy chocolate little girl bon-bon, a dinosaur's most favorite thing to eat (Willems 4). Willems' dinosaurs appear quite clumsy and inept, with rounded non-terrifying noses, bold lines that are colored in with a combination of pastel and comforting earthy tones, and basic clothes that represent female and male gender stereotypes. These dinosaurs do not appear threatening at all; although at times they do speak in loud booming voices. Children are quickly made aware that these predators are nothing to fear, and that Willems' monsters are absolutely going to fumble their best laid plans.

Goldilocks appears as an "Other" in their story, which is interesting since Goldilocks is a blonde Caucasian girl. However, in this tale she is the interloper. Children see her immersed into a situation that is completely unexpected, and quite different than what she is used to. Indeed, she is doing wrong by frolicking into a home uninvited, but what makes her stand out as an "Other" is the fact that she is the only human in the story—she is different. This can be read as a nod to how children from minority groups feel when watching films or reading texts that feature people who look physically different than themselves. Though it is a situation that people get used to over time, it can be startling at first for children. It is important for children that are considered part of an ethnic majority to experience how people living in minority groups feel. It not only helps build empathy, but can also affect how children interact with those different than them. Goldilocks has to critically think about her surroundings in order to survive her situation. Though her near tragic tale is told with humor, it can be compared to how many minority children feel in real life—parceling together information to both survive and positively interact with different environments.

Not to be outdone, the dinosaurs also have an "Other" character in their own home. Willems replaces the infamously whiny Baby Bear with "some other Dinosaur who happened to be visiting from Norway" (Willems 1). The Norwegian Dinosaur is played by a small orange triceratops who frequently sports a cap, carries a suitcase stuffed with toys and clothes, and speaks in a different language. Willems gives nod to the notion of people considered foreign being evil when he writes, "Then the other Dinosaur made a loud noise that sounded like a big, evil laugh but was probably just a polite Norwegian expression" (6). Children, and adults, are pleasantly surprised by the replacement of the traditional baby bear character which adds to the humorous nature of the story. However, by replacing Baby Bear with the Dinosaur, and by making this dinosaur silly, Willems automatically makes it possible for readers to become comfortable with an "Other" character—in other words, Willems helps to both identify and normalize the "Other" very quickly. Indeed, children's literature "functions as a socializing agent through the normalization of attitudes and beliefs, the inclusion and exclusion of various people" (Gaeta 172). An exposure to literature, most especially literature that does not shy away from inclusion of the "Other," in the formative years of children is undeniably important. Jill Gaeta argues that children can be thought of as blank slates, or neutral, as such they absorb what they read and are affected by it (2). Gaeta further suggests: "Children's literature possesses tremendous power in perpetuating or rejecting dominant social structures, and plays a key role in a child's ideological development and self-image. Such literature facilitates the inclusion of values and beliefs representative of the society into which a child is to be initiated" (2). Parents that read Mo Willems' stories may simply be choosing a tale full of humor and sarcasm, something to read that will both entertain the child and themselves. Yet, these parents are also choosing books that feature the Other in positive and inclusive ways. Instead of being afraid of the Norweigan Dinosaur, he simply is a part of Mama and Papa Dinosaur's family. His strange words, "Har! Har! Horjkfs! Huugrk!" are nothing to be troubled about, but instead add a level of welcome excitement to the story (Willems 8).

It does not get more exciting than a trio of Dinosaurs setting an obvious trap, and the book is full of page turning moments. Children find themselves wondering if Goldilocks will figure out that she is not in a Bear's house, but instead in a Dinosaur's house. Her fate teeters on the edge of sharp dinosaur teeth. Thankfully, she is able to critically analyze her surroundings and come to the realization that she is in fact in a dinosaur's house, and the wrong story. Her quick exit from the house, and back into the seemingly happy arms of the three Bears, leaves the dinosaur trio all forlorn. Willems provides the Dinosaurs a humorous moral "lock the back door" at the end of the story and the dinosaurs sadly slouch off to continue setting their trap for another wandering child (Willems 1–27). Although the dinosaurs should appear ignorant and incompetent, instead they come off as forgetful (a trait that nearly everyone can connect with). The trap they had set definitely had worked, but because of a slight mistake they miss out on their chewy bon-bon time. Willems' decision to not make the dinosaurs appear ignorant, but instead a tiny bit forgetful, is a wise one because then the "Other" is not discounted. Instead, his characters have helped Goldilocks to realize her own very important moral, "If you ever find yourself in the wrong story, leave," and are reminded of their own "Lock the back door!" in a comedic way.

The task of being a moral messenger appears to be too much for humans in Willems' books. Instead, his exciting and very animal/dinosaur characters, become moral messengers. Ultimately, the take-away from this is that children see that sometimes important lessons can be learned from someone different than themselves, and that differences are not to be feared, but instead welcomed. Research suggests that the way a culture is represented influences how a child views that culture (Gaeta 24). As such, featuring loveable monsters that do not scare, but instead appear silly and non-threatening, can be connected to how children view and interact with people different than themselves in real life outside of their fictional adventures.

The Monster at the End of This Essay

Though John Stone has not achieved the same "rock star" status as Mo Willems has, he is responsible for writing a beloved classic: *The Monster at the End of this Book* starring the goofy blue monster Grover from Sesame Street.

Many a child has happily read through this book alongside their parent, giggling with excitement as they turned the page, against Grover's increasingly drastic protests. The book itself has a simple premise; Grover does not realize that he is the monster that will be at the end of the book. The story beings with Grover breaking the fourth wall (when a performer or character acknowledges the existence of the audience by speaking to them directly) and talking directly to the reader: "On the cover, what did that say? Did that say there will be a monster at the end of this book??? IT DID? Oh, I am so scared of Monsters!!!" (Stone 1). Throughout the story Grover builds various traps to keep the reader from turning the page, in an attempt to protect the reader from the monster that lurks at the end of the book, only to find out that *he* is the monster, and children familiar with Grover know that he is far from scary.

Though Grover truly is terrified that the reader continues to turn the page, bringing him ever closer to the monster at the end of the story, what stands out most is the pains he goes to in order to keep the monster at bay. Grover constructs rope pulleys and builds brick walls to hide behind, all delightfully destroyed by readers. Grover even begs the reader to stop reading, but the reader continues sending Grover into fits of despair. Indeed, the famous "There is nothing to fear but fear itself" rings true in this text, as Grover has nothing to be afraid of. However, Grover has been taught that monsters are bad; his fear appears silly but at the same time understandable.

Though the book itself is quite silly and meant to bring laughter to both children and parents, it is also poignant. Grover is terrified simply because things that are different can be scary, he has no idea what to expect in this forth-coming monster, and instead of wanting to calmly approach the situation, he seeks to avoid it. Though certainly not applicable to all people, avoidance can be a common behavior trait when dealing with people different than oneself, and can sometimes lead to panic. Grover also fails to realize that the answer to the problem he has encountered is right in front of him— he is the monster which is not a problem after all. Grover's inability to deal with his situation and accept the fact that he may encounter a monster is an example of panicked avoidance. This behavior can be used to interpret how real people behave in situations where they feel uncomfortable due to the knowledge that they may encounter a cultural group different than their own—the correct tem for this is Xenophobia.

Xenophobia, loosely defined as the intense and unreasonable fear of people from different cultures, is what Grover suffers from in this classic text, and currently appears to be alive and well in 2015 United States culture. According to Ayesha Mian, M.D., and Andres J. Pumareiga, M.D.:

> Xenophobia has significant adverse impact on child/adolescent ethnic identity formation, which can result not only in marginalization, but also negative identity formation and deviant behavior. Images of immigrants in popular culture and media are

often negative and inconsistent; they are often stereotyped into roles depicting criminality, illiteracy, terrorism and gang culture. For children and adolescents, there is risk of acute stress and post-traumatic stress symptoms, being exposed to bullying by mainstream youth, and exposure to ethnic slurs, which lead to challenges in ethnic identity formation and, at times, ethnic self-hate [par. 2].

Mian and Pumariega further suggest that white children run the risk of envisioning themselves as perpetrators of violence towards people different than them, which ultimately is a traumatic self-view that affects others as well as themselves (par. 2). Indeed, when a child is raised with parents who suffer from Xenophobia then it can be argued that the child will also display xenophobic character traits. Although, children typically seem to be more accepting of people different than themselves (at least at a very young age), it is not always a given. Janet Penn, executive director of Youth Lead, argues that "change takes effort and sometimes it means confronting our own prejudices and assumptions ... what many parents find surprising when they take this journey is not how well their kids respond, but how much richer and more interesting their own lives become" ("Teach Your Kids to Connect with Those Who Are 'Different'" par. 20). Certainly, some parents fail to purchase books that feature people of different ethnic groups, in these instances monsters happily jump in and play the role of the "Other." Though parents may not realize it, when they purchase a Children's book that features monsters, they are unconsciously championing the acceptance of cultural differences.

Though Grover's hilarious story is no example of cannon inclusive literature, it is still important. Indeed, this beloved tale has been read by children and parents alike for decades. Perhaps Grover's self-fear is lost upon audiences. However, a critical reader cannot help but notice how Grover is afraid of monsters simply because he has been taught that they are bad. This directly connects to xenophobia and children. Though many a parent may wish to argue this point, typically children do listen to their parents—most especially when self-preservation is in question. Children are urged not to talk to strangers, and sometimes for safety reasons are told not to interact with groups different than themselves. True, self-preservation is very important to teach to children, most especially in a world rampant with violence toward them. However, conversations about inclusion and acceptance need to be had as well in order to combat possible xenophobic fears. Sometimes parents shy away from these types of conversations for fear of saying something wrong, or possibly bringing something up that they think may be a non-issue (Olson par. 12).

Ultimately, Grover's tale endorses the very important philosophy of not judging a book by its cover. Grover certainly feels silly, and somewhat relieved, when he realizes that his knee jerk reaction and judgment of the word "monster" caused him to overreact in exuberant ways. This feeling can be compared to real people who fear others, and then quickly discover that their fears were unfounded. In this time of political turmoil, rampant racism, and xenophobia Grover's message rings loud and clear—do not jump to conclusions about people, take the time to get to know them. *The Monster at the End of This Book* will, arguably, continue to be a favorite of many children through the years to come. Undoubtedly, the book can be used to entertain but it is also a valuable conversation starter in regard to acceptance and understanding.

Conclusion

The 2015 Caldecott Medal winner boasts a monster, of sorts. *The Adventures of Beekle the Unimaginary Friend* by Dan Santat is the delightfully colorful story of Beekle, an imaginary being (or monster) seeking a very real unimaginary friend. Beekle hails from a faraway island where all imaginary friends are born, some look quite monstrous while others appear less threatening. Beekle appears to be a non-threatening creature, he is a small, rounded, all white, friendly looking creature with very few sharp lines who resembles an animated cloud wearing a crown. Beekle searches throughout the book for his friend, someone who will accept him that he can have adventures with. Thankfully, after a seemingly long time, Beekle finds his special friend and the two become devoted to one another (Santat 1–27). Santat's beautifully illustrated story features monsters and their "real" friends having wonderful adventures together without being afraid of their noticeable differences. In this way, Santat emphasizes differences in order to amplify the fun that can be had when people who are dissimilar become friends.

Santat is no stranger to monstrous fiction having illustrated several monsters in picture books. Aside from *Beekle*, Santat has illustrated other popular children's texts including Samantha Berger's *Crankenstein*, a hilarious Valentine's Day adventure that features a very cranky version of Frankenstein's monster. Throughout the tale the monster is used to teach the importance of love, and how people express their love differently. Though Santat is definitely not the only person using monsters in Picture books, he is one of the most popular contemporary artists embracing these monstrous messengers. However, monsters have become prevalent in children's films as well: *Monsters Inc.*, *Monsters University*, *Hotel Transylvania*, *Frankenweenie*, and *Monster House* all reveal the often heart-warming, and sometimes heart-wrenching, stories of these creatures who ultimately seek to be understood.

Jacques Derrida, famous philosopher and author, argues that "monsters cannot be announced. One cannot say: 'Here are our monsters,' without immediately turning the monsters into pets" (80). Announcing their presence and uttering the word "monster" does remove some of the power these imaginary beasts wield. Laying claim to the word is almost a taming of it. This is especially powerful for children because it can teach them to state what they are afraid of, to face their fears, to tame them, or to simply learn how to live with them. Though they may be scoffed at for being fictional and therefore lacking in seriousness, monsters in picture books are important literary devices that not only help to teach a moral, but also help to combat xenophobia. Yes, indeed these monsters look very different than the children holding the books, and that is what makes them so pivotal. Rick Riordan once wrote, "The real world is where the monsters are"; thankfully fictional monsters are there to prepare children, and adults, to navigate those real monsters lurking outside the pages of a book.

NOTES

1. The "Other": "The Other is an individual who is perceived by the group as not belonging, as being different in some fundamental way. Any stranger becomes the Other. The group sees itself as the norm and judges those who do not meet that norm (that is, who are different in any way) as the Other. Perceived as lacking essential characteristics possessed by the group, the Other is almost always seen as a lesser or inferior being and is treated accordingly. The Other in a society may have few or no legal rights, may be characterized as less intelligent or as immoral, and may even be regarded as sub-human" ("The Other" n.pag).

2. I hail from a small farming community in central Illinois. I did not meet a person from a different ethnic group until I went to college when I was 17. I was terrified of people that were different than myself.

WORKS CITED

Ackerman-Barger, Kupiri, and Faye Hummel. "Critical Race Theory as a Lens for Exploring Inclusion and Equity in Nursing Education." *Journal of Theory Construction & Testing* 19.2 (2015): 39–46. Academic Search Elite. Web. 9 Dec. 2015.
Chester, Lonnie. Personal Interview. 9 Nov. 2015.
Derrida, Jacques. "Some Statements and Truisms About Neologisms, Newisms, Postisms, Parasitisms, and other Small Seismisms." *The State of Theory*, ed. D. Caroll. New York: Columbia University Press, 1989. 63–94. Print.
Fulgham, Robert. *All I Really Need to Know I Learned in Kindergarten.* New York: Ballantine, 1990. Print.
Gaeta, Jill M. *In the Eye of the Hurricane: Antillean Children's Literature, Postcoloniality, and the Uneasy Reimagining of the Self.* Diss., Michigan State University, 2008. Web. 3 Sept. 2015.
Harris, Violet. "Applying Critical Theories to Children's Literature." *Theory into Practice* 38.3 (1999): 147–54. Business Source Elite. Web. 24 Oct. 2015.
Lynch-Brown, Carol, Carl M. Tomlinson, and Katy G. Short. *Essentials of Children's Literature.* Boston: Pearson, 2011. Print.
Mian, Ayesha, and Andres J. Pumareiga. "Tackling Xenophobia: Are We There Yet?" *MD. MD Magazine*, 25 Feb. 2011. Web. 17 Oct. 2015.
"monster, n., adv., and adj." OED Online. Oxford University Press, Nov. 2015. Web. 11 Nov. 2015.
Olson, Kristina R. "Are Kids Racist? (Not) Talking about Race with Your Children." *Psychology Today.* HealthProf.com, 2 Apr. 2013. Web. 23 Oct. 2015.
"The Other." *The Other.* CUNY.edu, 4 Feb. 2009. Web. 11 Nov. 2015.
"Peter Hunt." *Anfal—The Ambitious Learner.* Anfal, 2014. Web. 10 Nov. 2015.
Santat, Dan. *The Adventures of Beekle: The Unimaginary Friend.* New York: Little, Brown, Books for Readers, 2014. Print.

Slotnik, Daniel E. "How Often Do You Interact with People of Another Race or Ethnicity?" *The Learning Network*. The New York Times, 18 May 2012. Web. 8 Nov. 2015.
Stone, Jon. *The Monster at the End of this Book*, 2d ed. New York: Little Golden Books, 2003. Print.
"Teach Your Kids to Connect with Those Who Are 'Different.'" *NYMetro Parents*. Davler Media, n.d. Web. 1 Oct. 2015.
"This Day in History." History.com. A&E Digital, 10 June 2015. Web. 7 Oct. 2015.
Willems, Mo. *Goldilocks and the Three Dinosaurs*. New York: Balzer + Bray—HarperCollins, 2012. Print.
Wrenn, Jill Martin. "Jealousy, Joy and Driving a Bus: The Secret's to Writing a Hit Children's Book." CNN.com. Cable News Network, 23 Apr. 2013. Web. 14 Sept. 2015.

"You can't get rid of the Babadook"
The Supertextual Supernatural

Lloyd Isaac Vayo

On the surface, Jennifer Kent's 2014 film *The Babadook* is a fairly standard variation of the monster-in-the-closet narrative of childhood terror, where a seeming figment of the child's imagination crosses over into reality. Samuel, whose father Oskar was killed in a car accident while driving his mother to the hospital to give birth to him, is already a high-strung child, and is rendered even more highly strung by the unexplained appearance of the picture book *Mister Babadook* among his other books one day. At first appearing almost as a shadow, the Babadook, the picture book's (and film's) protagonist, is a gaunt, human-like form with long Noseferatu-like claws and a top hat, a threat to those who ignore his (gendered male in both text and film) existence; he grows stronger and stronger with each appearance in the real-world, and he cannot be banished once he arrives. Once the book *Mister Babadook* appears, the Babadook himself is soon to follow, and the presence and resilience of the text attests to the impossibility of eliminating the monster once he enters Samuel and Amelia's lives.

Though Samuel, Amelia, and the Babadook are the ostensible main characters in the film, the real star and prime mover is the book *Mister Babadook* itself. For Samuel, the book is a how-to guide in everyday terror, a warning that one must be wary of the world around them, as well as an indirect lesson in "stranger danger" and more. The book's form is instructive; as a pop-up book, paper versions of the Babadook leap from the page, an action mirrored in the supernatural leaping performed when the real, paranormal, Babadook crosses the border from fiction to reality. Through his transmutation from a fictional character limited to the confines of the book *Mister Babadook* to a manifest being unchained from the paper medium, the Babadook becomes supertextual, containing all that the text suggests and more. Amelia's efforts to destroy the book are unsuccessful; it reassembles itself, reappearing on the doorstep after one effort at banishment. The lesson of the book and film, to the extent that there is one, is present in the final scene, where the Babadook takes up residence in the basement, half-tamed, to be fed by Amelia; it has become a part of the family forever. One's monsters may be controlled, it seems, but never eliminated, forever strange, forever monstrous, forever traumatic, and yet always close, like family. The picture book *Mister Babadook* is a rude awakening, disturbing sleep and the innocence of youth; a sort of serenity may be restored, but the manifested Babadook will always lurk beneath.

A Question of Audience

It is worth pausing for a moment to consider who exactly *Mister Babadook* is intended for, who is involved in the book's reception, and how that expanded reception might broaden understandings of the book's purpose and effect. Though nominally a children's picture book, which would suggest an audience of primarily, if not nearly exclusively, younger children, it is important to consider that Samuel, though of reading age himself, interacts with *Mister Babadook* along with his mother, Amelia. Indeed, he is never depicted as reading the book by himself, only absorbing the narrative with the aid of Amelia, and receiving its message largely in her voice (though he does read ahead of her in some moments, particularly when the book offers climactic threats of terror to come). With this dual reading in mind, Amelia's perspective on the book is instructive. Judith Yanov's work on the maternal reader offers a foundation for examining that mindset. Yanov first suggests that "parents ... do not always know what will be meaningful for their children or what will be overwhelming to them," hinting at Amelia's initial and, in retrospect, somewhat surprising lack of trepidation at the first appearance of the book which mysteriously appeared on her bookshelf. She displayed this lack of awareness of the possible impact on her son for most of its first reading. Only when the threat in the text of the book became explicitly threatening did she begin to alter the words of the text to suit her son's needs reflecting on the unique relationship between mother-reader and child. This is certainly the case with Samuel and Amelia, who first lack this resonance due to Amelia's doubts about the existence of the Babadook, then finally relocate it once the Babadook is subjected to domestic control. Finally, Yanov notes that "children do best when their feeling states are recognized and reflected on by the mind of another ... [t]his recognition helps children to trust the reality of their own experience, to be able to reflect upon their mental life,

80 Part 2: Normalization of the "Other"

and eventually to be able to recognize and understand the minds of others." This is certainly the case with Samuel and Amelia, who first lack this resonance due to Amelia's doubts about the existence of the Babadook, which Samuel asserts does exist. This lack of shared belief causes friction. Only when Amelia's belief system begins to include the real-life existence of the Babadook does Samuels fragile mind even out. This recognition only occurs between Samuel and Amelia near the film's conclusion when they fully understand each other. While Samuel may be the intended audience for *Mister Babadook*, its reception is mediated by Amelia, and her initial skepticism towards the book informs much of its early impact on Samuel and the eventual messages that it yields.

The Material Book

Before engaging more directly with the ostensible message of *Mister Babadook*, it is important to examine both the physical particulars of the book (including its overall material composition, its color scheme and illustration style, and its use of pop-ups and pull tabs) and the varied content of the story it contains (the story becomes longer and more specific in the second iteration after the book returns intact from her attempt to burn it) to establish the foundations of that message. Looking first at the basic physicality of the book itself, beyond the gravity of the narrative contained therein, the book itself is weighty; Samuel struggles to handle it in some moments, and Amelia herself has to engage in some minor gymnastics to both prop up the book for reading purposes and to manipulate the pages and devices therein. Perry Nordelman states, "The size of a book influences our response to it. We tend to expect rambunctious, energetic stories [from larger books]" (44) and the impact of this book on the two readers is indeed far-reaching as the Babadook living up to that energetic expectation; in this case literally popping off the page. Physically, it is a large text, especially in a children's book, allowing for a greater area of illustration since it also tends to cover the entire field of vision of the reader. This engrossing reach creates a further tension insomuch as it prevents the reader from perceiving what lies beyond the frame of the book itself, suggesting by implication that the Babadook may reside there unnoticed. Appropriately, the book is also bound in a deep red cloth (given the potential bloodshed to come), and the outer cover bears no distinguishing marks save for the title and a silhouette of the eponymous monster. This relative blankness extends to the opening and concluding pages; a clutch of all-black pages appear at the book's outset and a similar series of all-white pages appear at the end, as though the textual ending is waiting to be added to the ending. Although typically a frontispiece (the illustration which is opposite the title page of the book) bears an illustration, the opening pages of *Mister Babadook* function in a like-minded manner, abstractly illustrating the darkness to follow and offering a glimpse into the black interior of the Babadook. Lawrence R. Sipe speaks to the potential of these pages which are "commonly referred to as the 'peritext,'" noting that "children [are] highly engaged in using the front endpapers for predictive purposes, and often [assume] that the endpapers in some way [are] a prelude or preparation for the story" (30). Samuel is similarly engaged, reading the pages as meaning-bearing, presaging the dark descent in to the Babadook's world, as well as the Babadook's supertextual transcendence of the bounds of the book.

Amelia twice attempts to alter the basic physicality of the book, first by tearing its pages (including the opening and concluding pages) from the spine and then tearing them into smaller pieces, and then, after the book appears, reassembled, by dousing it in lighter fluid and burning it on a barbecue grill. After this second attempt, the book does indeed disappear (the white of the final pages possibly presaging the ash they become), though by that point its protagonist has been released from the pages to darken the horrified family's world. Dawnene D. Hammerberg addresses the unique phenomenon of internalization in relation to picture books, where "the relationship between images and printed text can also be one of synergy ... where the message must be read through images-as-text in ways that make it difficult to say where meaning lies" (209). In this instance, meaning lies in that interstice, in the space between image and text, a space that only exists in the mind of the reader(s) (Samuel and Amelia). Hammerberg goes on to suggest that "the genre of children's literature repositions the reader today as someone who does more than decode the words" (210), and in this case that "more" is the process not only of decoding those words through their companion images, but, as a function of the active, engaged nature of that practice, internalizing the book (*Mister Babadook*) and its message such that the text is no longer necessary to perceive its import.

The darkness of the Babadook and the potentially horrible demise that he promises to bring to those who refuse to believe in him is mimicked in the color scheme of the book itself, which is composed of decidedly muted tones that lend the text and illustrations a sense of creeping dread. As a color palette, the drab grays, blacks, and sepia shades that mark the book's pages lend the narrative a claustrophobic air, with nearly all of the light, both literal and metaphorical, being sucked out of the pages and the readers who gaze upon them. Corporate consulting firm Colour Affects describes gray as being "quite suppressive," and black as being "menacing" and creating "a perception of weight and seriousness" ("Psychological"), reinforcing the heaviness produced by the book's color scheme. The pages themselves resemble a sort of grayed out parchment, suggesting both age (and, by implication, the timeless threat posed by the Babadook) and a seriousness befitting influential historical documents committed to the same type of paper. That gray, touched with tan and brown hues, seems weathered, soiled, marked by repeated thumbings. It is almost as if the book may have existed prior to its appearance in Samuel's room, suggesting a broader reach and influence of the Babadook narrative, a monster existing beyond the pages of the book and beyond the walls of Samuel's room and Amelia's house. The only moment in which vivid color graces the pages of *Mister Babadook* is in its second iteration, where an illustration depicts Amelia slitting her own throat, with an accompanying pull tab moving the knife and loosing blood from her jugular. As the blood emerges, it is a deep crimson, at once capturing the darkness of the rest of the surrounding colors (rather than a primary, fire engine red) while adding a (literal) splash of life, vitality and its ebbing. Again, Colour Affects offers a reading of the shade in question, calling red's effect "physical; it stimulates us and raises the pulse rate ... and can activate the 'fight or flight' instinct" ("Psychological"), a visceral impact consistent with the vital gushing it marks and the terror it instills in both Samuel and Amelia. This moment of brightness marks the culmination of the Babadook's intended vengeance on the family, following the suggestion that Amelia will kill first the family dog, and then Samuel. The blood functions as a crescendo of sorts that empties out into the all-white final pages, though returning to red in the form of the back cover, which is itself an illustration of the swelling pool of blood coming from Amelia's neck.

The blocky limitations of the narrow color palette of the book's text and illustrations are mirrored in the illustrations themselves, which are drawn in chunky lines that convey a crude, nearly cartoonish version of the Babadook narrative. Rather than using crisp, clean pen strokes, *Mister Babadook* is rendered in uneven, nearly filthy forms, a fitting manner of capturing the dank, looming tone of the narrative and the monster that it describes. At times, the illustrations seem less drawn than carved, hewn from the pages themselves or pressed from woodcuts, adding additional credence to the perception of age that surrounds the book. Those illustrations, in their thickness and weight, paradoxically leap from the page (sometimes with the help of a pop-up), emerging from the murk of the parchment and producing a sort of negative space, the blackness of the lines less marked upon the page than cut from it to reveal the void-like substratum beneath. Given this dimension of the illustrations' style, the second component, the cartoon-like nature of the images, is almost counterintuitive. However, the tension between the festively merry aesthetic of the cartoon and the subtle but unrelenting terror of the blocky line-work serves to amplify the impact of the narrative, making it at once more palatable, able to reach and retain a broader audience, and more dreadful, able to enthrall that audience once they arrive. In isolation, either component would be insufficient, straight cartooning undermining the severe tone of the narrative and crooked scrawling alienating all but the most committed of readers; in combination, the pair offers a disarmingly simplistic, sinister feel, initially unthreatening enough to invite, and then menacing enough to captivate, to at once draw the reader into the page while exceeding its bounds.

Pop-ups and pull tabs are used to great effect in *Mister Babadook*, literalizing the leaping from the page suggested by the realistic threat of the narrative in the form of paper projections, while also allowing that projection to move beyond the literal paper on which it is printed or drawn into the very center of Samuel and Amelia's lives. In the book's first iteration, two chief pop-ups serve to magnify key moments of the text: the first accompanies the insistent Babadook's first arrival in the anonymous child's room, swooping over its bed with claws outstretched, and the second marks the penultimate pages' caution to consider the narrative, with the Babadook spreading his arms and baring his teeth frighteningly. The second iteration is considerably more kinetic, compounding the impact of the pop-ups with a liberal use of pull tabs. Alongside a warning against the dangers of ignoring the Babadook, he once more bursts from the pages, this time in a forebodingly dark form that occupies a two-page spread, though more devastating use of the two devices is yet to come. As the narrative becomes more personalized, chronicling the intended fate of Amelia to murder all and sundry, pull tabs come to the fore, first as she strangles the dog, animating the suffocating act, then as she strangles Samuel, similarly tightening her grip, and finally as she slits her own throat, yielding the aforementioned geyser of blood. In total, these pop-ups and pull tabs signal the culmination of the Babadook's infiltration of Samuel and Amelia's lives, transcending the textual (via the Babadook's supernatural nature) into the supertextual, a progression that may be traced across both iterations of the book.

Two Narrative Iterations

In her article "One and Inseparable: Interdependent Storytelling in Picture Storybooks," Denise E. Agosto identifies the mutually reinforcing nature of text and image in picture books, calling that phenomenon "augmentation ... [where] the texts and illustrations each amplify, extend, and complete the story that the other tells" (269–70). That augmentation may take two forms: humor and irony (270), and in the case of *Mister Babadook*, where the intermarriage between text and image produces amplified terror, the first iteration appears faintly humorous, while the second confounds the conventional expectation of a harmless narrative with a realization of that very terror. *Mister Babadook*'s first manifestation, spanning from Samuel's discovery of the text on the bookshelf in his room to Amelia's first attempt at destruction via tearing, functions largely as an informative warning against the threat of infiltration by the Babadook, a not altogether benign but not overwhelmingly menacing presentation of the Babadook narrative. At the outset, the brief tale is somewhat humorous; the text that accompanies an illustration of the Babadook from the waist up, focusing on his top hat, asks, "He's funny, don't you think?" as if he should be a figure of at least potential amusement at this point (*The Babadook*). The text takes a somewhat darker turn from there, but not drastically so, in the warning "see him in your room at night / And you won't sleep a wink" (*The Babadook*), though mere sleeplessness is a minor threat compared to the Babadook's full capacity for terror. Returning to the notion of the Babadook as a figure of fun, the text informs the reader that "I'll soon take off my funny disguise" (*The Babadook*), that worse is yet to come, though even then the promise is not exceedingly grave, given that it is offered in first person. After all, to reveal one's true monstrous abilities in that manner ruins all of the fun. It is only in the concluding words, presented in all caps, that the book presses its point, following the hint "and once you see what's underneath" with the imprecation "YOU'RE GOING TO WISH YOU WERE / DEAD" (*The Babadook*). In this form the book announces the Babadook's existence to the world of children (and adults), offers a shorthand summary of the threat that he poses, and somewhat counter intuitively warns readers of the impending nature of that threat, though the threat's positioning as a consequence of not believing in the Babadook underlines the true import of this iteration: to spread the Babadook's infamy far and wide.

The book's second manifestation, spanning from its unexplained arrival on the house's doorstep in reassembled form, complete with additional and more specific pages, to Amelia's impromptu incineration of the book itself, marks the moment when things become personal, and when the Babadook ceases to be bound between the covers of *Mister Babadook*. Where the first iteration is more general, giving a thumbnail version of who the Babadook is and what the nature of his business might be, the second iteration is chillingly specific, primarily in the form of its illustrations and their animation via the pop-ups and pull tabs. While the lines "You start to CHANGE when I get in; / the Babadook growing right UNDER YOUR SKIN" are menacing in and of themselves (*The Babadook*), they are even more so when accompanied by an illustration of Amelia, who now casts a shadow in the shape of the Babadook. The next pages, which call to the reader, "Oh come! Come see! What's UNDERNEATH" (*The Babadook*), display the deeds that the Babadook will incite within Amelia, in this case her strangling of the family dog, with the use of both a pop-up and a pull tab, making more severe the already murderous future posited for her due to her failure to truly believe in the monster. The notion of an underneath, while redoubling the shadowy and infernal nature of the Babadook, also reflects the degree to which he might penetrate Amelia, such that beneath her otherwise unchanged veneer, something more sinister is lurking, waiting to exact its violence upon those entities most near and dear to her. After the first attempt at destroying *Mister Babadook*, the book is literally fractured, riven with tears and cast into pieces in the dustbin; once it reappears, the book has at once sutured those fractures and externalized them. The book is now whole, at least temporarily (prior to Amelia's pyrotechnics), but the world around it is subject to a more thoroughgoing rupture, one presaged from the moment of the book's very arrival.

The Book's Arrivals

Mister Babadook appears first somewhat innocuously on Samuel's bookshelf, perhaps a more physically imposing volume than some of the others found there, but with little hint at its sinister contents. One evening, while getting ready for bed, Samuel pulls the book from the shelf as his selection for the night's reading from Amelia, and nothing about that process seems out of place. Samuel does not dwell for an unusual amount of time at the bookcase, shows no surprise at finding the book there, and considers it perfectly natural that the evening's bedtime story should come from its pages. There is no suggestion of anything untoward until Amelia starts reading the story itself, at which point Samuel begins to express a growing sense of fear, a sentiment that also evinces the fact that he has not read the book on its own and has no prior knowledge of the Babadook narrative. In this moment, Samuel and Amelia's world (an ordering that reflects his priority as the center of her life after the death of her husband) is largely untouched; the presence of *Mister Babadook* is inexplicable, but not yet inescapable. It remains a book among other books, at home alongside the *Three Little Pigs* and princes and princesses, somewhat unsettling in its unknown origins and ominous warnings, but not an engrossing threat in the manner that it will soon become. The book may be closed, put away, filed among the others; its narrative also being subject to at least temporary closure (though Samuel's mind races with the implications of the cautionary tale therein), and while the Babadook may be making halting steps towards escaping its pages, he is not yet a free-range monster.

The book's second appearance is more troubling; after attempting to rend the very fabric of the book by tearing it to shreds and tossing it in the trash, Amelia ignores the doorbell, but cannot ignore a pounding at the door that, when opened, reveals the reassembled book on the doorstep. Yet, what is delivered so insistently, an insistence that moves from polite use of the doorbell to a less courteous thumping, is not the *Mister Babadook* of the first appearance. Instead, though the original pages are there, with content and order unaltered, additional pages have been added, making the book's arrival less a return than a new turn, an intensification of the warning of the original version with a more specific understanding of the fate that faces the family if the Babadook is not properly respected. The timing of this arrival is also telling; where the book originally makes itself known in the evening, at bedtime, when monsters normally reign, and the presence of another might not draw particular notice, *Mister Babadook*'s second appearance happens in broad daylight. After discarding the book the previous day and considering the matter closed, Amelia is confronted with the renewed existence, the augmented presence of the book the next day. Though she opens the door to find no one there, there is indeed a presence, the titular Babadook who may be lurking somewhere in the margins (or might be invisible, as Samuel often experiences him). However, the Babadook is less marginal than central, the subject and potential author of his own text, as well as the primary preoccupation for Samuel and, increasingly, Amelia. Brief earlier manifestations aside, it is only when Amelia's more decisive efforts to destroy the book by fire go forward that the Babadook is able to fully liberate himself from its pages, to roam free, menacing all who might doubt his existence. In this case, he only has eyes (and claws) for Samuel and Amelia, even if his creator might still reside in the very shadows from which he has emerged.

Locating the Author

The question of attribution, of who exactly is responsible for authoring *Mister Babadook*, remains seemingly unresolved, the book instead appearing mysteriously from the ether, without any designation on its cover or elsewhere within the book. Given the message of the book itself, that the Babadook is not a figure to be trifled with, and that he will exact a cruel vengeance upon any and all who fail to recognize his existence, it would seem paradoxical for the narrative to have been penned by the Babadook himself. The difficulties of writing with such long claws aside, there is a counterintuitive dimension to a monster who would potentially want to cultivate an unwary pool of potential victims warning those among that very pool of what faces them. Yet, for a monster to signify, to truly and thoroughly terrify, it must be at once known and unknown, its vague outlines discernable, with some mystery left for the fertile imaginations of its youthful targets. With this process of victim creation in mind, the book functions as a business card of sorts for the Babadook, a *carte de visite* marking his first appearance in Samuel's room (though far from the last), a keepsake or reminder for his victims that further and more elaborate victimhood will ensue if his warning is not heeded. The book bears his name in bold type upon its cover, gives a succinct summation of his vocation, and includes contact information (do not call him; he will call you). Though far from pocket-sized, the book does facilitate the Babadook's networking efforts, enabling him to turn his connection with Samuel into a connection with Amelia, and suggesting that similar such connections might have existed, or might presently exist, in other homes around the town and broader country. It would make a certain sense for the Babadook to pen *Mister Babadook*, part memoir and part *aide de memoire*, though there may be an equally likely author a bit closer to home.

Amelia's initial dismissiveness towards Samuel's preoccupation with the Babadook may be evidence of parenting tactics, of a desire to quell her son's fears. However, she may also be deliberately encouraging both a dangerously blasé attitude towards the Babadook (such that he might seek vengeance) and an amplified preoccupation (telling someone to forget about something is the surest way to make them remember) as a means of increasing the effect of her own creation, *Mister Babadook*. When attending a birthday party for her niece, Amelia mentions to the assembled mothers that "I did some articles, magazines, kid's stuff" (*The Babadook*), positioning herself as not only an author, but an author of material for children, the very same category in which one might easily place *Mister Babadook*. While the exact nature of her previous writing remains unclear, the darkness of the book is similar to the all-consuming grief that comes out of her husband's death, and the book might function as an outlet for some of that emotion. After the reappearance of *Mister Babadook* following Amelia's first attempt to destroy the book, she seeks out police intervention, thinking that the book's endurance might point to a stalker. While at the police station, in the midst of describing the book (by now burnt to cinders) as evidence of the hypothetical stalker, Amelia's right hand is covered in ink, in much the same way as one's hand might become darkened when dragged across still wet illustrations and text. Though she did vigorously tear up the book not too long before, at which point some ink might have transferred, and she has even more recently burned it, during which some ash or smoke might have transferred (though she does not appear to interact with the book as it is aflame or afterwards), a more likely explanation is that she herself is its author. By potentially creating the Babadook out of whole cloth, Amelia produces a means of teaching Samuel, and perhaps herself, a myriad of lessons.

Lessons on Offer

In light of the potential for Amelia-as-mother-as-author-as-monster, a number of possible lessons may arise from *Mister Babadook*, the first of which is the evergreen threat often referred to as "stranger danger." At his core, the

Babadook is a stranger, beyond the basic strange that a child might encounter in the run of its daily life, a creature seemingly from another world, and one that is difficult to place within the quotidian landscape, even for the fertile imagination of a child. The Babadook is initially enticing, not going so far as to lure children into his grasp with the promise of candy or some other such amusement, but first presenting a face that is far less menacing than what follows, his top hat suggesting whimsy before the true nature of its wearer is made evident. As a means of making the danger associated with unknown adults real and impactful, *Mister Babadook* doubly succeeds, both by offering a gruesome hypothetical scenario of what might happen if a child should fall into the hands of such a stranger, and also by placing the omnipresent awareness of that threat as a means of staving it off at the very center of its narrative. That the Babadook, once loosed from the book itself, eventually comes to reside in Samuel and Amelia's basement, and is kept and fed there, also suggests an augmented reading of the stranger danger possibility. By keeping the Babadook on hand, partly as a necessary means of ensuring control, Amelia also positions him less as a one-time expression of the threat of stranger danger than an omnipresent warning for Samuel, always lurking just beneath the floorboards of the house. If the Babadook can be domesticated to some degree, perhaps his threat is diminished somewhat, though his ongoing proximity may offset that decline. This domestication suggests not only the continued threat posed by strangers, but also an internalization of that threat into Samuel and Amelia's shared home, such that any visitors (neighbor Mrs. Roach, coworker Robbie, representatives from Child Services), even those already known, are seen as threatening the mother-son dyad, to the point of potentially tearing the family apart.

Beyond the more specific rendering of the Babadook-as-stranger, consistent with the childhood-centric threat posed by stranger danger, the book may also be gesturing towards the larger problem of monsters that plagues individuals perpetually throughout their lives, not so much in supernatural form like the Babadook, but terrifying nonetheless. In this sense, *Mister Babadook* functions as a working through of a process that Samuel will likely repeat many more times in childhood, adolescence, and adulthood: facing an unexpected and largely unknown threat, becoming familiar with the dangers that it poses, and finding that an awareness of that threat may be the best way to prevent its realization. In his contribution to *Monster Theory: Reading Culture*, Jeffrey Jerome Cohen addresses the notion of perpetuity, concluding that "the monster always escapes because it refuses easy categorization" (6), while also observing that "they [monsters] bring not just a fuller knowledge of our place in history and the history of knowing our place, but they bear self-knowledge, *human* knowledge" (20). For Cohen, the presence of the monster is unavoidable, even necessary, but not evil, instead allowing its audience an opportunity for knowledge unavailable elsewhere. This process of identifying and familiarizing oneself with, though not realizing, threats might appear in childhood when a child has a public performance of some sort (a play or a music recital, perhaps) with the potentially negative audience reaction seeming monstrous until the generally friendly nature of that audience is appreciated. In adolescence when a teenager faces down the prospect of their driver's test, the vehicle itself and its capacity for destruction in inexpert hands appears monstrous until practice allows for more qualified command; and in adulthood, when an individual anticipates a performance review at work where the review panel seems made up of cackling ghouls until professionalism smoothes the way forward, self knowledge occurs. If Samuel takes this broader template from *Mister Babadook*, viewing it as a how-to manual for approaching life's other monsters, then the book will have done its job, making itself useful beyond the more elementary bounds of a particularly chilling childhood memory of a terrifying bedtime story into a cautionary tale that may endure beyond childhood and provide a model for dealing with what adulthood has to offer. That tale applies to not just one monster, but to a whole realm of monsters threatening to derail one's life not with blood and brutality (other than in the case of a thorough failing of the aforementioned driver's test), but with embarrassment or a generalized sense of failure, a minor trauma that mirrors the greater trauma at the heart of Samuel and Amelia's experience.

The notion of a wider field of monsters, present in perpetuity, parallels the chief monster in Samuel and Amelia's lives, a monster that precedes, intercedes, and supersedes the Babadook: Samuel's dead father/Amelia's dead husband, Oskar. Oskar's death is sudden and unexpected, much like the arrival of *Mister Babadook*, as Oskar is plucked from life in a car accident on the way to the hospital for Samuel's birth. Once present, the trauma of that initial moment lingers, burrowing its way into the minds and hearts of Samuel and Amelia, the actual text (the moment of death and its aftermath in the form of the funeral and subsequent mourning) needing not to be present for its presence to be felt and a creeping sense of dread to be produced. With this reading in mind, the book may posit an understanding where Samuel and Amelia need to be always aware of Oskar's absence, lest that absence become more gnawingly heartrending or, perhaps worse, permanent, with Oskar slipping from their thoughts entirely. For Samuel, Oskar is much like the Babadook: a figure that he does not know and has never met, who comes to life only via words and images offered by Amelia and, though possibly not as frightening as the Babadook, may be just as foreign and generally foreboding. If Oskar is indeed somewhat monstrous to Samuel, then perhaps this is the one monster that you do let in, that you do welcome into your life, as proves to be the case with the manifested Babadook. In their article "Cultural Variances in Composition of Biological and Supernatural Concepts of Death: A Content Analysis of Children's Literature," Ji Seong Lee et al. suggest that "children's literature has been used legitimately as a therapeutic and didactic tool for grief counselors, teachers, and school administrators to aid children in bereavement, as well as a useful means to communicate with their children on the subject of death" (538). Whether as author or as mother-reader, Amelia may be using *Mister Babadook* to that end, providing Samuel and herself with the tools needed to maintain Oskar's memory while not allowing it to dominate their lives. The trauma of Oskar's death is as enduring as the threat posed by the Babadook, and may be dealt with similarly, though dealing with that trauma will still not render Samuel's parents fully comprehensible to him.

Beyond its invocations against stranger danger, its modeling of how to deal with life's monsters, and its mimicking of the trauma of paternal loss, *Mister Babadook* also provides a glimpse through a child's eyes at the oftentimes terrifying and inexplicable relationship with one's parents, those who hold so much power with so little transparency. The very name of the Babadook suggests a nearly pre-verbal level of comprehension: if a child's first words are often "mama" and "papa," it is a short journey from those syllables to "baba," the root of evil in the narrative. When the Babadook announces himself in the book, he does so with a drawn out "ba ... ba ... DOOK DOOK DOOK" (*The Babadook*), as if figuring out his naming in the moment; the relatively innocuous nature of the first words meeting with the abrupt and guttural balance. To a child with little real understanding of the world around it, parents may seem terrifyingly inexplicable: they resemble the child, but are larger, stronger, and more advanced in many regards, and possess control over eating, sleeping, and numerous other daily functions, producing dependency in the process. Without the benefit of a deeper understanding of the complexities behind parenting, many decisions may seem totally arbitrary, and may go unexplained to the child's comprehension and/or satisfaction, a monstrous intervention that is sweeping and permanent, with no effectual grievance structure to which to appeal. Given that the narrative of *Mister Babadook* concludes in Amelia's suicidal throat slitting, it is possible that the fragility of parenthood more generally, and parental authority more specifically, is being suggested, though a more likely reading positions the book as a sympathetic voice for the child who finds itself the charge of seeming monsters.

Conclusion

Mister Babadook is, to all appearances, a book like any other, offering a narrative about a decidedly sinister monster who feeds on the denial of those who come to, but refuse to, know him. It is a bit dark for a children's book maybe, but not altogether remarkable otherwise. Yet, upon further examination, the book and the narrative it contains prove to be anything but mundane, calling on a particularly powerful visual aesthetic and textual brevity to produce a narrative of stunning simplicity, a mere few pages in its first incarnation that manage to speak, and to exceed the binding of, volumes. The Babadook is clearly supernatural in both form and behavior, taking on a looming, almost insect-like stature and movement, and through *Mister Babadook*, manages to become supertextual as well. While within the pages of the book, the Babadook is powerful, but his movement is restricted to that offered by the pop-ups and pull tabs of the book's physical construction, making him somewhat kinetic, though not as much as the narrative promises. It is only when Amelia attempts to destroy the book, first by tearing and then by fire, that the Babadook is able to shed his papery chains, dropping the polite "Mister" and becoming something else entirely. In motivating his own liberation by so thoroughly frightening Samuel that Amelia feels the need to put a literal stop to the narrative, the Babadook also generates a four-part reading of that narrative origin and its associated lessons: the Babadook-as-stranger, the Babadook-as-first-monster, the-Babadook-as-repressed-trauma, and the Babadook-as-mama/papa.

Each of these readings adds untold depth to a deceptively simple narrative, expanding a children's story about a monster into a parable for confrontation with the unknown that goes beyond the bounds of childhood and into the very fabric of our lives. In their introduction to their edited volume *Monster Culture in the 21st Century: A Reader*, Marina Levina and Diem-My T. Bui argue that "monstrous narratives of the past decade have become omnipresent specifically because they represent collective social anxieties over resisting and embracing change in the twenty-first century ... monstrosity has transcended its status as a metaphor and has indeed become a necessary condition of our existence" (1–2). *The Babadook* is in some ways a film out of time, with few temporal markers placing it within a specific decade, as well as few moments of respite for the besieged Samuel and Amelia, and so its status as a 21st century film is oblique at best. Yet, in Samuel and Amelia's eventual tentative embrace of the Babadook, the film works through the very social anxieties ascribed to the new century and demonstrates the necessity of that very monstrousness. For the doubled readers of *Mister Babadook* (the picture book) and *The Babadook* (the film), the narrative on offer provides a way forward through the challenges of childhood and adulthood (as well as the meeting points between the two) that is at once timeless and distinctly of its time.

WORKS CITED

Agosto, Denise E. "One and Inseparable: Interdependent Storytelling in Picture Storybooks." *Children's Literature in Education* 30.4 (1999): 267–80. EBSCOhost. Web. 17 Dec. 2015.

The Babadook. Dir. Jennifer Kent. 2014. Shout! Factory, 2015. DVD.
Cohen, Jeffrey Jerome. "Monster Culture (Seven Theses)." *Monster Theory: Reading Culture*, ed. Jeffrey Jerome Cohen. Minneapolis: University of Minnesota Press, 1996. 3–25. Print.
Hammerberg, Dawnene D. "Reading and Writing 'Hypertextually': Children's Literature, Technology, and Early Writing Instruction." *Language Arts* 78.3 (2001): 207–16. Print.
Lee, Ji Seong, et al. "Cultural Variances in Composition of Biological and Supernatural Concepts of Death: A Content Analysis of Children's Literature." *Death Studies* 38 (2014): 538–45. EBSCOhost. Web. 17 Dec. 2015.
Levina, Marina, and Diem-My T. Bui. "Introduction: Toward a Comprehensive Monster Theory In the 21st Century." *Monster Culture in the 21st Century: A Reader*.
Levina, Marina, and Diem-My T. Bui, eds. *Monster Culture in the 21st Century: A Reader*. New York: Bloomsbury, 2013. 1–13. Print.
Nordelman, Perry. *Words About Pictures: The Narrative Art of Children's Picture Books*. Athens: University of Georgia, 1988. Print.
"Psychological Properties of Colours." *Colour Affects*. Colour Affects, 2008–15. Web. 15 Dec. 2015.
Sipe, Lawrence R. *Storytime: Young Children's Literary Understanding in the Classroom*. New York: Teachers College Press, 2008. Print.
Yanov, Judith. "Books and Feelings: The Power of the Picture Book and the Inner Life of the Child—A Joint Conference by the Boston Psychoanalytic Society and Institute and PEN New England's Children's Books Caucus." *Robie H. Harris—Children's Book Author*. Robie Harris, 19 Oct. 2002. Web. 15 Dec. 2015.

Monsters Like Us

Gerald Raymond Gordon

Monsterland Japan

Japan is a culture rich with monsters. Mysterious creatures have crept in and out of the human world throughout its history. Appearing within traditional and regional folktales, Shinto animism myths, Buddhist cosmology, modern manga comic books and hugely popular animated TV programs, films and video games, monsters remain fascinating inhabitants in the imaginations of Japanese children and adults. The different types of monsters that exist in Japan's traditional and pop cultures are too numerous to list, and new ones are regularly being discovered and created. Owing to their popularity, there is even a certification system to qualify Monster Experts. In a testing program that may be more focused on regional PR than genuine monsterology, the Sakaiminato City chamber of commerce in Tottori Prefecture regularly administers 50-question exams for certifying applicants' introductory and intermediate level monster expertise. The advanced level requires an essay. A 5-year-old girl recently made news by passing the introductory level test ("Okayama").

And there is no lack of variety and details that any would-be Japanese monster expert might need to master. Monsters in Japan range from inanimate objects that have come to life—such as *karakasa* (an angry broken-down or forgotten umbrella that has one leg, one eye and a long greasy tongue, which sneaks up on people and gives them an oily lick)—to mythical hybrid beasts—like the *baku* (a tapir-inspired creature with the amalgamated anatomy of an elephant's nose, bear's body, tiger's claws and rhino's eyes, which exists to beneficently eat people's bad dreams and is occasionally found depicted on objects related to sleep, such as pillows or medieval head rests)— to humanoid creatures—like the *kappa* (a species of green, reptilian-skinned river dwellers which are commonly blamed for riverside mishaps ranging from pranks to drowning, but have also been accused of kidnappings and rapes). *Kappa* are one of the most common and widespread monstrous creatures in Japan, having more than eighty names related to it in different regions of the country (Foster 3). And, there are a great many other monsters that lurk and live in close proximity with human beings in Japan's cities, villages and wilds.

The popularity of monsters in the Japanese imagination and visual culture goes back many hundreds of years. Visual evidence of this history can be seen in the online International Research Center for Japanese Studies' Yokai Database, which stores thousands of images of Japanese monsters culled from paintings and other visual sources produced by various artists from different time periods. One particularly enchanting series is a group of paintings called the *Bakemono Zukushi* (Monster Variety) by an anonymous artist in the Edo Period (18th and 19th centuries) depicting twenty-three different monstrous characters (Bakemono).

However, from among the many intriguing supernatural creatures, I want to direct our attention onto one particular monster called *oni*, which regularly appears in Japanese traditional, mainstream and popular culture. Physically comparable to ogres in western cultures, *oni* are untamed barbarians who appear in folktales, seasonal festivals, Japan's version of Hide-n-Seek, proverbs, architectural ornamentation and advertising campaigns. Typically serving as villains in folktales, *oni* embody bad behavior and a lack of civilized enculturation. As well, they are used to instructionally suffer the tragic outcomes that await beings who act too wildly. The *oni* character has historically been cast in stories as an antithetical model of preferred social norms, teaching correct behavior by negative example. Don't do X, or bad things will happen to you. Also, *oni* in traditional stories are used as a vehicle for telling bawdy tales of vice and debauchery, often times with the *oni* being defeated in the end by a simple trick which restores the moral order after a brief flirtation with chaos. The listener can be titillated by a vicarious brush with a risqué topic without humanity being indicted for enjoying such lusts. In addition, *oni* are often used as a scare tactic to frighten children into obedient behavior. In some villages, there are New Year's traditions in which men costumed as *oni* come into people's homes to terrorize the children and reassert the power of the father or parents as the protectors and authority in the household. The children learn the parents are what hold back the forces of chaos and terror, thus one should submit to their authority. This practice also gives the parents a tool they can use to threaten children away from future disobedience for fear that the monster could be called back to punish them or to take a bad child away to live within the *oni*'s population. This sort of forced adoption—as well as the fact that almost all *oni* are male—raises a question that has no clear answer: How are new *oni* produced? While there is no official generative method for it, the most common explanation follows a logic of regressive spiritual evolution. Basically, when a person is so bad that he exhausts his potential for rehabilitation back into civilized humanity, he transforms into an *oni*, usually at death—where he then serves as a tormentor of souls in hell. But, for the very worst bad people, they become *oni* while still alive ("Oni"). Such in-life *oni* are the ones who appear as troublemakers in many folk tales.

In contemporary Japan, *oni* can be seen almost every day along the sidewalks and in the supermarket aisles. They live among us, depicted on the products for sale and as modes of attracting point of purchase attention. While contemporary images of *oni* are more varied than in the past and can be commonly found to portray a wider range of emotional moods, the most common images of *oni* depict them as either powerful or cute. For example, if a local government is running a PR campaign about how it is getting tough on crime, it might use an angry-looking *oni* with its identifiable massive muscles and iron club to convey the municipal message of seriously doing its duty. However within the realm of cute, a pre-school advertising itself might produce a colorful poster of many smiling *oni* children in the school's uniform happily playing together in the sandbox. As well, images of *oni* appear regularly on products, such as a particularly cheap brand of *sake* that is called *Oni Koroshi* (*Oni* Kill) which regularly updates its packaging illustrations to show different *oni* exhibiting a variety of *oni*-associated emotions and activities, ranging from angry, to chilled-out-drunk, to child-like mischievous, to comically bemused while partying at a regional winter festival. A Google image search of Oni Koroshi (鬼ころし) will provide you with an assortment of such cultural contextualization.

The myth of *oni* is very old in Japan. The Chinese character of *oni* (鬼) originally had more of a general meaning akin to "demon" and was used for a wider variety of monsters, ghosts, haunting spirits, etc. Later, the Chinese character came to be associated more exclusively with the ogre-like creature we know today. Typically, an *oni* is depicted as having a human male anatomy but being massive in size, muscle-bound, and with one or more horns growing from his head. *Oni* are usually bright red, but blue ones are also common. There are other colors as well, but these are more rare. *Oni* typically reside apart from human beings, such as deep in forests, in distant mountains or on isolated islands. But, it is important to note here that there are very similar creatures which play a role in Buddhist cosmology as tormentors in hell (Japan 1151). These beings greatly inform peoples' commonly held images and fears regarding *oni*. As alluded to above, the demons which torment the human damned in the Buddhist hell realms share many of the same characteristics as terrestrial *oni* found in folklore. In Buddhist paintings, these demons are virtually indistinguishable from *oni*—and very well may have enough cross-over to make them one and the same. Demons in hell are depicted enacting incredibly graphic punishments upon the frail and frightened forms of the damned. They eat "the dead" alive, flail off their skins, burn them with hot tongs and even torment unborn children by knocking down the piles of stones that they are required to perpetually build up like sobbing little Sisyphuses (Sadakata 167). These hell images often show the demons enjoying their sadistic employment. And, for the most part, these hell demons and the *oni* of folktales are viewed by the lay-person as the same thing, both as willing to enact the same terrible and terrifying behavior. For the typical adult and child in Japan—particularly before Japan's post World War II modernization—*oni* are synonymous with inhuman "Otherness."

Red Oni Cries: Deterritorialization of the Child-Reader

Against the above cultural background, I wish to examine how Hirosuke Hamada's story *Red Oni Cried* (泣いた赤おに—*Naita Aka Oni*) humanizes the *oni* "Other" and deterritorializes the child-reader, but also critiques society in ways similar to the work of Gilles Deleuze and Felix Guattari in *Anti-Oedipus*. Hamada's story was originally published in 1933 as an unillustrated text. *Red Oni Cried* became a popular children's story and came to be adopted as a reading in many elementary school textbooks. Over its years of use, the story's text became widely known to a large number of young readers. The story has also been published in several picture book versions, of which I am using the one illustrated by Toshio Kajiyama, published by Kaiseisha in 1992. The illustrations feature Kajiyama's broad-lined, rather art-brut painting style using a limited palate of earthy flat reds, greens, browns, and yellows. Kajiyama's approach to the images conveys the primitive nature associated with *oni* culture, but also imbues the objects depicted with an abstract quality that allows the reader to fill in the emotional details and nuances conveyed by the text. For an apparently tragic story, the writing has humor and playfulness. Hamada's language is more casual than formal, again in keeping with the theme that *oni* don't care so much about social sophistication. But, these "less sophisticated" aspects of the language and illustrations also function to meet the child-reader on his or her level, echoing the child's own instability, awkwardness, and lack of fluency in matters where social sophistication are maybe expected. And, while the story is commonly interpreted and taught in Japanese schools as expressing cultural ideals of friendship—with Blue Oni being held up as a role model of self-sacrificing loyalty because he willingly banishes himself to protect Red Oni's chances to live out his dream—the story is far from exhausted by this rather moralistic interpretation alone.

Monsters Like Us (Gordon) 97

The story is much more open and rich with possibilities for meaning, and I hope my writing here serves to explore some of the tendrils that connect within its extensive rhizome of potential understandings.

To summarize, the story portrays the friendship of Red Oni and Blue Oni and the sad outcome that follows Red Oni's efforts to connect with and nurture friendship with human beings. The story opens by locating Red Oni in the small wooden house where he lives in a remote mountainous region ambiguously described by the narrator as "somewhere in some mountain, but I don't know where" (Hamada 2). We learn of Red Oni's long-held hope to become friends with human beings. A village of people exists not too far away, in a less remote area of the mountains, at the base of a cliff. To realize his dream, Red Oni puts up a hand-painted sign welcoming people into his house for tea and snacks. The sign is seen and analyzed by two passing woodcutters. They consider accepting the invitation, but become afraid and flee. The woodsmen then inform the village about the *oni*'s invitation. The villagers are surprised and curious but ultimately too scared to accept the idea of a friendly *oni*, and thus reject his offers of hospitality. Frustrated by these rejections, Red Oni has a fit of anger and breaks up the sign of welcome. At this moment, a friend named Blue Oni flies in on a rain cloud for an unannounced visit and sees how uncharacteristically wild Red Oni is acting. He asks why and upon hearing of Red Oni's experience and thwarted hopes, offers to help Red Oni get accepted by the villagers. Blue Oni's plan is for the two of them to stage a fake fight, with Blue Oni pretending to play the stereotypical role that human beings have of *oni*: that they are wild and violent and love to terrorize human beings. With hesitation, Red Oni agrees. They go to the village and Blue Oni enters a human house, scares the residents out and starts wildly busting the place up. As planned, Red Oni arrives shortly after, pretending to be the defender of the people. He joins into a mock-fight with his blue friend and chases him out of the house and away from the village. Blue Oni's noisy show of destruction in the house, and the subsequent *oni* fight, successfully attract the villagers, who quickly regard Red Oni as their hero and protector. After this, the human beings start visiting Red Oni's house and enjoy being his guests, drinking tea and eating snack together, fulfilling the image of Red Oni's dream. However, over time, Red Oni wonders why he has not seen Blue Oni since the fight. He worries that something might be wrong and goes to visit his friend in the even more remote location where Blue Oni lives. Red Oni climbs over some mountains to get to Blue Oni's house. Upon arriving, Red Oni sees a letter posted on the wall. It is addressed to Red Oni. In the message, Blue Oni says he had worried that if the human beings ever found out that Red Oni and Blue Oni are actually friends, the people would stop trusting Red Oni. So, in order to protect Red Oni's relationship with the humans, Blue Oni has decided to go away somewhere even more remote. Upon reading this letter, Red Oni cries and the story ends in a quite ambiguous way. No specific explanation for Red Oni's tears is given, so the reader is left to imagine the cause. The book's final illustration is a double-page spread showing a small Red Oni walking amidst many mountains, forests, and clouds. We don't know where he is going, and maybe he doesn't know either.

One of the story's obvious themes is about difference, but not really the expected difference of *oni* and humans. *Oni* and humans serve as the context within which to explore differences between individuals and groups, guiding the reader to look at society and himself or herself in new ways. Through the special omniscience granted as the story's reader, the child gets to see the familiar human culture from a more objective perspective and also take an empathizing look into the monsters' world. Hamada's sensitive depiction of Red and Blue Oni as individuals doesn't merely "humanize" them in the eyes of the child-reader, it works to suspend some of the stabilizing elements in the child's identity upon which stereotypes and culturally-centric judgments are grounded, providing the child with an experience of deterritorialized openness. The child-reader experiences the monstrous "Other" as familiar and worthy of respect or even emulation. The child sees that the monsters are actually good and this creates a chance for the child to identify with the "Other" through seeing shared values and sensitivities. The child-reader gets to witness Red Oni's particular hopes and concerns and see that his sincerity is so deep that it motivates him to act. In pursuing his dream, Red Oni expands himself beyond what his own culture presumes, and the story facilitates the same type of expansion within the child-reader, giving her the ability to see beyond her culturally-centric perspective. Red Oni gives us a peek into what *oni* culture is like when he tells us about his dream: "I was born as an oni, and I want to try to do things that are good for oni people. But, actually, if possible, I want to make friends with human beings and get along nicely with them" (Hamada 6). From this we can imagine that *oni* culture has its own norms against mixing with humans. Red Oni's use of "But, actually, if possible" shows that befriending human beings is not a typical action in *oni* culture. But, another way to read this is that it may be just understood to be difficult for an *oni* to be accepted by humans. Regardless of the reason why *oni* culture isn't on good terms with humans, the child reader sees that Red Oni is willing to go beyond what is normal or easy in order to experience more than what he already knows. Red Oni puts his hope into action—setting up his friendly invitation sign and preparing tea and snacks for possible visitors. Even though his efforts fail to attract human visitors, they show he is working in his own way to realize a condition of radical difference, to change his world. Red Oni's hopes are to go beyond the limits that are usually associated with his culture, and in this effort we can see the narrator's words are accurate, "this red oni's feelings are different from other oni" (Hamada 6). The child can empathize with Red Oni's feelings of kindly hoping to make friends with others but being rejected due to prejudices held by them. This empathy with Red Oni serves to recontextualize how the child-reader feels about the villagers. The humans become the demons. While the child would naturally self-identify with the villagers in the story, their unkind behavior makes the child side with the *oni* and feel that the humans are "Other." The monsters become humanized and the humans become demonized. And, suspended in between, the child-reader experiences deterritorization.

Red Oni's goodness as an individual has a powerful effect on the child-reader. Even though the child can probably understand the villagers' cautious rationale for rejecting Red Oni, the child feels it is unfair. Red Oni's sincerity makes him special, gives him an openness that places him on the same level as the child and makes him worthy of respect and admiration. So, when the villagers fail to fulfill the qualities that are touted as hallmarks of human society—qualities such as hospitality, kindness, appreciation, etc., qualities that the child has quite likely been taught are of great importance—the child becomes suspended between worlds, with monsters living on both sides. The child-reader feels an emotional affinity with the *oni* monster "Other" and a degree of alienation from the demonizing human culture. In this way, the child-reader becomes situated in between—in a place not stably identifiable as here or there. The child can self-identify with both the monsters and the humans. In this way, the child becomes something of a hybrid and his sense of strictly belonging to one distinct group becomes less self-evident or natural. As Patricia MacCormack describes, "Hybrids present an encounter of self as more-than-one [and] challenge the belief in unity, phyla (classification) and absolute differentiation of elements, species, things and subjects" (136). In this way, with his stability of identity-associations in flux, the child-reader has the chance to be momentarily suspended outside of prejudicial stereotypes and culturally bound expectations based on societal values. The child-reader can look down from a higher place, a deterritorialized perspective less bound by biases that are informed by cultural identifications. The story somewhat magically transports the child (in a way not dissimilar to how Blue Oni travels from place to place via rain cloud) to an unknown "somewhere in some mountain," a location that is lost because it is without reference or territorialized values, lost because it doesn't maintain a fixed or determinable nature, isn't stabilized by external meanings that are defined, delimited and reinforced by cultural standards and norms, but rather is a unique and wholly individuated condition. The child hovers in singularity: a moment unlike any other moment—which is true for each moment. The child becomes a schizo.

Desire, Schizophrenia and Anti-Oedipus

The condition of singularity that the child-reader can experience occurs because the societal factors that usually inform, stabilize, and dictate her identity become briefly suspended or deterritorialized. This temporary condition of radically individualized insight can be seen most fully embodied in the story by the character of Blue Oni. In examining *Red Oni Cries*, I was struck by how much the story presents a similar analysis of society as that put forth by the French thinkers Gilles Deleuze and Felix Guattari in their book *Anti-Oedipus*. In 1972, the pair published a radical critique attacking Freudian psychoanalysis, society, and capitalism. In *Anti-Oedipus*, this duo of philosopher and psychiatrist (respectively) develop an approach that flips many of the traditional understandings that are put forth by Freud and held as established truth within the institution of psychoanalysis. Deleuze and Guattari reinterpret the ways to think about such things as society, desire, reality, and the term schizophrenia. In this way, *Anti-Oedipus* becomes something of a handbook for pulling ourselves out of what Deleuze and Guattari view as a trap.

One of Deleuze and Guattari's fundamental critiques regards desire. Traditionally, desire has been characterized as an unwelcome urge to acquire something that is lacked, to fulfill some need, or a sense of being incomplete. In this way, desire came to be categorized as a negative. In contrast, Deleuze and Guattari say desire is a positive force of production which is actually what creates reality through its process of making connections. Desire reaches out and joins with others. In *Red Oni Cries*, we can see that Red Oni's desire for making friends is the driving force that transforms his world. For Deleuze and Guattari, desire is a revolutionary force that transforms what is into what becomes by way of making new connections. Desire brings about an unstable multiplicity of shifting unions known as reality. In contrast to the model that views it as negative, desire is not something that arises within the individual or social structure due to some error in psychological upbringing or out of some sin planted into our original programming. Rather, desire is a continuously flowing force extending the network of new combinations it then flows even more extensively through. Through desire, reality is always becoming. And, thus Deleuze and Guattari critique how the powers of capitalism and psychoanalysis repress the free flow of desire by shaping it into limits via the erected systems that structure society. In actuality, capitalism and psychoanalysis are offspring's of desire—just as everything is—but they have become like a cancer that works to subsume the very body-system it grows out of. Thus, Deleuze and Guattari offer tools to help individuals and groups stop "fight[ing] for their servitude as stubbornly as though it were their salvation" (Spinoza 6). In critiquing psychoanalysis' primacy of the nuclear-family's mother-father-child triad as both the fundamental building block of society and also the incestuous Oedipal melodrama within which every feeling is felt, idea is thought, and dream is dreamt; Deleuze and Guattari say, "If desire is repressed, this is not because it is desire for the mother and for the death of the father; on the contrary, desire becomes that only because it is repressed, it takes on that mask only under the reign of the repression that models the mask for it and plasters it on its face" (*Anti-Oedipus* 118). And one of the tools they offer for turning off this TV situation-tragedy—which serves as a mouthpiece for capitalism—is the critical approach they call schizoanalysis.

Now, to make clear, Deleuze and Guattari's use of schizophrenia as a theoretical concept is not to romanticize the experience and very real suffering of clinical schizophrenics or argue that mental illness is a form of freedom. Far from it; inspired by Guattari's extensive work with clinical schizophrenics in the psychiatric clinic at La Borde, Deleuze and Guattari developed the critical practice of schizoanalysis based on seeing that schizophrenia mirrors the developmental trajectory of capitalism. In their theory, the schizo becomes the heroic guide for living true to desire rather than "trapped within the residual or artificial territorialities of our society.... The schizophrenic deliberately seeks out the very limits of capitalism: he is its inherent tendency brought to fulfillment, its surplus product … and its exterminating angel" (*Anti-Oedipus* 35). For Deleuze and Guattari, the schizophrenic is the model for deterritorialized individuality, an undefined and undefinable becoming who allows herself to be radically drawn by desire beyond limiting societal norms and to facilitate new connections.

Spectrum of Characters

In *Red Oni Cries*, the different characters and character groups can be seen as corresponding to the general spectrum of forces at play within Deleuze and Guattari's image of capitalist society. On the one end of the spectrum, territorialized society is represented in the story by the villagers. On the other end, a fully-formed schizophrenic life is modeled by Blue Oni. In the middle we can see that the two woodsmen and Red Oni represent different degrees of deterritorialization flowing between the two ends of the spectrum. All the characters provide a context for viewing how Red Oni navigates through this spectrum of forces. Through the story, we can see that Red Oni follows his desire and gets potentially trapped within society's roles. At the conclusion of the story, he is moving into an unknown future beyond the last page and we wonder whether he will follow the path of the schizo in the footsteps of Blue Oni, return and accept the role dictated for him by human society, or follow his desire towards something else.

Starting our analysis on the territorialized end of the spectrum, we see that the villagers represent society and they live according to the social norms that bind them—both bind them to each other through the mutually shared associations that identify them as members within the same group, and also bind them to themselves by enabling them to construct and recognize their own identities through the values that the group maintains. Their sense of a shared identity leads them to try to maintain social stability and continuity, and to resist change. It territorializes them and gives rise to fears that the stability is always under threat, either from an outside "Other" or from turbulences or differences within the group. In the story, the villagers are repeatedly seen discussing things, deciding as a group what is true and what isn't, even though we as the readers know that all the villagers' assessments of situations are inaccurate. For example, after witnessing the fake fight between Blue Oni and Red Oni, the humans discuss what happened and agree that Red Oni must be the only kind *oni* that exists. This understanding is false because in fact both of these *oni* are kind. In addition, the villagers' agreement of this "truth" is undermined as simply a re-entrenching of shared social assumptions because they fail to realize the fundamental fact that the *oni* fight is a performance designed to trick them. As a society, humans agree to mutually believe in and follow assumptions, regardless of what is the actual truth. Using these constructed beliefs, they reinforce and check their identities with and against others' approval and disapproval. This establishes a society's territorialized norms and values. And above everything else—above hospitality, generosity, appreciation and the lessons they teach their children—security is shown to be the human society's highest priority. Thus, Red Oni is wrong when he thinks the value of hospitality can connect him with human beings.

The welcoming invitation sign Red Oni makes doesn't work, and thus he breaks it into pieces. His failed efforts reveal that hospitality—this supposedly prized human practice—is less valued in society than security. The practice of hospitality is actually a deterritorializing practice which creates openings for potential connections between "Others." Within the context of ritualized giving and receiving, hospitality facilitates an exchange between different people, ways of thinking, cultures, etc. This is how Red Oni hoped to use it. However, in a security-oriented society, difference is viewed first and foremost as a threat, and thus Red Oni's hospitality is viewed as a potential trick. But, why then do the villagers accept Red Oni after he "defeats" Blue Oni in what ironically is an actual trick? Blue Oni understands that humans will only admit difference into their territorialized space if it is either subservient, enslaved, or beneficent. Humans will resist an unknown if it is stronger than them. So, when Red Oni appears to vanquish the proven threat exhibited by Blue Oni's rampage, the villagers create a middle-space category in order to deal him. They make him into something that reinforces their security-centered view of the world. They treat Red Oni not as a human, but not as an *oni* either. They treat him as a gift bestowed on them, as a miraculous protector for their increased security. Red Oni then, in the words of Rosi Braidotti, "represents the in between, the mixed, the ambivalent as implied in the ancient Greek root of the word monsters, *teras,* which means both horrible and wonderful, object of aberration and adoration" (77). In line with this, the humans treat Red Oni as a special security barrier that exists between their fears of the deterritorialized and themselves. The humans can't accept Red Oni as the unique individual he is. They can only fit him into their territorialized system as their savior protector, and this becomes his societal category and role. But Red Oni's complexity of feelings and sincere concern about Blue Oni reveals the degree to which the humans only deal with a limited aspect of him. He is genuinely a being of extraordinary powers, but the strongest one isn't physical. It is his caring. But the villagers cannot grant him that level of humanity. They can't drop their categories and let Red Oni just be himself, in the same way they can't let themselves exist outside of their categorical societal roles. And, thus, their only option is to keep him at a distance by making him their protector.

Deleuze and Guattari would describe the above behavior by the villagers as neurotic, saying, "The neurotic is trapped within the residual or artificial territorialities of ... society, and reduces all of them to Oedipus as the ultimate territoriality—as reconstructed in the analyst's office and projected upon the full body of the psychoanalyst (yes, my boss is my father, and so is the Chief of State, and so are you, Doctor)" (35). Just as with the neurotic on the analyst's couch, the people in the village must create a secure territorialized space to stabilize what is unknown, or uncategorizable. They do this by fabricating a role for Red Oni as their protector, stabilizing him with a function inside their self-centric myth. This then justifies their mistaken sense that they are in danger, which further justifies their need of a massive security apparatus. Of course, the ultimate irony is that Blue Oni and Red Oni are not actually any threat to the human beings. The escalation of the humans' false narrative of danger becomes woven deeper into their social norms, increasing their neurosis and the growth of paranoia. And the potential for a further irony can be imagined from this situation. Should Red Oni return to the village after the end of the story and the humans continue to require him to play the role of their savior, how long will it be until he becomes enculturated and views this role as "true," that he is above them and their protector? From here it seems a short logical evolution until he could morph into the role of king, at which point the villagers will have—fulfilling the words of Spinoza—established "their servitude as stubbornly as though it were their salvation" (6).

Turning now to two other characters situated along the spectrum of Deleuze and Guattari's image of society, we can examine the woodcutters.

They are the first humans who have contact with Red Oni. The two of them read Red Oni's sign and discuss what it means. They even analyze the brush strokes, saying:

> WOODSMAN 1: Hmmm. This is strange. It's obviously an oni's handwriting.
> WOODSMAN 2: No doubt. It's clear. You can see the power in his brush stroke.
> WOODSMAN 1: Yeah, the brush stoke shows he wrote this with a serious feeling.
> WOODSMAN 2: So, that means these words are sincere.
> WOODSMAN 1: Shall we go inside?
> WOODSMAN 2: No. Wait! Let's just peek inside [Hamada 12].

These woodsmen are a potential real connection between human society and the *oni* world. The woodsmen consider extending beyond their own territory and taking Red Oni up on this offer of hospitality. Like the child-reader, the woodsmen are given a chance to see beyond the superficial, as their analysis of Red Oni's writing shows. Looking beyond the invitation's surface message, they use special techniques to read layers of secret information that are revealed behind the meaning of the words. This method of reading the energy of a writer's brush strokes implies that there are meanings that can't be hidden, truths that even the writer can't lie about or keep secret. In this way, the woodsmen serve like psychoanalysts, looking for unconscious signs that can reveal Red Oni's deepest motivations. And, the two of them do in fact get the correct understanding. Red Oni is indeed sincere. Unfortunately, they reject that knowledge.

The woodsmen serve as something of a bridge between the human society and the world of the *oni*. Their way of living even shares some qualities with the *oni*, such as spending a lot of time outside of the social territory, working and moving through the deterritorialized spaces of the mountains. As well, they work in much more autonomous ways, needing to rely on themselves without external help. However, they are in fact firmly a part of human culture, their particular societal role being to go into the forests and cut wood for houses and other human needs. Ultimately, the wood-cutters rely on human culture and identify with it. They work outside of it, but are like extended tentacles of human society which reach out in order to pull back needed materials for facilitating human life. And, as with the other members of their society, the woodsmen ultimately find reason to doubt the evidence of Red Oni's sincerity that they find in his writing. They approach Red Oni's house and look inside, but then run away in terror when Red Oni appears. They, like the villagers, show that security is ultimately the deciding factor.

Now, we come to examining the Red Oni character in relation to Deleuze and Guarttari's spectrum from society to schizophrenia. Being the main character, Red Oni is the most actively involved in transformation. We can see that he follows his dream to make friends with humans, and this embodies desire's function to make connection with difference. His desire leads him out of his secure condition and brings about an expansion of his world, transforming his awareness into one of greater complexity. He previously had an idealized image of what friendship with humans would be like. An example of Red Oni's idealization is a painting he made and displays in his house. The painting is of a happy red *oni* with a happy human child sitting on his shoulders, depicting an image of casual and accepting openness. This is obviously what Red Oni had hoped for himself. But, those hopes are simplistic and naïve compared to the more complicated new condition Red Oni experiences with respect to humans. Rather than being welcoming and friendly, Red Oni discovers that humans are conditioned to fear difference and will only accept him if he pretends to be their special protector. They require him to play a defined role which fits within and reinforces their territorialized construct of the world. So, while Red Oni's contact with the humans fulfills the image of his dream, the limitations they place on him make him aware of more complex forces at play within human society. The price Red Oni is expected to pay to have human "friends" is to give up his authenticity as an individual. He is required to reduce himself to the simplified view the humans construct for him and play a role as something he isn't in order to be accepted within the territorialized and anthrocentric narrative of human culture. Red Oni knows who he is and what he wants, but he has to keep his honest self hidden for fear that it will burst the bubble of human societal norms. Red Oni knows that he isn't the evil monster characterized in the humans' fears, but he's not a hero either. Red Oni is just himself, simply a friendly *oni*. But that isn't acceptable. Being himself doesn't work within the human society's demand for fixed roles and structures.

As Red Oni spends more time with humans, he begins to think about Blue Oni. While not stated directly, the difference between real friendship and role playing must be something Red Oni ponders before he sets out to visit Blue Oni. And, there is some evidence for this revealed in what Red Oni does not tell the humans when he departs. He posts a note to the villagers when he leaves his house, but he doesn't give them any indication of where he is going or who he will visit. He has obviously not been able to tell his human "friends" that he is not really their protector and that Blue Oni is actually his friend. Red Oni has had to keep these facts a secret. So, when Red Oni reads the message that Blue Oni posted on the wall, Red Oni's hidden concerns may also be what flow out from his tear-filled eyes.

The story gives us no specific indication of what causes Red Oni's tears, but the last image in the book shows what happened after Red Oni cried. In the final double-spread illustration, Red Oni is walking alone, dwarfed by the scale of the vast deterritorialized space of mountains, forests, and clouds. The world is huge and full of unknowns. He isn't crying any longer, and he has the wrapped bundle of his travel belongings still gripped in his hand. He is going somewhere, but we don't know where. Life didn't turn out like Red Oni imagined, but that is the nature of life. The reality that Red Oni's desire created is filled with more actualities than could be predicted. Red Oni sees that human beings are not merely the simple things he expected. Rather, they are complex creatures driven by their own measures, fears, myths and logics. In short, each human is a point of connection into multiplicitous webs of complexity, and the intensity of their fears requires Red Oni to look more deeply at not only what he really wants, but also at how he wants to be. Choices bring about changes. Blue Oni hints at this crisis of confronting difference when, just before he and Red Oni stage the fight, he forebodingly says, "To achieve anything, we have to lose something or go through some pain" (Hamada 20). This statement appears at the turning point and the middle of the story and foreshadows the story's end. On the last page we can see that Red Oni has indeed lost something and gone through some pain, but also that as an individual he is free to choose his next direction.

Will Red Oni continue to search for Blue Oni? Will Red Oni set up a new home in some deeper reaches of some mountains? Will he search out a new group of human beings and try again? Will he return to his house as he wrote in his note and try to change the human society he is a part of? Will he come back and play his scripted role in the humans' narrative and be their hero/protector in exchange for a chance to be their friend? I doubt anyone would want to come back and try to make things work within the institutional repression of the dysfunctional and co-dependent village society. Once seeing beyond the false limits constructed and propped up by society, it becomes nearly impossible to believe in them again. And, this is possibly why schizophrenics—both clinical and Deleuzian/Guattarian—have difficulty accepting what society says is real and maintaining a stable and uniform identity.

Now we have reached the schizophrenic end of the spectrum and the character of Blue Oni. Blue Oni serves as an image of radical individualization and contextualizes Red Oni's initiation into schizophrenia. Blue Oni is a model of what Deleuze and Guattari characterize as a fully individualized schizo. He is a rule unto himself, without any territory to protect, expand, or belong to. He lives in the singularity of being, not bound or delimited by anything outside of himself. He fits Deleuze's description that "individuals find a real name for themselves ... only through the harshest exercises in depersonalization, by opening themselves up to the multiplicities everywhere in them, to the intensities running through them. [This is] a depersonalization through love rather than through subjection" (6). In schizophrenic fashion, we see that Blue Oni is free enough to even serve as his own "Other," able to be in flux and defy identification—even an identification with himself. Evidence of this is his ease in assuming the role of the "violent *oni*" in the fake fight. Blue Oni doesn't worry about how he will be viewed or judged by others. He assuredly trusts that Red Oni knows that his performance is just play, that he can pretend to be something he is not in order to help his friend, or just for the heck of it. And, as for the human beings, Blue Oni doesn't seem to care what they think of him, sensing that they wouldn't understand his willingness to play into their fears as a way to trick them into letting Red Oni fulfill his dream. Blue Oni doesn't need to maintain a consistent image because, in the words of Deleuze and Guattari, "continually wandering about, migrating here, there, and everywhere as best he can, he plunges further and further into the realm of deterritorialization.... It may well be that these peregrinations are the schizo's own particular way of rediscovering the earth" (35). In addition, Blue Oni is free enough to let life change in an instant. He knows the fake fight will bring about a change in his and Red Oni's lives, as his comment about loss and pain being the price for everything new indicates. But, he doesn't hesitate or hedge his bets. He doesn't try to predict how the fight will positively and/or negatively impact him. He doesn't plot trajectories. He just enters the moment fully. But, Blue Oni reveals that he has a deep understanding of how the human culture works. He knows that the human beings will not be willing, or perhaps incapable, of accepting Red Oni as himself. Rather, Red Oni must perform a role that is valued and recognized within human thinking. Blue Oni correctly sees that the human beings only accept things that fit the logic of their own narrative, a storyline that keeps them at the center of their drama. And, because he exists so far outside of the human beings' needs for living inside of the orderly rules of their social myth, Blue Oni has no hesitation about either compounding the human narrative with a new chapter or scrambling it. He'll be long gone by the time they even agree on what they think happened. Deleuze and Guattari say that "the schizophrenic escape itself does not merely consist in withdrawing from the social, in living on the fringe: it causes the social to take flight through the multiplicity of holes that eat away at it and penetrate it ... make fall what must fall, make escape what must escape, at each point ensuring the conversion of schizophrenia as a process into an effectively revolutionary force" (341). Blue Oni fulfills this model of withdrawing without rejecting anything overtly. He seems to know that it isn't worth the effort to try and change others. Rather, his actions let other engage their false stories as they will. When the time comes, their story will exhaust them in a way that is accurately balanced to their belief in it. We can see this dynamic also at work within Red Oni in the final scene. Blue Oni's written message doesn't confront Red Oni directly with a lesson or theory about life. The message isn't prophetic or expert in tone. Blue Oni simply helps Red Oni fulfill his dream and then lets him live out the effects. This kind of autonomy is what enables Blue Oni to just leave home without notice or ceremony, and might also be what guides Red Oni after the end of the story as he moves through the deterriorialized space beyond the last page. Without any influence from external pressures over his behavior or identity, Blue Oni is a model of free flux. Fully autonomous, he needs no support from agents that might place expectations on him in return for their help or approval.

Conclusion: Zen's Schizo Hints

The drama of *Red Oni Cries* derives from a conflict between differences. Initially, these differences appear to be between *oni* culture and human culture, but with closer examination we see that the conflict is really between individuals and societal groups. Childhood is the time when society begins to profoundly shape a person's identity, understanding, and expectations. Within this context, *Red Oni Cries* serves as a subtle allegory exposing the processes of both social persuasion and radical individuality. Facilitating the child-reader's deterritorialization, the story enables the child to observe how Red Oni negotiates the different forces that offer to initiate him into either a strictly defined social role or what Deleuze and Guattari define as schizophrenia.

Hamada's story was written more than forty years before Deleuze and Guattari's *Anti-Oedipus*, which makes the similarities of their societal critiques interesting rather than related to each other. They were not writing from the same background or in response to each other, but rather I think they were responding to patterns that are evident within human society regardless of time or culture. Deleuze and Guattari say they were inspired by how clinical schizophrenia mirrors capitalism. In Hamada's case, Japanese Zen Buddhism is a potential theoretical background for *Red Oni Cries*. Zen concepts echo many of the key traits practiced by Deleuze and Guattari's profoundly secular schizo hero. As well, in Zen, and Buddhism in general, there is a well known tradition of extremely independent hermits who live in mountain caves and secluded forest huts. These figures could well have informed Hamada's character of Blue Oni as they too float away from the world to exist beyond the reach of human society, critiquing the norms and values of society while serving as a model for living beyond such limitations. Following the example of the historical Buddha by leaving the pressures of society, as well as its distractions, Buddhist hermits strive to face their real self more directly through the moment to moment engagement with life in singularity. Deleuze and Guattari contextualize this struggle between individual freedom and societal limitations through ideas that were suitable for their time (and possibly ours), but the forces of desire that facilitate radical individualization and deterritorialize social norms transcend any particular culture or time.

Works Cited

"Bakemono Zukushi." *Yokai Database*. International Research Center for Japanese Studies, 6 May 2010. Web. 22 Nov. 2015.
Braidotti, Rosi. *Nomadic Subjects: Embodiment and Sexual Difference in Contemporary Feminist Theory*. New York: Columbia University Press, 1994. Print.
Deleuze, Gilles. *Negotiations*. Trans. Martin Joughin. New York: Columbia University Press, 1995. Print.
Deleuze, Gilles, and Felix Guattari. *Anti-Oedipus: Capitalism and Schizophrenia*. Trans. Robert Hurley, Mark Seem and Helen R. Lane. Minneapolis: Minnesota University Press, 1983. Print.
Foster, M. D. "The Metamorphosis of the Kappa: Transformation of Folklore to Folklorism in Japan." *Asian Folklore Studies* 57.1 (1998): 1–24. Print.
Hamada, Hirosuke. *Red Oni Cried (泣いた赤おに—Naita Aka Oni)*. Illus. Toshio Kajiyama. Tokyo: Kaiseisha, 1992. Print. Trans. Gerald Gordon and Rie Hase. Unpublished 2015. http:/moontriangle.blogspot.jp/2015/12/oni-translation.html.
Japan: An Illustrated Encyclopedia. Tokyo: Kodansha, 1993. Print.
MacCormack, Patricia. "Unnatural Alliances." *Deleuze and Queer Theory*, ed. Chrysanthi Nigianni and Meri Storr. Edinburgh: Edinburgh University Press, 2009. Print.
"Okayama Girl, 5, Youngest to Be Deemed 'Yokai' Ghost World Expert." *Japan Times* 26 Nov. 2015. Web. 26 Nov. 2015. http://www.japantimes.co.jp/news/2015/11/26/national/okayama-girl-5-youngest-deemed-yokai-ghost-world-expert/#.Vlwr33vOCk1.
"Oni." Yokai.com. Yokai.com, 2013. Web. 31 Oct. 2015.http://yokai.com/oni/.
Sadakata, Akira. *Buddhist Cosmology: Philosophy and Origins*. Tokyo: Kosei, 1997. Print.
Spinoza, Baruch. *Theological -Political Treatise*. Trans. Michael Silverthorne and Jonathan Israel. New York: Cambridge University Press, 2007. Print.

PART 3. FOSTERING HETERONORMATIVITY,
AGENCY AND RACIAL SUPERIORITY

The Scars of Dracula
Count Dracula and the Undead Meaning in Children's Early Readers

SIMON BACON

With the current popularity of vampires in popular culture, and particularly for young adults (YA), it comes as no surprise that they have also found their way into picture books, readers and primers for younger children. Texts such as *Bunnicula, Fangs: Vampire Spy, Araminta Spook: Vampire Brat* and *Mona the Vampire* to name a few, all utilize the figure of the vampire to represent ways of forming one's own unique identity, accepting difference, and negotiating one's place in society. Within many of these texts the figure of the vampire represented is not that of the new breed of the sparkly or "fangless" undead, as seen in YA narratives, but that of the seminal bloodsucker himself, Count Dracula. However, while these texts often reference Bram Stoker's text or, more often than not, Bela Lugosi from the 1931 film *Dracula* by Tod Browning, they make no mention of the biases and prejudices that originally created the undead monster in 1897 London or 1931 America respectively. This study will explore this potential dichotomy in relation to children's books to see if their surface topics of the acceptance of difference and non-normative identities are primary to their ultimate meaning, or whether they might be, subliminally or otherwise, reinforcing the mores of racial discrimination and white ethnic superiority.

Monsters are a staple of children's literature, with well-known texts such as *Little Red Riding Hood, Jack and the Beanstalk*, and *Cinderella* featuring monstrous creatures and humans that perform both a didactic function as well as establishing forms of societal difference and otherness. Vampires are less common in such works, maybe because of their categorization as an irredeemable and particularly horrific monster, at least up until the middle of the 20th century, as rather excessively noted by vampire scholar Montague

Summers: "In all the darkest pages of the malign supernatural there is no more terrible tradition than that of the Vampire, a pariah even among demons. Foul are his ravages; gruesome and seemingly barbaric are the ancient and approved methods by which folks must rid themselves of this hideous pest" (vii).

Written only 32 years after Bram Stoker's *Dracula*, Summers' description seems part of the 19th-century gothic tradition that the Vampire Count was a product of. Part of the vampires monstrosity was based on its predilection for children as a source of food, as shown in Stoker's novel, where the Count throws a sack on the floor in front of his three brides: "One of the women jumped forward and opened it. If my ears did not deceive me there was a gasp and a low wail, as of a half-smothered child" (43). This view remained largely unchanged, at least in terms of the figure of Dracula, until the 1970s and the creation of the self-reflexive vampire,[1] most obviously seen in Anne Rice's "Vampire Chronicles" series, which began in 1976 with *Interview with the Vampire*. Here, arguably, for the first time the vampire speaks for itself, something which was not available to Count Dracula back in 1897, as he, and the other vampires of the 19th century, could only be heard through the voices of others and mainly those that used it as a container for all their own prejudices and anxieties. This is predominantly the case for most monsters who are constructed from the fear of those within the narrative as well as the larger society from within which the novel was produced. As noted by Judith Halberstam, monsters, and vampires in particular, are ideological blueprints for all a society sees itself as not being:

> Monsters are meaning machines. They can represent gender, race, nationality, class, and sexuality in one body. And even within these divisions of identity, the monster can still be broken down. Dracula, for example, can be read as aristocrat, a symbol of the masses; he is predator and yet feminine, he is consumer and producer, he is parasite and host, he is homosexual and heterosexual, he is even lesbian. Monsters and the Gothic fiction that creates them are therefore technologies, narrative technologies that produce the perfect figure for negative identity. Monsters have to be everything the human is not and, in producing the negative of human, these novels make way for the intervention of human as white, male, middle class, and heterosexual [21–22].

This monsterization, however, is not an isolated point and its economies continue beyond the period that a particular monster is created in, and, as Halberstam goes on to note, "monsters may be exiled, beaten, shot, stabbed, obliterated and still they always return; but the returns are not 'like' the return of the repressed: the returns of monsters are always economic" (188). Consequently, any specific monster that returns is integrated into later monstrous forms and carries with it something of its original symbolism—i.e., societal prejudices from which it was constructed. For this study the figure of Count Dracula will be used, and as will be shown, the various reincarnations he has undergone since the publication of Stoker's novel make the body of the vampire something of an "'undead' archive of memory" (Bacon and Bronk xviii) as well as becoming "a way of finding the commonalities and connections between our experiences of the past and the ways it informs our presents" (ibid., xxi). In this study it will be used more to show the links between the negative aspects of earlier versions of Count Dracula and more recent ones.

The vampire Count is an amazingly resilient figure and is continually referenced, knowingly or otherwise, in a large number of vampire related texts. Yet the majority of them do not actually reference Stoker's work, but rather Browning's film from 1931, which itself does not use the novel as its source but the official stage version of the work by John L. Balderstone and Hamilton Deane. And so before discussing what the figure of Dracula might be bringing with it into the children's books in which it appears, it is necessary to look at what and where the undead memories he embodies came from.

Undead Memories

Bram Stoker's novel contains very little information on what the vampire Count wears but it does contain a rather lengthy description of what he looks like, as relayed by the young English solicitor, Jonathan Harker, upon arriving at Castle Dracula after a very long journey to the land beyond the forest:

> His face was a strong—a very strong—aquiline, with high bridge of the thin nose and peculiarly arched nostrils; with lofty domed forehead, and hair growing scantily round the temples, but profusely elsewhere. His eyebrows were very massive, almost meeting over the nose, and with bushy hair that seemed to curl in its own profusion. The mouth, so far as I could see it under the heavy moustache, was fixed and rather cruel-looking, with peculiarly sharp white teeth ... his ears were pale and at the tops extremely pointed; the chin was broad and strong, and the cheeks firm though thin [Stoker 19–20].

This is a considerably different picture of what most people might think of when describing the image of Dracula in the popular imagination, with maybe the most striking aspects being the large mustache and bushy eyebrows. In fact the face fits more closely that of woodcut portraits of Vlad Tepes, or Vlad the Impaler, the Wallachian voivoide, that Stoker is popularly believed to have used as inspiration for his Count. It then configures a very particular configuration of difference as being from the uncivilized and backward Eastern part of Europe, but more than that, it also symbolizes immigrants from the outside "invading" the Empire and contaminating its bloodlines. Stephan Arata sees this in terms of "reverse colonialism" (108), but Halberstam is more specific about what the look of Dracula signifies. He "resembles the Jew of anti–Semitic discourse in several ways: his appearance, his relation to money/ gold, his parasitism, his degeneracy, his impermanence or lack of allegiance to a fatherland, and his femininity" (92). Other than just referencing features of other derogatory constructions of the Jew at the time, such as Fagin from Charles Dickens *Oliver Twist* (1838) and Svengali from George du Maurier's *Trilby* (1895), this "look" also corresponds to descriptions by anti–Semites, such as Eduard Drumont, quoted in Halberstam, who identified the characteristics of the Jews as "the hooked nose, shifty eyes, protruding ears" (93). These are the points that Harold Malchow corroborates and further links to the idea of "the eternal [wandering] Jew" (Malchow 153), and which is further observed by Jules Zanger's on the correlation to migration and the greater visibility of Jews in London towards the end of the 19th century: "Eastern European Jews from 1880 on had begun to appear in England in increasing numbers […] following the assassination of Tsar Alexander II, the government sponsored pogroms, expulsions, and anti–Jewish legislation precipitated a massive exodus of Jews, not only from Russia but from the Austrian Empire and Rumania into Western Europe and the Americas" (3). Stoker's novel encapsulates this notion of an invader from outside—outside society, outside normativity, and outside the limits of safety—and is one that stays with the body of the vampire as it moves from the page to the stage.

Hamilton Deane wrote the official adaption of the novel and severely curtailed the action shown in the book so that the production costs were kept manageable. Subsequently, the play was predicated on the "drawing room drama" style which, as observed by Bacon, "here the 'star' of the show is required to stand centre stage and interact with the other characters, predominately in an interior setting" (5). This required the Count to no longer be a creature of darkness but a lounge lizard, and so his unkempt hair become a greased back widows peak; the facial hair disappeared so that his pale complexion and fangs were more visible; and he donned the now iconic evening dress and cape. The cape has a particular story behind it, as during the performance the vampire was required to mysteriously disappear. This was facilitated by such a long cape with a high collar that obscured the actor so that when he turned his back to the stage as a puff of smoke erupted, he could vanish unobserved down a trap door. As the mist cleared the cape would flutter to the floor empty. This set in place what Alan Silver and James Ursini identify as the "very genuine stereo-typification of the Dracula figure" which is typified by "dark clothes and full-flowing red-lined cape, the hair brushed back straight and flat from the forehead, the lips extraordinarily crimson and distended in an eerie smile which reveals abnormally long canines" (9). The play was taken to Broadway in 1927 by Horace Liveright and the script revised by Jon Balderstone, but the most important part of this production, at least for this study, was the hiring of a young Hungarian actor in his first English speaking role, called Bela Lugosi, to play the role of Dracula. Lugosi went on to star in Tod Browning's film *Dracula,* and it was the image of him walking down the huge staircase in his Transylvanian Castle and uttering the iconic words "I am Dracula" in his thick Hungarian drawl, alongside his greased back hair, evening dress and cape, that have become burned into the public consciousness (though it should be noted that at no point in the film are the vampires fangs visible). *Dracula* was released at a very specific point in American history. After the nation had lost many of its young men in the war in Europe between 1914 and 1918, events across the Atlantic threatened to draw the United States into another conflict that was not theirs once again. Many wanted to continue a state of isolationism for America, and Browning's film gave voice to that anxiety, showing how this degenerate parasite from the Old World wanted to feed on the New World—lines actually used in *Son of Dracula* by Robert Siodmak released in 1943, during World War II. Lugosi's vampire represented a decadent aristocracy that would charm itself into the heart of the new Empire and seduce its women and contaminate its blood—taking many signifiers from Stoker's undead Count and recycling them for a new age. Whilst not explicitly anti–Semitic, Browning's *Dracula* still has at its core the fear of immigrants—as noted by Zanger above, many had already started traveling from Europe to the United States by the time the film was released—who would emasculate its men, contaminate its women and steal their money. After World War II, mutant monsters and aliens from space become the creatures to be most afraid of, replacing the classic monsters such as vampires, werewolves, and mummies possibly due to the atom bomb and the new anxieties around science and the future. Yet it was not until the 1970s, and the humanization of the undead at the hands of Anne Rice, that vampires became acceptable fare for groups other than purveyors of horror films and literature—though one should not forget the highly popular television series' *The Munsters* and *The Addams Family* that both ran from 1964 to 1966 and featured comic versions of the classic monsters representing a countercurrent to the reinvented vampires seen in the contemporary Hammer Films.

Suitable for the Children

The 1970s were something of a turning point in the popularity of the vampire. After the revitalizing of Dracula, and indeed the vampire, under the hands of Hammer films, with the last in the series being *The Satanic Rites of Dracula* directed by Alan Gibson from 1973,[2] the Count suddenly became a figure of relevance again in popular culture, a point confirmed by the appearance of Count Chocula breakfast cereal in 1971; Count Von Count in Sesame Street, the hugely popular children's program from America, in 1972; the first overtly romantic Count on film played by Frank Langella in *Dracula* (Badham 1979); and the first comedic one played by George Hamilton in *Love at First Bite* (Dragotti 1979). It is within this milieu that one of the first books for children featuring a vampire, *Bunnicula: A Rabbit Tale of Mystery* by James Howe, was published in 1979, and it is part of a series that ran until 2006. Written for 8- to 12-year-olds, it tells the tale of a new pet in the Monroe household that just might be a vampire rabbit. The Monroes go to see the movie *Dracula* and their son Toby finds a small rabbit wrapped in a bundle on his seat. Beguiled by the little rabbit they take it home and, in honor of where they found him, call him Bunnicula—mixing the words Bunny and Dracula. However, it quickly transpires that there is more than meets the eye to this little bunny that sleeps all day, as discovered by Chester the cat and told, rather dramatically, to Harold the dog: "I noticed the peculiar marking on his forehead. What had seemed an ordinary black spot between his ears took on a strange v-shape, which connected with the big black patch that covered his back and each side of his neck. It looked like he was wearing a coat ... no, more like a *cape*" (20).

And further, "but as I watched, his lips parted in a hideous smile, and where a rabbits buck teeth should have been, two little pointed fangs glistened" (23). The rabbit's vampire credentials are reinforced by the note found with him and written, as identified by Harold, in an obscure dialect from the Carpathian Mountains, saying, "Take good care of my baby" (9). There is also the sudden appearance in the kitchen of white vegetables that have been totally drained of their juices. Chester's overzealous imagination gets the better of him and does all he can to "save" his family from the menace that has been invited into their bosom. Harold realizes that the rabbit means them no harm and only needs the juice of vegetables, which he sucks out with his fangs, to survive. Harold manages to save Bunnicula, and Chester's overactive imagination earns him a series of visits to a pet psychologist, who helps him to find himself, and to accept the rabbit into their home. Harold brings the story to a close, as it was he that was writing it, illustrating the acceptance of the new member of their family and "the mysterious stranger who is no longer quite so mysterious and who is definitely no longer a stranger" (98). *Bunnicula* contains many tropes taken from Dracula: the other who does not speak for himself; the movement from outside or beyond, into the heart of the family (empire); and the cape and fangs that mark him out as dangerous or non-normative. The fanged bunny carries the markings of the ethnic outsider that singled out Dracula as the Other who had to be destroyed, and Chester the cat, who is the consumer of sensationalist novels, is the one that reacts in the exact same way as proscribed in the books he reads. Interestingly, the Monroes are a professional family—the father is a professor of English—revealing them to be the same kind of middle-class readers identified by Tabish Khair as the intended audience for such gothic novels as *Dracula*. Subsequently, the forms of monsterization portrayed within such novels are specifically meant to resonate with that audience, as represented by Chester, and so Harold's defense of Bunnicula offers something of a reaction to that and the acceptance of difference that is not life threatening—or at least does not endanger the integrity of the family unit.

A similar construction is seen in *Vlad the Drac* by Ann Jungman from 1982, the first in a series of six books, except the action is moved from suburban America to suburban England. Written for 7- to 9-year-olds, it shows an English family traveling to Transylvania where, outside Dracula's castle, their children Judy and Paul discover a baby vampire hidden beneath a stone: "a tiny creature with a comical face, two sharp fangs, long ears and a hurt expression" (10). He speaks perfect English, due largely to overhearing the tourists that come to the castle and, not unlike Count Dracula before him, has a huge desire to go to England. He has a green complexion, which is never explained but is used to mark out his difference, and is also nameless as his Great Uncle Ghitza, who was a "real" vampire, and refused to come to his christening. After talking to Judy and Paul he decides to call himself Vlad the Drac—a mixture of the names of Vlad the Impaler and Dracula—and they decide to take him home; They pretend he is a model vampire so that they can get him through customs. Once home they keep him hidden in a drawer in their bedroom, but it soon transpires that, for all his brave talk, he does not like blood and actually likes to eat soap, washing liquid and polish. However, Vlad does not like being kept in the children's bedroom and, after almost a year in the house is shown to Judy and Paul's parents. Interestingly, this does not seem to faze either of the adults who accept him quite readily and decide to help Vlad to get back home to Romania. The children's Mother, who is a doctor, gets in touch with the Ministry of Tourism for Romania, who was "very impressed by Vlad and ... immediately offered him the post of resident vampire at Count Dracula's castle, with a lifetime's supply of soap, washing-up liquid, shoe polish or whatever he wanted" (118). Vlad returns home and Judy, Paul and their parents visit him two years later, by which time Vlad has found himself a wife and has had 5 children, although, rather worryingly, one of them is just like Great Uncle Ghitza. As in *Bunnicula*, Judy and Paul's family are professionals, their mother is a doctor and their father a violinist, and their easy acceptance of Vlad would seem a positive thing, except perhaps for their eagerness to get him back home rather than have him in their house. Equally, while Vlad's unusual diet posits him as a safe kind of vampire, it also signals his outsider status and as something non-human, just as does his green color.

These last two themes play a large part in the next story, as well as the notion of rebellion against one's elders and/or social expectation. *Gruesome and Bloodsocks* by Jane Holiday from 1984, is part of a three-book series meant for 7- to 9-year-olds. It tells the story of Augusta (Gruesome Gussie) and her cat, Bloodsocks—named so as he is all black with rust-brown paws. Gruesome is an embarrassment to her family who are descended from a long line of Transylvanian vampires (11), as she is allergic to blood and likes to sleep at night. She leaves them on their churchyard home to go and live in the town of Trumpington. Unlike the previous two books there is no professional family to live with as the story is set in the north of England during the 1980s, when unemployment was rife, and so Gruesome with no home of her own is told to go to the DHSS (Department of Health and Social Services) where she is given a council flat and then instructed to go to the unemployment office, where they seem oddly unperturbed at her being a vampire or being green. They tell her to collect her giro (unemployment benefit) from the local post office once a week. And so Gruesome and Bloodsocks move into 52A Wellington Street, where she hangs viper skins on the walls and black bin bags over the windows, and buys a coffin on credit to sleep in. Her upstairs neighbors, the Joneses, are one of the few families that have jobs, and Gruesome becomes friends with their son Leotard. Not unlike Vlad the Drac before her, Gruesome enjoys odd mixtures of food such as chocolate biscuits spread with fish paste, and this more "human" diet soon begins to change her green pallor to that of a more normalized pink. Gruesome gets caught up in a pet kidnapping scam when Bloodsocks is taken from her garden, and she enlists the help of her vampire family to catch the villains when she leaves the ransom in a phone box. However, all the other families in the street are also leaving the ransoms for their own pets at the same time and chaos ensues. The crooks are caught and the vampires are lauded as heroes, and so Gruesome becomes friends with the other occupants of Wellington Street. The vampires are offered a job as night security guards at a warehouse in Dieppe, France, and want Gruesome to go with them. She refuses wanting to stay in her new home and with her new friends. Whilst Gruesome does not directly follow in the footsteps of Dracula in the same way as Bunnicula or Vlad, she does reflect the "Daughter of Dracula" narrative as seen in the sequel to Browning's 1931 film, *Dracula's Daughter* by Lambert Hillyer from 1936. Here the girl tries her best to resist patriarchal authority, which would see her continue her life as a bloodsucking monster, but all her attempts to do so fail. Gruesome is more successful and the further she gets away from her vampire past, the more human she gets, as one of the vampires observes: "your face … has gone a most healthy shade, and you've been *washing* your hair" (74–75). When the story begins she is marked out as inescapably other—as either a homeless person, a traveling gypsy or an immigrant—as also seen in her peculiar skin color and unusual diet. Yet the more assimilated she becomes, the more "human," i.e., like everyone else, she looks.

118 Part 3: Heteronormativity, Agency and Racial Superiority

These books very much see the vampire as a metaphor for forms of otherness and the possibility of being able to accept or assimilate it, usually through some form of socialization, as seen in Gruesome. Before looking at more recent books that continue and evolve this idea, it is worth mentioning a separate thread of vampires in children's books that purposely keep the otherness and difference of Stoker's and Browning's Draculas. All of these can be put in the bracket of activity books which tend to have less coherent story but often require some kind of physical interaction by the reader. *Vampires* by Colin Hawkins and Jackie Hawkins from 1982, meant for 9- to 12-year-olds, has a rather dark sense of humor. It suggests that, although vampires were originally confined to Eastern Europe, they are now everywhere—"even your best friend could be a vampire" (4). A vampire can be identified as anyone having eyebrows that meet in the middle, or hairy palms, or sleeps in a coffin. The illustrations extend this to anyone with a large hooked nose—which links it back to the original Count's anti–Semitic visual construction. *The Gorys*, by the same authors, from 1999, uses the same characters but in an extended format, stretching the vampire puns even further. Yet it does nothing to change its depiction of otherness. *Marceline's World of Vampireness* by Kirsten Mayer from 2014, is part of a larger series of story books and also linked to a series on the Cartoon Network. It invites 9- to 12-year-old "henchmen" to challenge their "skills in the areas of art, musicality, vampireness, smartability and being a good henchman" (back cover). *Marceline* is meant for the older end of the 9- to 12-bracket with more word games and puzzles, but bares strong relation to the earlier *The Little Vampires Diary* from 1995 by Sonia Holleyman which relies more on cut-out vampire glasses and mobiles and interactive flaps to lift and explore rather than quizzes. Both books are interesting as one can acquire vampiric traits just by wearing special glasses or completing a puzzle successfully, intimating that the otherness bestowed by them is positive rather than something to be avoided, something which links them to *Mona the Vampire*, a book that will be mentioned in more depth later on. *Dracula Junior and the Fake Fangs: A 3-Dimensional Picture Book* by Julianna Bethlen from 1996 is for 7- to 9-year-olds. It tells of Dracula Junior who is forced to eat proper "red vampire food" (4), which he hates, by his extremely strict and grumpy grandma. He runs off to his coffin but returns later to play with grandma's false fanged teeth that are kept on the mantelpiece. He puts them into his pet rabbit's mouth, which promptly runs out of the room with the false fangs before Dracula Junior can stop him. The following pages tell of his adventure in trying to get them back before his grandma wakes up, which he does only after finding them with a spider that was hiding under a hat. No longer being forced to eat by his grandma, Junior decides to eat his supper and goes to the kitchen where his soup is still warm and full of "the most toothsome vampire reds: radishes, red beans, pickled peppers and lots of red chilies" (18). This friendly twist to the vampires is further emphasized through the look of the vampires themselves which tend more toward the plumpness of stereotypical images of the British middle-class rather than ethnic or racial difference.

A Vampire Is Coming to Dinner: 10 Rules to Follow by Pamela Jane from 2010 is supposedly suitable for 3 years upwards but feels aimed at older children. The story is about a young boy who is left a note from a vampire, telling him he is coming to dinner and what follows are 10 fold out pages with the appropriate rule on the front, i.e., "Rule 4: Greet the vampire with a friendly handshake—vampires love to make new friends!" (6) with an amusing image revealed behind each flap. The final Rule, number 10 advises that "if the vampire is sleepy, find him a quiet place to rest—vampires love to take naps" (12) but this then has a secondary rule, number 11, saying that "if the vampire can't sleep, throw out all the rules and have a monster good party" (13), accompanied by a pop-up showing the boy and a vampire wearing a nightshirt dancing to a mariachi band. The "rules" are made up from pieces of popular vampire lore, such as the aversion to garlic mentioned above, but also not appearing in mirrors or being able to cross moving water (a favorite of Hammer films), all mixed in with vaguely comic observations, like "dress up for the occasion" as "vampires always wear capes" (4). However, the image of the vampire used is an unusual one, not referring to Dracula but to Count Orlok from the 1922 film *Nosferatu: Symphony of Terror*, the unofficial remake of Stoker's book by a German filmmaker, F.W. Murnau. The vampire in Murnau's film is a creature of darkness, with his name, Nosferatu, literally meaning "plague bearer" (Butler 157). As described by Eric Butler: "Orlok is tall and gaunt, and makeup accentuates his angular features to make them appear exaggeratedly sharp; in particular, his eyes have been outlined and his nose and fingers elongated to reach beyond natural proportions. He wears a long black coat and a hat resembling a turban. His dress evokes indeterminate foreignness" (Ibid.).

Yet it is not so indeterminate as it first seems. As mentioned previously in relation to Count Dracula, the hooked nose and drawn features symbolize Jewishness, as do the 'money grabbing' claws and the long black coat. Further, the correlation between Orlok, vermin (he looks like a large hairless rat) and disease expressed inter-war anxieties in Weimar Germany that saw the Jewish contagion as an easy scapegoat for its own troubles. As Butler further observes, "Nosferatu is not an antisemitic film. However, it draws on cultural anxieties and uses strategies of representation that inform the worst forms of contemporary antisemitic rhetoric and art. Therefore it provides a ready allegory for the vampire as a Jew" (162). This provides the undead memory that hangs around the figure of the vampire used in Jane's book, which is unsettling at best. The illustrations showing the vampire with a large hooked nose and long clawed fingers echo rather too strongly signifiers utilized in the earlier manifestation of this image, which even the comedic dance with the mariachi band in the final pages cannot dispel—not least as Mexicans provide another source of unwanted immigrant that has connections to images of vermin.

The next two books continue the evolution of the friendly vampire, but reverse the ideas of it being an outsider and tell their stories from the undead perspective, with humans as the invaders from another world. *Dear Vampa* by Ross Collins from 2009, for 7- to 9-year-olds, follows the epistolary tradition of Stoker's novel and is a letter from young Bram Pire to his Grandad (Vampa), telling him about their new neighbors, the Wolfsons. The Wolfsons are terrible as they stay awake all day making noise, shut their windows at night, and their pet dog barks at the Pires all the time. And to add injury to insult, the Wolfson's children pelt the Pires, in their bat form, with stones using catapults. As the story ends the Pires, finding their new neighbors unbearable, are forced to move out back to Transylvania to get some peace and quiet, with the final twist being the Wolfson being sad to lose their neighbors and revealing themselves as werewolves. The Pires, while dressing in a very gothic, Addams family–esque manner share the feature of pointed ears with the original Dracula, making them less representative of ethnic difference, although the move back to the "homeland" suggests otherwise. The Wolfsons turning out to be werewolves is an interesting twist, intimating that even the most average of families is different in some way and that otherness works both ways. A point which is the basis for *Vampire Boy's Good Night* by Lisa Brown.

Published in 2010 and for an audience of 7- to 9-year-olds, *Vampire Boy's Good Night* tells of Bela, the vampire, and his friend Morgan, the witch, who go out on Halloween for an adventure. Bela has pointed ears, fangs and no reflection, and does not believe there are such things as children "with rosy cheeks and shiny white teeth" (10). Whilst flying on Morgan's broom they spy a Halloween party and join in. Once there Morgan is the only witch without warts, and, although a vampire wins the fancy dress prize, it is not Bela. But the best part of the night is when the other children take off their disguises and Bela sees their rosy cheeks and little teeth. He and Morgan quickly leave the party and return home, and when Bela goes to bed he dreams of the wondrous things he has seen. Highlighting the otherness of humans is an interesting approach, but we see Bela drinking blood for breakfast, and at the end of the book we see his butler wearing a plaster on his neck—the traditional site of a vampire bite—suggesting the nice little boy is more monstrous than he first appears. This is something seen in *Fangs Vampire Spy: Operation: Golden Bum* by Tommy Donbavand.

Published in 2013 for 7- to 10-year-olds and part of a series of six books, *Operation: Golden Bum,* features Fangs Enigma the self-proclaimed best spy in the world. The book introduces us to Fang and his sidekick, Puppy Brown, who is a werewolf. Fang wears a tuxedo and a silk lined cape; is very pale with dark patches around his eyes; has two white fangs protruding from his mouth; and pointed ears. The stories themselves are something between James Bond and Sherlock Holmes, with a large helping of *The Munsters* and *Austin Powers*, played by Mike Myers in his series of spoof spy films—which is also responsible for the one feature that differentiates Fang from Dracula—his 1970s swinger type hairstyle as worn by Austin Powers. Fang works for Monster Protection 1st Unit—MP1—in a world where both monsters and "normal" people exist, with his job being to control the out-of-control monsters. His positioning within the world of the narrative, and indeed the novel itself, attempts to normalize monstrosity, but is at best ambivalent, and although Puppy Brown tries to explain it, the monsters are never really anything else than that. In explaining her turning into a werewolf—unlike most she is human on the full moon and a wolf for the rest of the time—she says how her parents tried "to make me look like a "normal" person" (18) but it in a monologue later on states: "Supernatural creatures do exist. They have just spent centuries hiding away in dark castles and moldy dungeons because humans kept attacking their homes, armed with pitchforks and flaming torches. But that's all history now. Ever since the supernatural equality laws were passed, people of all shapes and sizes have lived happily side by side" (17). This is not strictly the case as the book shows that people are still divided between those that are "normal" or "human" as opposed to those that are not. This is further confirmed by Fang himself, but not in what he says—which is not an exaggerated Eastern European accent—but in how he looks. He manages to contain elements of both Stoker's and Browning's creations, with the pallor and ears of the old world vampire and the dress of Lugosi. It is possibly the face and ears of Fang that mark out the main points of difference for the vampire and which bring the most amount of undead memory with them. Whilst Fang's nose—small and pert—goes against the anti–Semitic stereotypes of his color and ears, they also mark him out as different even to the other monsters around him. This is shown by his seductive approach to women and a predilection for human blood, the source of which is never mentioned. Consequently, though never explicitly stated, in comparison to the other comic monsters shown in the stories, Fang is actually a real monster.

Araminta (Minty) Spook, a series begun in 1994 by Angie Sage, continues this trend of mixing the vampire with the detective story where ones outsider status allows for a more objective eye on the world around one, and is also a useful device for extending a single story into a series of novels. *Vampire Brat*, published in 2007 and aimed at 7- to 9-year-olds, shows Araminta living with her Aunty Tabitha (Tabby) and Uncle Drac in their home, Spook House—

a large gothic American Victorian pile in the style of the home of the Addams family—alongside Wanda Wizzard and her mum Brenda, the cook, and Barry, the butler. The house and its visitors provide many adventures for Araminta, and in this story she is on the trail of a werewolf and out to prove that Max, Uncle Drac's nephew who is staying with them, is a real vampire. Minty herself is not a vampire, but has gothic leanings as shown by her wanting to dress largely in black and her easy acceptance of the ghosts that live in Spook House. Her Aunt and Uncle are of vampiric ancestry, and Minty describes the difference between them and real vampires, which she believes Max to be, as follows:

> There is the nice kind, like Uncle Drac, who does vampire stuff like not long daylight, hanging around with bats, and having cute pointy teeth at the sides of his smile. This is the kind of vampire who would not dream of biting you ... they just happen to come from a vampire family ... so you can look like a vampire but not behave like one. Then there is the horrible kind of vampire ... the nasty, biting kind whom you could not trust one inch. You can generally tell the nasty ones as they are extremely creepy ... *and they have extremely sharp teeth* [80–81].

Uncle Drac certainly does not look like Lugosi's Dracula, other than having pointed ears; whereas Max has greased back hair and wears aristocratic style (posh) clothing. Araminta invents the "Combined Werewolf and Vampire Trapping Kit" to solve both mysteries but, in the manner of Chester in *Bunnicula*, they are seen to be more the product of her overactive imagination. The werewolf is in fact the missing cat "Pusskins" sitting on a bag of bat poo, while having kittens, and Max only has sharp teeth, because all young vampires do and the blood, which Minty saw dripping off them, was actually juice from the cherry sweets the little boy eats. Araminta largely avoids the pitfalls of the undead memory of the vampires past by creating a difference that is purposely disassociated from its past and promoting the idea of not judging a book (vampire) by its cover. The last book/series to be considered here brings together this and many of the earlier, more positive, ideas regarding otherness together, in that things are rarely as they first seem and that there aspects of the vampire that allow for greater autonomy and that look forwards rather than backwards.

Mona the Vampire, written by Sonia Holleyman—who also write *Little Vampires Diary*—was published in 1990 and later spawned a television series in 1999, and further books from that. The stories are meant for 3 years upwards, and the book used here is *The Robot Babysitter* from 2001. All the stories are about a young girl called Mona Parker who has a very vivid imagination and believes her home town is being overrun by various kinds of monsters, which she, her friends Charley and Lily, and her cat Fang manage to fend off. Mona, like Minty, is not a vampire but she wears a vampire costume that helps to focus her vampire-premonitions and come up with ideas on how to save the town. In this story, Mona ends up at home with, what she believes is, a robot babysitter. The only way to save herself is to change into her vampire costume and call Charley (Zapman) and Lily (Princess Giant) to come over in their superhero costumes to save the day. However, in trying to break the connection between the robot and its controller, they give her an electric shock which only makes it/her more angry. The babysitter sends Charley and Lily home but Mona's vampire senses tell her to use the remote control from the television to reprogram the robot, and it works, so that they become the best of friends. Mona is interesting as in donning the cape and fangs of a vampire—as well as a rather outlandish wig—gives voice to her sixth sense about people and situations, a part of herself that would otherwise be deemed unacceptable or uncontrollable. In this way, the guise of difference helps her to normalize/utilize her own sense of otherness, but this is achievable only because she identifies with the largely non-racialized aspects of Dracula—though not necessarily the class-based ones—and the fact that her parents, not unlike those in *Vlad*, readily accept her vampiric performativity.

Conclusions

This study is something of an exploratory venture into the world of the undead in children's books, and while not covering all instances of the appearances of vampires, either as main or subsidiary characters, begins to set out the terrain of what kinds of baggage—undead memory—certain monsters bring with them from the Old World into the New. Vampires, as a perennially popular classic monster which, to paraphrase Nina Auerbach, are recreated by/for every generation (5–6) and with such readily recognizable features—the cape, the widow's peak, the fangs, the accent—are easily transposed into contemporary situations and storylines to signify otherness and difference. However, as noted above, these are anything but empty signifiers, and the types of difference they were originally employed to encapsulate was not designed to be a vehicle of understanding and inclusion, but exclusion and vilification. When these signifiers are transposed into other narratives, they do not instantly lose that meaning but, as seen in *A Vampire's Coming to Dinner*, can make what is meant as a comic story into something much more ambiguous, if not disturbing which, hopefully unknowingly, continues derogatory racial stereotypes.[3] An interesting aspect of this provisional study is the role of girls who exceed the roles/restrictions that are traditionally placed upon them by patriarchal ideologies within the narratives, and as seen in Gruesome, Araminta and Mona, manage to more successfully represent forms of difference that use aspects of the undead past to create their own forms of agency. Mona in particular utilizes and controls the signifiers of patriarchal otherness, the cape and fangs, to become herself and help the community around her. In this way the more successful stories/characters/series examined here are the ones that are aware of the signifiers of the past but use them to create new forms of significance in the present or, as Kimberley Reynolds observes, "the stories we give children are blueprints for living in culture as it exists, but they are also where alternative ways of living are often piloted in recognition of the fact that children will not just inherit the future, but need to participate in shaping it" (14). In this way the monsters of the past might not only be positive influences in the present but role models for the future.

Notes

1. Arguably Varney from *Varney the Vampire, or The Feast of Blood* by James Malcolm Rymer, that was a serialized vampire tale in 19th century penny dreadfuls and ran from 1845–47, is one of the first self-reflexive vampires as by the end of the tale he can no longer live with himself and decides to end his dead life by jumping into the volcanic lava of Mount Vesuvius. However, Varney's tale is not written in the first person in the way that's Rice's vampire monologues often are and so is more observed by a narrator rather than recounting personal experience.

2. *The Satanic Rites* was the last of the Hammer films featuring Christopher Lee as Count Dracula, a series that had begun with *Dracula* by Terence Fischer in 1958, there was however one later film, *The Legend of the Seven Golden Vampires* by Roy Ward Baker from 1974 where John Forbes-Robertson played the Count.

3. Writers such as Jeffrey Cohen in the introduction to his book *Monster Theory* and Leslie Ormandy in the introduction to this present volume, suggest that monsters are palimpsestic signifiers whose meaning can be re-written with the passage of time. However, the present study contends that this is not strictly the case and as argued by Bacon and Bronk in *Undead Memory*, the past meanings of monsters often act like ghosts in the machine which lay in wait to resurface at unexpected moments in the future. One might say that all future uses of the signifier of the monster are haunted by the trauma of its previous meanings.

Works Cited

Arata, Stephen. *Fictions of Loss in the Victorian Fin de Siecle*, Cambridge: Cambridge University Press, 1996. Print.
Auerbach, Nina. *Our Vampires, Ourselves*. Chicago: University of Chicago Press, 1995. Print.
Bacon, Simon. "Exactly the Same but Completely Different: The Evolution of Bram Stoker's Dracula from Page to Screen." *The Journal of South Texas English Studies* 2.1 (Dec. 2010): 1–21. Print.
Bacon, Simon, and Katarzyna Bronk, eds. *Undead Memory: Vampires and Human Memory in Popular Culture*. Bern: Peter Lang, 2014. Print.
Bethlehem, Julianna. *Dracula Junior and the Fake Fangs: A 3-Dimensional Picture Book*. London: Tango Books, 1996. Print.
Brown, Lisa. *Vampire Boy's Good Night*. New York: HarperCollins, 2010. Print.
Butler, Erik. *Metamorphoses of the Vampire in Literature and Film: Cultural Transformations in Europe, 1732–1933*. Rochester: Camden House, 2010. Print.
Collins, Ross. *Dear Vampa*. London: Hodder Childrens Books, 2010. Print.
Donbavand, Tommy. *Fangs Vampire Spy: Operation: Golden Bum*. London: Walker Books, 2013. Print.
Dracula. Dir. Tod Browning. Universal, 1931. DVD.

Dracula's Daughter. Dir. Lambert Hillyer, Universal, 1936. DVD.
Halberstam, Judith. "Technologies of Monstrosity: Bram Stoker's Dracula." *Victorian Studies* 36.3 (1993): 333–52. Print.
Hawkins, Colin, and Jackie Hawkins. *The Gorys.* London: Collins, 1999. Print.
_____. *Vampires.* London: Collins, 1982. Print.
Holiday, Jane. *Gruesome and Bloodsocks.* London: Young Lions, 1984. Print.
Holleyman, Sonia. *The Little Vampires Diary.* London: Orchard Books, 1995. Print.
_____. *Mona the Vampire*: The Robot Babysitter. London: Orchard Books, 2001. Print.
Howe, James. *Bunnicula: A Rabbit Tale of Mystery.* New York: Atheneum Books, 1979. Print.
Jane, Pamela. *A Vampire Is Coming to Dinner: 10 Rules to Follow.* New York: Penguin Young Readers, 2010. Print.
Jungman, Ann. *Vlad the Drac.* London: Collins, 1982. Print.
Khair, Tabish. *The Gothic, Postcolonislism and Otherness: Ghosts from Elsewhere.* London: Palgrave Macmillan, 2009. Print.
Malchow, Harold L. *Gothic Images of Race in Nineteenth-Century Britain.* Stanford: Stanford University Press, 1996. Print.
Mayer, Kirsten. *Marceline's World of Vampireness.* New York: Price Stern Sloan, 2014. Print.
Nosferatu: A Symphony of Horror. Dir. F. W. Murnau. Film Arts Guild, 1922. DVD.
Reynolds, Kimberley. *Radical Children's Literature: Future Visions and Aesthetic Transformations in Juvenile Fiction.* London: Palgrave Macmillan, 2007. Print.
Rice, Anne. *Interview with the Vampire.* New York: Ballantine, 1976. Print.
Sage, Angie. *Amarinta Spook: Vampire Brat.* London: Bloomsbury, 2007. Print.
Silver, Alain, and James Ursini. *The Vampire Film: From Nosferatu to Interview with the Vampire.* New York: Limelight Editions, 1997. Print.
Son of Dracula. Dir. Robert Siodmak. Universal, 1943. DVD.
Stoker, Bram. *Dracula.* 1897. London: Signet Classics, 1996. Print.
Summers, Mondegue. *The Vampire in Lore and Legend.* Mineola, NY: Dover, 2001. Print.
Zanger, Jules. "A Sympathetic Vibration: Dracula and the Jews." *English Literature in Transition* 34 (1991): 33–44. Print.

Misogyny, Monsters and Malice
Dismantling Troy Cummings' The Notebook of Doom *Series*

Holly A. Wheeler

The eight books that currently make up Troy Cummings' *The Notebook of Doom* (*NoD*) series seem progressive: the heroes who protect a small town from monsters attempting a variety of nefarious acts, including trying to steal all the air and blotting out the sun, are not strapping young noblemen who go on a quest and defend the honor of captive maidens; instead, the series' heroes are three elementary school children. The monsters, too, are not classical dragons or ogres, but ridiculous fiends like a dinosaur-shaped piñata and a warrior made of bubble wrap. These monsters have funny names (the former, for example, is called a P-Rex) and are often comprised of common sights for child readers who know that flappy balloons from the car dealership and bubble wrap are decidedly *not* alive; they are, therefore, safe from the monsters in the series. The three children are familiar character types: Alexander is the shy but smart leader, Rip is the tough bully, and Nikki is the quiet girl. Together they defend the town from villains that (mostly) only the town's young children can see. The series sounds like archetypal childhood fantasies come true: everyday kids are smarter than their parents, they make important choices, and they demonstrate bravery and daring beyond their years. However, not all is as it seems in the anagrammed town of Stermont.

Each book in the series works the same way: something unusual happens, and Alexander consults an old notebook he found with S.S.M.P. on the cover, later revealed to stand for Super Secret Monster Patrol. The notebook is brimming with cartoon-like illustrations of monsters like the Rhinoceraptor, "an armored beast with a large horn and massive swan-like wings" (*Goon* 44) and Blinkers, "a typical, everyday giant floating eyeball" (*Vegetables* 44). Each book is filled with entertaining and amusing drawings: the story itself is illustrated with black and white drawings, and the S.S.M.P. notebook provides a picture of the monster and additional information: description, habitat, diet, warning, behavior, and, often, a funny fact. For example, book two introduces a Socktopus, "a woven monster with eight mismatched arms" (*Smashers* 56), accompanying an illustration of what children will recognize as an octopus with socks for legs (*Smashers* 56). The details of each monster are equal parts funny and frightening: the Hittin' Mittens eat only lint, fuzz, and fur balls and "look cute" like "warm fuzzy mittens" (*Mummy* 40), but once an unsuspecting child puts them on, they "turn into boxing gloves" (41) which force the child to punch his or her own face.

The ending of each book is the same: Alexander, Rip, and Nikki confront the monster with a combination of nerve and quick thinking—at Alexander's direction—and the monsters are thwarted. The adults are unaware and uninvolved in the attacks and, once everyone is safe, the heroism of the children is not recognized. Lastly, Alexander adds the new monster to the S.S.M.P. notebook. However, as with most things in literature written for children, appearances are deceiving; underneath the funny Blubber-duckies, Purple Slurpers, and Forkupines lurk something much more sinister: the potential for everyday objects to be evil; underrepresented and (sometimes) monstrous females; and a lack of agency by the very people young children look to for protection: parents and teachers.

Child readers new to the *NoD* series will find it familiar because of its many fairy tale archetypes. Fairy tales are the most well-known stories read to and by children. It is through these stories that children are granted, in the words of psychoanalyst Bruno Bettelheim, "access to deeper meaning and that which is meaningful for him at his stage of development" (4). That is, these stories encourage imagination and develop readers' minds while helping them work through emotional anxieties and overcome their fears. According to scholar Jack Zipes, fairy tales may be "the most important cultural and social event in most children's lives" (1). These "universal, ageless, and eternal" stories (6) demonstrate social order, appropriate behavior in that social order, and conflict-resolution (7). While fairy tales have multiple versions spanning the globe, the reoccurring patterns of behavior, symbols, and characters they portray are universal archetypes. Carl Jung's use of the term *archetype* relates to his conceptualization of the "collective unconscious" containing "contents and modes of behavior that are more or less the same everywhere and in all individuals" (287); thus, providing an explanation for why fairy tales from all over the world have similar character types, settings, and conflicts.

The evil stepmother, the hero, the trickster, and the witch are immediately recognizable characters. Similarly, the journey away from home, the forest, and the absent (or dead) parent—usually the mother—will be familiar to children who have been exposed to fairy tales. The archetype of the number three is that is "universally seen as a special number" (Ashliman 7), as is the universal time and place, the "once upon a time" opening which could be anywhere except "the concrete world of ordinary reality" (Bettelheim 62). Lastly, the least favored position in the family is usually the protagonist of the fairy tale (Ashliman 45) so that the youngest, the smallest, or the simpleton is the focus of the tale and is often given a nickname. Child readers will find these familiar folktale tropes tucked into Cummings' pages, immediately taking comfort in their presence.

Book one establishes the archetypal pattern for the *NoD* series: Alexander Bopp is coded as the "special" one: his birthday is on leap year and he is singled out at school because he is new, late, covered in construction dust, and forced to wear one sneaker and one froggy rain boot. If that wasn't enough, he tells his classmates that he has "'been lost, yelled at, crushed by bricks—and attacked by monsters! [...] Huge, ugly, terrible, walking balloon goons'" (*Goons* 39), causing uproarious laughter. Further, he is left to walk to school on the first day alone, following a convoluted map taking him through most of the small town, only to find the school abandoned and under construction. There, he is confronted by balloons that use "their long wobbly arms" to grab him (*Goons* 19), serving as his initiation into the world of monsters. Rounding out the archetypes, Alexander lives with his single father near the proverbial forest and receives a nickname. His teacher, Mr. Plunkett, tells the class that a nickname has to "'count'"; he assumes that Alexander "'likes slimy green things'" after noting his "'silly frog boot'" and, therefore, dubs him "'Salamander Snott'" (*Goons* 39).

Books written for children may serve multiple purposes from entertainment and education to socialization and transmission of culture. Children may also learn any number of values, behaviors, or skills from reading. The values that are coded as positive include those values Field and Weiss examined in *Values in Selected Children's Books of Fiction and Fantasy*: cooperation, courage, friendship and love of animals, friendship and love of people, humaneness, ingenuity, loyalty, maturity, responsibility, and self-respect—most of which are demonstrated by Cummings' series. However, the controversy of potentially dangerous or subversive texts is always lurking in the background of the genre; the debate of which is beyond the scope of this argument. Instead, the values and lessons that can be safely labeled as either positive or negative are examined here. To be sure, Cummings' books promote various positive and desired behaviors for socializing children, but they also promote equally dangerous ones.

The Day of the Night Crawlers teaches children that teamwork will safeguard them and that everyday items can save the day. *Attack of the Shadow Smashers* educates children of the value of friendship with people different from themselves, and *The Charge of the Lightening Bug* demonstrates that lessons learned in school are applicable and potentially life-saving outside of the classroom. The main values espoused in the series, ingenuity, courage, quick thinking, critical thinking, and teamwork, are reinforced in each book. Book after book, each child plays a role in thwarting the monsters and expresses both willingness and a responsibility to do so. Alexander declares, "'Stermont needs us'" (*Smashers* 63); Nikki later echoes, "'I took an oath to protect my town, and I intend to keep it'" (79), demonstrating their commitment to their town.

Other more minor values are reinforced by the series as well. Punctuality is clearly important as Alexander's continual lateness is frowned upon; order and conformity are valued as children at school must, understandably, follow rules like listening to their teachers and other rules expressed for child reader amusement: "'students must wear both shoes at all times'" (*Goons* 32). Respect for animals is demonstrated when Alexander admonishes Rip who wants to step on the worms saying, "'Rip, when we fought those balloon goons, we helped everyone in Stermont—even those tiny worms. If we go around squishing 'em, we're no better than the monsters we were trying to stop'" (*Crawlers* 7). However, lurking underneath feel-good lessons about loyalty, teamwork, and friendship are sinister messages. Child readers learn that school is not really a place for learning and that their parents have no idea what is happening around them and cannot offer protection; therefore, the very survival of the town and its people relies on the children.

If a school is only as good as its investment in teachers, Stermont Elementary School is all but bankrupt. On the surface, the series promotes learning: in every book, except for *Snombies* which is set in the summer, the children attend school. However, the repeated failure of the teachers to instruct their charges demonstrates that Stermont places little value on education. The first teacher in the series and the one most often mentioned is Mr. Plunkett; he is funny, wearing a "pink-and-orange flowery shirt, green pants, and purple shoes" (*Goons* 36), but he does no actual teaching. In the next book, he *plans* to teach about worms, but as with the previous book, offers no instruction. The same is true in later books. He says he will teach the children table manners and napkin folding in preparation for a community dinner, but in the course of that entire week, the only instruction he offers is to put a chart on the board with picture of different napkins and asks which fork would be best for spearing a pickle. However, in book six, he does teach the class about the ruby scorpion, Stermont's "greatest treasure" (*Mummy* 18) in preparation for a field trip. Another teacher, Coach Gill demands of her students: "'watch [...] stand like this. And hold your foils like this'" (*Crawlers* 37). But, her instruction is brief and poor; instead of correcting their "'terrible'" work and providing further instructions, she dismisses class and promises a quiz. But, the worst example of teacher is Ranger

Harry, counselor at Campy Gloamy. Under the pretense of teaching the children survival skills, he hands them sheets of directions and a tool (varying from the innocuous fire-safety booklet and compass to the potentially dangerous bow and arrow) and sends them off to learn on their own. He takes them out at night, splits the children up in the dark, and leaves them alone; worse, he doesn't realize the snowmen are *not* the campers. So while he, like other adults likely can't see the monsters, he does notice the snombies when they are not moving. He presumably can count, so he *should* know there are more snowmen than campers and, therefore, that something is amiss. By book eight, however, Cummings redeems himself, albeit briefly. Dr. Tallow shows the children the "'brand-new, state-of-the-art classroom-pet zone'" (*Lightening Bugs* 41) and begins to teach about cocoons. While her lesson is soon interrupted by a loss of power, the next day, she demonstrates the first real lesson of the series: during an electrical storm, she tells the class not to be scared and instructs them about how to stay safe during a storm. This lesson directly influences the outcome of this book.

While the focus of the series is obviously not what the children learn *in* school, it is still *the* major setting of the series. Its utter lack of concrete attention to the children having learned anything sends a clear lesson: education is not valued in Stermont. More time is spent in the books describing the movement of the children from place to place than on them being in class. This is established immediately in book one when, for example, as soon as Alexander receives his nickname, the children are sent to lunch followed by early dismissal because the tires on all the buses are deflated. In book three, the children take school pictures and go right to lunch. Even when Alexander is mentioned being in math class no teaching or teachers are mentioned—just that he is looking at the S.S.M.P. notebook. Instead of classroom development, the lessons that Alexander, Rip, and Nikki learn are mostly those they acquire from monsters fighting, not from school.

Texts written for children are filled with various types of authority figures: family members, teachers, and friends, among others. Vardell says, "Some authors weave adult characters into the story in a way that makes them integral to the narrative. Their interactions with the child characters help the readers to see the dynamic growth of the young hero or heroine" (173). Of the authority figures in the *NoD* series, only Mr. Hoarsely is "integral to the narrative" because his refusal to help the children with the town's monster infestation directly forces the growth of the children as they take on the responsibility of the S.S.M.P. Even Alexander's father, Mr. Bopp, is a more one dimensional prop, save for a few scattered moments of, mostly accidental, aid.

Although Mr. Bopp wears a tie to work as a dentist and likes to grill, he serves as what Mallan calls "a softer, more caring domesticated male" (16).

He makes sure Alexander goes to bed on time, cooks all their meals, plants tulips, and reads to Alexander. He is kind and involved in Alexander's life as he encourages his son to invite new friends to his birthday party and serves as a school chaperone to the overnight field trip. However, he does not do so in typically male ways. Instead, he makes animal figures out of Alexander's lunches, wears space pajamas to the field trip, and serves breakfast in the shape of a funny face while wearing an apron. Vardell suggests that in single parent families, fathers have "take[n] on more 'feminine' attributes" (166), a mantle Mr. Bopp has definitely taken up, though, unlike Mr. Hoarsely who hides at the sign of danger, this is not negative. Mr. Bopp demonstrates what Mallan characterizes as a "feminized masculinity" that is the "caring, sensitive, domesticated father/partner" (24). Despite his role as caretaker, Mr. Bopp often allows his son to go out on his own with his friends, sometimes in the dark and in the woods. When reading with his son, he labels a comic book swamp-yak "'scary'" (*Smashers* 1) and when Alexander contradicts him, "A real monster would be way smarter,'" Mr. Bopp replies, "'Oh, Al. You take this monster stuff too seriously'" (2), and he finds Alexander's school ant-farm project "'creepy'" (*P-Rex* 3). Although Mr. Bopp does not know about the monsters, it seems unlikely, then, he would be helpful even if he did.

Other adults in Stermont are equally as problematic as authority figures. In *Flurry of the Snombies*, Ranger Harry demonstrates an utter lack of appropriate camp counselor abilities as well as guardianship. He sends the children off alone and does nothing to supervise. The parents of the other children are just as ignorant. Rip explains that after one of the Balloon Goons threw a rock and chased him after school, "'I ran home. I tried to tell my parents, […] 'but they didn't believe me'" (*Goons* 62). Worse, when Rip is taken prisoner by an evil broccoli stalk masquerading as a nurse, he does not attend school the next day, yet no alarm was raised; there is no mention of anyone (like his parents) other than Alexander and Nikki noticing he is missing. In *Smashers*, Alexander and Rip notice that everyone is "casting strange shadows. Some had horns, some had wings, some had tentacles" (65). Rip observes a child trying to show his mother who "didn't seem interested" (66) and a jogger in *P-Rex* "bounded past" the dinosaur piñata, causing Nikki to say, "'the dinosaur thing is *right there*' […] how could she not have seen it?!'" (42). It is no surprise, then, that Alexander never considers talking to his father about the monsters, choosing, instead, to keep this immense secret. Alexander's choice could have implications for child readers who learn here that adults really do not understand or believe children and that sometimes secrets have to be kept from parents.

More problematic are the two other constant adults: Ms. Vanderpants, the school principal and Mr. Hoarsely who serves as school secretary, gym teacher, bus driver, and nurse., Mr. Hoarsely is the only confirmed adult who knows that monsters are real and yet will not help the children. He leaves Alexander a note in *Goons* saying, "I know about the monsters" (46) and shows up as a clown at Alexander's birthday party, seemingly to protect him; instead, he offers this helpful advice, "'Their secret is in the woods, behind your house [...] they'll do anything to protect it. RUN FOR YOUR LIVES'" (6), and promptly runs away. Despite this not-so-helpful approach, he did teach Alexander how to make a "'very important balloon animal'" (64), which Alexander uses to tie up the giant snake Balloon Goon, allowing his father to accidentally pop it. In book two, Alexander tries to talk to Mr. Hoarsely about the worm infestation, but Mr. Hoarsely hides, putting the children and town in danger that he could have helped prevent. When the children find his hiding spot and inform him that Tunnel Fish that "swim" underground are coming, Mr. Horsely immediately realizes that "'she'" tracked him down (71). Instead of telling the children that the *she* is a Fish-Kabob, "a scaly monster with a sword for a face" (90) who is after him for revenge, Mr. Hoarsely deserts the children and hides. At the end of *Night Crawlers*, Mr. Hoarsely tells the three children that he quit the Super Secret Monster Patrol: "'Congratulations. You kids are in charge now. You've already got the notebook'" (87). The narrator's assessment of Mr. Hoarsely holds true for the rest of the series: "Mr. Hoarsely seemed to be the only grown-up in Stermont who could see monsters. But he refused to talk about them" (*Vegetables* 60). Later he tells Alexander, "'I don't want to hear the *M*-word'" (88). In a later book, when Alexander tries to talk to him about monsters, he says, "'HEY! We had a deal! *You* run the S.S.M.P. now! My monster fighting days are over'" (*P-Rex* 18), a stance he holds throughout the series without explanation; again, leaving the children on their own with a grave responsibility.

While Mr. Hoarsely previously fought monsters, it is difficult to imagine him as aggressively masculine. Instead, he seems to demonstrate more stereotypically female characteristics as he refuses to talk about the monsters, avoids confrontation, and hides when confronted by monsters. While a male taking on characteristics of the traditional female could be positive in literature written for children, the fact that by doing so he privileges himself over the children he is supposed to protect is a significant problem.

Of the six main characters, four (Alexander, Rip, Mr. Bopp, and Mr. Hoarsely) are male, leaving females in the series numerically underrepresented and, for the most part, frightful. Ms. Vanderpants, the other significant school authority figure, is textbook stern principal. She wears all gray and has hair "in a long braid, coiled on top of her head like a snake" (*Goons* 26); she regularly hints about something, but comes just shy of revealing what it is. In *Goons*, she tells Alexander that the school is closed "'to deal with—'" (27) but never finishes her sentence, and she chastises the children for being at school on a Saturday because they are "dealing with a major [...] pest problem'" (*P-Rex* 88). Principal Vanderpants is pictured in all of the books except *Snombies* which takes place over summer vacation; however, of the thirteen drawings of her, she is depicted only frowning or yelling.

The problematic position of women in this series continues when examining the monsters. Of twelve monsters that the children face, only two are gendered—the rest are simply "it" or the collective "they." The two gendered monsters are female: Coach Gill is a Fish-Kabob who wants to kill the children, and Nurse Brock is a people-eating stalk of broccoli who kidnaps and imprisons Rip, both monsters demonstrating to child readers that women, at least in this series, are to be feared.

However, *NoD* does present two positive women characters, albeit briefly. Unsmiling Ms. Sargent tries to protect the museum and the children in *Pop of the Bumpy Mummy*, but ultimately proves ineffective and, instead, is saved *by* the children. In the most recent book, *Charge of the Lightening Bugs*, Dr. Tallow is, finally, a responsible adult who is always depicted teaching, thereby, softening what up to this point in the series is an utter lack of education and aid by adult figures. Her positive depiction may well mark a turning point in the series away from frightful women and inept teaching.

The two main characters, Alexander Bopp and Rip(ley) Bonkowski, are studies in opposites but represent different sides to traditional hegemonic masculinity. Alexander is bookish and worried about his first day of school. He's described as a "mop-haired, bug-eyed, gut-filled bag of bones" (*Goons* 2) who is "scared to death" (2). The New Age Boy, according to Stephens, adapting concepts from David Buchbinder, breaks up the binary between aggressive Old Age Boy and privileged Mommy's Boy with a boy who likes to read, acts "without self-interest" and lacks "physical prowess and physical courage, though his moral courage and other-regardingness will prompt him to act courageously" (44). Alexander fits this middle position. To be sure, he is brave through the series, but he is thoughtful first. While Rip and Nikki participate in the monster fighting, Alexander is the one who puts the pieces together to figure out *how* to defeat their foes and displays a variety of heroic qualities. He knows, for example, that something isn't right when the school is freezing and a new chef serves them ice cream for lunch. Whereas Nikki and Rip indulge, Alexander questions. He investigates and follows clues alone to protect others, despite possible danger, demonstrating significant critical thinking. He applies lessons learned in school to defeat the Candy-Saurus and Thunderbug and regularly develops a plan and assigns roles for Nicki and Rip. For example, in *Whack of the P-Rex*, Alexander puts together the pieces of paper that keep getting stuck on his shoe, to the purple taffy that it is attached with, to the purple finger prints in the S.S.M.P. notebook and discovers the Pinata-Saurus Rex. He realizes, "Everything made sense now: the giant footprints, the piles of candy, the smashed buildings—even the paper stuck to his shoe" (50). He creates a plan to turn the three children into "'a little piñata monster'" so they can "'fool the P-Rex'" (53). He hatches the plan, they build the piñata, and he leads the way. He orders his friends around so they, together, defeat the P-Rex. Unexpectedly, the P-Rex turns into a new monster—the Candy-Saurus Rex. Again, it is Alexander who figures out how to destroy it.

Despite his role as hero, Alexander is a fairly flat character with one significant weakness: he is solely focused on the S.S.M.P. notebook. Any time something is different around him, he immediately makes two assumptions: whatever it is must be a monster and, secondly, that the monster will be in the book. In *Vegetables*, he sees a new coat rack in the kitchen. Instead of asking his father about it, he consults the book, sees a related monster, assumes the coat rack is nefarious and "'leap[s] from the counter, scream[s] a battle cry and snap[s] a wet dishtowel at the coat rack'" (8). Instead of thinking his way to a new monster, Alexander assumes he can find the answers in the book. Despite a description of mega-worms as small blue loner worms that "shrivel up" after "any loud screeching sound" (*Night Crawler* 9), Alexander continues to think the "'millions'" of "'pinkish gray'" worms that do not respond to his screeches as mega-worms (11)—so much so that he goes to great lengths (stealing a bathroom pass and a chalkboard and risking the wrath of Principal Vanderpants) to test his theory. While this could be read as him being thorough, it actually demonstrates a lack of critical thinking or a lack of trust in his own skills of deduction. Like the protagonists of many series books before him, Alexander remains largely unchanged through the course of the series, a hallmark of early reader series for children.

Whereas Alexander thinks before acting, Rip acts first. His introduction in the series is to open the classroom door with a "jerk" and "barg[e] into the room and demand, 'Who's the weenie?'" referring to Alexander (*Goons* 38). The accompanying picture is captioned with physical descriptions, depicting his "spiky hair, squarish head, fake tattoos, and missing teeth," the latter of which could be missing "baby teeth or possibly lost in a fight" (38). Thus, Rip represents, as his nickname would suggest, the Old Age Boy, "the child who is either aggressive or something of a rascal, self-regarding and physically assertive" (Stephens 44). Immediately following class, Rip throws a dodgeball at Alexander, hoping it would "bounce off [his] nose" (41) and then shows everyone Alexander's "Who's a Big Boy?" Birthday invitation, chiding him by saying, "'Salamander Snott is having a birthday party tomorrow! Looks like he's turning two!'" (47). When he shows up at Alexander's party the next day, Alexander expects Rip to "'throw something'" or to call him "'names or whatever'" (61), demonstrating Alexander's understanding of Rip as a bully. Surprisingly, Rip, although he admits Alexander's suggestion "'sound[s]'" like fun," is really there to tell Alexander that he got attacked by a balloon on the way home from school, and that he believes what Alexander said about the monsters (62).

In the rest of the series, Rip proves to be equal parts brave and reckless. When confronted by the Balloon Goons, Alexander proposes running; Rip says, "'I say we fight'" (*Goons* 69). In *Vegetables*, gym class is suddenly plunged into darkness, children are pelted with "'some sort of volleyball,'" and Rip's immediate response is characteristic: "'Dodgeball in the dark!? [...] This is awesome!'" (39). He doesn't care about the quality of his homework, carelessly throwing his ant farm in the air; he eats candy found on the ground; and despite what he's learned, he is dismissive of mysterious happenings—like when all the children are mailed striped boxes with bubble wrap, commenting, "'yeah, yeah—soooo spooky,'" accompanied with an eye roll (*Mummy* 16). Rip acts as we expect a child bully to act: he calls everyone a "weenie," dismisses Nikki's claim that she can read cursive, asserting, "'If *I* can't read it, then neither can you!'" (*Night Crawlers* 41), has been in trouble, "'I got five warnings per day in kindergarten,'" (*Lightening Bugs* 39), and stomps carelessly through a neighbor's flower bed. He taunts monsters by yelling, "'HA! [...] WHAT A DUMMY'" (*P-Rex* 64) which results in Alexander, Rip, and Nikki being attacked. He even sticks "his thumb on his nose and wiggle[s] his fingers" at the Snombie saying, "'you can't get us, slushbucket'" (*Snombie* 46).

Despite his reckless behavior and behind his hard shell, Rip hides a sweeter, gentler side. He visits Stermont Stella, the town's resident gopher, every day before school because she was scared by the Shadow Smashers, but then in keeping with the tough, aggressive picture of the Old Age Boy, he dismisses his act by saying, "'Stella's just a gopher'" (*Vegetables* 12) after Nikki asks if he was doing something nice. His tough exterior is further thwarted when all the children are forced to wear coats from the Lost and Found because the school is freezing and Rip is stuck with the panda bear snow suit, making him the "'fuzziest, wuzziest panda'" at school (17).

Rip is naturally a significant contributor to their monster battles. He is the one who figures out that the Goons are eating air, fences the Fish-Kabob, and discerns that Snombies stay away from fire. In *Lightening Bugs*, when the lights go out and his classmates are "freaked out and screaming" (63), he says, "'You need light, weenie? [...] Stand back. It's *my* time to shine'" (63). While he was referring literally to the light-up shoes he used to help his frightened peers to safety, the emphasis on *my* indicates the sidekick role he plays to Alexander. "Rip Bonkowski was quick, strong, and good at shoving people to the ground. So without thinking, he shoved Alexander and Nikki aside" (*Lightening Bugs* 77) and took the zap of the Thunderbug right to his chest to save his friends. He is even taken prisoner by monsters twice within the series—unlike Alexander and Nikki.

Despite his questionable behaviors readers like Rip, partially because we are supposed to. He is morally ambiguous in that while he takes mostly positive actions, he does behave in questionable ways (Krakowiak and Oliver 117). He usually wants to run headlong into danger but by book eight, he wants to heed the warning to stay off the roof. While the *NoD* books are, as Stephens describes, "Narratives in which performance, role-play, or the playing of games are key elements [which are] broadly comic or incorporate comic elements" (40), they are also progressive—at least in terms of rejecting heteronormative structures of masculinity. The same cannot be said for the depiction of females, especially for the series most significant female—Nikki.

The third member of the monster-fighting trio, Nikki, is more cryptic than the boys. Readers' first glimpses at her are fleeting: she is the "hoodie-wearing kid in the back row" scribbling in her notebook on Alexander's first day of school (*Goons* 40); she tries to talk to Alexander about having seen his S.S.M.P. notebook but is interrupted and, then, she promptly disappears for the rest of the book. In book two, Alexander sits next to her because "she was the only kid who had been nice to him on his first day of school" (*Night Crawlers* 17); however, they don't speak until she becomes the passive note passer for the active two boys. Later, she says she wears the hoodie because of a "'condition'" (32) she doesn't name. She confronts the boys after class; after explaining that she was "'chased by a fish creature the size of an alligator'" Nikki indicates that she wants to work with the boys because she has "'useful, um, skills'" and has been "'interested in monsters since ... well, forever'" (53).Whereas by book one Rip's character is well-defined, here Nikki is still mysterious and not just because she is a girl. While Alexander recognizes her intelligence and bravery and wants to work with her, Rip is decidedly not a fan. He calls Nikki "'hoodie head'" (54) and "'weird'" (55) because, he says, "'she's always by herself'" and is following them around (56). While Rip reluctantly agrees to work with Nikki, the mystery of her character does not end with the official forming of the trio.

Much has been written about the depiction of girls in the media, indicating that since gender identity is developed early by societal beliefs and attitudes, that literature written for children serves as one vehicle through which child readers learn about gender. Anderson and Hamilton's study of gender in picture books reveals that traditional gender binaries can affect attitudes and behaviors of readers (145). Nikki, then, is cause for concern. First, Nikki is clearly the third member of the trio. As the odd (wo)man out, she is always listed after Alexander and Rip in any action: "Alexander, Rip, and Nikki stood back-to-back-to-back as the small angry tunnel fish closed in" (*Crawlers* 82). Alexander tries to convince "Rip and Nikki" the school has been turned into a giant refrigerator in *Vegetables*, and Alexander considers "Rip and Nikki" his best friends. "Rip and Nikki" wave to Alexander—despite the picture depicting Nikki on the left so readers *see* her first, they read her name only after her male counterpart (*Lightening Bugs* 24). Her status as *last* of the group and the less vital role is further demonstrated by her actions which are more passive than those of the boys, therefore reinforcing traditionally female stereotypes. In *Smashers* at S.S.M.P. headquarters she organizes their supplies while Rip draws pictures of himself single-handedly fighting the monsters they've faced together; she studies a map while Rip eats candy in *P-Rex*. When everyone in class is "sobbing" because of the onion smell, including Nikki, she is singled out negatively two paragraphs later as she "wept like a baby" (*Vegetables* 19), a designation assigned to no one else. The privilege of male action over female inaction is best demonstrated in the children's interaction with monsters. When the boys are busy making observations that lead to action, Nikki comments. For example, Rip notices that the P-Rex moves slowly and Alex figures out how they can defeat it, while Nikki merely observes its "'claws'" and "'smashy tail'" (76). In *Snombies*, despite the screaming campers, Nikki "whispered" (67) and "asked" (69) while Rip "scrambled" (68) and "grabbed" (69). Nikki's stereotypically female behavior is further evident in her emotional reaction to the boys' discussion of her future in the club, where instead of talking to them, she quits and storms off (*Smashers* 37). She is also the only one of the three who wants the stereotypical female external validation from Ms. Vanderpants, for saving the school and the town. Finally, she is the only child of the three who lacks a last name, further demonstrating her diminished significance. If children are socialized by the types of characters to which they are exposed, *NoD* readers learn that boys are stronger, active, and important while girls conform to gender stereotypes by following and observing.

Despite the oversimplified gender binaries of the children, Nikki does have a few shining moments. In book six, she is the reason, not Alexander, that they are saved. Despite a subordinate role early in the book where Rip interacts with Alexander three times before Nikki says anything at all, it is Nikki who realizes all the missing shiny objects are related. She is the one who wants to chase the mummy, and later acts on her own—for the first time without Alexander's direction. Demonstrating her own agency, she leaves the boys alone to fight the mummy while she runs up the ladder, gets the gift shop ruby scorpion, and returns to yell, "'Drop my friends, bubble brain,'" to the Bubble-Wrap Warrior, currently in octopus mode and squishing the boys (82). She threatens the monster with dropping the scorpion into the gears of the clock, thereby, destroying what it is after. When her threat is called as such, she does it, causing the monster to get caught in the clock gears. Her actions are diminished, however, as this is not the end of the monster. While it is caught, it is not dead; once again, Alexander figures out how to pop it for good. A child reading this series who is still formulating conceptions of gender identity learn that while girls and boys can be friends and work together, the boys make the plans and go first, while the girls bring up the rear and take direction.

Nikki's added complication as a female gender model is more problematic than the series' presentations of hegemonic masculinity, however, in book three, she rips a page from the notebook as Alexander says he remembers "'seeing a long-tooth monster,'" shouting, "'NO!'" and rushing out without explanation (*Smashers* 6). When forced to smile for picture day, Nikki does so but reveals "extra long" and "pointy" teeth (19). Alexander notices that she "barely move[s] her lips when she talks" (27), covers her food with ketchup, and storms out of the cafeteria after Rip says, "'Bloodsucking monsters are the *worst!* With their fangs and—'" by yelling only "'ENOUGH!'" (24) and splashing her juice box in Rip's face. Later she interrupts Alexander and Rip to reveal that they need to talk about "'*another* monster'" whom she reveals is herself (42). She holds up the pages she'd ripped out of the notebook which proclaim that a Jampire is a "terrible undead monster" who spends time in graveyards, eats blood, and is evil (44–45). However, Nikki declares that "'the entry was all wrong, so [she] fixed it'" (43). The drawing of the pointy-eared vampire-like fanged creature is scribbled out and replaced with the word "wrong," the description is modified from "a terrible undead monster" to a "smart, brave girl" who hangs out in grade schools and eats "anything red and juicy: ketchup, fruit punch, raspberry jam, jelly donuts, strawberry gummies" (45). She changes the behavior to read that they are friendly and can see in the dark. The only characteristics that remain uncorrected by Nikki are the warning to keep Jampires out of the sun and the indication that they do not possess shadows. The boys vow to keep her secret, but the problem with her character as representing females as "monster" is not so easily remedied.

The purpose of the S.S.M.P. and, by extension, the focus of the series is on children who fight monsters and save the unsuspecting town. According to Bettelheim, children are not yet able to "comprehend intermediate stages of degree and intensity" so that the clear dichotomy between good and evil enables children to "make sense of the world" (74). The series lays a very specific good versus evil foundation: monsters are evil and must be destroyed. Monster fighters are good and what they do is not only important, but necessary to the survival of the town. Whereas adult readers understand that characters are complex and sometimes contradictory, child readers, especially early readers may not do the same. They do not understand that one could be "good and obedient, yet bad and rebellious" at the same time (74). Therefore, the one-dimensional characters in the good versus evil dichotomy allow children to "comprehend its actions and reactions easily" (74). They know the hero is good and the villain is bad. However, having a monster fighter as a monster calls into question the very dichotomy on which the series is predicated.

Garry and El-Shamy summarize the good/evil dichotomy in traditional stories: "the characters are not only good or evil, but also courageous or cowardly, jealous or innocent, kind or unkind, self-sacrificing or greedy, self-effacing or arrogant" (461), and almost always the good characters defeat the evil one in traditional tales. While *NoD* is a bit more complex than the flat characters of folktales in that Rip is not always as nice as he might be and he acts without thinking, he is still coded as a good character: he is a righteous monster fighter who, with Alexander and Nikki, selflessly protect their town. Rip's less than desirable behavior is overshadowed by his heroic deeds. In their study of good, bad, and morally ambiguous characters, Krakowiak and Oliver found that people like bad characters the least, good characters the most, and morally ambiguous characters, those who do both good and bad things, somewhere in the middle (129). According to their study, Krakowiak and Oliver found, "character liking, in turn, predicted affective enjoyment and, to a lesser extent, cognitive enjoyment" (129). Their study concluded that morally ambiguous characters are as enjoyable as those coded as good, and the same could be said for Nikki. A girl-monster fighter who helps save the town by putting herself in danger definitely pushes against the male-dominated system, but her position as both good monster fighter and as monster, coded in the series as evil, is problematic.

For child readers, still making sense of the "turmoil" of feelings (Bettelheim 5) an ambiguous character "can cause uncertainty" (Krakowiak and Oliver 118), exactly the opposite of the safety and certainty series books offer. The fact that Nikki is the one who "corrects" the S.S.M.P. notebook to make the Jampire "good" is even more questionable and is related to the very problem of the book itself: Alexander takes the notebook as absolute truth. He doesn't question whether the monsters in it are real or whether they can be defeated as explained in the book. The notebook itself, however, as guide and teacher is relatively untested. Of the eleven monsters the children face by book eight, the notebook only helps them defeat three: Tunnel Fish (book 2), the P-Rex (book 5), and Snombies (book 7). The S.S.M.P. notebook gives Alexander a false sense of security as whenever anything different happens, he immediately consults the book and, despite the number of monsters he has added to the book himself, he always tries to fit a monster from the book to meet whatever monster they are facing—even in the face of evidence to the contrary. While this does not actually cause many problems as he will move on after an attempt or two, it has the potential to do so.

However positively the boys react to Nikki's revelation by vowing to keep her secret, it lasts only until Rip realizes she has lied to them. While Alexander is stunned into silence at Nikki's bravery, Rip asks Alexander, "'So when are you going to kick her out of the S.S.M.P.?" (47). He recognizes the inherent contradiction of having a "'*monster* in the Super Secret *Monster Patrol*'" (48). After reluctantly thinking about it, Alexander agrees to do so, but Nikki quits, saying, "'I don't want to be in your stupid monster-hating club anyway'" (67). While her reaction is emotional and child-like, she is, after all, a child, it also hits on the very issue at the heart of this conflict—the S.S.M.P. does *hate* monsters and have taken an oath to fight them. More uncertain is Nikki's declaration that Jampires are good and now, according to the book, are both children and female. Does this mean that all other monsters in the notebook are not, in fact, monstrous? Could additional entries in the book also be in need of *correcting*? Problematic, too, is the boys' lack of critical thinking regarding this, belying their age and inexperience. Just because Nikki is "good," does that mean, then, that all Jampires are no longer "terrible undead monster[s]"? (*Smashers* 45). These significant problems are not resolved by book eight in the series, thereby calling into question the very basis on which the series is predicated.

While the series does address most of the values identified by Field and Weiss, potentially providing positive messages to child readers, those lessons are overshadowed by what lies beneath: misogyny, ambiguity, and an utter lack of parental supervision. Despite the humorous nature of the monsters that the children face, their seriousness cannot be overlooked. Both the Meat-eating Vegetables and the Ice Crusher literally want to eat people. In the former, the new school chef reveals himself to be a hungry carrot who, with his vegetable friends, "'plan to eat everyone'" (*Vegetables* 59) and the latter calls humans "'silly meat creatures'" (*Snombies* 83). Some monsters also want revenge: the Fish-Kabob is after Mr. Hoarsely, the vegetables plan to eat the town's adults "'for forcing kids to eat [them] in the name of health'" and "'munch kids for using [them] as noses on their snowmen!'" (*Vegetables* 78), and the Bubble Wrap Warrior "'did it all for payback!' ... 'for all the times humans' use bubble wrap to 'protect [their] shiny treasures'" and then pop them when they are no longer needed (*Mummy* 75). Maybe Dr. Tallow's introduction in book eight signals a changing tide regarding both the value of education and women. Despite the success of series books and the positive experiences they can provide, especially for early or reluctant readers, Cummings' *NoD* series communicates dangerous messages to child readers that are not as easily overcome as the monsters he writes about.

WORKS CITED

Anderson, David A., and Mykol Hamilton. "Gender Role Stereotyping of Parents In Children's Picture Books: The Invisible Father." *Sex Roles* 52.3/4 (2005): 145–51. Web. 21 Nov. 2015.
Ashliman, D. L. *Folk and Fairy Tales: A Handbook*. Westport, CT: Greenwood, 2004. Print.
Bettelheim, Bruno. *The Uses of Enchantment: The Meaning and Importance of Fairy Tales.* New York: Random House, 1975. Print.

Cummings, Troy. *The Notebook of Doom 1: Rise of the Balloon Goons*. New York: Scholastic, 2013. Print.
_____. *The Notebook of Doom 2: Day of the Night Crawlers*. New York: Scholastic, 2013. Print.
_____. *The Notebook of Doom 3: Attack of the Shadow Smashers*. New York: Scholastic, 2013. Print.
_____. *Notebook of Doom 4: Chomp of the Meat-Eating Vegetables*. New York: Scholastic, 2014. Print.
_____. *The Notebook of Doom 5: Whack of the P-Rex*. New York: Scholastic, 2014. Print.
_____. *The Notebook of Doom 7: Flurry of the Snombies*. New York: Scholastic, 2015. Print.
_____. *The Notebook of Doom 8: Charge of the Lightening Bugs*. New York: Scholastic, 2015. Print.
Field, Carolyn W., and Jaqueline Shachter Weiss. *Values in Selected Children's Books of Fiction and Fantasy*. Hamden, CT: Library Professional Publications, 1987. Print.
Garry, Jane, and Hasan M. El-Shamy, eds. *Archetypes and Motifs in Folklore and Literature: A Handbook*. Armonk, NY: M.E. Sharpe, 2005. Print.
Jung, C. G. *The Basic Writings of C.G. Jung*. Ed. Violet S. DeLaszlo. New York: Modern Library, 1959. Print.
Krakowiak, K. Maja, and Mary Beth Oliver. "When Good Characters Do Bad Things: Examining the Effect of Moral Ambiguity on Enjoyment." *Journal of Communication* 62.1 (2012): 117–35. Web.
Mallan, Kerry. "Picturing the Male: Representations of Masculinity in Picture Books." *Ways of Being Male: Representing Masculinities in Children's Literature and Film*, ed. John Stephens. New York: Routledge, 2002. 15–36. Print.
Stephens, John. "'A Page Just Waiting to be Written On': Masculinity Schemata and the Dynamics of Subjective Agency in Junior Fiction." *Ways of Being Male: Representing Masculinities in Children's Literature and Film*, ed. John Stephens. New York: Routledge, 2002. 38–54. Print.
Vardell, Sylvia M. "Parent Characters in Children's Novels: Lessons Learned." *Beauty, Brains, and Brawn: The Construction of Gender in Children's Literature*, ed. Susan Lehr. Portsmouth, NH: Heinemann, 2001. 162–75. Print.
Zipes, Jack. *Fairy Tales and the Art of Subversion*. New York: Routledge, 1983. Print.

PART 4: EVOLVING MONSTERS

Ogress, Fairy, Sorceress, Witch
Supernatural Surrogates and the Monstrous Mother in Variants of "Rapunzel"

MELISSA MULLINS

Let me tell you a story.

A woman is beset by a craving for parsley, rapunzel, rampion, radishes. She wants to be pregnant. Or she may be pregnant. Or she is pregnant. She spies the very thing she craves in the beautiful but forbidden garden next door. The garden is tended by an ogress, a fairy, a sorceress, a witch. She steals into the garden and feasts on the stolen goods. Or, her husband, distraught by seeing his wife withering away, creeps in for her. And again. The thief is caught in the act. The woman, the husband, is forced to promise away the unborn baby. The baby is snatched at birth and the parents are never mentioned again. The fairy, the sorceress, the witch promises to raise the child as her own. The baby is not snatched at birth, but cast off when she is seven years old. She is locked in a tower without stairs when she turns 12. The tower is full of beauty and light, with everything a young girl could wish for except company. She sings. The tower is dark, with one small window. She is alone. She lets down her hair. And again. She is surprised by a prince climbing her hair. She consents to let a prince climb her hair. There are declarations of love. There is intimacy. Perhaps there is intimacy. The girl betrays her secret belly because her cloths are too tight. She betrays her secret lover because the sorceress is too heavy. The ogress, the fairy, the sorceress, the witch cuts off her braids in horror, in rage, in disappointment, in grief. The girl is cast out, exiled. She is magically transported to a seashore with a basket full of self-replenishing bread. She's banished to a desolate land and lives in grief and misery. She bears twins. She doesn't bear twins. The prince throws himself from the tower in despair. He is pushed out of the tower. He stumbles and falls out of the tower. The prince is blinded. He wanders for many years, for one year, for some years. The lovers reunite. Her tears restore his *vision. The fairy turns their food to stone. Then she forgives them. Or the fairy, the sorceress, the witch is never mentioned again. Or the ogress chases after the lovers but is eaten by a wolf. They return to his kingdom. It is all happily ever after for everyone. Except the original parents. And the ogress, the fairy, the sorceress, the witch.*

If this convoluted tapestry of threads woven from the disparate textual manifestations of the "Rapunzel" tale directs our critical eye to anything, it is that this narrative, in the hands and mouths of storytellers from a multitude of time periods and cultural and social backgrounds, is utterly complex. Taken as such, with a number of voices rising in a multivalent cacophony, it seems a tale resistant to distillation. It is certainly not the only tale to be variously shaped by hands from different backgrounds, but it is, perhaps, one of the few well-known tales that so obviously resists easy demarcation into clearly defined character roles. Although 20th- and 21st-century writers and directors have creatively adapted any number of pre–20th century folktales and fairy tales into pieces that explore alternate perspectives and write "against" the text, we see in the mélange of voices above that this particular tale has been repeatedly and dramatically re-inscribed from the point of its very earliest textual sources. Unlike, for example, tales like "Cinderella" or "Snow White," where villainy is rendered more obvious, manifestations of the "Rapunzel" tale boast no such easily defined victim and villain. Are we encouraged to blame the biological mother for her unreasonable cravings? The biological father for his thievery? The surrogate (whose name changes with every version, from ogress, to fairy, to sorceress, to witch) for kidnapping a child? The prince for taking advantage of a young and inexperienced girl? The girl, herself, for betraying the trust of a woman who raised her (whether in finery or abject isolation)? Is the surrogate the villain simply because she is defined by her supernatural descriptors and is, thus, the "Other" to this human cast of characters? Is the biological mother exculpated of her transgression because she is merely following the urges naturally dictated by her pregnancy? The husband for appeasing his ailing wife? Are the prince and the young girl guiltless because they are following the urges set in motion by some noble and pure concept of true love? There are no simple answers for this line of questioning except to assert that the magnificence of this tangle of variations rests in the very multiplicity of its perspectives and possible interpretations. We have no easily defined villain here (if such a thing exists), just as we have no hero. And yet, at a certain point in the 19th century, there is a confluence of textual and visual decisions, as the tale is translated into English and illustrated to engage a child audience, which serve, inexorably, to forge a more singular delineation of good and evil. By pulling a broad (and by no means exhaustive) history of the pre–20th century "Rapunzel" variants toward several distinct observations about translation and illustration choices in the

19th century and beyond, I hope to show how seemingly innocuous textual and visual decisions have dramatically shaped how audiences of all ages have come to receive and understand this ubiquitous narrative.

Although there are many surviving (and ever-evolving) literary versions of what has been categorized Type 310, or "The Maiden in the Tower," in the Aarne-Thompson-Uther system of organizing folktales, English speaking audiences generally recognize the elements in the Grimms' "Rapunzel" (from their *Kinder und Haus-Märchen*[1]) more than any other variant. Many readers may be unaware that the Brothers Grimm published multiple editions of their now famous collection or that there are significant differences between the first two-volume edition, first published in 1812/1815 and the seventh, published in 1857. In fact, the differences between the two editions, especially in "Rapunzel," are astonishing. To begin, the writing style veers from "blunt and unpretentious" to increasingly dialogue-driven and explanatory (Zipes, "Rediscovering" xx). Jack Zipes, who recently published the first full English translation of the first edition, notes, "The Grimms had not yet 'vaccinated' or censored them with their sentimental Christianity and puritanical ideology" (xx). Also, there are actual plot differences, exegetical changes that explain problematic scenes or issues, including, most notably, the method of discovering the love affair between Rapunzel and the prince. In the first edition, the *fee* learns of Rapunzel's pregnancy because the girl innocently wonders out loud why her clothes are increasingly tight around her belly. Wilhelm Grimm, the driving force behind the continual purification of the tales, ultimately orchestrates the discovery to occur after Rapunzel asks *frau* Gothel why she is "so much harder to pull up than the young prince. He gets up here in a twinkling" (Grimm, Tatar 60). Ironically, although the discovery scene is cleaned up, Rapunzel still goes on to give birth to twins in all editions of the Grimms' tale. Subsequent editions do not merely give us minor plot and stylistic alterations. There are shifts in language choice, including references to Rapunzel's supernatural kidnapper/surrogate mother. In the first edition, Rapunzel's surrogate is referred to as a *fee* or "fairy," a word that is replaced as early as the second edition of the tale in favor of *Zauberin* and *frau Gothel* as, Zipes argues, is a "gesture of protest against the French occupation and a gesture of solidarity with those people who wanted to forge a unified German nation" (Zipes, "Rediscovering" xxv). Terry Windling concurs: "[T]he Grimms often edited fairies out of their stories, for they considered them too French" (2). The Grimms' editorial decision to alter *fee* to *Zauberin* and *frau Gothel* is only the first step in understanding how seemingly minor textual decisions have radically affected how "Rapunzel" has been received and interpreted. The later translation of these words—*Zauberin* and *frau Gothel*—into English would prove particularly important to the tale's later reception and adaptation.

Of course, these changes may seem subtle compared to the changes the tale has undergone as it has been woven into and out of oral and literary variants. In Zipe's translation of Giambatista Basile's 17th-century Neapolitan version of the tale, "Petrosinella," it is an ogress who demands payment for the parsley-stealing woman's act of thievery, but she doesn't collect the girl until she's seven years old. In spite of Basile's use of the term "ogress," cannibalism is not on the agenda; rather, although the ogress is not especially kind to Petrosinella—she "seiz[ed] her by the hair and took her into a forest where not even the horses of the sun entered because they did not pay to have the right to graze in the shade" (Zipes, *Great Fairy Tale* 476)—she assumes something of a protective role when the biological mother casts the girl aside in impatience. First published in 1634, Basile's version sets the precedent for a Rapunzel who is impregnated by a prince intent on his own acts of thievery. The tale includes a number of other plot elements that test the courage and quick-thinking of its young lovers, including an escape scene in which the ogress' gall nuts, magical objects she uses to keep Rapunzel in the tower, are used against her, ultimately leading to her destruction. Charlotte Rose de la Force's 1697 "Persinette" provides the first literary variant of the tale that most closely resembles the sequence of events popularized through the Grimms' versions, mostly due to the fact that Friedrich Schulz provided a close translation of the tale in his 1790 "Rapunzel." The Grimms used Schulz's version as the primary source for their own retelling, assuming (mistakenly) that Schulz had, himself, called upon German sources. The de la Force/Schulz manifestation of the story elaborates heavily on problematic details in Basile's version, while eliminating much of the bold agency of Basile's lovers. This is a critical turn in the evolution of the tale, where active protagonists constructing their own happy ending are replaced with passive victims who stumble into a fortunate ending, graced by the mercy Persinette's/Rapunzel's former guardian. In these versions, the fierce yet protective ogress is replaced by a fey/fee, who, having taken charge of the girl baby from birth, "wrapped her in sheets of gold and sprinkled her face with some precious water [...] that immediately made her the most beautiful creature in the world [...] took little Persinette to her home and raised her with the utmost care imaginable" (480).

Returning to the Grimms, who purge the florid versions of de la Force and Schulz of much of their exegetical qualities, and certainly strip Rapunzel's tower and living conditions of some comfort and charm, we return to a less nurturing version of Rapunzel's surrogate supernatural mother, who is yet far more complicated than Basile's depiction. De la Force's fairy might be cut from the fabric of Greek tragedy, as we are told she "was fully aware of what fate had in store for [Persinette], [and] she decided to shield her from her destiny" (480). Schulz veers toward the supernatural, the rune-reader, when his fairy "knew that there had been a bad constellation of the stars when

Rapunzel was born, [and] she decided to do all she could to protect the girl" (485). The Grimms' expurgate the specific use of the term "fairy," but, interestingly, they replace it with a name far more fitting to de la Force and Schulz's description. *Zauberin*, the word the Grimms' most often used to describe Rapunzel's surrogate mother, is best translated as "sorceress," an appropriate term for a complex character who might not fit well into more decisive terminology. Although she shows none of the mercy and forgiveness seen at the end of the de la Force/Schulz versions (in fact, after she exacts revenge on Rapunzel and the prince, she disappears altogether), in an echo of those variants she states at Rapunzel's birth, "'You needn't fear about the child's well-being, for I shall take care of it like a mother'" (490). Indeed, the other term the Grimms occasionally use for her is *frau Gothel*, which sometimes goes untranslated in English versions that mistake it for a name. Maria Tatar, in her annotations of her translation of the tale explains, "the term is a generic one in Germany, designating a woman who serves as godmother" (Grimm, Tatar 112).

A *Zauberin* is a figure, which, while associated with sorcery and magic, isn't laden with the connotations (in the 19th century and present day) that we might find with the use of the word "witch." In Friedrich Kluge's seminal 1883 *Etymologisches wörterbuch der deutschen sprache*, we see the stark difference between the two German words *Hexe* and *Zauberin*. *Hexe*, or "witch," which the Grimms use frequently in other tales, has a long association with the occult and the Devil, whereas *Zauberin*, as mentioned above, is far more neutral, describing a practitioner of *Zaubercraft* or magic, one who can read *Runen* or runes (Kluge 307, 875). This seemingly subtle linguistic difference was entirely overlooked by 19th-century translators of the Grimms' collection, who were introducing these tales to an eager English-speaking audience. As early as 1853, Rapunzel's *Zauberin* was conflated with every other reference made to *Hexe*, and, I would argue, mistakenly translated as "witch." This precedent would initiate not only a trend in future translations to use the term "witch," it would irrevocably shape the way story-tellers interpreted, illustrated, and, in general, adapted the tale into the mind-boggling plethora of "Rapunzel" variants available today, not to mention the ways in which English speaking audiences, specifically children, received the tale.

It would be a mistake to place the onus of this trend entirely on a 19th-century translation foible, as illustrations of earlier "Rapunzel" variants, like "Petrosinella," could have served as an influence on future translators and illustrators of the tale. A number of scholars have pointed to the power of illustration to shape our interpretation of texts. Susan R. Gannon argues that "it is clear that the reader's own narrativity is susceptible to the powerful impact of an illustrator's vision," while Ruth B. Bottigheimer asserts that illustrations are capable of multiple functions; they may decorate, interpret, and "may even reformulate the text by supplying information different or absent from the text" (Gannon 90, Bottigheimer 52). Bottigheimer goes on to say, "For the reader who glances at the illustration and even more for the listener whose eyes linger on pictures while someone else reads, the power of pictures to recast the text into memorable images is formidable" (52). Patricia Ciancolo goes so far as to argue that each act of illustrating a fairy tale creates a new variant of that tale, because "[W]hat is expressed is a selective interpretation, an illusion rather than a miniature reality" (98). As early as 1848, George Cruikshank, the well-known illustrator of the work of Charles Dickens and caricature artist for the satirical publication *Punch*, rendered a single illustration for J. E. Taylor's English translation of Basile's *Pentamerone* depicting "Petrosinella," as part of a number of plates for that work. In the illustration, he conveys several scenes in one (and, actually, three tales in one plate), with the biological mother's encounter with the ogress consuming the left half of the frame, the mother gazing longingly out her window at the forbidden garden in the center, and the prince climbing Petrosinella's tresses on the left. What stands out most in this depiction is Cruikshank's ogress, whose head is at least triple the size of the other heads in the picture, and is dominated by an enormous open mouth, full of shark-like teeth. Her eyes are set in a fierce scowl, and, although she is wearing a standard bodice and skirt, like the biological mother, we can see a knife protruding from a pocket in her skirt. She is clutching a walking stick with one hand and with the other she is pointing an accusatory finger at the supplicating figure of the mother. Cruikshank's illustration corresponds directly with a particular interpretation of the term "ogress," based, presumably, on the term's historical implication of cannibalism, and has little to do, as we've seen above, with Basile's depiction of this character. There are no textual cues pointing to this kind of extreme monstrosity, which demonstrates just how powerful illustration is in providing distinct interpretations (even diverging into its own adaptations) of the text.

The first English translation of the Grimms' "Rapunzel," appeared not long after the Taylor/Cruikshank *Pentamerone* in the 1853 *Household Stories*, illustrated by Edward H. Wehnert. Although tales from the Grimms' *KHM* had been translated as early as 1823, Edward Taylor's popular collection (also, incidentally, illustrated by Cruikshank), failed to include "Rapunzel" in any of its many reprints. In Wehnert's *Household Stories*, the translator(s) are not credited, but we see here the first instance of the problematic translation of *Zauberin* that would continue to shape popular reception of the tale, and specifically the interpretive illustrations and other forms of adaptation that would inform our reading of Rapunzel's surrogate. In this translation, the character is referred to as a "Witch [capitalized] who possessed great power, and who was feared by the whole world" (Grimm, Wehnert 81). In spite of M.L Davis' translation of the term as "magician" in the 1855 *Home Stories*, the Wehnert version continued to be churned out, with five additional editions appearing before 1882, when Lucy Crane first translated a collection (which included the tale) illustrated by her husband, famed illustrator Walter Crane, and introduced by John Ruskin. Crane also refers to her as a "witch," one "of great might, and of whom all the world was afraid" (Grimm, Crane 87).

Recent translations by folklorists Jack Zipes, Maria Tatar, and D.L. Ashliman have proven far more sensitive to the subtleties of the original German, and these translations serve, in part, to rectify the problematic choices of the tale's first translators by opting for "enchantress" or "sorceress." In spite of these recent efforts, however, the choice of the word "witch" as a translation for the Grimms' *Zauberin* and *frau Gothel* in these early translations (and in the majority of retellings, which often use these translations as their touchstone) is worth noting, although it is rarely even noticed. Tatar admits, "Some translations of the story into English change the enchantress into a 'witch.' In accordance with the ascendency of the darker versions of the tale, the move from 'fairy' to 'witch' has a certain logic" (Grimm, Tatar 57). Max Lüthi, in his seminal study *Once Upon a Time: On the Nature of Fairy Tales*, is openly dismissive of the choice as he describes the Grimms' editorial changes, stating, "The mistress of the garden and the tower he no longer calls by the good name 'fairy'; he calls her 'a sorceress'; we can safely say 'a witch'" (111). Peter Hunt offers invaluable insight into this issue of translation as he explores the problematic history of children's literature in translation, including, at the forefront of this discussion, the translation of fairy tales. He states: "The situation is complicated by the phenomenon of the 'retelling.' The low literary status of children's books, and their intimate integration into popular culture means that stories are commonly reworked to suit the ideologies of an age, or its image of childhood, and it is not always clear how far translation is involved" (107). We may gather from this that, although it may seem one of the more subtle translation points of the tale, a seemingly simple word choice may be executed deliberately to achieve a particular, desired effect. It is possible, too, that such a word choice might be made quite carelessly, yet still have the power to shape the translations that follow. In this case, the choice, deliberate or not, of the word "witch" sharply delineates the morality of the tale and de-emphasizes any interpretation in which a character's behavior might be portrayed in varying shades of gray. However we might explain or justify this translation choice, many of the subsequent adaptations—whether in the form of additional translations, retellings, spin-offs, illustrations, and animations—incorporate and expand on the darker connotations of the word.

To some extent, these connotations are based on what now seems like common knowledge. We associate the term "witch" with evil, with the "Devil," with stooped forms, and hooked noses speckled with warts. Other tales, especially other Grimms' tales (where, incidentally, the German *Hexe* is almost always the word chosen to describe them), relate instances of attempted cannibalism, as in "Hansel and Gretel," disfiguring spells cast, and sneaking old women luring innocents into the woods or "hover[ing] around pregnant women, waiting for the opportunity to snatch an infant" (Grimm, Tatar 58). Such impressions, now deeply rooted, have formed over many centuries during which, to put it simply, Christianity has paved its path through western civilization partially through the attempted erasure of any lingering remnant of pagan thought or belief. We can trace our current associations back beyond the Grimms, of course, to crazed witch trials conducted by Catholics and Protestants alike from the 15th to the 18th centuries in Europe and America; to the infamous tool of witch-hunters and Inquisitors, the *Malleus Maleficarum*, or "Witch Hammer," of 1487, which was written and used by its German author Heinrich Kramer to not only identify and condemn those who fit the definition of "witches," but also cast suspicion on anyone who didn't subscribe to the notion that such beings existed; to the *Canon Episcopi* of circa 906, which encourages bishops to uproot practitioners of witchcraft; "wicked women perverted by the devil, seduced by illusions and phantasms of demons" (Russell 76) to Biblical sources, including Deuteronomy from the Hebrew Pentateuch (here taken from the *King James Bible*), which dictates, "Here shall not be found among you any one that maketh his son or daughter to pass through the fire, or that useth divination, or an observer of times, or an enchanter, or a witch" (18:10). According to the English translation of Kluge's etymological dictionary, the history of the word *hexe* reflects this troubled journey, at once encompassing both "demon," and "forest woman" (147).

That is not to say "enchantress" or "sorceress" are terms completely free from negative connotations. Certainly, at the apex of witchcraft persecution, these terms might have been used interchangeably; however, as the fervor for this persecution began to die down in the 19th century, these more subtle distinctions could once more be asserted. Kluge's etymology of the term *Zauberin* demonstrates this late 19th-century distinction (as he traces the history of the word's usage), suggesting that the term is associated primarily with the ability to decipher runes and cast enchantments. Whereas a *Hexe* is often defined through what she is and with whom she associates, a *Zauberin* is predominantly defined by her skills. When closely comparing Rapunzel's surrogate with other characters translated into the English as "witch," it is hardly surprising the Grimms make this choice. Opting for *Zauberin* over *Hexe* suggests that the character differs from what we see in other Grimms' tales, the wicked witch, the "hideous old witch [...] with her long claws" (Grimm, Tatar 156), the cannibals with "red eyes [who] cannot see very far; but they have a fine sense of smelling like wild beasts, so that they know when children approach them" (Grimm, Wehnert 74). As Tatar argues, the Grimms' treatment of "Rapunzel" is darker than other earlier variants, and yet this *Zauberin*, for all her moments of seeming cruelty, is yet still much closer to the "fairy" of de la Force and Schultz—who provides the girl with every creature comfort needed—than to any "witch" figure in the Grimms' other tales. She cultivates a garden "filled with the most beautiful flowers and herbs"—a reference (combined with the biological mother's transgression) that recalls the depiction of Eden in Genesis 2 and 3, suggesting our *Zauberin* is more deity than witch (Grimm, Zipes 489). She responds to the husband's plea for mercy, not with violence, but with a deal. Her "anger subsided," she promises, "I will take care of it like a mother" (490). The *Zauberin* of "Rapunzel" does not engage in violence or ill-treatment for its own sake or to directly satisfy her own nefarious desires, at least as far as we can discern, but responds to the transgressions of others, as she perceives them. To begin, it is thievery (as the husband steals the greens), then deception (as Rapunzel fails to mention her lovers' trysts), then violation or, at least, another perceived act of thievery (as the Prince takes Rapunzel's maidenhood or declares her his bride). Considering the plot elements in this way, it is reasonable to wonder who the protagonists and antagonists of this tale truly are.

Blatantly disregarding the Grimms' distinct choice of the word *Zauberin* and choosing to translate the word as "witch" causes a monumental snowball effect that rolls with force all the way to the present day. As mentioned above, Lucy Crane produced the dominant translation of the late 19th century, which was famously illustrated by her husband Walter Crane. Although many other Grimm's collections were published during this time, only a handful included "Rapunzel" in their contents. The Cranes' version, which included the tale, went through ten editions between 1882 and 1920 with Hurst and Co., and Crane's illustrations were included in a number of other collections produced by different publishers. Although Lucy Crane translates *Zauberin* as "witch," at first glance, Walter Crane does not seem to emphasize this aspect of the tale. Rather, his centerpiece for the tale depicts the King's son climbing Rapunzel's tresses as they gaze intently into each other's eyes. There is a nagging insistence, however, in the seemingly de-emphasized portions of Crane's illustrations. His headpiece and historiated initial[2] both depict a scowling, hook nosed woman, and in the historiated initial we see her pointing a long fingernail at the backside of the trespassing husband as he clambers over her wall. The headpiece shows her clutching a pair of shears while also being framed by a giant pair of shears, and the frame of the centerpiece woodblock contains two symmetrically placed circles with scissors frozen mid-snip on a wavy lock of hair. Not only does the depiction of the scissor-wielding woman conform to stereotypes of how a witch ought to look, the extraordinary repetition of the image of scissors emphasizes the most vicious scene of interaction between Rapunzel and her guardian. If Crane's witch seems subtly stereotypical, Arthur Rackham's 1909 illustration of Mrs. Edgar Lucas' translation dispels with a good portion of that subtlety. Lucas not only uses the word "witch" in her translation, she chooses to capitalize the word (thus calling special attention to it), describing her as a "powerful Witch, who was feared by everybody" (Grimm, Lucas 80). Rackham, whose illustrations are notoriously full of dark, twisted villains with bulbous eyes, builds on Lucas' translation by depicting Rapunzel's guardian prominently in both of his color plate illustrations. In one, we see her lurking around the corner of her garden wall, spying on the husband in his act of thievery. She is a stooped figure in a dark, hooded cloak, which casts a shadow over hooked nose and lined face. The intensity of Rackham's witch is in her eyes, the pupils of which are rolled up so far that only the whites glare at the viewer, as well as her claw-like hands, which are extended out toward the viewer like a wild animal ready to pounce.

Danish illustrator Kay Nielsen offers, perhaps, the most visually dramatic interpretation of the witch in his single black and white illustration of the tale, found in a 1925 collection of Grimms' tales. Nielsen's witch fully embraces the monstrous and demonic angle of the witch stereotype. Choosing to illustrate the intense moment when the *Zauberin* "seized Rapunzel's beautiful hair, wrapped it around her left hand several times, grabbed a pair of scissors with her right. *Snip snap* went the scissors, and the beautiful tresses fell to the ground," Nielsen completes his gruesome image of the witch by rendering her as barely humanoid (Grimm, Tatar 60–61). She stands on two feet and clutches Rapunzel's hair with two hands, but Nielsen's witch is a conglomeration of animals—a pointed beak like a crow, elbows and legs spiked like a horned toad, and hair like snakes—all long associated with witches. The illustration emphasizes the distinction between the lithe and innocent Rapunzel, clad in a flowery gown with her hands flung above her head in surrender and the pouncing, pointed figure of the witch. Nielsen's witch is clearly not a nurturer, shows no mercy, and is purely monstrous. Few illustrations are as extreme as Nielsen's, but, I would argue, fueled, in part, by the problematic translation of *Zauberin* as "witch," many emphasize qualities associated with this term while de-emphasizing the more humane aspects of the character we see in the Grimms' text.

In his 1997 illustration depicting the witch climbing Rapunzel's blonde braid, the viewer looks down on P.J. Lynch's witch with dread (even as Rapunzel seems nonplussed by the sight), her boney feet clawing at the stone face of the tower, her monstrous, Golum-like face set in a snarling grimace, and mysterious bags of food or, perhaps, potions, hanging from her shoulders. Similarly, Julia Noonan's witch from illustrations in the 1997 collection *Classic Grimm's Fairy Tales*, her head wrapped in a turban-like headpiece, seems to howl in rage as she uses her sharp-nailed fingers to cut a lock of hair with giant scissors, her brow furrowed, her hooked nose red, her open mouth filled with fierce, jagged teeth. So too, the witch in Francesca Rossi's 2015

Rapunzel: A Fairy Tale Adventure, looks as though it might have been adapted from Noonan's, as she wears a white turban and clutches, not a giant set of shears, but a scimitar. Finally, Jeffrey Stewart Timmins' witch in Stephanie True Peters' 2009 graphic novel adaptation of the tale is, like Nielsen's witch, barely humanoid. Without any discernible gender, the round, hunched figure slouches through Timmins' frames with bulging white eyes and tufts of white hair poking out of either side of its head, which is adorned with a pointed carrot-shaped nose and a gaping, jagged-toothed mouth. Timmins, like Nielsen, draws a sharp contrast between this forbidding creature and the infantilized characters of the biological parents, Rapunzel, and the prince, who all possess abnormally large heads and wide-set child-like eyes and features.

Pointed, black hats, symbols of stars and moons on ragged cloaks, and hooked noses with scowling eyebrows are common choices made in illustrations as early as Anne Anderson's 1935 rendition of the tale, found in the collection *Old, Old Tales*. Anderson provides only two color illustrations for the tale, but she chooses to focus both on her witch. In the first, the witch is the only figure fully in frame, an old woman with a hooked nose, pointed hat and ragged red cloak climbing the hair of a Rapunzel whose head is out of frame. In the second, the witch is again at the center of the action, with Rapunzel's head and the heads of the prince and his horse barely visible in the far corners. One of Susan Suba's illustrations for the "Rapunzel" collected in the 1959 *Favorite Fairy Tales Told in Germany* focuses on the same scene of the ascending witch, although her witch dons striped tights in addition to the stereotypical pointed hat. Suba's second witch illustration is menacing and shows her hanging out of the tower window, a grimace on her face, holding Rapunzel's cut braids for the Prince to ascend. This version of the witch is almost identical in appearance and expression to Suba's witch from "Hansel and Gretel," showing that, at least in this particular collection and set of illustrations, no real distinction is being made between that cannibalistic, child-abusing *Hexe* and the *Zauberin* or *frau Gothel* who raises Rapunzel.

Old women with hooked noses dressed in pointed hats and some combination of striped tights or curled, clog-like shoes ascending Rapunzel's ladder of hair continue to form the focus of "Rapunzel" illustrations up to the present day. In Tracy Arah Dockray's 1997 collection *Grimm's Grimmest*, the ever-popular ascending witch is depicted with striped tights and a half moon perched on her pointed hat, whereas Julia Downing's witch ascends the tower in her striped tights, curled-toe boots, and pointed bonnet gripping Rapunzel's braid with long green fingernails in the 2005 *First Book of Fairy* Tales. Sarah Gibb's 2011 opus pays homage to Rackham's style by depicting a number of scenes in silhouette. The silhouettes of the witch call attention to her stooped figure, propped up by a twisted cane, her hair (as in Sansom's illustrations) and shawl flying up around her head. A raven, presumably her familiar, is also perched on the child's crib, mimicking the accusatory body language of the witch silhouette.

Whilst there are illustrators who depict the "witch" of their respective retellings sympathetically, these versions constitute an extreme minority. The colorful pastels of Bernadette Watts' 1975 "Rapunzel," for example, feature a white-haired, elderly witch who wears bright robes and a handkerchief tied over her head. Even as she brandishes a pair of small scissors in the direction of Rapunzel (we aren't shown the actual act of cutting), she continues to look like a kindly grandmother. In one frame, she is grasping a basket and appears to be instructing Rapunzel in the art of gardening. In her 1982 *Rapunzel*, Trina Schart Hyman also portrays her kindly witch in a scene of instruction, with a skein of yarn wrapped around her hands, sitting above a rapt-faced Rapunzel who is balling the yarn the witch is feeding her in a kind of reversal of the oft-seen tower-ascending witch scene. Hyman's illustrations are characterized by muted browns and greens, emphasizing the connection of her witch and Rapunzel to their forest environment. Finally, in Carol Heyer's 1992 *Rapunzel*, we see a woman, not benign and instructive as in the Hyman and Watts versions, but more like a Miss Haversham figure, once potentially beautiful in her purple satin ball gown, but driven wild and mad, her long, wavy black hair streaked with gray and disheveled. She is fierce, and Heyer does not shy away from depicting a close-up of her wrinkled and scowling eyes, yet the illustrative hints to her former beauty suggest a more complicated backstory. Other illustrations portraying a more humane and sympathetic *Zauberin* do so with the more accurate translation of "sorceress." Paul O. Zelinsky's 1997 *Rapunzel* strikes a ferocious pose as she catches Rapunzel's father in his act of thievery, but looks on the new infant lovingly as she carries the child away from its distraught parents. A later scene shows Zelinsky's sorceress, clad in a simple black robe and nun-like headpiece, sitting on stone wall on an Italianate hillside (complete with Roman ruins) and watching the young Rapunzel skip about in delight. Zelinsky, by his own admission, deliberately melds the Grimms' storyline with elements from Basile and de la Force, including an elaborately decorated tower in which Rapunzel is generously nurtured. Although these versions, which treat the figure of the Grimms' *Zauberin* as the more complicated figure she undoubtedly is, have been well-received, they are not only fairly recent additions to the conversation surrounding this tale, they are, as stated above, in the extreme minority.

While problematic translation choices certainly play a role in the illustration history of "Rapunzel," the fact that there is no true consistency in the use of the term "witch" as the translation for the Grimms' *Zauberin* and *frau Gothel* suggests that it is not solely the early translators of the text who are influencing the ways in which this figure is depicted and, ultimately received and interpreted. An overwhelming majority of authors retelling the tale (often retelling an unspecified translation) and the illustrators themselves (even working with the more precise translation "sorceress" or "enchantress") are offering interpretations of Rapunzel's guardian that actively work against the multivalent qualities of text. Although the Grimms' character is undoubtedly more harsh, less nurturing, and possibly less complex than Charlotte de la Force's *fey* or Friedrich Schultz's *fee*, there are very few adaptations that call attention, whether through exegesis, or, more commonly, illustration, to the fact that even the Grimms' *Zauberin* is more surrogate than jailer. The *Zauberin's* magical abilities, too, are, as we have seen, relegated to easy, stereotypical symbols of magic, like stars, crescent moons, and pointed hats. Laura J. Getty's thoroughly-researched and insightful piece, "Maidens and Their Guardians: Reinterpreting the 'Rapunzel' Tale," expands, in part, on the problematic issues posed by variants catalogued under this tale type, although her argument mostly centers around the interpretation of the earlier Mediterranean and French variants. Whilst she does not take particular issue with the problematic translation of *Zauberin*, offhandedly mentioning that "Wilhelm now calls the fairy a sorceress; later she would be called a witch," she does "question the very definition of a hero in a magic tale," and argues that "the fairy/ogress does a great deal more than oppose the maiden in 'The Maiden in the Tower'" variants (Getty). Ultimately, she is arguing that "this type of villain represents a different kind of threat" and encourages us to reexamine the distinctly female elements that employing a female hero in opposition to a female villain suggest (Getty). She further expands on this by pointing out:

> The beginning of the story, with its tie to original sin, makes the mother of the maiden a sinner [because of her thievery of the forbidden lettuce], and the loss of her child to the fairy/ogress a kind of punishment. The themes that run through the tale, focusing as it does on such issues as pregnancy, loss of innocence, and marriage, all relate to Christian attitudes toward proper/improper female behavior [Getty].

Getty makes a pronounced distinction between the symbolism of the fairy/ogress in Mediterranean variants, French variants, and German variants, concluding that, while the fairy/ogress might represent a nun in a convent, sequestering the girl away from her family and the prying eyes of men until she has reached a proper point of maturation, the Grimms' dismissal of the *Zauberin* figure (which she, at this point, has also willingly aligned with the term "witch"), indeed, the disappearance of the guardian after an escape has been made, reflects 19th-century German misogyny. That is, this "demonization of the fairy/ogress explains the limitations of her power in the Grimms' version, as well as why the wounds that she inflicts can be healed without her cooperation" (Getty).

Although Getty makes a compelling argument here, I don't think we can so easily dismiss the complexities that persist in the Grimms' variants of the tale. The Grimms offer versions of the tale in which the guardian figure is still significantly more invested in the act of mothering than we might expect given the common translation of "witch," yet the problematic translation issues coupled with a long legacy of illustrations that play into common stereotypes associated with those translation issues work to draw sharp lines between perceived protagonist and antagonist, between hero and villain. We also cannot dismiss the influence of intertextual assumptions in shaping our expectations of a tale. This is a fairy tale. It is common to anticipate clearly delineated characters, bifurcated by oversimplified moral lines. But as Elizabeth Wanning Harries argues, we "mistakenly expect fairy tales to be short and simple," to be concise and not "indulge in psychological exploration," but, she points out, "this paradigm is not typical of all fairy tales" (12). The possibilities for "psychological exploration" in any of the Grimms' variants of "Rapunzel" are numerous, and yet, rather than opening up the conversation, the translation and illustration choices discussed above invariably lock down interpretation to an alarming degree. When we take a second look at the Grimms' versions of the tale, I believe we cannot help but be aware of this. In every single English illustrated retelling, the biological parents are illustrated in a state of victimhood, completely de-emphasizing their transgression against the supernatural figure, not to mention the horrifying deal they are willing to forge. And yet it is neither the father nor the mother, with her unreasonable cravings, who are translated and illustrated as monstrous, it is the supernatural figure. The prince commits a gross act of deception by disguising himself as Rapunzel's guardian in order to climb Rapunzel's hair and enter her chamber (both literally and metaphorically) and yet he, too, is not rendered monstrous for these transgressions. The supernatural surrogate, on the other hand, demands payment (albeit a proportionally large payment) as recompense for a transgression that is justifiably punishable in all cultures in which this story is retold. In all variants, the form of this repayment, the child, is cared for in varying states of luxury, not even the least of which deprive her of her ability to grow and live. And yet Rapunzel herself, the often-cast victimized hero of the tale is universally willing to abandon her surrogate in favor of one of the key transgressors. Although she and her prince suffer for this final act of transgression, they are always ultimately rewarded for their pains. I would argue that even the Grimms' descriptions, although not as sympathetic as the earlier de la Force and Schulz variants, encourage their reader (who would have been thought to be primarily adult for the first edition and a mixed audience of child and adult alike in subsequent editions) to resist easy categorization and bifurcation. In the end, however, through seemingly innocuous yet problematic translations and a century and a half of mostly demonizing illustrations of the supernatural surrogate, the reader is encouraged to resist these easy categorizations. As the tale, in its many translations, retellings, adaptations through illustration (and even animations, which I have chosen not to address here) has woven its way firmly into the fabric of children's literature, into the sphere of the child and our constructions of how we encourage children to perceive the world, we must consider the impact of such seemingly inconsequential adaptation choices. As Peter Hunt argues, "All books for children reflect changing perceptions of what childhood is and should be; indeed, to have translations 'for children,' there had to be a recognizable concept of childhood, which scarcely existed until the 18th century" (108). Riita Oittinen adds to our understanding of this issue by positing, "Anything we create for children—whether writing, illustrating, or translating—reflects […] our respect or disrespect for childhood" (15). Donna Jo Napoli addresses this troubling trend in treatment of the "Rapunzel" tale, not in literary criticism but in her own fictionalized adaptation of the tale. In *Zell* she is able to give flight to a form of exegesis and interpretation which, still using the Grimms' version as a touchstone, offers a more balanced perspective, by, in fact, giving equal license to the multiple perspectives of the surrogate, Rapunzel, and the prince. Writers like Napoli and illustrators like Zelinsky, Hyman, and Watts who endeavor to reclaim what has been obfuscated in English retellings of the Grimms' original German versions (not to mention the many other variants of "Maiden in the Tower" that have fallen into obscurity in the wake the Grimms' success) have begun the interesting, and I believe important, process of re-inscribing new interpretations for current readers.

NOTES

   1. *Kinder und Haus-Märchen* is the original German title for *Grimms' Children's and Household Tales.*
   2. A headpiece is an illustration found in the blank space at the start of a chapter. A historiated initial is a decorated letter that is larger than the rest of the text. It is sometimes rendered so elaborate as to include figures as well as decorative objects, as in the case of Walter Crane's "T" which is mirrored in the shape of the husband climbing over the wall of the forbidden garden.

WORKS CITED

Anderson, Anne. "Rapunzel." *Old, Old Fairy Tales.* Illus. Anne Anderson. Racine: Whitman, 1935. Print.
Bottigheimer, Ruth B. "Iconographic Continuity in Illustrations 'The Goosegirl.'" *Children's Literature: Annual of the Modern Language Association Division* 13 (1985). Print.
Ciancolo, Patricia Jean. *Picture Books for Children.* Chicago: American Library Association, 1973. Print.
Gannon, Susan R. "The Illustrator As Interpreter: N. C. Wyeth's Illustrations for the Adventure Novels of Robert Louis Stevenson." *Children's Literature* 19.1 (1991): 90–106. Print.
Getty, Laura J. "Maidens and Their Guardians: Reinterpreting the 'Rapunzel' Tale." *Mosaic: A Journal for the Interdisciplinary Study of Literature* 30.2: 37–52. Proquest. Web. 29 Nov. 2015.
Grimm, Jacob, and Wilhelm. *The Annotated Brothers Grimm.* Trans. Maria Tatar. Ed. Maria Tatar. New York: W.W. Norton, 2004. Print.

_____. *Fairy Tales of the Brothers Grimm.* Trans. Mrs. Edgar Lucas. Illus. Arthur Rackham. New York: Doubleday, Page, 1909. Print.
_____. *Grimm's Fairy Tales.* Trans. Lucy Crane. Illus. Walter Crane. New York: Hurst & Co., 1882. Print.
_____. *Household Stories.* Newly Translated. Illus. Edward H. Wehnert. Vol. 1. London: Addey and Co., 1853. Print.
Harries, Elizabeth Wanning. *Twice Upon a Time: Women Writers and the History of the Fairy Tale.* Princeton: Princeton University Press, 2001. Print.
Henrickson, Linnea. "The View from Rapunzel's Tower." *Children's Literature in Education.* 31.4 (2000): 209–23. Print.
Hunt, Peter. "Children's Literature." *The Oxford Guide to Literature in English Translation,* ed. Peter France. Oxford: Oxford University Press, 2000. Print.
King James Bible. Project Gutenberg, 2d version, 10th ed. Champaign, IL: Project Gutenberg, n.d. Web.
Kluge, Friedrich. *Etymologisches Wörterbuch der Deutschen Sprache.* Hawthorne: De Gruyter, 2013. Ebook Library. Web. 4 Mar. 2016.
Kluge, Friedrich, and John Francis Davis. *An Etymological Dictionary of the German Language.* London: G. Bell, 1891. Print.
Lüthi, Max. *Once Upon a Time: On the Nature of Fairy Tales.* Bloomington: Indiana University Press, 1976. Print.
Oittinen, Rita. *I Am Me—I Am Other: On the Dialogics of Translating for Children.* Tampere: University of Tampere, 1993. Print.
Russell, Jeffrey Burton. *Witchcraft in the Middle Ages.* Ithaca: Cornell University Press, 1972. Print.
Windling, Terry. "Rapunzel, Rapunzel Let Down Your Hair." *Journal of Mythic Arts* 20 (2007). Dec. 2015. Web. 4 Mar. 2016.
Zipes, Jack, ed. *The Great Fairy Tale Tradition: From Straparola and Basile to the Brothers Grimm.* New York: W.W. Norton, 2001. Print.
_____. "Rediscovering the Original Tales of the Brothers Grimm." Introduction. *The Original Folk and Fairy Tales of the Brothers Grimm: The Complete First Edition,* ed. Jack Zipes, trans. Jack Zipes. By Jacob Grimm and Wilhelm Grimm. Princeton: Princeton University Press, 2014. xix–xliii. Print.

Swimming with Serpents
Dismantling Boundaries in Sea Monsters Picture Books

Rebecca A. Brown

In his discussion of Olaus Magnus' *Carta Marina* (1539), "a nine-sheet" chart which illustrates "northwestern Europe" (Van Duzer 81), Joseph Nigg offers an insightful observation that artistically links sea serpents to children's literature. For contemporary viewers, he claims, "the quaint figures rising in the northern waters of Olaus' map of Scandinavia could be illustrations in a children's book" (8). Nigg refers to a menagerie of marvelous creatures, such as sea pig, a crustacean, at least one serpentine beast, and several others, swimming in the Norwegian Sea. Their ferocious features—tusks, teeth, and claws—are tempered by their rounded bodies, playfully rendered in shades of green, gray, brown, yellow, and pink. They do not resemble the horror film monsters that haunt our cultural imagination, such as Godzilla or Jaws, even though the map depicts their malevolence towards ships and sailors. As Nigg may also allude to, and in tangent with ideas Sherrie Lynne Lyons has explored, "sea monsters defied easy categorization and transgressed the boundaries between the natural and supernatural, the real and the imaginary" (22). Thus Magnus' charming, animalistic creatures bear an especially strong connection with children's literature, especially since youngsters' expansive imaginations often easily elide boundaries between the fictional and factual.

Following on from Nigg's discerning statement, in this essay I examine three sea monster picture books: Lois and Louis Darling's *The Sea Serpents Around Us* (1965), Bill Peet's *Cyrus the Sea Serpent* (1975), and Chris Wormell's *The Sea Monster* (2005). The Darlings' work provides a history of sea serpents from a monster's perspective; in contrast, Peet's and Wormell's texts narrate suspenseful stories involving these creatures and humans. I analyze the ways that the author-illustrators reframe artistic and sociohistorically resonant sea serpents tropes from earlier periods, thereby creating benevolent beasts that use their physical and intellectual otherness to help humans rather than to frighten or destroy them. As a result, the monsters in these books implicitly provide young readers with models for dismantling social boundaries between themselves and the "Other." This skill is especially valuable in cultures where young citizens' socialization and exposure to diversity often begins early in life.

Marking Boundaries, Transgressing Boundaries

My use of the terms "sea serpent" and "sea monster" throughout this essay engages with a range of etymological and semantic connotations. "Sea serpent" may conjure the image of an overwhelmingly long aquatic snake whose elusiveness confounds scientists and sailors. Moreover, serpent, due to its biblical and mythic allusions, suggests wickedness and/or sin. "Sea monster" insinuates these associations and others. The word "monster" derives from the Latin monstrum, meaning "divine omen, portent, sign; abnormal shape"; it is "from [the] root of monere" meaning "warn" ("Monster"). Since the monstrous body is non-normative, frequently evincing aberrations in size and shape, monsters' physiques, alongside their behaviors, always disrupt or defy boundaries.[1] Thus, expanding on Lyons' remarks, the term sea monster invites us to imagine a hybrid creature—perhaps equal parts dragon, dinosaur, and serpent—of gargantuan size. Depending on the culture and text, sea monsters may warn of impending destruction or commit violence towards men, women, children, ships, and/or towns, cities. Throughout this essay I often use these two terms synonymously; however, I also employ these words more precisely to highlight the nuances of the illustrated creatures I investigate.

A brief overview of Medieval and Renaissance cartography as well as the 19th-century sea monster crazes reveals other reasons why these aquatic creatures are a compelling subject for children's picture books. Returning briefly to Magnus' *Carta Marina*, Nigg implies that while we may associate the chart's beasts with fairytales or perhaps Mercer Mayer picture books, Magnus' contemporaries would have interpreted them as signifiers of the horrifying unfamiliar. He explains, "The chart's giant lobster gripping a swimmer in its claws, a monster being mistaken for an island, and a mast-high serpent devouring sailors would have represented actual fears of the unknown deep" (8). Even as Columbus and his contemporaries began to re-map the world, suspicions about monsters in the sea and monstrous races on land persisted (Wright 3–7). The creatures Nigg addresses illuminate some of these fears. For instance, the lobster and monster "mistaken for an island" underscore the gargantuan aspects of monstrosity, which threaten to dwarf and delude humans. The crustacean and serpent also affirm the destruction conventionally associated with monsters, since the former entraps a swimmer and the latter invades a vessel with humans on it. As Nigg's remarks imply, sea serpents on maps "warned," in the etymological sense of the word monster; they marked uncharted regions, potentially "discourag[ing] ... exploration" (Van Duzer 13). Moreover, they symbolically represented universal fears of the sea that Matt Kaplan identifies, including drowning (80).

Chet Van Duzer offers another perspective about sea serpents that Nigg alludes to when he claims maps "provide glimpses of our understanding of the world at any point in time" (8). Van Duzer maintains, "One subtle and undiscussed effect of the representation of sea monsters on maps is the empowerment of the viewer: the cartographer reveals on the surface of the waters creatures which are normally concealed in the depths, allowing the viewer to participate in a privileged and supernatural view of the world. The monsters represent the revelation of hidden knowledge" (12). Sea monsters often functioned as commodities on Renaissance navigational maps; they were "decorative elements" commissioned by patrons or placed on the charts by the map-maker him/herself (Van Duzer 10–12). Despite their monetary value and the nautical warnings they offered, Van Duzer links these creatures to "an increased general interest in wonders and marvels" during this period (12). As he states, "The more exotic the creature depicted, the better; and the study of both maps and images of exotic creatures was thought to sharpen the intellect and [to] be educational [for the reader]" (12).

Despite their artistic and educational appeal, sea monsters' appearances on charts waned in the 17th century and became virtually obsolete by the 18th century for at least three reasons: there was "a general decline in interest in marvels and wonders" (Van Duzer 118), "nautical technology improved ... and human confidence in achieving dominion over the seas increased" (Van Duzer 119). Nonetheless sightings continued throughout these years, culminating in the 19th-century "sea serpent crazes," which channeled these monsters into a non-cartographic visual medium (2). As Paula A. Rotschafer explains, the renowned Gloucester, Massachusetts sea serpent(s) beginning in 1817, the *Daedalus* ship's sightings of a monster near the coast of South Africa in 1848, as well as less renowned viewings, spawned a market/platform for natural scientists, sailors, and the general public to see sea serpents and also to study them (3). Rotschafer argues that the prevalence of aquatic serpent "illustrations" in print sources created a fascinating phenomenon: "It is not only that people saw serpents that looked like serpents they had seen in pictures, but that the pictures offered a kind of template on which viewers could inscribe particular historical fears" (2).

Like the Medieval and Renaissance creatures on maps, sea serpents within 19th-century print culture still represented the unknown and terrifying, despite technological and imperial progress, but they gained a more politicized context. As Rotschafer contends, "The sea serpent motif could be adapted to different threats to social stability, whether those threats came from scientific theories about evolution or from secessionists" or the broader cultural climate of the U.S. (4–5). Overall, one might suggest that when sea serpents became familiar figures for the American and British public in print culture, their menace was at least slightly abated. They were visually and verbally manipulated to suit the needs of money-seekers, experts hoping to advance their professions, and those more generally seeking fame.

Ultimately, sea serpents resemble other monsters due to their non-normative bodies and behaviors as well as their commodity value; for these reasons and others, they find a welcome home within children's picture books. Similar to cartographers and savvy newspaper editors seeking to make a profit, children's artists as disparate as Virginia Kahl (*How Do You Hide a Monster?* [1971]) and M.T. Anderson and Bagram Ibatoulline (*The Serpent Came to Gloucester* [2005]) may use these creatures to sell their works. Beyond this publishing reality, the author-illustrators I discuss harness the sea serpent's body as a symbolic representation of the unknown, cultural fears, and child-centered themes, like cooperation and valuing otherness. In this respect, they reinforce Van Duzer's claim: knowledge gleaned from the monstrous body is knowledge gained. I begin my picture book analysis, then, with Darling's book, *The Sea Serpents Around Us* (1965), since it most explicitly interacts with the sociohistorical context and tropes I provide in this section.

Cold War Sea Serpents

The Sea Serpents Around Us capitalizes on its long, narrow physical shape to depict its subject. The illustrated serpents are consistently unframed and given expansive range to lay, cavort, swim, and sprawl from verso to recto, defying the gutter as a boundary between the sides of the double-page spreads. As Perry Nodelman suggests, "in narrower [picture] books ... there is less opportunity for depicting setting and, as a result, greater concentration on and closer empathy with the characters depicted" (46). Although the Darlings portray aquatic settings on several pages, the sea serpents are almost always foregrounded. This focus on character type and readerly identification may initially seem antithetical to the book's cool color palette of blacks, whites, and greys.[2] Nonetheless, through the narratorial voice of a sea serpent the Darlings establish empathy between the child and the "Other," suggesting that youngsters who gain knowledge about sea monsters can help preserve them and by extension, contribute to the improvement of a Cold War world.

The Sea Serpents Around Us begins by inverting conventional beliefs about sea serpents. In the preface, "The Story of How This Book Came to Be Written," the authors relay that one day when they were out sailing, a serpentine creature approached their boat. The beast explains why his brethren "cut ... [themselves] off from *Homo sapiens*": humans became too destructive; the monsters, who were merely "attempt[ing] to be friendly," were nearly eradicated due to their physical differences and presumed violence (vi; italics Darlings'). By emphasizing humans as aggressors, the Darlings allude to the aforementioned Gloucester sightings and others, such as Rio Bay (South America) in February of 1958, where the police "opened fire on the poor beast" (Heuvelmans 503–04), thereby becoming monstrous themselves. Yet, the authors also issue a veiled connection to the Cold War, a period of repressive, nuclear fear and violence directed at an othered threat (outside its borders, Soviet, Korean, and within its own borders, Communists, African Americans, and Hispanics). The monster's words channel timely fears of the non-normative and humans' unthinkingly violent actions towards the "Other." This opening foreshadows that the Darlings will capsize readerly expectations about people and sea serpents throughout their work, in an effort to stimulate the child reader's morality and imagination.

Following on from this opening statement, the serpent emphasizes children's important role in altering human knowledge and actions. He tells the author-illustrators, "We want you, with our help, to write a short description of sea serpents. The book will explain our true natures and explode forever the myth that we are dangerous to mankind!" (vii). "Explode," with its contemporary associations of war and atomic power, suggests a potent, forceful eradication of lies and in its place, the proffering of truth. Within the book's context, though, the verb has restorative rather than destructive connotations. This emphasis implies that the book's audience should be primarily children, and the Darlings' subsequent remarks reinforce this idea: "The old sea serpent knows full well that the hope and future of his kind lie in the hands of children now quite young. This is why he especially asked us to direct this book to them" (ix). Amy Ogata has explored the social value of creativity within Cold War children's culture. As she explains, "the creative child was a source of authentic imagination and insight and the regenerative answer to some of the many anxieties of postwar culture" (xvi). Her words echo with messages in the Darlings' book, that since youngsters are less judgmental, more open-minded than adults, and, by extension, more innately imaginative, they are in a unique position to understand and potentially save larger, old beings (in Ogata's analysis, adults, in the Darlings' book, sea serpents).

To reinforce the child's central role in understanding the "Other," the book continues with a white page bearing the title "The Sea Serpent's Story," the narrator's voice announcing, "Nobody believes in sea serpents much nowadays, especially adults—although a few do" (1). No illustration appears.

This artistic choice implies an association between lack of belief and lack of visibility, which is central to the book's subject. The homonyms see/sea underscore the idea that these monsters can be "seen" in the sea, but that they remain unseen by most land-locked humans, particularly those seeking corporeal proof of their existence. In short, "nobody believes in sea serpents much nowadays," and the accompanying white space relegate these creatures to the realm of mythology, folklore, and legend, privileging instead, a rational, adult, unimaginative view of the world.

However, the following double-page spread provides a written counterpoint to this perspective: paleontologists are among the few adults who place faith in sea monsters (2–3). Here, the authors temper disbelief with an area of study that, although "an inexact science" (Parsons xii), often relies on concrete evidence. They emphasize a scientific theory originating in the Victorian era and upheld by certain proponents in the 20th century: that sea serpents are descendents of the "*Ichthyosaurus* (fish-lizard)" and "*Plesiosaurus* (almost-lizard)" (Lyons 18; italics Lyons'). On the recto, above "Paleontologists," the Darlings illustrate the word's meaning by depicting a curious, plant-eating brontosaurs.[3] On the following double-page spread, the authors define the word paleontologist while the dinosaur's body stretches across it, above the words; the creature's tail continues onto the following page in this series. Words and images collude to illustrate the paleontologist's object of study, to bring the distant past back to life, and to additionally foreshadow that dinosaurs' enormous, spatially defiant bodies will parallel their supposed contemporary cousins, sea monsters.

Next, the narrator re-emphasizes adults' lack of belief in sea monsters, and then addresses the diversity and prevalence of these beasts in the world. Eleven sea serpents parade across a double-page spread, four violating the gutter with their bodies or necks. They resemble traditional dragons, dinosaur-like creatures, and even enormous snakes. Most of these gigantic, sharp clawed figures look directly at the reader, as if to say, "Here is definitive proof we exist." The double-page spread implies that much as there are different types of humans throughout the world, there is, likewise, an assortment of sea monsters within the Earth's waters. This idea has resonance with the book's color scheme. Nodelman maintains, "we commonly associate black and white with uncompromising truth" (67) and that there is a "documentary quality of certain sorts of black-and-white depictions—our faith [is] that they show us the real, unvarnished truth" (68). The narrator explicitly reinforces the idea of "unvarnished truth" when he states, "It just goes to show how dull people can be, because the truth is that there are still *thousands* of" sea serpents (11; italics Darlings'). The word "dull" ambiguously alludes to both people's "stupidity" as well as their lack of "imagination." Taken within the context of the previous double-page spread's assertion that even sailors no longer believe in these aquatic creatures, the words and image reinforce the idea that a creative, unbounded child's mind provides an anathema for the adult's overly constrained rational one.

Over the next twenty-two pages, the Darlings further develop these ideas by introducing the Loch Ness Monster. Stretched from verso and recto, the renowned creature is portrayed as sinuously long, pleasantly curved, scaley, and finned; she stares provocatively at the reader with her black, bulbous eyes. As Constance Whyte explores, people lucky enough to witness Nessie's appearances described her "head and neck" as "'like a serpent's head'; 'like a turtle's head'; 'like a bird in the water'; 'like a huge swan'; 'like a horse's head on a long neck…'" (92). While testimony (oral and written) is fluid, the Darlings fix the image of Nessie, offering a visual representation for children to invest in. Rather than stunting youngsters' imaginative process, the subsequent merging of visceral information about the sea serpent with fictional information parallels the dual terrain these creatures have always inhabited (real and mythical, as Lyons suggests). This amalgamation additionally illustrates why sea monsters are such a dynamic subject for picture books.

Barbara Bader writes, "As an art form … [a picture book] hinges on the interdependence of pictures and words, on the simultaneous display of two facing pages, and on the drama of the turning of the page" (n. pag.). The idea that this genre renders texts and images concurrently visible dramatizes the seen/unseen issue at the heart of sea serpent sightings. Because picture books bridge gaps between verbal and visual symbols, they are a medium which can provide pictorial testimony or proof to authors' words about sea monsters. For instance, the narrator discusses Mrs. Patrick Wall who "while diving with both aqualung and snorkel, saw Nessie from underneath!" and "made a discovery of the utmost importance to science but almost beyond belief" (26–27). These words are not illustrated; however, the next ones are: "Below the water line Nessie proved to be—TARTAN!" (28–29). The double-page spread shows Nessie's serpentine body under water, encased in plaid, alongside the tiny swimmer (Mrs. Patrick Wall). Much as Van Duzer addresses the idea that monsters on maps reveal hidden knowledge, the Darlings use the same method, showing a view from beneath the water that is whimsical (a sea serpent's version of clothing) and thought-provoking (Nessie's nationality may be encoded within her body). The merging of visceral and fictional details bolsters empathy with the child reader, and, at the same time, provides the youngster with a lesson in critical thinking. Unlike people who witnessed Nessie's appearances, the child reader can separate the "real" facts from the fictional ones, while still "seeing" the monster.

The remainder of the Darlings' book maps the wealth and diversity of sea monsters throughout the world, eliding temporal boundaries while linking geographical spaces. For instance, on one recto, the authors discuss the

Skrimsl, from Iceland, and the Lau, from Africa (54). Of the former Whyte explains, "Tales of an animal similar to the Loch Ness Monster were collected in Iceland by Rev. S. Baring-Gould who visited that country as a young man in the summer of 1861" (146). She indicates that descriptions of this creature may date back as far as 1345, but that "the fishermen of the tiny island of Grimsey, off the north coast of Iceland, believe that similar creatures occasionally come ashore there from the sea" (Whyte 149). The Lau in Lake Victoria also resembles Nessie, and testimony spans both past and present: "Known at first from native reports only ... [the monster] has been seen more recently by ships' officers, travellers [sic] and explorers. During and after World War II soldiers returning from East Africa to Fort George near Inverness brought stories of it" (Whyte 151). On the same page, the narrator additionally mentions two of the most famous Canadian sea monsters, the Ogopogo and Caddy (Cadborosaurus) (54), both of whom have origins in First Nations' legends (Garner 40–43). They proportedly reappeared multiple times in the Cold War era: Caddy surfaced as early as 1946 and again in the fifties and early sixties (Heuvelmans 473, 506–07); Ogo-pogo appeared in 1949, 1950, and in the early sixties (Garner 43–45). The Darlings, in yoking Canada, Africa, and Iceland, collapse boundaries between different nations, implying, once again, that if so many different countries and cultures harbor sea serpents within their waters than perhaps the "Other" is not so unfamiliar. They additionally reinforce the idea that the Cold War reappearance of these creatures forcefully implies their longevity, thereby starkly contrasting with destructive humans who, in holding the secrets of nuclear power, could quickly annihilate each other (like "real" monsters).

The book draws to a close with a reiteration of sea serpents' contemporary predicament, the black and white palette here reinforcing the "truth" of their endangerment. On the penultimate double-page spread, several ships hover close together on the top of the ocean. Below, a plethora of sea creatures, including a whale, sea turtle, sting ray, and squid, swim amongst scientific equipment and four divers. The authors emphasize the nefarious aspects of exploration and discovery: "Now scientists from many countries—oceanographers, hydrographers, geographers, *et al.* ...—have converged on the Indian Ocean. In time they hope to find out a great deal more about it that has never been known before" (66–67; italics Darlings'). The Indian Ocean was a popular location on Medieval and Renaissance maps to depict sea monsters, due to its other-worldly exoticism and inaccessibility (Van Duzer 48, 56, 80).[4] The "convergence" in this spot, portrayed in the crowded illustration, reveals that advancements in these disciplines will leave no corner of the world undocumented. Science in this illustration is aligned with its more destructive Cold War implications rather than its potentially beneficial ones, such as expanding minds and improving society.

Appropriately then, the book's final double-page spread shows a vast ocean with grey clouds suspended above the shoreline; only a few birds hover over the undulating waves. The narrator conclusively states that sea serpents must masquerade as "extinct" to survive in the contemporary world (68–69). The Darlings' work ends on a bleak yet implicitly hopeful note. The sea monster chooses to become *unseen* and the child reader, who now has knowledge, imagination, and perhaps morality surpassing that of adults, may, sometime within a more distant future, become its savior.

Sinking Boundaries with Cyrus

Bill Peet's picture book, *Cyrus the Unsinkable Sea Serpent* (1975), offers a different perspective than the Darlings' work since the author-illustrator fashions his titular serpent as a fairytale hero. Cyrus is a serpentine creature with a long, green black spotted body as well as head and neck fins. His verdant features may be interpreted within the context of the color's more positive connotations of "growth and fertility" (Nodelman 61). At times in the narrative, as I discuss below, he even resembles a dragon—the serpent's cousin as Van Duzer, the Darlings, and Kaplan have addressed—because of his shape, color, and feats.[5] Cyrus, unlike some of the Darlings' creatures, is more serpent than monster due to his humanitarian impulses. Although he *initially* seeks to behave destructively, the aquatic snake uses his vast size and physical prowess to help a boatload of oppressed Europeans journey to (an implied) colonial America. *Cyrus* thus teaches the child reader about shattering stereotypes by rewriting fairytale heroism, and in the process promotes values—cooperation, freedom—which, upon the brink of the country's centennial, might have had especial resonance for young citizens.

Cyrus begins by introducing the main character in a familiar fashion: "Once upon a time there was a giant sea serpent named Cyrus. Even though he was a horrible looking monster he wasn't the least bit fierce. All he did was wander about in the sea with no idea of where he was going" (1). The "Once upon a time" fairytale opening sets the story in the distant, magical past in which ferocious monsters roamed freely amongst humans. Yet Cyrus is neither fierce nor horrible looking; the initial illustration portrays a disgruntled looking creature, bounding along on top of the waves. As the text and image imply, like an uninspired fairytale hero (Jack before he experiences the beanstalk, for instance), he suffers from boredom. After Cyrus voices his desire for a lifestyle change, to "have some fun," a ferocious grey shark offers him unsolicited advice: "why don't you go out and wreck a ship, then eat all the passengers?" (2). Peet's shark expresses a common stereotype concerning sea serpents that the Darlings' book sought to undermine; the word "shark" also has human connotations as a rogue, rascal, trickster, or swindler.[6] Peet's vicious creature catalyzes Cyrus' adventures, playing the rogue by issuing insults: "You've got no more spunk than a jelly fish.... You're nothing but a big sissy" (2). The serpent's appearance is androgynous yet the word "spunk," with its connotations of power and energy, and the term "sissy," with its emasculating overtones, evokes Cyrus' powerfully masculine response. He vows, "I can be as rough and tough as anyone ... and if I have to wreck a ship to prove it, that's what I'll do" (3).

In an effort to harness his new masculine role, Cyrus lies in wait at the docks of a European kingdom, stealthily observing a group of people boarding a large vessel. As the narrator explains, "the ship was called the *Primrose*, and she was bound for a new land far across the sea. The passengers were all poor people who were going there to seek their fortunes" (6). These impoverished Europeans embody the "Other" within their own land, thereby foreshadowing a connection to Cyrus, who, as the shark indicates, is a non-normative sea serpent. As the boat departs, an old man exclaims, "'You'll never make it! You'll run into the doldrums and be stranded forever! Or a storm will take you under! And if a storm doesn't get you the pirates will!'" (8). This fairytale-inspired curse evokes Cyrus' empathy for the people. He becomes "worried about the *Primrose* and all her passengers," and as a result, he decides to follow the ship, harnessing a new masculine role as its protector (9). His incipient heroism is reinforced by the fact that the ship is coded as the damsel in distress: like most large boats, the vessel is engendered as "she," and "she" bears the name of a flower, a conventional feminine symbol which may wither and die without proper care.

True to the old man's words, the *Primrose* is eventually beleaguered by three trials, and its passengers are in need of a hero's protection. Three, the magic number, frequently structures the feats/trials of fairytale heroism. Loyal Cyrus collapses spatial boundaries between himself and the ship, saving the passengers at each turn of trouble. However, he does so mostly *unseen*. First, to unfetter the ship from the doldrums, late at night "he slipped up close behind the *Primrose*, then very gently began puffing at the sails.... Soon she was sailing along over the shimmering sea in a smooth, easy glide" (15). Already dragon-like due to his shape, color, and features, these aspects combined with the physical prowess of "puffing" suggest a homage to "Puff the Magic Dragon" (1963) who "lived by the sea," a beast that befriended yet never saved a human (Lipton and Yarrow). Cyrus' actions further suggest an association with other forms of these mythic animals, such as those from "the Han dynasty" who were "good and whimsical godlike creatures" (Kaplan 115), rather than a more conventional dragon, which, Margery Hourihan maintains, ferociously besieged heroes in "Western mythology" (111–12).

Peet again capitalizes on the association between serpents and dragons

168   Part 4: Evolving Monsters

when the *Primrose* sails out of the doldrums, encountering a terrifying storm. Cyrus' ploy for aiding the vessel and its passengers is to wrap "his great serpent body around [the ship's] ... hull and then, gulping in air, ... puff[s] himself up into a huge life preserver" (23). The sea spreads across both verso and recto in this double-page spread, waves high, black clouds looming, while Cyrus magically supports the boat, showcasing his physical fortitude and his quick thinking. This image affirms a connection between dragons and the sea that Hourihan relays: "Some dragons, like the one from which Perseus rescued Andromeda, came from the sea and thus suggest the power of ocean forces" (113). Here, Cyrus is allied with oceanic power in a regenerative rather than destructive sense. Simultaneously, he revises the image of the serpent on Magnus' *Carta Marina* that Nigg discusses. "[I]nstead of indicating the dangers to human navigation on the sea" (Van Duzer 76), Cyrus becomes essential to humans' survival against perilous natural forces that defy their own navigational skills. The sea serpent, who was once a symbol of foreboding, is now an agent of exploration and assistance.

Cyrus' final feat, saving the *Primrose* from a pirate ship, takes an even heavier toll on his physical and cerebral prowess. Hourihan identifies pirates as one of several evil forces that threaten epic heroes due to their status as "lawbreakers, or at least [people] hostile to the social establishment" (144). However, she concludes that in many tales, there may be as many commonalities as differences between hero and villain (144–45). Peet's vagabonds are coded as destructive when they tell the *Primrose*, "'Heave to! Or we'll blast your tub to splinters!'" (30). Cyrus, from the foreground of the verso, witnesses a horrifying spectacle dramatized across the gutter. The pirate ship fires several cannons across the double-page spread into the recto, annihilating the *Primrose*'s sails, causing the ship to tilt. Foreseeing disaster, on the next double-page spread, the sea serpent finally takes the shark's advice: he becomes a conventional sea monster with all the destruction that the word "monster" implies. The recto depicts Cyrus' long neck extended out of the water; his head serves a weapon, making forceful impact with the hull, ensuring that the pirates tumble into the water. The Jolly Roger flag is now parallel with the sea, perhaps (again) in homage again to "Puff the Magic Dragon": "Pirate ships would lower their flags when Puff roared out his name" (Lipton and Yarrow). Cyrus, in sum, affirms Hourihan's contention, here ironically adapting the same quality as the pirates themselves in order to protect/save the humans.

When Cyrus eventually surfaces, the narrator states, "The [*Primrose*'s] captain and his crew had seen the giant sea monster destroy the pirate ship with one might blow, and they feared their ship would be next" (38). Playing upon the homonym see/sea, the humans, swayed by popular stereotypes rather than rational thinking, employ the word "monster" to associate Cyrus with drowning. He, in turn, grabs the boat's anchor and begins to pull it. The pilgrims, as a hysterical mass scream, "'It's the monster! The sea monster! He's stealing the anchor! No! No! He's pulling us! He's hauling us off to his cave! He'll eat us alive!'" (41). This horror film inspired hysteria recalls culturally coded fears of the sea and the unknown that these aquatic creatures represented during the Renaissance. However, the ship's captain notes that the monster is trying "'to help'" (41). Indeed, Cyrus' aid is provocative in its narrative and symbolic import. Initially serpent, then dragon, then sea monster, as Cyrus drags the ship, he becomes an equine mode of transportation: "Like a high-stepping steed hitched to a fancy carriage Cyrus galloped over the sea, picking up speed as he went" (42). Monsters bodies, in their defiance of boundaries, are frequently subject to transformation. Here, much as a knight might come "galloping" on his steed to slay a dragon or save a princess, Cyrus becomes both horse and knight. The verb "hitched" also carries romantic connotations—attached or married—which reinforces the masculine/feminine, serpent/ship association Peet's words and illustrations have implied. Again, the monster crosses boundaries to become the book's hero, one that the child reader may identify with.

The penultimate double-page spread portrays the happy Europeans standing atop a rock on a shore, likely representing Plymouth; green trees cover the hills behind them. The text makes the serpent's final transformation evident: "As he swam on his way the captain and his crew and all the passengers gathered on a huge rock, and they gave their sea serpent hero a rousing cheer" (44). Cyrus is a now explicitly a hero, the pilgrims' object of desire and affection. Having not only accomplished his three gallant tasks, but additionally brought the ship to its goal—a new home, the typical space of "closure" for heroes in epics (Hourihan 51-53)—the shattering of cultural stereotypes is complete. The monster, rather than marking unknown territory, has now fully mapped mysterious aquatic spaces. Etymologically, Cyrus has even earned his moniker. While "the origin of the name is not known, but in the early Christian period it was associated with Greek *kyrios* 'lord,' and borne by various Greek saints, including an Egyptian martyr and a bishop of Carthage" (Hanks, Hardcastle, Hodges 66; italics editors'). Less lord than saint or martyr, Cyrus dissolves barriers between himself and humans, ultimately contributing to their own livelihood and prosperity in their verdant new land where they can perpetuate cooperative, culturally respectful values, like the child reader him/herself.

A Real Monster

British author Chris Wormell's *The Sea Monster* (2005) is an adventure tale that features a truly hybrid creature. The monster has a round head, prominent nose, large Muppet-like mouth, green eyes, and scraggly hair. His body is both human and amphibious, featuring long gangly arms and scaly webbed hands. However, the most provocative aspect of the creature's corporeality is that his unboundedness surpasses Cyrus' own transformative body. The monster not only appears different in color and appearance on virtually every page of the book, but his behavior is equally unfixed. Unlike the Darlings' and Peet's books, the aquatic creature's interactions with humans do not promote cross-species understanding or explicitly pave the way for a new, better world. Instead, Wormell's text offers subtle moral lessons, rendering its subject an ambiguous hero to reinforce the idea that while sea monsters can help humans, their longevity is intimately bound with their own, separate environments. As a result, it ultimately represents the monster and the sea he lives in as unknowable, mysterious "Others."

The Sea Monster, like *The Sea Serpents Around Us*, uses its shape advantageously. In contrast to the Darlings' work, the book is unconventionally large and square shaped. Perry Nodelman contends that "[t]he extra width of wider [picture] books" can help readers "focus on relationships between character and their environment" (46). While Wormell's work is almost equally high and wide, it nonetheless creates a more intimate connection between environment and character than the other works I have examined. *The Sea Monster* opens with an expansive double-page spread of the ocean floor, portraying the monster emerging from a bed of seaweed, looking at a boat sailing on top of the blue waters. The undulating plants provide a striking visual parallel to the creature's waving hair and webbed hands. Wormell's text further reinforces the connection between the monster and his milieu when the narrator explains, "Barnacles and limpets clung to his scaly skin and seaweed grew from every wrinkle" (n. pag.).[7] Indeed, he seems essential to the ocean floor ecosystem, thereby underscoring a more harmonious way of living and being in the world than humanity. The distance between the monster and the sailboat visually emphasizes the differences between the two worlds and two ways of living, below the water and above.

By the book's second recto, Wormell's creature reveals his ability to cross boundaries, to survive both in the sea and on land. On the fourth double-page spread the importance of this spatial transgression becomes evident when two new characters enter the story: a boy and his dog who seek "to sail a little boat in the tide pools." Here, and in the succeeding two double-page spreads, the monster looms behind the beach's massive rocks, watching the child and animal play. Although he is clearly divided from these beings, the child at one point senses that "*he* was being watched" (italics Wormell's). The illustrations make an implication from the previous pages explicit: the looming beast is menacing because he traverses land and sea. Nonetheless, the monster does not signify the violence that certain sea monsters did on

Medieval and Renaissance maps or within Cold War horror films. Instead, like the sea itself, he is dangerously distracting. When the boy spots the monster's green eye, the boat is "carried ... out among the waves ... far out of reach." In the youngster's attempt to save his toy, he is "caught" by "the current"; shortly thereafter, "he was far out in the deep water beyond the bay." The monster causes this unfortunate mishap and in this respect, becomes the catalyst for the boy's adventures within the sea. Notably as well, the creature becomes invisible for the book's next several double-page spreads.

A retired fisherman, who lives on a cliff above the sea, overhears the boy's dog barking and subsequently becomes the child's hero. The man's white hair and beard, although stereotypical, suggest wisdom and experience. These features connect him to the white dog, who has also cleverly stayed ashore while his young master pursued the boat. Although the fisherman is "old" and has not been out to sea for years, he is nonetheless prepared for adventure. His age shows no toll on him as he takes his "boat hidden among the rocks" and "pull[s] through the waves like in the old days." The hero's strength and vitality is illustrated in a circular framed picture: he is bent forward rowing while the waves crash against his boat. Much as the sea itself suggests endurance, timelessness, and even rebirth, the old fisherman's stalwart rowing suggests that his residence by the water and his former career has imbued him with the same features as the otherwise unknowable sea, enabling him to fearlessly navigate it.

The fisherman and dog eventually encounter the youngster, "there, on a round rock covered with barnacles and limpets, and with seaweed growing from every crack." As the repeated words imply, the "round rock" is the back of the sea monster, its arms, face, and legs hidden beneath the sea. Wormell offers an homage to earlier sea serpent imagery in this illustration. Nigg explicitly addresses a monster posing as an island on the *Carta Marina* while Van Duzer contends that "the myth that whales could be mistaken for islands goes back to the *Physiologus*, an anonymous book about animals, plants, and magic stones composed sometime between the second and fourth centuries, and appears in medieval bestiaries" (48). This particular type of sea monster is generally portrayed as inimical because it dupes humans, masquerading as a safe place in the sea and subsequently causing destruction or drowning. However, in Wormell's book, the monster's back saves the boy. Brown bears "earth[y]" connotations (Nodelman 61), and the brown rock/back emerging amongst the crashing waves signifies the stability of land as well as safety, for the color is further identified with the brown boat the fisherman and dog travel in. The only partially visible sea monster thus maintains its intimate connection to the aquatic environment while briefly overstepping boundaries to play a valiant role.

Upon reaching shore and drying off in the fisherman's cottage, the boy says to his newfound savior, "'That's strange.... It's low tide, isn't it? And yet there's no sign of that rock where you found me.'" The two stare off from the top of the cliff into a beautiful expanse of serene blue sea. The fisherman responds, "'Some rocks *are* strange.... They pop up just when you need them and then you never see them again.'" His sage comment shows an understanding of the aquatic environment and the harmony one can attain by respecting and living in synch with the sea. It is a remark the Darlings' serpentine narrator might have hoped to hear from humans in the distant future. After pondering these words for a moment but not grasping their significance, the boy laments his material loss. The kindly fisherman, who creates model ships in his cottage hands the boy his most recent vessel: a sailboat with a sturdy brown hull and white sails, a larger replica of the boat he lost at sea. The fisherman's role, by the end of the picture book, thus shifts from heroic protector to creator of future adventures. Through the toy vessel he symbolically perpetuates the boy's interest in the sea and the mysteries it holds.

The final page of Wormell's book makes the hitherto mysterious, invisible sea monster visible. Suspended/framed by an excess of white space, a centered circular illustration resembling a portrait portrays the smiling creature, his green eyes dancing as he holds the boy's boat in his enormous hands. Dwarfing the tiny vessel and, due to the picture's framing, even the sea surrounding him, the illustration offers an ambiguous conclusion. On the one hand, Wormell's sea monster clearly deviates from the other aquatic creatures I have investigated in this essay. Here, he appears as a large child himself, delighted to play with the toy, which may establish a comforting connection with the child reader. On the other hand, read within larger sociocultural context of sea serpents/monsters, Wormell's picture bears slightly more menacing undertones. The creature is "down at the bottom of the ocean, among the wavering kelp." Symbolically, the monster has captured and sunk a boat, much in the vein of his Medieval and Renaissance map predecessors. Wormell's picture book both identifies with the child reader, and additionally rewrites artistic and cartographic tropes that have maintained their relevance into the 21st century.

Monstrous Conclusions

Sea serpents have joined a pantheon of monsters parading in children's picture books since (at least) Maurice Sendak's *Where the Wild Things Are* (1963). As I have discussed, these aquatic creatures have a long-standing relationship with other visual texts. Their images appear on Medieval and Renaissance maps and manuscripts, circulating, as well, in nineteenth- and 20th-century newspapers, magazines, and books. Although they have often been used to mark and maintain boundaries between the known and unknown, between humans and non-humans, in the works I have explored, these boundaries dissolve in enlightening ways. In one respect, this dissolution reinforces theories about the picture book as a "form." David Lewis maintains,

> What we find in the picturebook is a form that incorporates, or ingests, genres, forms of language and forms of illustration, then accommodates itself to what it has swallowed, taking on something of the character of the ingested matter, but always inflected through the interanimation of the words and pictures.[8] The immediate result of this ability to ingest and incorporate pre-existent genres is that already existing forms are represented—that is, re-presented—and in the process re-made [65].

Lewis' statement casts picture books as monsters due to their ability to ingest, consume, and transgress boundaries. In addition, highlighting the notion of "re-present[ation]" and "re-ma[king]" underscores aspects of monstrosity, which harken back, at least to Mary Shelley's *Frankenstein* (1818). Victor Frankenstein famously fashioned a monster from pre-existing human parts; in the process he re-made and re-presented both humanity and monstrosity.

Sea monsters and all their attendant symbolism find an apposite home within a form that reconstitutes what has already been produced, demolishing rather than erecting boundaries in the process and enabling the reader to empathize with or know the "Other." The young reader's exposure to diversity through books, school, and culture is a potent part of the socialization process that bears especial value in the 21st century since the "Other" has become, more so than in recent years, an outsider, a figure to project fear on rather than to embrace within our own borders. In the Darlings' work, the reader is positioned as the educated observer, the hope for the future. In Peet's picture book, the child reader can identify with Cyrus as a hero. However, Wormell's book importantly draws the child into the action, thereby more explicitly upsetting boundaries between child and monster. Other recent picture books follow suit with these works, such as A.W. Flaherty and Scott Magoon's *The Luck of the Loch Ness Monster: A Tale of Picky Eating* (2007) and Kate Messner and Andy Rash's *Sea Monster's First Day* (2011). With luck writers and artists will continue to explore these monsters just as humans will continue to explore the unfathomable and often unconquerable sea.

NOTES

1. My comments in this paragraph are influenced by Jeffrey Jerome Cohen's discussion in *Monster Theory*: monsters "are disturbing hybrids whose eternally incoherent bodies resist attempts to include them in any systematic structuration. And so the monster is dangerous, a form suspended between forms that threatens to smash distinctions" (4).

2. The creatures may pay homage to B-horror films from the era, such as *It Came from Beneath the Sea* (1955) and the television cartoon *Beany and Cecil* (1958–1962), which features a harmless, dim-witted aquatic creature's adventures with a human child.

3. The Darlings' brontosaurs are physically similar to the kindly, prehistoric creature in Syd Hoff's storybook, *Danny and the Dinosaur* (1958) and innumerable plastic toys from the era.

4. Van Duzer implies the inaccessibility/unfamiliarity of the Indian Ocean in his

discussion of Medieval and Renaissance maps. He more explicitly identifies this body of water's cartographic associations with "exotic wonders" (56).

5. Kaplan offers a "similarity" between serpents and dragons dating back to Babylonian myth (100). Also, the Darlings place dragons on their sea monster family tree (13).

6. The sharks may profit from misguided beliefs about these beasts, inspired by the recent release of Peter Benchley's novel *Jaws* (1974) and its subsequent film adaptation (1975).

7. Wormell's picture book does not include page numbers. For the first quotation, I include "n. pag." in parentheses. Thereafter, I just provide quotations without parenthetical citations.

8. Lewis defines "interanimation" as "the process by which, in composite texts such as picturebooks, comics and graphic novels, the words and images mutually influence one another so that the meaning of the words is understood in light of what the pictures show, and vice versa" (169).

WORKS CITED

Bader, Barbara. *American Picturebooks from Noah's Ark to The Beast Within*. New York: Macmillan, 1976. Print.
Cohen, Jeffrey Jerome. "Monster Culture (Seven Theses)." *Monster Theory: Reading Culture*, ed. Jeffrey Jerome Cohen. Minneapolis: University of Minnesota Press, 1996. 3–25. Print.
"Cyrus." *Oxford Dictionary of First Names*, ed. Patrick Hanks, Kate Hardcastle, and Flavia Hodges, 2d ed. Oxford: Oxford University Press, 2006. Print.
Darling, Lois, and Louis. *The Sea Serpents Around Us*. Boston: Little, Brown, 1965. Print.
Garner, Betty Sanders. *Canada's Monsters*. Hamilton, Ontario: Potlatch Publications, 1976. Print.
Heuvelmans, Bernard. *In the Wake of the Sea-Serpents*. Trans. Richard Garnett. New York: Hill and Wang, 1969. Print.
Hourihan, Margery. *Deconstructing the Hero: Literary Theory and Children's Literature*. London: Routledge, 1997. Print.
Kaplan, Matt. *The Science of Monsters: The Origins of the Creatures We Love to Fear*. New York: Scribner, 2013. Print.
Lewis, David. *Reading Contemporary Picturebooks: Picturing Text*. London: Routledge, 2001. Print.
Lipton, Lenny, and Yarrow, Peter. "Puff the Magic Dragon." *Songfacts*, 2016. Web. 5 Dec. 2015.
Lyons, Sherrie Lynne. *Species, Serpents, Spirits, and Skulls: Science at the Margins in the Victorian Age*. Albany: State University of New York Press, 2009. Ebook. ProQuest Ebrary. Web. 2 Oct. 2015.
"Monster." *Online Etymology Dictionary*. Douglas Harper, 2001–2015. Web. 18 Nov. 2015.
Nigg, Joseph. *Sea Monsters: A Voyage Around the World's Most Beguiling Map*. Chicago: University of Chicago Press, 2013. Print.
Nodelman, Perry. *Words About Pictures: The Narrative Art of Children's Picture Books*. Athens: University of Georgia Press, 1988. Print.
Ogata, Amy F. *Designing the Creative Child: Playthings and Places in Midcentury America*. Minneapolis: University of Minnesota Press, 2013. Print.
Parsons, Keith M. *Drawing Out Leviathan: Dinosaurs and the Science Wars*. Bloomington: Indiana University Press, 2001. Print.
Peet, Bill. *Cyrus the Unsinkable Sea Serpent*. Boston: Houghton Mifflin, 1975. Print.
Rotschafer, Paula A. "Serpentine Imagery in Nineteenth-Century Prints." MA Thesis, Spring 2014. Digital Commas at University of Nebraska. Web. 20 Oct. 2015.
Van Duzer, Chet. *Sea Monsters on Medieval and Renaissance Maps*. London: The British Library, 2013. Print.
Whyte, Constance. *More Than a Legend: The Story of the Loch Ness Monster*. London: Hamish Hamilton, 1957. Print.
Wormell, Chris. *The Sea Monster*. London: Jonathan Cape, 2005. Print.
Wright, Joyce M. "True Peoples and Their Monsters: Speculations on the Other in the Age of Exploration." *Terrae Incognitae* 37.1 (June 2005): 1–15. Maney Online. Web. 15 Oct. 2015.

PART 5: MONSTROUS MONSTERS

The House That Drac Built
Faith-Based Qualms About Halloween Picture Books

CORWIN R. BADEN

A board creaks. A chain rattles. A windy blast blows on rusty hinges, tossing aside a broken shutter or opening a forbidden portal. These clichés have signaled the scary since *The Castle of Otranto* and *The Mysteries of Udolpho* inaugurated the Gothic novel genre in the 18th century. In fact, the "haunted house" surely dates back within Western tradition to before Pliny the Younger's depiction of a spiritually "possessed" villa in Athens or the Eastern tale "Ali the Cairene and his Haunted House" in *1001 Arabian Nights*. In at least some respects, such "orientalized" or "arabesque" tales were an inspiration for Western horror writers such as Edgar Allan Poe and H.P. Lovecraft, firing the imagination with their descriptions of the Brass City, the awful jinn, and the demonic *ghūl*.

Today, haunted houses are "happy haunts" found even in children's books. Their boiling cauldrons and black cats have been thoroughly groomed, sanitized, and domesticated. One could even call these dilapidated domiciles "cozy." In Natasha Wing's *The Night before Halloween*, child readers are invited into a haunted house by a brotherhood of bashful beasts. In the end, it is the friendly monsters whose hospitality is rejected, yet the brotherhood find a way to party on alone. This, along with a whole coven of picture books, has reinvented Dracula's castle.

Somewhere along the time the haunted house became a national icon in the United States. Chris Heller in *Smithsonian Magazine* writes about its "holy" genesis: "The idea behind haunted houses is not new, of course—people have entertained themselves with spooky stories for centuries—but haunted houses are different because they are inseparable from the holiday that vaulted them to cultural prominence. The tradition could not exist without Halloween; Halloween would not be the same without it." Specifically, today's haunted-house "attractions" bear a clear genealogical ancestor in 19th-century Western culture. The phenomenon can be traced back to Madame Tussaud's Chamber of Horrors and Parisian theater-house "dismemberments." In addition, the "ghost house" became a common fairground attraction immediately after Victoria's death in 1901, a symbol for the haunted new century.

The Money Mansion

And yet it wasn't until the 1940s, when Walt Disney embraced the idea of the haunted house and finally brought an attraction to life (or death?) two decades later, that the haunted house as "money mansion" took hold and returned horror. Yet haunted houses have only rarely cropped up on the edge of town as children's book authors and comic book artists have danced around censorship efforts and ethical dilemmas as they have sought the industry's most coveted award, the Caldecott Medal. In fact, no Caldecott winner has ever depicted a haunted house, although numerous children's stories have capitalized on monster-house motifs, framing such dark dwellings as a transitional phase on the path toward overcoming fears and facing conflict.

Recent controversies regarding the intensity of commercial haunted houses and an upsurge in violent occult or anti-social practices on Halloween have led people of faith to reconsider both the roots of the holiday—originally a Christian holy day—and the purposes to which it is directed today. Yet there are many rooms within Western Halloween's "haunted house" milieu. Christian children's book writer Madeleine L'Engle was perhaps one of the first to include a meta-analysis of the traditional haunted house within her work. The edifice in question, found in her Newbery Medal–winning children's book *A Wrinkle in Time*, is ironically used as means to keep out prying eyes. It is the sanctuary of three "witches," one of whom is whimsically named "Mrs. Which." These extraterrestrial visitors (some would say a portrayal of angels) use the abandoned building to construct a joyful reminder of the self-parody Halloween represents for most American homes. A time of carving pumpkins, bobbing for apples, and roasting pumpkin seeds, the autumnal candy harvest is a remembrance of joy. But apart from these benign aspects, Christian children's writers L'Engle, C.S. Lewis, G.K. Chesterton, George Macdonald, and Charles Williams also embrace the frightening dimensions of All Hallows' Eve, originally a Christian feast day, as a means for representing spiritual themes in their novels, such as Williams' narrative about a woman who discovers she is dead. These authors are also able—having emerged from a British society replete with folk culture layered with pagan predecessors—to embrace the festive aspects of non–Christian celebrations without feeling threatened by spiritual incursion. They are joined today by Ted Dekker and Frank Peretti, American authors who have re-framed the Christian Gothic as a vehicle through which to communicate with young adults.

Halloween: Wholly Unholy?

Despite its reputation as a breeding ground for the unholy, All Hallows' Eve and its tradition of haunted houses has latent potential for bringing communities together, and it is this potential which children's authors and publishers seek to tap as they create Halloween and monster-themed narratives for young children. First, such books are able to remind readers to cherish their families as they share a kind of sanctified space with them. Second, they open doors to all who are different, choosing treats rather than tricks. Finally, and perhaps most significantly, "Hallowed-Evening" monster narratives lead readers of all ages to reflect on the fragility of life, the need for joy, and the embrace of what J.R.R. Tolkien calls the "eucatastrophic" (meaning "happily catastrophic") turn, a life-preserving shift that reminds believers of the hope of salvation and resurrection.

The problem is that such an unconditional embrace is precisely what people of faith have long feared: a secularly sanctioned push to homogenize society causes parents in faith communities to wonder what will enter if windows are left open. History has taught us that those things that should be left to conscience are often colonized by powerful government and social forces. This is what Friedrich Wilhelm III did in 19th-century Germany, driving many Confessional Lutherans to leave their homeland. It is difficult—even contrary to conscience—for many devout believers to marry the sacred with the secular. Meanwhile, Halloween decorations have become as ubiquitous as Christmas lights, while Halloween candy and anthropomorphized or tamed monsters such as Count Von Count and vampire bunnies smack strangely of wolves in sheep's clothing. While it's been relatively easy for people of faith to engage with *Sesame Street* creations without even acknowledging (or realizing) their monstrosity, the monsters who climb through open windows these days are not always warm and fuzzy.

Where the Wild Things Aren't

It is worth mentioning that religious communities have long engaged with monster figures as an ironic matter of course. Gothic cathedrals were adorned with monsters who might protect against ... monsters. Bayer-

Berenbaum writes that "[t]he gargoyles and other carvings on the building designed to frighten away evil spirits are an obvious allusion to divine malevolence. The presence of pagan symbols on religious buildings also underscores a psychological connection between a sense of God and a sense of the grotesque, between religion and Gothicism" (58). Gargoyles, Golems, and Jinn have creatured stories for centuries, seemingly compatible with Angels and Saints.

Yet within Judeo-Christian-influenced American culture, only one ghost story and one monster story have won the coveted Caldecott Medal since those awards were first presented. Of religiously inspired monster tales, only the Jewish "Golem" narrative has been embraced, mainly within the Jewish-American community, as a "member of the family." David Wisniewski's 1997 Caldecott-winner was a monster smash, seeking to break down religious and ethnic barriers. It tells the story of Rabbi Leow, a legendary Bohemian figure who is attended by a monster he creates, Adam-like, out of clay. This Golem protects a Jewish community under siege by Christians who place credence in a blood lie regarding Jewish ritual and is only destroyed once the Jewish people have been reassured of their safety by the powers that be. Safe to say, religious monster stories have been the exception rather than the rule. Even young adult literature has only recently produced two monster Newbery Medal winners: *The Graveyard Book* by hot Gothic author Neil Gaiman and Laura Amy Schlitz's *Splendors and Glooms*. Of course, monster stories continue to proliferate beyond the awards platform.

Such official kid gloves regarding monster stories continues a tradition begun in Victorian England, a time when, despite the overwhelming popularity of Gothic literature in the periodical press and books, relatively few Gothic images appear in early children's books from the late eighteenth and nineteenth centuries. Instead, didactic Victorian children's books taught lessons about social norms and religion. Nevertheless, against this tradition arose a subversive adult culture of Gothic tales we know best today.

The Catharsis of Monster Houses

Haunted Halloween houses found in today's children's fairy-tale picture books take on a rehabilitated educational role. Here are some possibilities—some wholesome and others opportunistic—for the current uses of monster-enchanted dwellings:

- Haunted "monster houses" can be co-opted for "fun"—or commerce—as Disney and DreamWorks have profitably discovered, both on cereal boxes and at the box office.

- They can serve as means for comforting children who fear the grotesque in domestic grottoes, the proverbial bogeys beneath the bed, by demystifying the dark corners of their minds.
- Monsters in these houses can be portrayed as reflections of ourselves, and the result can be a reimagining of difference itself: a rapprochement between hostile parties and people who are deterred by difference.
- The houses themselves are portrayed as being cleansed and renovated, made whole by fellowship and community and by the ebb and flow of natural life cycles that dispel the fear of death.
- The quality of redemption which is depicted in numerous "monster tales" lies at the heart of religious life, and it is a focal point that specifically defines many religious narratives.

This does not necessarily quell the qualms that people of faith have regarding Halloween, scary stories, and haunted houses. Their reservations signal a need for democracies around the world to continue to protect religious expression ... and religious boundaries. While it may not be true that "good fences make good neighbors," a disrespect for boundaries (such as the recent surrounding of an American mosque in an act of intimidation, or a swastika on the side of a church or the wall of a bathroom) must be regarded and policed as hate crimes.

As much as we may seek to dissociate ourselves from religious hostility that seeks to brand alterity and crucify it anew, we can still embrace the freedom that protects Christian, Wiccan, and even Satanic or explicitly anti–Christian or anti-religious expressions of belief within the bounds of our Constitution. It is precisely this freedom that allows us a space in which to interact with even hostile others and an opportunity to communicate with them—without coercion—what we personally believe to be the fullness of life.

The Sign of the Cross

The freedom to "produce" monsters and the liberty to leave them behind: this is the doppelgänger nature of our first amendment rights. People decorate and celebrate the Halloween holiday with Gothic gravestones, rotting corpses, and even depictions of unmentionable acts of violence. Others close their doors to this culture or provide alternative events for community members. Furthermore, as this debate spills over into picture books, the stakes are generally raised. Picture books have power, and—as primary movers of young minds—they can leave lasting impressions which the guardians of those minds may resist.

Respect for the borders and boundaries of faith are a headstone and cornerstone of a democratic community and the mythical Plymouth Rock on which the United States was founded. Of course, the Pilgrims and later-arriving Puritans themselves tried to claim those boundaries in a new, discriminating hegemony, leaving others in the outer darkness, but the principles of religious freedom and religious tolerance have arguably strengthened our society.

But does this "freedom" extend to the embrace of truly evil beings that are depicted as doing (and encouraging) truly evil deeds? There were plenty of Manson Family, Jeffrey Dahmer, and hardened "terrorist" costumes worn this past Halloween night, glorifying their originals for young minds. There is a fine aesthetic line between the rehabilitated monster and the monstrous evil, resident in human actions around the world and across time. Ironically, it is the sign of the Christian cross that has historically been believed to ward off such evil. In response (and some would say defiance), creative marketing minds have co-opted this cross to draw evil like some sort of monster magnet. After all, what would a monster story be without a graveyard replete with cruciform headstones that serve as stools for monster meetings?

Even C.S. Lewis, author of *The Lion, the Witch, and the Wardrobe*, utilizes the power of the desecrated sacred to set the scene for the apparent triumph of evil. His White Witch commands, "Summon all our people to meet me here as speedily as they can. Call out the giants and the werewolves and the spirits of those trees who are on our side. Call the Ghouls, and the Boggles, the Ogres and the Minotaurs. Call the Cruels, the Hags, the Spectres, and the people of the Toadstools. We will fight" (140). Shortly afterwards, this Witch's counterstrike is brought to a climax:

> A great crowd of people were standing all round the Stone Table [...] But such people! Ogres with monstrous teeth, and wolves, and bull-headed men; spirits of evil trees and poisonous plants; and *other creatures whom I won't describe because if I did the grownups would probably not let you read this book*–Cruels and Hags and Incubuses, Wraiths, Horrors, Efreets, Sprites, Orknies, Wooses, and Ettins [157 emphasis mine].

Lewis, in self-censorship, declines to describe these denizens of darkness, conjuring them merely with his laundry-list of monstrous epithets. He understands that monsters scare children, yet he is not willing to efface their presence entirely. Key to this episode is their presence in the story's most sacred space, the cracked Stone Table which, in Narnian terms, represents Mosaic law and divine justice. The monsters are no respecters of persons, or places.

Holy Toledo!

For many the actual boards of a holy house themselves must not be violated. Yet this injunction is often ignored or seen as an invitation to mischief.

A clever entrepreneur near my town obtained access to a church slated for demolition on a street called Toledo. The result was a clothing boutique named "Holy Toledo!" This, of course, is a dramatic shift within contemporary culture, a gradual slip-sliding by which parody is increasingly tolerated. Yet it is also true that most contemporary Christian worshippers do not see the "church" as a sacrosanct building decked out in steeple, but as a body composed of people with Jesus Christ as head. No longer is the desecration of a church building seen as an existential threat to most members of a Christian community. All of this was severely tested when a racist gunman chose a predominantly African-American church to murder nine people in Charleston. Amazingly, even that community responded in grace, demonstrating that a building can never match the strength of a spiritually bonded people.

Still, as unshakeable as buildings of worship stand in our collective psyche, there is something about the home that points to an even more tender faith space, especially for those for whom public discrimination has been a lived daily reality. Encroachment on that domestic space is not easily ignored or answered with high-minded principles.

Roman Catholic and Protestant versions of communal worship have, of course, created modified versions of this sacred space. The Roman Catholic confessional and the Protestant parlor both convey intimacy—with both God and man. They are spaces of reconciliation where relationships can be restored in abject humility or around a raucous dinner table.

In particular, Protestantism, from Martin Luther's day forward, has erected the home as a holy sanctuary in which parents are free to teach their children the tenets of their faith. The re-establishment of the hearth as a center for religious and cultural instruction has most certainly been an impetus for the growing homeschool movement. The home, a house with a heart, has long been—at least for Protestant Christians who have, in essence, decentered their faith spaces by no longer requiring attendance at a specific parish church or cathedral that legitimates their worship—a church of its own. Colleen McDannell writes:

> Domestic sacred space is not merely an abstract category. Homes are places where real people interact with one another in the hopes of promoting specific religious and cultural values [...] The home, like all space, is contested space that changes meaning over time. Future studies will further refine how the sacred space of the home is created and maintained across religious, political, and social boundaries [214].

There is tension between those evangelicals who wish to set their homes apart and those who see their faith as centered in the more traditional "public" sphere. Then again, there are many members of faith communities who hold both spheres, the private and public, to be sacred and advocate for increased awareness and sensitivity to the needs of their communities. In "Parlor Piety," McDannell again writes:

Like the church, the home as a physical space and a kinship structure was sacred. During the second half of the nineteenth century, mainstream Protestant Americans sought to make their domestic space holy by elaborating an ideology which placed the home, and not the church, at the center of the creation of religious and patriotic values. By adapting Gothic Revival architecture for house construction, they emphasized the connection between the design of homes and the design of churches [162].

It is this connection between domestic spirituality and the Gothic that is a fascinating dichotomy, creating an intriguing interplay between faith and the principles of the Gothic genre.

Guy Debord and the Contesting of Sacred Space

Across the street from these perspectives stands Guy Debord's weather-worn treatise, *Society of the Spectacle*. Famous for his establishment of psychogeography as "the study of the precise laws and specific effects of the geographical environment, consciously organized or not, on the emotions and behavior of individuals" (qtd., in Coverly 88), Debord is quite eager to establish "sacredness of space" as a false idol inspired by a class-based, corruptly capitalist society:

> Separation is the alpha and omega of the spectacle. Religious contemplation in its earliest form was the outcome of the establishment of the social division of labor and the formation of classes [...] [M]ass allegiance to frozen religious imagery was originally a shared acknowledgment of loss, an imaginary compensation for a poverty of real social activity that was still widely felt to be a universal fact of life [25].

It would be easy to conclude that people of faith are deluded if they feel that their space is any more sacred than any other space; such beliefs, explain critics, expose a desire for control and power. The "frozen imagery" that homeowners or churchgoers seek to protect is an illusion in a society that has come to honor the likeness (or the hyper-reality) above the corrupted actual. So does this mean it is pointless—and even unprincipled—for faith communities to seek to protect themselves from a cultural onslaught that normalizes imagery and ritual contrary to their consciences?

Helaine Becker's *The Haunted House That Jack Built* (illustrated by David Perkins) highlights the sometimes arbitrary lines that are drawn between the sacred and the profane. On Becker's cover we see the eponymous house: It's façade sports lighted lead-glass windows sometimes associated with church structures and its peak is capped with a skull—rather than a cross or the typical rooster (also derived from Protestant Christian tradition). Perkins' imagery, in contrast to the more innocuous tendencies of other books mentioned in this chapter, generally seeks to scare. Ghosts are truly ghouls in this Jack's (or we might say "Jack o' Lantern's") house. In addition, the last page includes a recipe for "Halloween Skeleton Stew." The image of a skeleton merrily stirring another skeleton into his pot (a striking image of not-so-friendly cannibalism?) is backgrounded by the typical cemetery scene. At the graveyard's height is a cross, a symbol powerful enough to make some think the entire image sanctioned within that faith community. Some would prickle at such a depiction.

On the other hand, many people of faith would explain that the fetishizing of skulls and gravestones runs counter to the principles of freedom and an abundant life that believers proclaim. Is a skull or cross desecrated simply by appearing alongside a "creepy" narrative? Indeed, there seems to be symbolic power flowing both ways. Some would even say that the mere depiction of a cross is crossing a line in favor of religion. The Gothic landscape is truly a complex patchwork. Most likely, those who protest such depictions harbor concerns that their symbol system has, in some way, been devalued through such portrayals.

Religiously inspired iconoclasm has shaken the Western world since the Reformation swept through the German countryside and dissolved plenty of English abbeys—in both a literal and ecclesiastical sense—as Henry VIII took possession. Christ was a builder, the son of a carpenter. Yet even he overturned tables ... within what he saw as his Father's House. There are sacred spaces that must be protected, and respected, by those of us who claim to be speaking on behalf of freedom from persecution, lest we ourselves might someday face equally appalling threats. A Golem must rise in defense of the spiritually oppressed.

Sadly, it is also true that orthodox Christian and Wiccan voices cannot, by doctrine and definition, raise themselves in common spiritual hymns. By no means does this foreclose the possibility of earthly reconciliation and brotherly love. Both Christians and Wiccans speak openly of tolerance and forgiveness. But it would be ludicrous to imagine a Wiccan embracing Christian texts and rituals that delimit beliefs to one God and proscribe participation in occult practice. This has been demonstrated recently within the U.S. armed forces, where Wiccans have successfully lobbied for their religion to be recognized and for a release from Christian rituals even now embedded in secular branches of our government,[1] just as Satanists have lobbied to have their own monuments erected on lawns marked with crosses or living nativities. For this reason, as outlined by national constitutions and human reason, we have different houses for different spiritual bodies. Clearly both Wiccans and Christians would confirm the wisdom in this provision of the Constitution to separate church and state.

Such reminders of our common humanity and, for Christians, reminders of a tradition of open dialogue and engagement (represented by those first ninety-five theses on a Halloween church door) may not lead all evangelical or fundamentalist believers to open the door for all Halloween costumes and customs, at least not on secular terms. Yet "Fall Fun Nights" and "Harvest Festivals"—often with gentle but explicit reminders to eschew the guises of witches, ghosts, and zombies—have cropped up nationally (and even internationally) as a demonstration that Christians are seeking to welcome all as an expression of their own beliefs and on their own terms. In addition, fundamentalist branches of Christianity have sought to co-opt the haunts of Halloween houses by constructing them to tell their own narratives. Controversial "Hell Houses," begun at Liberty University by Jerry Falwell, have sought to scare visitors straight and prepare them for the peace of the Bible's gospel (Heller). While this may not be the welcome that some feel entitled to, it shows efforts to change approaches rather than withdraw from cultural exchange. Specifically, efforts to invite visitors to peaceful gatherings—and the community's response to them—is a sign that brotherly love is a universal need and an appropriate goal, no matter what a person's faith narrative might be. A tent housing a church-sponsored fun night on Halloween can remind us of an image Lewis tries to capture in *Mere Christianity*: "[Faith] is more like a hall out of which doors open into several rooms. If I can bring anyone into that hall, I have done what I attempted. But it is in the rooms, not the hall, that there are fires and chairs and meals. The hall is a place to wait in, a place from which to try the various doors, not a place to live in. For that purpose the worst of the rooms (whichever that may be) is, I think preferable" (xv). Faith communities seek to share an abundant life with others. While sectarian differences must not be whitewashed and cannot simply be wished away, the traditional fences that have sometimes barred entrance for "outsiders" are almost universally being dismantled in favor of a welcome mat that invites all to join the party.

Having Candy and Eating It, Too

On the other hand, Christian and other religious groups often push back against calls for ecumenical religious unity, at least when it comes to doctrine or the most intimate elements of faith, seeing such efforts as an attempt to dilute genuine religious expression in the name of social (and perhaps political) harmony. Most contentious would be a government-instituted call across faiths, and not simply across denominational differences. There is ample historical precedent for the uneasy tension between the secular and the sacred.

Specifically, the medieval festivals that often filled the markets erected alongside towering Gothic cathedrals were seen as signifiers both of bounty and of cultural fragmentation, a crossing of the line between church power and community freedom. These festivals were thus kept out of the sanctuary, although they certainly provided the revenue needed to support the management of the ecclesiastical community. Interestingly enough, these markets were an offshoot of chancel dramas that were eventually relegated to external "sacred" spaces, and which evolved into community events. Gene Veith writes that "[s]oon these plays became too long and ambitious to fit within the confines of a church service. They moved outside" (155). These dramas became increasingly secular and blended with the cacophony of vendors selling their worldly wares. In particular, the Saturnalian tradition of the Feast of Fools, with its Lord of Misrule's once-a-year overturning of ecclesiastical and political power at Christmas, demonstrates the ease with which churchgoers became partygoers in order to "observe" Fat Tuesday before Ash Wednesday or the "Fastnacht" before "Fastenzeit" (Feast before Lent). During the Tudor period, John Stow wrote about this extended time of Misrule: "[i]n the feaste of Christmas, there was in the kinges house [...] a Lord of Misrule, or Maister of merry disports [...] [t]hese Lordes beginning their rule on Alhollon Eue [Halloween]" (qtd. in Nares, Halliwell-Phillipps, and Wright 573). For people of faith, there can emerge both a kind of desired release and an implicit threat in such non-church rituals. It is at these moments that the competing impulses to enable and discipline produce societal monsters that can overshadow joy with fear and loathing.

Literary Tradition and the "Drac Shack"

Prompted during the mid–1700s by Walpole's *Castle of Otranto* and Radcliffe's *Mysteries of Udolpho*, *Frankenstein* and *Dracula* staggered through the door of Western discourse over the course of the succeeding century. By the turn of the 20th century, Thomas Hardy's *Return of the Native* and Henry James' *Turn of the Screw* had demonstrated the thorough domestication of the Gothic. The effect was mixed: the threat of monstrous evil was familiarized, yet the narratives of the 20th century (*1984* and *Clockwork Orange* come to mind) re-framed the Gothic in futuristic terms that never seem to die. The obsession with pre-possessed properties continues with "The Haunted House," a no longer extant Lovecraft story from 1902—a narrative event which points to a cultural Barnumesque/Ripleyesque romance with the grotesque and is corroborated by a contemporary "Ghost House" attraction at Coney Island in 1904.

Yet oddly enough the haunted house has not made an appearance in over eighty years of Caldecott Medals and almost a century's worth of Newbery Medals. Most importantly, within this selected subgenre "the home" has been considered sacrosanct. Consider Virginia Lee Burton's 1943 Caldecott Medal winner *The Little House*, an idyllic tale presenting a domestic facade that has been intentionally drawn to look like an expressive face that changes with its surroundings. The home must be protected at all costs: it is ultimately removed from the "Gothic" and industrial urban center that has grown up around it (and turned its happy facade into a disconsolate frown) and is replanted in a new pastoral setting. In the same vein, 2009's winner, Susan Marie Swanson's *The House in the Night*, is a "home full of light," free of fears and tremors. Nevertheless, as any child growing up in the 1970s would know from movie trailers titillating on after-school TV, any façade can be twisted by the creative mind into an *Amityville Horror*.

Horror Comics: An Oxymoron?

Over the first half of the 20th century, and especially after World War II, the comics industry—which can never be legitimately separated from the children's book industry—saw a fertile market in the monster/horror genre. Yet the controversial *Seduction of the Innocent* (1954) by Fredric Wertham decried the violence, as well as sexual content, and what the author interpreted as gender perversions which the author claimed were being promoted within comics targeting children (and by the popular EC Comics in particular): "Horror, crime, sadism, monsters, ghouls, corpses dead and alive—in short, real freedom of expression. All this in comic books addressed to and sold to children" (386). In that same year, a Congressional inquiry into comic book content led to a voluntary Comics Code Authority adopted by the industry to self-censor comic book production.

Twenty years later, in 1971, the Comics Code Authority began to relax their restrictions regarding the depictions of horror to align with traditional school curricula:

> Scenes dealing with, or instruments associated with, walking dead or torture shall not be used. Vampires, ghouls and werewolves shall be permitted to be used when handled in the classic tradition such as *Frankenstein*, *Dracula*, and other high-caliber literary works written by Edgar Allan Poe, Saki, Conan Doyle, and other respected authors whose works are read in schools around the world ["Comics"].

This resurgence coincided with the introduction of monster-themed cereals by General Mills: Count Chocula, Franken Berry, and Boo Berry. As a result of this cultural convergence, my younger self (at age six) was soon perusing issues of *Ghostly Haunts*, *The Unexpected*, *Black Magic*, *Weird War Tales*, and *House of Mystery* that had been discarded by my neighbors.

It would be easy to conclude that there are good and bad monster stories, with the good being those which open haunted houses to the light and invite monstered beings to participate, thereby telescoping sacred space. To the contrary, Bruno Bettelheim indicates that, at some level, children need the monsters to be evil:

> There is a widespread refusal to let children know that the source of much that goes wrong in life is due to our very own natures—the propensity of all men for acting aggressively, asocially, selfishly, out of anger and anxiety. Instead, we want our children to believe that, inherently, all men are good. But children know that they are not always good; and often, even when they are, they would prefer not to be. This contradicts what they are told by their parents, and therefore makes the child a monster in his own eyes [7].

The preceding discussion leads us to this threshold: can haunted houses themselves be redeemed as valid subjects for children's picture books? Even in the comics code changes, we see that monster stories can carry unintended baggage. The "high-caliber literary" monsters that were first allowed grudgingly into the comics industry represent forces that can be painted over with innocuous children's illustrations. Nevertheless, the origins of these creations, just like the origins of Halloween itself, give faith communities pause.

Monsters of All Stripes and Scars: Enabling Fiends and Disciplining Zombies

In order to understand the deep-seated iconography that monster depictions represent, it may be helpful to divide monster figures into two main types: those which enable and those which discipline. As emblems for these types we need only turn to the Fantastical Four of horror fiction: Dracula, Wolfman, Frankenstein, and the Mummy. These four alone have generated unimaginable wealth for the entertainment industry and seem to be the gifts that just keep unwrapping (at least in the case of the Mummy).

First there are monsters that enable. Here I won't use the word empower, although some believe it to be so, because such an assertion would be an affront to those whose faith contradicts the very "power" sought: for self-fulfillment in spite of the needs of others, and for a modernity that often seeks to efface religious belief. On this side stands Count Dracula, emblem of self-preservation and parasitical sadism. Dracula is the poster child for elitist, class-based oppression, domination, and exploitation of women; modern technologies that enhance power and facilitate cosmopolitanism and globalization; cultural hegemony and linguistic superiority; and sexual promiscuity. The fact that Dracula cannot see himself in mirrors is indicative of a deflection away from any accountability for the Self even as the Self is indulged. This is the Id at its rawest. Alongside Dracula is the Wolfman, the werewolf figure of numerous stories beginning (most publicly) with Reynolds' *Wagner the Wehr-wolf* in 1847. Representing raw human passion in contrast to disciplining restraint, it is the wolf inside which wins the day. Like Dracula, there are distinctly sexual undertones to his story on which Hollywood has capitalized with nearly every iteration—from Michael Landon's *Teenage Werewolf* to John Landis' *An American Werewolf in London* to Michael J. Fox's *Teen Wolf*. Literally the "wolf in sheep's clothing," it is this wild side that has been celebrated recently, the Id in ascendancy as the moon exercises its mythical powers for transformation. It is this radical change—change in all its forms—that we simultaneously crave and fear.

The implications of appearances of these monsters in narratives for children can be important: domesticated depictions—both as "tamed" monsters and as visitors to the home—create the impression that all sins have been arbitrarily forgiven and there is no need to worry about excesses and extremes such as these monsters originally represented. They have been defanged and declawed. This is what Bayer-Berenbaum calls "[t]he incorporation of the incredible into the everyday world" (123).

On the side of the Superego are those monsters who remind us of our limits even as they transcend theirs. These disciplining monsters, including the Mummy and Frankenstein, represent the desecrated sacred even as they become abominations themselves. The mummy, ancient policeman that he is, must punish for the crossing of boundaries, must curse with every letter of the law. He responds to the invasion of sacred space and seeks to restore order. In a similar sense, Frankenstein is the archetypal zombie, a revenant or "re-animant" who reminds us of our own fear of death. Yet it is the overreaching of science that is here being disciplined. Even the creature's justice, the creation of a female to be his companion (a project that Victor Frankenstein concludes will be an abomination in itself), reminds us of our own hubris in seeking to order our own world. When these types of monsters are subdued and employed to tell a different story, especially the carefree narratives designed for children, it seems that the signals are being crossed.

Four Houses with Happy Haunts

And now, for a glimpse through the broken shutters of the "domesticated" haunted house, we must take a look at a handful of picture books designed to inoculate children against the fear that has traditionally been inspired by ghosts and goblins, and specifically by the "movie monsters" enumerated above.

In *The Night Before Halloween* by Natasha Wing, the monsters are getting ready for their big Halloween day. Dracula is primping himself in a mirror, Frankenstein's bride is fretting over what to wear, and the mumm(ies) "unraveled and put on new wraps." In this personal narrative, dedicated to the author's father who "was born on the night before Halloween," Wing seeks to overturn nearly every taboo regarding monsters. Dracula can see his own smiling reflection—although his literary forebear's less-than-visible purposes are subtly invoked as he "grinned, and slicked back his hair." The bride is no abomination, but rather a sympathetic (if stereotyped) female figure with sad eyes who fears for her unfashionable future. In contrast, the witches, ghosts, and mummies of the tale have undiversified smiles on their faces—the smiles of neighbors rather than nemeses. The illustrated images, rounded and vibrantly colored, contrast with the story's Gothic ancestors. The storyline set to the meter of "'Twas the Night Before Christmas,'" like other Wing books celebrating various Western holidays, is simple: the monsters are decorating their communal home for Halloween trick-or-treaters they hope will drop by. Yet when children actually do come to the door, those guests are still haunted by the monsters conjured by their minds and end up running away. But the party must go on: the monsters decide to have their own mash-bash, dancing the night away in monstered bliss.

The second and third tales in this quartet involve ghosts in residence. *Ghosts in the House* by Kazuno Kohara is a work reminiscent of Japanese anime, and the author-illustrator creates classic woodcut-type images to tell her story. While this tale is not directly connected to Halloween, it has been illustrated with the now standard orange and black colors of that holiday. It tells the tale of a girl who happens to be a witch that captures ghosts, throws them in the washing machine, and hangs them as curtains or spreads them as tablecloths with smiling, contented faces. One oral reading of the book uploaded onto Youtube.com records a Taiwanese mother sharing the book in bilingual modeling for her daughter. The most striking portion of this is her commentary (in Mandarin) at the end of her reading: "Aren't the ghosts cute?" (Lin). Such a statement works against thousands of years of fear and ritual within Chinese culture that has sought to appease spirits in order to keep their influence at bay. Apparently this text has succeeded in exorcising traditional qualms. Another text involving spirits is Jennifer O'Connell's *Ten Timid Ghosts*. A "counting" narrative, the story explains how, when a witch moves into a haunted house, the ghosts, one by one, are scared, too. As the determined witch uses one monstrous device after another to frighten off the frighteners, no more ghosts remain and the witch can comfortably enjoy her haunted house ... except that the final ghost sees through her flimsy costume. In the end, the original ghosts return with a comical, glorious vengeance.

The last book recasts a cumulative tale—that is, a tale in which repeated phrases build to a climax—based on the first story that Randolph Caldecott published in 1878: *The House That Jack Built*. Even more to the point, *The House That Jack Haunted* by Pamela Conn Beall (like Becker's book mentioned earlier) actually rests on the foundations of Judeo-Christian belief and practice. Caldecott's original picture book was an adaptation of an Aramaic hymn called "Chad Gadya" in the *Sepher Haggadah* of 1590 (*Trübner's*), and any subsequent retelling essentially co-opts that sacred textual space, just as Wing's narrative and Tim Burton's *Nightmare Before Christmas* have co-opted Christmas frames for their Halloween stories.

As in Becker's book, Beall's *House* (illustrated by Charles Reasoner) parades elements of a "typical" haunted space, essentially demystifying them for the child reader. There is little to be frightened of here, except for any associations a child may prepossess regarding bats, black cats, and big eyes. Reasoner's images in this board book are lit by a massive, ever-present moon that casts a cheery glow from its rounded edge across every page. The house, too, is tidy. In fact, each critter that populates the place is downright cute, and the wavy ghost-owner smiles out through the cover's cut-out window, enjoying the aftertaste of his steaming cocoa.

Nevertheless, Beall's narrative (like Kohara's and O'Connell's) involves "home invasions" that ironically turn the tables by casting traditional home-wreckers as craving their own sacred domestic space. Startled awake by the accumulation of bats, cats, witches, and goblins, the ghost has finally had enough. His vengeful "BOO!" sends the invading parade packing and the rightful owner presumably goes back to his cocoa and easy chair. Yet even this final confrontation is a mere hiccup in an otherwise idyllic scene. It is easy to imagine father and child counting together the numerous pairs of peeping eyes that provide their own additional light to an already very illuminated book.

In essence, all four of these picture books involve a haunted house that is almost ritualistically sanitized or satirized so that children may engage with a deeper revelation of the human condition through such a construct. By peeping through the window of a humorously exaggerated haunted house to watch frightened ghosts and uncomfortable witches, children and adults see their own silly, satirized shadows. In the process, a space designed to house fears and to compartmentalize "Otherness" is rededicated for different purposes. It might seem almost laughable to compare gory horror comics or Gothic aberrations to these pastel-printed children's books. Nevertheless, we must acknowledge the power of iconography at work whenever ghosts, Dracula, or Frankenstein are invoked. The question remains: how much of the original traditions linger as children consume, and are influenced by, these innocuous-seeming works?

Tricks Among the Treats

All of the preceding discourse can be boiled down to two qualms that parents in faith communities have about Halloween haunted houses in children's picture books. First, they do not want to be party to producing monsters. In their minds, such narratives may promote the belief that fairy-tale or movie monsters actually do exist just down the street. Such monster-mongering creates fear when those parents believe in peace. Second, parents don't want to be seen as abetting monsters: Concerned caregivers make the case that actual evil—evil that does exist and is carved on the foreheads of madmen—is repressed, masked, costumed, even consumed through monster children's books. By re-fashioning monsters as consistently friendly and neighborly, a very important—and healthy—boundary between the home and the unknown is potentially undermined. Finally, parents in faith communities are specifically wary of real or perceived threats to their way of life. They fear the eroding of fast-held moral boundaries as their children "play" with the occult, including anything "magical." They fear a disrespecting of boundaries on which they have founded a home that they consider sacred. Most controversially, they see moral differences as lines of demarcation, and they feel that the broad-stroke effacing of difference at the expense of closely held beliefs and norms forces them to compromise who they are and who they want their children to be.

People of faith—and here we are speaking of devout believers who have embraced a holistic faith-based worldview—see their religion as a set of life or death moral imperatives. Regarding children's stories, G.K. Chesterton reminds us that "[i]f you really read the fairy-tales, you will observe that one idea runs from one end of them to the other—the idea that peace and happiness can only exist on some condition. This idea, which is the core of ethics, is the core of the nursery-tales." How then can we assuage faith-based qualms while embracing the "treats" that can come from a community drawn together to discuss differences openly and respectfully? It is through non-discriminatory humor; self-reflection, including open parody such as that found in *Goodnight, Goon* by Michael Rex; the restoration of community; and a forgiveness that comes only by addressing real fears and wrongs, as well as perceived offenses, that we will overcome fears of being overcome.

A Violent Turn of Channels

Today's Halloween attractions include extreme haunted houses (also known as "horror houses"): room upon room that would make Bluebeard blush, including physical contact (and assault), nudity, electric shock, forced ingestion of substances, fake water-boarding, and sexual undertones or themes throughout ("Seven"). I will never forget when I first entered an extreme haunted house virtually, on Taiwan television. My twelve-year-old host brother, watching nightly news that included features from abroad, was subjected to images that were wholly unwholesome.

In today's increasingly complex (and commercial) cultural milieu, the blueprints for Bluebeard's mansion have been redrawn, and the lines have been crossed. The random killing of house pets, the desecration of places of worship, and the glorification of elements that have gained cultural stature only as a function of their opposition to religious belief or practice have made some faith communities fearful, and perhaps even furious. One might conclude, particularly within the Academy, that such opposition is precisely the business of books … even (or especially) children's books. The goal of some is to dispel religiosity and superstitious fear by confronting it head on.

On the other hand, most reasonable citizens, by means of genuine empathy, can understand faith-based trepidation—or outright opposition—to cultural elements that directly oppose the values they seek to teach their children. The trouble comes when one camp or another desires to speak on behalf of all within the public "tent." This is the (perhaps everlasting) nature of a society based on religious plurality and democratic public discourse.

Practicing Wishcraft

Interestingly, the corporate, sanitized observance of Halloween does not satisfy the neo-pagan worshippers that Christians have feared will use the holiday as a platform to influence others, including their own children. Domestication of the monstered isn't what witches want: a door-to-door Halloween is actually frowned upon by Wiccans who seek the woods for their religious expression.

We, all of us, live in a common haunted house in which the ghosts of dead ideas remain. For people of no faith or those of non-Christian belief, the danger has always been hegemonic domination by Christian tradition, even a corrupted version that we witness on Halloween night. For Christian believers, the question is whether or not those who are within can safely open their doors without being swallowed by a new hegemony: a secularized (and pluralized) national culture that may run counter to their belief systems. For those believers, the domestication of "Haunted Space" smacks of capitulation, as if the Jewish Maccabees had actually welcomed a statue of Zeus in their temple and its concomitant pig's blood on the altar of their faith. Or perhaps it would be, to Christians, as if the Romans had welcomed the Goths as invaders of their sacred domestic and public spaces. In either case, it must be remembered that children seek joy, and adults are the ones left holding the bag—or in this case, the book. It is the power of picture books that can help all of us open doors and cross bridges. While we won't agree with everything we see on store shelves, it is always true that the opening of a picture book at any age opens a conversation that has the potential to enliven every home.

A house is only haunted if books are banished or sit unread on shelves. As we seek to come together to respect various traditions, we must also exercise restraint and sensitivity toward all who are different, monstered or monstering, as they seek to raise their children to build rather than tear down.

NOTE

1. Discussed in "Air Force Academy adapts to pagans, druids, witches and Wiccans," a *Los Angeles Times* article by Jenny Beam from 26 Nov. 2011.

WORKS CITED

Amityville Horror. Dir. Stuart Rosenberg. MGM, 2014. DVD.
Bayer-Berenbaum, Linda. *The Gothic Imagination.* Cranbury, NJ: Associated University Presses, 1982. Print.
Beall, Pamela Conn, and Susan Hagen Nipp. *The House That Jack Haunted!* New York: Price Stern Sloan, 2003. Print.
Beam, Jenny. "Air Force Academy Adapts to Pagans, Druids, Witches and Wiccans." *Los Angeles Times* 26 Nov. 2011. Web. 20 June 2016.
Becker, Helaine. *The Haunted House That Jack Built.* Toronto: Scholastic Canada, 2010. Print.
Bettelheim, Bruno. *The Uses of Enchantment.* New York: Vintage, 1989. Print.
Burgess, Anthony. *A Clockwork Orange.* London: Heinemann, 1962. Print.
Burton, Virginia Lee. *The Little House.* Boston: Houghton Mifflin Harcourt, 1978. Print.
Caldecott, Randolph. *The House That Jack Built.* 1878. Alcester, UK: Pook Press, 2015. Print.
Chesterton, G.K. "Fairy Stories." SurLaLunefairytales.com. Web. 10 Dec. 2015.
"Comics Code Revision of 1971." *Comic Book Legal Defense Fund.* cbldf.org. Web. 10 Dec. 2015.
Coverley, Merlin. *Psychogeography.* Harpenden, UK: Pocket Essentials, 2006. Print.
Debord, Guy. *Society of the Spectacle.* Detroit: Black and Red, 1970. Print.
Gaiman, Neil. *The Graveyard Book.* New York: HarperCollins, 2010. Print.
Hardy, Thomas. *The Return of the Native.* New York: Modern Library, 2001. Print.
Heller, Chris. "A Brief History of the Haunted House." *Smithsonian Magazine.* Smithsonian.com, 28 Oct. 2015. Web. 10 Dec. 2015.
James, Henry. *The Turn of the Screw.* New York: Modern Library, 1991. Print.
Kohara, Kazuno. *Ghosts in the House!* New York: Roaring Brook, 2008. Print.
L'Engle, Madeleine. *A Wrinkle in Time.* New York: Square Fish, 2007. Print.
Lewis, C.S. *The Lion, the Witch, and the Wardrobe.* Grand Rapids: Zondervan, 2005. Print.
_____. *Mere Christianity.* Grand Rapids: Zondervan, 2001. Print.
Lin, Ching. *Ghosts in the House by Kazuno Kohara Zhong Ying Wen.* Online video clip. Youtube.com, 19 Oct. 2013. Web. 10 Dec. 2015.
Lovecraft, H.P. "The Haunted House." Non-extant, 1898/1902.
McDannell, Colleen. "Creating the Christian Home: Home Schooling in Contemporary America." *American Sacred Space,* ed. David Chidester and Edward Tabor Linenthal. Bloomington: Indiana University Press, 1995. Print.
_____. "Parlor Piety." *American Home Life, 1880–1930: A Social History of Spaces and Services,* ed. Jessica H. Foy and Thomas J. Schlereth. Knoxville: University of Tennessee Press, 1994. Print.
Nares, Robert, James Orchard Halliwell-Phillipps, and Thomas Wright. *A Glossary: Or, Collection of Words, Phrases, Names, and Allusions to Customs, Proverbs, Etc.: which Have Been Thought to Require Illustration in the Works of English Authors, Particularly Shakespeare and His Contemporaries.* Vol. 2. London: J.R. Smith, 1876. Print.
The Nightmare Before Christmas. Writ. Tim Burton and Michael McDowell. Walt Disney, 2010. DVD.
O'Connell, Jennifer. *Ten Timid Ghosts.* New York: Scholastic, 2000. Print.
Orwell, George. *1984.* New York: Signet, 1962. Print.
Radcliffe, Ann. *The Mysteries of Udolpho.* London: Penguin, 2001. Print.

Rex, Michael. *Goodnight, Goon: A Petrifying Parody*. New York: G.P. Putnam's Sons, 2012. Print.
Reynolds, George, W. *Wagner the Wehr-Wolf*. 1847. New York: Dover, 2015. Print.
Schlitz, Laura Amy. *Splendors and Glooms*. Somerville, MA: Candlewick, 2014. Print.
"The Seven Most Extreme Haunted Houses in America." *The Raven and Black Cat*. ravenblackcat.com. Web. 10 Dec. 2015.
Swanson, Susan Marie. *The House in the Night*. Boston: Houghton Mifflin Harcourt, 2011. Print.
"The Thousand and One Nights." Trans. Husain Haddawy. *The Norton Anthology of World Literature*, ed. Sarah Lawall. New York: W.W. Norton, 2002. 658–93. Print.
Trübner's American, European, and Oriental Literary Record. London: Trübner, 1889. Print.
Veith, Gene. *Reading Between the Lines*. Wheaton, IL: Crossway, 1990. Print.
Walpole, Horace. *The Castle of Otranto*. New York: Dover, 2004. Print.
Wertham, Frederic. *Seduction of the Innocent*. New York: Rinehart, 1972. Print.
Wing, Natasha. *The Night Before Halloween*. New York: Grosset and Dunlap, 1999. Print.
Wisniewski, David. *Golem*. New York: Clarion, 1996. Print.

Wicked "Others"
Christian Conservatism and the Rejection of the Supernatural

BRENDA S. GARDENOUR WALTER

From the witches of traditional fairy tales to ghosts, monsters, and mythical creatures, the supernatural is a popular theme in children's picture books. Paranormal stories and characters offer young listeners and beginning readers entry to a wondrously fluid realm where anything is possible and everything is connected by silvery strands. From a liberal perspective, the fluidity and interconnectedness of the supernatural as a category makes it a perfect medium through which children might begin to investigate seen and unseen worlds and the creatures, human and otherwise, that populate them. Nestled safely in the lap of the reader, the child ventures into haunted spaces and meets strange beings, often only to discover that the supernatural or monstrous "Other" is not an evil enemy but a misunderstood—and ultimately very human—creature in search of acceptance and love. Many supernatural children's narratives, both textual and visual, are told from an internal focal point, in which the story unfolds through a first-person perspective. Other supernatural tales are told from dual focal points, in which the story unfolds from both internal and external perspectives. In addition to these multiple focalizations, children's picture books are negotiated between the child who controls the pace of the story by interpreting pictures and asking questions, and the adult reader who provides his or her own explanations and interpretations while narrating the text (Nodelman). This dialogic process facilitates the communication of liberal values such as empathy, equality, and a respect for differing worldviews and experiences, all while encouraging the autonomous child to create his or her own meanings and ideals.

While supernatural characters such as ghosts, witches, monsters, and magicians are delightful additions to the tale for many liberal readers, inspiring wonder and presenting opportunities for the discussion of issues of such as alterity and acceptance, supernatural themes are all but absent from conservative texts. Conservative reading lists for young children feature books with Christian themes that move beyond Bible stores to embrace pro-life agendas (Cockerell) and the "Christian history" of the United States (Olsen and J. Sherman). More pervasive are the often-intertwined themes of patriotism and militarism, both of which are reflected in books such as *American Soldier Proud and Free* (2007) and *With My Rifle by My Side: A Second Amendment Lesson* (2010), both written by Kimberly Jo Simac, an active political member of the Wisconsin Tea Party. *The Fisherman's Catch: A Conservative Bedtime Story* (2010) delves into right-wing socio-economics, arguing that capitalism is fair and that any redistribution of wealth, including social services such as welfare, is an affront to all. Unlike liberal children's books, which feature multiple viewpoints and first person perspectives, conservative narratives are often zero-focalized. In zero focalization, "a godlike narrator," voiced by the adult reader, and the ideology espoused in the text both gain "the status of an undeniable authority and the authenticity of an objective presentation" (Yannicopoulou 76). This framework does not allow for multiplicity of viewpoints, nor does it encourage children to explore and make new meanings of the internal and external worlds in which they live. The singular and authoritative nature of conservative texts is reinforced by the inclusion of "follow up questions" at the back of each book, meant not to promote open questioning and free discussion, but to reinforce the conservative ideologies of the adult reflected and affirmed in the text.

At the very heart of conservative children's picture books is a reductive binary cosmology in which the Christian nuclear family, often white and middle class, is not only "the seedbed of emotional life" but also the only place of safety and sanctity in an inherently sinful world populated by evil enemies (Wilcox 797). In books such as *Help! Mom! There Are Liberals Under My Bed!* (2005), *Help! Mom! Hollywood Is in My Hamper!* (2006), and *Help! Mom! The 9th Circuit Nabbed the Nativity!* (2007), all by Katharine DeBrecht, liberals are depicted as monstrous "others" who have crept into the Christian home to lurk in dark spaces and poison it with their non–Christian agendas (Abate 152–73). In the conservative imagination, liberal politicians, welfare recipients, communists, and atheists appear to be in solidarity with one another, a collective of dangerous outsiders seeking entry to the middle class fortress in order to destroy the patriarchal family unit from within. To protect the conservative status quo, children are taught that their Christian beliefs and values are right, pure, and good, and that all those who think or look differently than they do are impure, corrupt, and evil. At an extreme, they are likewise taught that the binary categories of Christian goodness and non–Christian evil have forever been and will always be at war, at least until the End of Days.

A militant fear of "otherness" and the potential penetration of the Christian domicile is reflected not only in the absence of supernatural characters such as ghosts and monsters in conservative children's books, but also in the repeated attempts on the part of many Christian conservatives to ban supernatural-themed books from public libraries and schools. In recent years, series such as *Goosebumps, Harry Potter,* and *Twilight* have come under attack by conservative Christian groups who have argued that they are morally and spiritually dangerous to children (Willey). While all supernatural themes are suspect, the depiction of wizardry and ritual magic in children's books and young adult fiction are believed to be the most perilous of all, in particular because the very act of reading these texts and the spells that they contain aloud is analogous to occult practice. Even more terrifying, "the child and the book can be or can become one"; as the child enters the world of the text, he or she repeats incantations, becomes familiar with forbidden practices, and may even "become an evildoer while reading" (Purkiss 30; 19). For conservative parents, supernatural children's books are circumspect not only because the they might seduce vulnerable minds and hearts into occult practice, but also because they frequently contain tropes and codes culled from gothic horror, including the color black, nighttime, tempests, forests, graveyards, Ouija Boards, occult rituals, candles, and monstrous beings, all of which are signifiers for Satanic evil. Liberal parents see these codes as good creepy fun, offering children an escape from the mundane world, an opportunity to step into Huizinga's magic circle where there is "no formal difference between play and ritual," a realm where they might experience something akin to transcendence (Huizinga 19). For this very same reason—the transformative power of the text—conservative parents see the inclusion of ritual magic, the tropes of gothic horror, and the supernatural in general as a gateway to Satanic evil that might sever the child from core family values.

The pervasive fear that Satanic "others" are actively seeking to destroy the conservative Christian family through the manipulation and penetration of its children is taken to an extreme and writ large in *Don't Make Me Go Back, Mommy: A Child's Book about Satanic Ritual Abuse* (1990). Written by Doris Sanford, *Don't Make Me Go Back* tells the harrowing tale of a young girl named Allison who is victimized by the Satanic cult that runs her daycare center. While in their "care," she is stripped naked, forced to perform sexual acts in the "movie star room," and fed strange foods, including "magic juice." One illustration features a sylvan Halloween ritual in which the daycare witches, clad in flowing black robes, gather naked children into a circle near a stone altar complete with pentagram, red candles, and black book. A horrifying narrative, *Don't Make Me Go Back* was published a the height of the Satanic Panic, a time in which conservative Christians across the Anglo-American world lived in abject terror of a Satanic New World Order, embodied in the liberal left, that sought the destruction of the Christian family. While Sanford's book can be seated in the historical context of the 20th-century Moral Panic, the signifiers of evil it contains—as well as the far more pervasive conservative narrative of evil "Others" seeking to pervert, penetrate, and in some cases consume innocent Christian children—can be traced to a specific rationality originating in 13th-century Europe. Using an Aristotelian binary cosmology as their foundation, scholastic theologians codified rigid categories of Christian goodness and inverted Satanic evil. This binary construction has remained a deep structure in Western discourse and continues to serve as the primary lens through which conservative Christians read their world, both to themselves and their children. An archaeological analysis of these deep structures reveals the otherwise hidden discourses that inform the production of conservative children's books, the absence of supernatural characters and themes in those books, and the lensing of liberal tales of the supernatural as corrupt, dangerous, and potentially demonic.

Dark Roots: The Medieval Construction and Codification of Evil

The binary cosmology that serves as a deep structure for modern conservative Christian mentalities has its roots in the academic milieu of the 13th century. It was then that scholastic theologians such as Thomas Aquinas and William of Auvergne conflated the natural philosophy of Aristotle, recently translated from Arabic into Latin, with authoritative Christian texts in an attempt to create a syncretic and all-encompassing system for explicating seen and unseen worlds. The foundation of this system was a bifurcated cosmos, inherited from antiquity, in which the moon served as a sacred boundary (Grant). Above the moon, planets embedded in crystalline spheres spun in perpetual harmony through the ether. Beyond the planetary spheres sat the sphere of the fixed stars, and beyond that the Prime Mover, who set the cosmos in to motion out of love (Aristotle *Metaphysics*, 6:7; *Physics* 8). In opposition to the superlunary realm, the sublunary realm was dominated by both the violent motion of physical bodies and the chaotic transformation of the four elements (fire, air, water, and earth), the latter of which facilitated the material processes of generation and corruption. Earth, the heaviest and most corrupt of the four elements, was the dross of the cosmos and therefore sunk to its very center, farthest in distance from the ethereal perfection of the Prime Mover. For Aristotelian and later Neoplatonic philosophers, the realms above and below the moon were neither "good" nor "bad," but part of an essentially neutral cosmic whole.

Beneath the quills of medieval scholastics, the ancient pagan cosmic model was baptized and codified. The superlunary realm became one of divine perfection, with the Prime Mover-cum-Christian God enthroned beyond the sidereal sphere in his heavenly Empyrean. Radiating downward from the Godhead were choirs of angels, moving in harmonious circles, utterly obedient to God's will (Aquinas *Summa Theologica*, Q57; A4). Theologians created the category of divine goodness as a reflection of this heavenly realm, codifying it as singular, white, translucent, warm, weightless, Christian and male. Following the logical precepts of Aristotelian contrariety, theologians constructed the sublunary realm as a radical inversion of Christian perfection, a place of dark Satanic evil (Clark). At the earth's icy dark core, far from the warmth and radiant light of the Christian God, sat the fallen Lucifer and his fellow disobedient angels, the leathery-winged black demons who wreaked havoc in an already chaotic world. While heavenly angels obeyed God and protected His people on earth, demons acted as free agents, floating on the air, manipulating the elements, and causing phantasms in weak human minds, all in an attempt to seduce Christians away from God and His Church and into the service of Satan (Aquinas *De Substantiis Separatis*). Constructed as a radical inversion of Christian goodness, Satanic evil was marked by multiplicity, the color black, darkness, coldness, and heaviness; it was likewise coded as non-Christian and female (Azouvi). The binary codification of Christian goodness and inverted Satanic evil promulgated by scholastic theologians left no room for ambiguity. Following the dictates of radical inversion, all individuals, entities, or ideas that did not conform to the patriarchal Christian paradigm were *of necessity* classified as Satanic and "other."

The medieval Church was the ultimate example of Christian perfection here on earth, led by authoritative men charged with maintaining the purity of the sheepfold. After the Fourth Lateran Council of 1215, all those who did not abide by the Church's ever-more-closely circumcised patriarchal dictates were labeled heretical, potentially wicked, and subject to punishment. Throughout the thirteenth and fourteenth centuries, church authorities became increasingly concerned with the presence of heretics, such as the Albigensians, and non-Christian "others," such as Jews, who were believed to be poisoning the Christian body (Rubin; Moore). Chaotic events in the Church, such as the existence of three men who claimed to Pope and the horrors wrought by the Black Plague, served as evidence for scholars and popular preachers alike that the power of Satan and his demons was increasing and that they were recruiting followers to their cause at an unprecedented rate. Fears that the Church body was under attack from Satanic enemies were articulated at the Council of Basel, which among other things discussed the heresy of witchcraft (Bailey and Peters). In response to these concerns, Johannes Nider wrote the *Formicarius* (1475), which argued that weak women were being seduced into heretical witchcraft by demons and other wicked women (Bailey). In order to curb the growth of this strange new heresy, Nider advocated for increased pastoral care in rural communities where such deviant practices were purportedly taking hold. Published just over a decade later, the *Malleus Maleficarum* (1486), an inquisitor's manual written by Heinrich Kramer, took an opposite approach, arguing that Satanic witches were irredeemable and should be mercilessly destroyed in order to protect innocent Christian families, in particular their young children.

Despite being denounced by the Church in 1490, the *Malleus* grew in popularity and inspired an entire tradition of witchcraft literature, in part because it affirmed what many already believed—and had long been taught—about the nature of inverted feminine evil and the Satanic "others" in their midst. Across witchcraft texts, from the *Malleus* to Nicholas Remy's *Demonolatry* (1595) and Pierre Lancre's *On the Inconstancy of Witches* (1602), the construction of Satanic evil is devilishly consistent, marked by blackness, nighttime, heaviness, coldness, and demonic duplicity. At the wicked heart of Satanic witchcraft lurk corrupt, irrational, and sexually rapacious women who actively worship the Devil through inverted rituals, such as trampling the cross, blaspheming, and the performing the *osculum infame*, all of which were meant to mock the patriarchal Church and its liturgy (Lancre 153). In the clerical imagination, witches sought the destruction of male authority, not only at the institutional level but also in the domestic sphere—the very heart of the Christian home. For example, in male-authored witchcraft treatises, witchy women are often accused of performing spells to control male sexuality, in some cases causing impotence, in others making the penis seem to disappear altogether (Smith 85–117). Men who rejected the sexual advances of witches or who were happily married to good women appear to have been the main targets of such spells. As inversions of obedient and modest Christian women, power hungry and rapacious witches were not only disobedient and toxic wives but also bad mothers. As midwives, they were accused of killing infants as they emerged from the womb and stealing their unbaptized corpses for use in the concoction of ointments; living babies and children were stolen for use in Sabbath rituals or to be raised as witches (Guazzo 34; Lancre 139). Critically, these evil women did not act alone but were imagined to be in concert with an ever-expanding network of Satanic "others," including scholarly practitioners of learned magic and "blood thirsty" Jews, all of whom were believed to be under the tutelage of demons and to serve in an organized Synagogue of Satan that sought the destruction of institutionalized Christian goodness (Rubin). The witchcraft paradigm, replete with the signifiers of inverted "otherness" first codified in the 13th century, would be transmitted from generation to generation through witchcraft, anti-woman, and anti-Jewish treatises, all of which shared the same message: the patriarchal Christian

Body, the Christian family, and its most vulnerable members—*the children*—must be protected from the penetrating and corrupting forces of inverted and Satanic evil.

Twisted Branches: The Modern Satanic Panic

The binary codification of good and evil and the construct of Satanic others seeking to penetrate the pure and patriarchal Christian body—be it the body of the Church, the family, or the child—have remained salient features of conservative culture in the West (Frankfurter). Like a current running just below placid waters, these paradigms bubble up most notably during periods of intense cultural change, most recently in turbulent 20th-century America (Smoczynski). The century began with the growing popularity of Spiritualism, a movement that sought communion with invisible entities through Ouija boards, automatic writing, table tapping, séances, and spirit photography (Melechi; Weisberg). These practices were combined with Eastern philosophies and non–Christian ideologies that had been sifted together in the esoteric works of authors such as William Keats, Aleister Crowley, and Madame Blavatsky. While fin-du-siècle Spiritualists saw the occult arts as valid paths to closure and transcendence, conservative Christians saw them as portals through which demonic entities—for in a binary cosmology neutral spirits have no place—might enter the world and corrupt society, home, and body. Dominated by women, Spiritualism likewise represented a rift in mainstream culture, a sign that good people were being seduced away from the singular, patriarchal, Christian ideal that, for traditionalists, served as the backbone of civic life. World War I, the Great Depression, and World War II followed on the heels of Spiritualism, traumatic events that confirmed conservative Christian suspicions that demonic forces were gathering strength for a global attack on American Christian freedom. At home, the death of sons due to warfare, the financial ruin and displacement caused by the Depression, and the disruption of the nuclear family as women entered the wartime workplace all contributed to a sense of despair and a concomitant rise in alcoholism, physical abuse, and suicide. For conservative Christians, especially members of the Pentecostal movement, these seemingly natural responses to violent cultural change were construed as demonic afflictions, evidence that the Devil sought the destruction of Christian America from within (Poole 100–02). In order to free good Christians from these demonic forces, pastors performed exorcisms, hoping to heal the afflicted with the power of the Holy Spirit (Cuneo 2001). By coding all mental illness and human suffering as potentially demonic, many Christians found evidence for the proliferation of evil and the coming of the End Times that they already believed to be upon them. Through this lens, the more exorcisms that they witnessed, the more apparent Satan's increasing power became.

In the second half of the 20th century, already-embattled conservatives saw the further dissolution of the patriarchal Christian ideal in the growth of the Counter Cultural movement and rise of the liberal left. The Civil Rights movement, the Gay Liberation Front, and Anti-War protests were evidence that the younger generation were willing to question institutionalized authority with little to no respect for the status quo. Even more telling, the 1960s saw the introduction of oral contraceptives, Women's Liberation, and the Equal Rights Amendment, all of which struck at the bastion of conservative culture—the patriarchal family and the middle class home. In this strange and inverted new world of "hippies," women controlled their own fertility and worked outside of the home if they wanted to; subverted men might stay home and care for children, do laundry, cook and clean. Communal living reshaped popular conceptions of the American family even further, rejecting nuclear and "heteronormative" structures for expanded socio-sexual networks that included homosexuality and polyamory. Conservative fears that these New Age communes were not only dangerous but also potentially evil were confirmed with the conviction of Charles Manson and his Family for the brutal murders of several individuals, including Sharon Tate and her unborn child, in the summer of 1969. At two separate crime scenes, strange symbols and sayings were scrawled on the walls in human blood. "If you're going to do something," said Charles Manson, "do it well. And leave something witchy." The violent turn of the Counter Culture, fueled in part by the introduction of methamphetamines as a new drug of choice, was likewise evident in the Altamont Free Concert stabbing in December of that same year. Popular culture capitalized on this growing concern that America's youth were not just liberal, but frenetic agents of Satanic evil. The Satanic supernatural permeated horror films, from the grindhouse classic, *I Drink Your Blood* (1970), in which Satanic hippies terrorize a small conservative town, to William Friedkin's *Exorcist* (1973), in which a pubescent girl is possessed by a demon while her divorced mother pursues a career outside of the home. For conservative Christians who lined up to see the *Exorcist* again and again, the film served as a confirmation for what they already believed—that the Devil had penetrated the Christian family, infected the children with liberal evil, and caused the horrors that were then unfolding in modern America.

In the 1980s, the pervasive fear that demon-possessed youths and Satanic conspirators lurking just out of sight were wreaking havoc on the predominantly white middle-class American family escalated into a "Satanic Panic" (Victor; Ellis *Lucifer Adcending*, 20). In conservative culture, these fears were fueled by Hal Lindsey's bestselling books *The Late Great Planet Earth* (1970), *Satan is Alive and Well on Planet Earth* (1972), and *The 1980's: Countdown to*

Armageddon (1980), all of which argued that Satanists were plotting the End of Days and that Christians and their way of life were under direct attack. Mainstream Americans beyond conservative Christian circles began to draw the same conclusions, in part because of the multi-media attention given to Satanic issues. In books such as *Michelle Remembers* (1980), written by Dr. Lawrence Pazder and his patient and future lover, Michelle Smith, and *Satan's Underground* (1988), written by Lauren Stratford, women claimed to have recovered memories of Satanic Ritual Abuse (SRA), which would soon receive its own diagnostic label in the clinical world. In these books and in televised exposes such as *20/20's* "The Devil Worshippers" and Geraldo Rivera's infamous "Exposing Satan's Underground," women claimed that they had been forced to participate in Black Masses, to bear and murder infants, and to consume their flesh and blood, all for the glory of Satan. Readers and viewers readily accepted the stories of these women because—like the *Malleus Maleficarum* five hundred years before—they confirmed what they already believed was true, that Satanists were everywhere and that children, especially those exposed to "others" outside of the family home, were vulnerable to corruption.

The Satanic Panic reached its peak with a series of scandals, including the now-infamous McMartin Preschool case, in which daycare providers were accused of abusing children in the service of Satan. The McMartin case, which would become the longest and most expensive trial in United States history, began in 1983 when a woman named Judy Johnson suspected that her three year old son who complained of a painful bowel movement had been sodomized at daycare. When she asked him what happened, she claimed that he told her that Ray Buckey, an attendant at the McMartin preschool, not only sexually abused him and the other children but also flew through the air and forced them to participate in strange blood rituals. Johnson brought her complaints to the police, charges were filed against Buckey, and precautionary letters were sent to dozens of parents whose children attended McMartin. Panicked parents demanded a full investigation, which involved the intensive questioning of very young children by Kee MacFarlane and her children's advocacy group, Children's Institute International. Upon questioning, the children all seemed to tell the same bizarre story—that members of the McMartin preschool were black-robed Satanists who performed sex acts on children, tortured them, and forced them to participate in the ritual sacrifice of infants and to consume their blood, all of which took place either in the tunnels beneath the school or in an abandoned church. Panicked parents believed that the children were telling the truth; how else would their stories all match so clearly? Skeptics argued that, by asking leading questions and promising rewards, the children were coerced into providing answers that affirmed a familiar narrative—that of the witchcraft paradigm—reshaped only slightly to fit a new age. Conservative Christians, however, many of whom were themselves terrified parents wracked with guilt at leaving their children in the hands of strangers, saw proof of what they already believed about the perils of modern life, the dissolution of the nuclear family, and the pervasiveness of Satanic others who sought to destroy their children. Even now, over thirty years after false imprisonment and release of Ray Buckey and the exoneration of the McMartin preschool, many still believe that Satanic ritual abuse took place and that the physical evidence, including the tunnels and the bodies of sacrificed infants, has merely been spirited away by dark forces. For conservative Christians, the threat of Satanic penetration never disappears but is forever lurking, waiting for an opportunity, looking for a place to plant its seeds and grow (Victor).

Dreadful Seeds: Evil "Othering" in Conservative Children's Books

The binary cosmology that fueled the Satanic Panic of the late 20th century continues to shape the worldview of conservative Christians and informs their production and consumption of children's books. In conservative Christian ideology, the category of goodness is defined as patriarchal, patriotic, and Christian—a paradigm established in picture books such as *America's Forgotten Heritage*, which establishes the hegemony of the Christian right, and *American Soldier Proud and Free*, which preaches patriotism and glorifies war as holy. Everything that does not fall within the closely circumscribed parameters of conservative American Christian goodness is *of necessity* associated with Satanic "otherness." This suspicion of individuals and ideas that fall outside of the conservative Christian ideal explains the xenophobic bent of many conservative children's books, which feature white middle class children almost exclusively. When non-white non–American children do appear in conservative children's texts, they are often depicted as helpless and requiring American intervention. In *Saving the Vietnamese Orphans: Heroes of the Vietnam War, Book 2* (2012), for example, the only hope for the children's survival is to be adopted into good American families and thereby be redeemed. Those who cannot and will not be converted to the conservative Christian agenda, such as liberals, are demonized as the hated "other." By their very nature, liberal viewpoints are myriad, multivalent, and focused on diversity rather than conformity. From a conservative perspective, this very multiplicity serves as an indicator of evil "otherness," a belief reflected in books such as *Mom! Help! There Are Liberals Under My Bed*, in which the scary monsters of childhood are replaced with liberal figures seeking to divert children from the singular and absolute path of Christian conservativism. The zero-focalization of these narratives confirms the authority of the all-knowing adult reader. Liberal monsters are not to be understood; their voices are not to be heard. Instead, they are at all costs to be shut out of the conservative home for the sake of protecting the purity of the children and patriarchal hegemony.

This binary cosmology likewise explains the near absence of supernatural themes in conservative books for children and young adults. By its very definition, the supernatural resides beyond the bounds of natural law. For conservative Christians, the only entity that can supersede natural law is the author of that law—the Christian God. A seemingly supernatural event, then, is either a miracle of God or a deception performed by the Devil or one of his evil agents, human or demonic. A radical binary system has no room for ambiguity, no neutral place for monsters, witches, or magic, all of which do not conform to the singular Christian ideal and are therefore cast into the inverted category of Satanic evil. Even ghosts have no purchase in this conservative world. The souls of the dead either rise to Heaven, descend to Hell, or await final judgment at the Second Coming of Christ. If the souls of the dead seem to wander the earth, it must be a mere phantasm, a demonic lie meant to fool weak human minds. In the conservative worldview, the supernatural is associated with Satanic evil and has no place in books for children, which are meant to teach them how to be good conservative Christians. A chilling and telling exception to the conservative rule against the use of the supernatural in picture books is *Don't Make Me Go Back, Mommy: A Child's Book About Satanic Ritual Abuse*. The book centers on a young girl named Allison whose mother sends her to daycare. While there, Allison becomes a child bride of Satan, drinks "magic juice," has pornographic pictures taken of her in the "movie star room," is penetrated by a demon through "magic surgery," and participates in a Samhain-Halloween ritual with other naked children while her teachers, clad in black robes, prepare a Satanic altar for sacrifice. While *Don't Make Me Go Back* is very much an artifact of the Satanic Panic and the daycare scandals at its height, it is nevertheless a manifestation of more general conservative Christian concerns. For example, the world outside of the patriarchal home—including the "alternative" female-dominated family of the daycare center of educational system—is depicted as a dangerous place where good Christian children are targeted by evil entities and taught to disobey their parents. Good Christian mothers should stay at home with their children under the watchful eye of the patriarch rather than dropping them off at daycare and subjecting them to evil "others." Likewise, *Don't Make Me Go Back* reflects the persistent conservative belief that magic, witches, Halloween, and anything associated with the supernatural imagination is of necessity Satanic and dangerous to young bodies, minds, and souls.

The conservative Christian lensing of liberals as monstrous others and the supernatural as Satanic evil goes a long way in explaining the vehement rejection of children's books with supernatural themes. From spooky picture books such as *A Dark, Dark Tale* (1992) and *The Littlest Witch* (1962) to series such as *Goosebumps*, *Harry Potter*, and *Twilight*, the supernatural is fundamentally liberal, an invitation into an alternate reality, a world of wonder and alterity. Liberal children's books feature both first person and multiple focalizations, allowing the child to see and hear the narrative from a variety of perspectives. Reader and listener navigate these different narratives together, a process that facilitates dialogue and fosters a respect for divergent views and co-existing truths. This is especially powerful in picture books about monsters who are shunned for "not fitting in." In seeing the story from the monster's point of view, the child experiences empathy and compassion for beings that might otherwise appear scary. While monsters serve as a vehicle for teaching kindness, respect, and acceptance, ghosts offer an opportunity to discuss the existence (or not) of life after death. Presented with a variety of religious, spiritual, and secular viewpoints, the child is left to wonder what he or she believes as an individual; there is no right answer. The fantastic realm of wizards, witches, and magic is perhaps the most profoundly liberal of all; here, individuals harness cosmic forces and manipulate nature, thereby shaping their own destinies and acting as agents of change in the world around them. These narratives often feature incantations, spells, and rituals that children might perform, chanting memorized words and mimicking gestures in an attempt to connect with unseen powers, to invent their future selves. As every sorceress knows, books themselves are magic; they are spells with the power to transform the hearts and minds of children and adults alike. It is the transformative power of the text that conservative Christians apparently fear the most—for books, like demons, might creep into the conservative home and corrupt their children from within.

Works Cited

Abate, Michelle Ann. *Raising Your Kids Right: Children's Literature and American Political Conservatism*. Rutgers: Rutgers University Press, 2011.
Azouvi, François. "The Plague, Melancholy, and the Devil." *Diogenes* 27 (1979): 112–30.
Bailey, Michael D. *Battling Demons: Witchcraft, Heresy, and Reform in the Later Middle Ages*. Philadelphia: Pennsylvania State University Press, 2002. Print.
Bailey, Michael D., and Edward Peters, "A Sabbat of Demonologists: Basel 1430–1441." *The Historian* 65.6 (2003): 1375–95.
Barkun, Michael. *A Culture of Conspiracy: Apocalyptic Visions in Contemporary America*. Berkeley: University of California Press, 2003. Print.
Boureau, Alain. *Satan the Heretic: The Birth of Demonology in the Medieval West*. Chicago: University of Chicago, 2006.
Broedel, Hans Peter. *The Malleus Maleficarum and the Construction of Witchcraft Theology and Popular Belief*. Manchester: Manchester University Press, 2003. Print.
Clark, Stuart. *Thinking with Demons*. Oxford: Oxford University Press, 1997. Print.
Cockerell, L. *The Miracle*. Kinderfable Press, 2014. Print.

Cuneo, Michael W. *American Exorcism: Expelling Demons in the Land of Plenty.* New York: Doubleday, 2001. Print.
De Brecht, Katharine. *Help! Mom! Hollywood Is in My Hamper!* Los Angeles: Kids Ahead Press, 2006. Print.
_____. *Help! Mom! The 9th Circuit Nabbed the Nativity!* Los Angeles: Kids Ahead Press, 2007. Print.
_____. *Help! Mom! There Are Liberals Under My Bed!* Los Angeles: Kids Ahead Press, 2005. Print.
Ellis, Bill. *Lucifer Ascending.* Lexington: University of Kentucky, 2004. Print.
_____. *Raising the Devil.* Lexington: University of Kentucky, 2000. Print.
Frankfurter, David. *Evil Incarnate: Rumors of Demonic Conspiracy and Ritual Abuse in History.* Princeton: Princeton University Press, 2006. Print.
Grant, Edward. *Planets, Stars, and Orbs: Medieval Cosmos, 1200–1687.* New York: Cambridge University Press, 1996. Print.
Guazzo, Francesca Maria. *Compendium Maleficarum.* Trans. Montague Summers. New York: Dover, 1988. Print.
Huizinga, Johann. *Homo Ludens: A Study of the Play Element in Culture.* Boston: Beacon Press, 1955. Print.
Lancre, Pierre de. *On the Inconstancy of Witches.* Trans. Joseph O'Connor. Tempe: ACMRS Publications, 2006. Print.
Lindsey, Hal. *Satan Is Alive and Well on Planet Earth.* Grand Rapids: Zondervan, 1972. Print.
Lindsey, Hal, and Carole C. Carlson. *The Late Great Planet Earth.* Grand Rapids: Zondervan, 1970. Print.
Mackay, Christopher S. *Malleus Maleficarum.* Cambridge: Cambridge University Press, 2006. Print.
Massey, Jeanne. *The Littlest Witch.* New York: Knopf, 1962. Print.
Melechi, Antonio. *Servants of the Supernatural: The Night Side of the Victorian Mind.* London: Random House UK, 2009. Print.
Moore, R. I. *The Formation of a Persecuting Society,* 2d ed. Oxford: Blackwell, 2007. Print.
Nodelman, Perry. "The Eye and I: Identification and First-Person Narratives in Picture Books." *Children's Literature* 19 (1991): 1–30.
Olsen, C., and J. Sherman. *America's Forgotten Heritage.* Minneapolis: Riding the Truth Press, 2011. Print.
Poole, W. Scott. *Satan in America: The Devil We Know.* Lanham, MD: Rowman and Littlefield, 2010. Print.
Purkiss, Diane. "Books of Magic." *Magical Tales: Myth, Legend and Enchantment,* ed. Diane Purkiss and Carolyn Larrington. Oxford: Bodleian Library Press, 2013. Print.
Remy, Nicholas. *Demonolatry.* Trans. Montague Summers. New York: Dover, 2008. Print.
Rubin, Miri. "Europe Remade: Purity and Danger in Late Medieval Europe." *Transactions of the Royal Historical Society* 6.11 (2001): 101–24.
Simac, Kimberly Jo. *American Soldier Proud and Free.* Wisconsin: Great Northern Adventure Co., 2007. Print.
Simac, Kimberly Jo. *With My Rifle By My Side: A Second Amendment Lesson.* Eager River, WI: Nordskog Publishing, 2010. Print.
Smith, Michelle, and Lawrence Pazder. *Michelle Remembers.* New York: Congdon, 1980. Print.
Smith, Moira. "The Flying Phallus and the Laughing Inquisitor: Penis Theft in the Malleus Maleficarum," *Journal of Folklore Research* 39.1 (2002): 85–117.
Smoczynski, Rafal. "Persecuting Witches in the Early Modern and Late Modern Eras: Similarities and Differences in the Sabbath Myth." *Anthropological Notebooks* 19.2 (2013): 25–38.
Stratford, Lauren. *Satan's Underground.* New York: Harvest House, 1988. Print.
Thomas Aquinas. *De Substantiis Separatis.* Turnhout: Brepols, 2013. Print.
Victor, Jeffrey. "Fundamentalist Religion and the Moralist Crusade Against Satanism: The Social Construction of Deviance," *Deviant Behavior* 15:3 (1994), 169–98.
_____. *Satanic Panic: The Creation of a Contemporary Legend.* Chicago: Open Court, 1993. Print.

Weisberg, Barbara. *Talking to the Dead: Kate and Maggie Fox and the Rise of Spiritualism.* San Francisco: Harper One, 2005. Print.
Wilcox, W. Bradford. "Conservative Protestant Childbearing: Authoritarian or Authoritative?" *American Sociological Review* 63 (1998): 796–809.
Willey, Jessica. "Pastor Wants 'Demonic' Books Removed from Public Library." 22 Aug. 2014. http://abc13.com/religion/pastor-wants-demonic-books-removed/275930/.
Wright, Thomas. *The Fisherman's Catch: A Conservative Bedtime Story.* Ivory Dusk Publishing, 2010. Print.
Yannicopoulou, Angela. "Focalization in Children's Picture Books." *Telling Children's Stories: Narrative Theory and Children' Literature.* Ed. Mike Cadden. Omaha: University of Nebraska Press, 2010.

Part 6: Moral Agencies

The Fantastic in the Everyday
Growing Up with The Mysteries of Harris Burdick

Mariaelena DiBenigno

In December 2012, while last-minute holiday shopping, I encountered a ghost from my youth in the children's section of an independent bookstore. The ghost was elegant and striking, with a thick hardcover and crisp pages. It was a recently published anthology, entitled *The Chronicles of Harris Burdick*, containing fourteen image-caption combinations accompanied by short stories. I was unfamiliar with the short stories, but I recognized the image-caption combinations. They reminded me of a dusty bookshelf in my childhood bedroom and a slim, haunting, hard-backed portal into my childhood imaginings. I remembered my first wide-eyed forays into a literature where the answers were not nestled neatly in pre-packaged conclusions and morals. Viewing the image-captions as an adult, I still felt wonder and curiosity.

These image-caption pairs were from a much older book, Chris Van Allsburg's enigmatic *The Mysteries of Harris Burdick*, published in 1984. In the original *Harris Burdick*, Van Allsburg distanced himself from the picture book bearing his name in a decidedly grown-up "Introduction." Van Allsburg wrote that the image-caption pairings came from a shadowy individual named Harris Burdick, who disappeared without sharing the connective narrative that explained each image-caption. Instead of stories, Van Allsburg and the reader were left with aesthetically inventive black and white images. Suggesting the photographic work of Eugène Atget or Alfred Stieglitz, the images "feel" pictorial due to a "sculptural realism, ... chiaroscuro and the shifting perspectives from picture to picture" (Neumeyer 6). Like the work of Atget and Stieglitz, *Harris Burdick* encourages—nay, requires—an expansive imagination in its reader. Without a willingness to wonder, *Harris Burdick* might be a frustrating experience for young readers. In the original "Introduction," Van Allsburg asks (perhaps more of the reader than of Burdick): "What are the stories that went with these drawings?" This is a picture book that begs for storytelling *from* its audience rather than offering it.

In the spin-off *Chronicles of Harris Burdick*, well-known authors such as Stephen King and Lois Lowry entered the world of Harris Burdick to answer Van Allsburg's question. In each new story, "the authors use the pictures and their captions as mere jumping-off places for richly imagined stories" (Coats 277). However, these stories do not attempt to offer the "definitive" word on Burdick's authorial intent; instead, they are about "starting more conversations and opening more possibilities than they close" (Coats 277) which was Van Allsburg's intent when publishing the image-captions in 1984.[1] Obviously, this is all a beautifully maintained farce.[2] Van Allsburg created the exquisite black-and-white images, titled them accordingly, and wrote their enigmatic captions. He then presented them to millions of readers as a postmodern ghost story. With each eerie image-caption, the reader crosses over into magical territory and creates his or her own fantastic story—perhaps centered on a magical harp ("The Harp"), or a glowing pumpkin ("Just Desert"), or a ghostly schooner ("Captain Tory")? In the *New York Times Book Review*, Leonard S. Marcus wrote how Van Allsburg's oeuvre concerned "Jump-starting the imaginations of world-weary 6-and-7-year olds"—and none of Van Allsburg's spectacular picture books jump-start the imagination more than the enigmatic *Harris Burdick*.[3]

Harris Burdick presents supernatural openings within familiar settings to show its audience that morals are not always simply handed to the audience. These spectral, fragmented image-captions act as a transition for readers ready to move beyond neat and tidy storytelling. Unlike wordless picture books or "choose your adventure" texts, where text-images direct meaning for the reader, *Harris Burdick* allows its audience to be the moral messenger and provides the child audience with an adult agency not found in many picture books. Though it has often been explored as a pedagogical tool, I propose to look at *Harris Burdick* as a postmodern picture book without traditional transitions and without overt authorial power over the narrative. In its postmodern-ness, *The Mysteries of Harris Burdick* uses familiar, domestic settings to reveal spectral boundaries within traditional narratives. Using actual windows, doors, and other familiar openings, the reader must imagine moral conclusion(s) based on the textual and visual threads provided by Van Allsburg. Using five specific image-captions from the *Harris Burdick*, my essay will first address notions of spectrality and mystery, then move into a discussion of childhood imagination and the postmodern picture book. I will conclude with a close reading of supernatural openings into the traditionally demarcated domestic spaces of *Harris Burdick*.

In my essay, I rely on the Oxford English Dictionary's definitions of "morality" and "moral." First, morality relates "to the distinction between right and wrong, or good and evil, in relation to the actions, desires, or character of responsible human beings" ("Morality, n"). It is a way to behave or rules of conduct that help impart culturally normative behaviors. Second, a moral is "[a]n exposition of the moral teaching or practical lesson contained in a literary work; that part of a work which expounds or contains the moral meaning" ("Moral, n"). As the vehicle for the development of morality, individual morals help create meaning for the developing child. In postmodern *anything*, morality—if it exists at all—is self-constructed and unbounded by socio-cultural norms. Thus, the postmodern picture book is a mode for young children to construct their own morals using familiar, if fragmented, narratives. We often arrive at the moral of a story by asking, without irony, sarcasm or animosity, "What's the point?" Using these definitions, readers are always moralizing when perusing *Harris Burdick*. They must create "the point."

Spectrality and Mystery

The *Mysteries of Harris Burdick* is a tour de force in the picture book industry.[4] It lingers with readers for years after they first encounter the soft, charcoal and black pastel drawings (Kiefer 670). The images have a spectral quality that suggests the tenuous boundary between the natural and the supernatural. In *Harris Burdick*'s very first image-caption, "Archie Smith, Boy Wonder," two ghost orbs hover over a sleeping child and three more approach the child's open bedroom window. These orbs are bright and, according to the caption, are sentient speakers: "A tiny voice asked, 'Is he the one?'" (Van Allsburg). This is the most overtly spectral image-caption in *Harris Burdick*. Ghostly orbs are widely accepted as evidence of the supernatural and they are often captured on film in haunted places.[5] However, a recent turn in cultural theory proposes to look more closely at the spectral as more than a spooky moment. In the important anthology, *The Spectralities Reader: Ghosts and Haunting in Contemporary Cultural Theory*, Maria Del Pilar Blanco and Esther Pereen define spectrality as "a conceptual metaphor capable of bringing to light and opening up to analysis hidden, disavowed, and neglected aspects of the social and cultural realm, past and present" (21). When witnessed, the spectral begs for an interrogation of knowledge formation—what we know and how we know it (*Spectrality* 9). This interrogation is what French philosopher Jacques Derrida calls "hauntology," a play on the term "ontology." With hauntology, an existence materializes only when we acknowledge its absence. Hauntology considers "the effectivity or the presence of a specter, that is, [...] what seems to remain" (Derrida 10). When we study "what seems to remain" we engage in hauntological analysis of fragmentary, narrative residue. By its very structure, *Harris Burdick* calls for the hauntological approach, as it is a text filled with absences: an absent author, missing stories, and no tidy moral. When middle-school teachers prepare lessons that use the *Harris Burdick* image-captions, they are asking their students to engage in this sophisticated analysis.[6] In order to find meaning, student writers confront the narrative absences and resurrect the spectral residue from the mysterious image-captions.

Mystery, at the heart of *Harris Burdick,* requires an awareness of hauntology. In "Archie Smith," the reader is asked to interrogate the absence of an explanation for the ghostly orbs. We know *who* they want, but *what* do they want? How will they affect, or perhaps infect, Archie? These questions seek answers from the reader because the author offers none. Thus, *The Mysteries of Harris Burdick* is a study in how the supernatural subsumes the rational. In their Introduction to *Mystery in Children's Literature: From the Rational to the Supernatural,* Adrienne Gavin and Christopher Routledge define two subgenres within mystery. First, "[r]ational mysteries ... are solved to the satisfaction of a character's and/or reader's intellect" (2). I am reminded of the Nancy Drew and the Boxcar Children mysteries, which rarely haunt the reader post-dénouement. Their endings are neat, tidy, and logical. I am more interested in Gavin and Routledge's second category, "the 'supernatural' in which mysteries are generally resolved to the satisfaction of a character's or reader's instincts and in which the mystery remains" (2). Encountering this latter form encourages intellectual development and "provides room for more than one truth" (Gavin and Routledge 3). *This* is the mystery of *Harris Burdick*: we all examine the same enigmatic image-captions and construct a different set of morals. We tell different stories because *Harris Burdick* is not rational; instead, it is supernatural and requires the "acceptance of the mystery as an inexplicable element of human life" (2). At any age, this is a decidedly mature moral to learn and process. We must acknowledge the absence of ontological truth and delve into hauntological unknowing. *The Mysteries of Harris Burdick* certainly opened new narrative possibilities for my own cognitive development. I was—and still am—blown away by the "plotlessness and indeterminacy [in] Van Allsburg's book" (Gavin 217). There is simply nothing like it in the picture book world. Before *Harris Burdick,* I had never experienced an authoritative and authorial shift when reading. I always trusted the author to resolve the story into an uncomplicated moral. *Harris Burdick* completely subverted that paradigm for me, as the picture book "clearly moves into 'the unknown,' as far from the 'rational,' solved world ... as it is perhaps possible to go" (217). It is an eerie, unbounded, enigmatic puzzle that cannot be resolved without reader input and there are no hard answers, morals or value judgments. These are constructed through individual imaginative processes.

Childhood Imagination and Postmodern Picture Books

In *The Uses of Enchantment: The Meaning and Importance of Fairy Tales*, Bruno Bettelheim argues that children use literature to "find deeper meaning" (3). Specifically, in order to "enrich" a child's life, this literature "must stimulate his imagination" (Bettelheim 5). Within such stimulating literature, the child finds necessary "ideas on how to bring his inner house into order"— or what Bettelheim refers to as "a moral education" (5). Bettelheim argues in psychoanalytical terms, but he usefully suggests that the child become familiar with his or her own moral code by creating his or her own stories using familiar literary elements (7). In other words, this stimulating literature—perhaps supernatural in genre—provides "new dimensions to the child's imagination which would be impossible for him to discover as truly on his own" (Bettelheim 7). The developing child requires a text to stimulate these "new dimensions" which then create a new moral code. Bettelheim identifies the folk fairytale as the best literature for stimulating the childhood imagination. Broadly defined, folk fairytales use magical, supernatural elements to illustrate an "existential dilemma briefly and pointedly" in simplified or familiar situations where "all characters are typical rather than unique" (Bettelheim 8). The folk fairytale uses these stock characters to showcase the grown-up lesson that "evil is as omnipresent as virtue" (Bettelheim 8). Within the folk fairytale, the "duality" (Bettelheim 9) between good and evil poses a moral problem to the child reader, who usually projects himself or herself on to the fairy tale hero. In this projection, the child reader adheres to the hero's moral code and struggles to make sense of (and perhaps conquer) evil in the world (Bettelheim 9). I would offer that *Harris Burdick*, disjointed and spectral, is a self-constructed fairytale lacking the "follow the hero" formula. For example, the aforementioned "Archie Smith, Boy Wonder" contains magical elements that a reader might recognize from familiar folk fairytales: ghostly orbs associated with fairies, a sleeping child, the promise/dilemma of adventure beyond the home. While we may recognize these familiar elements, "Archie Smith, Boy Wonder" lacks a clear-cut resolution helmed by a moral-driven hero. This makes it an intriguing read for child and adult alike.

In stimulating literature like *Harris Burdick*, "our sense receptors get turned up, not off; they work harder, rather than shutting down" (Spitz, *Brightening Glance* 8). *Harris Burdick* captures the reader's imagination because the reader recognizes familiar elements, but imagines the story's meaning using his own experiences. This can be an uncomfortable sensation because there are no pre-packaged morals. We must then imagine the moral to make meaning. In his encyclopedic study, *Landscapes of Fear*, cultural geographer Yi-Fu Tuan writes, "If we had less imagination, we would feel more secure" (6). Yet we encourage imagination in the child, especially via shared literature, so perhaps we also use literature "to teach [children] fear" (8). Tuan also suggests that this fear can have a positive affect in that "we turn curious" (10). For Tuan, looking at what we fear helps "To understand growth, daring, and adventure" (10)—three words I would use to describe *Harris Burdick*'s mysterious, postmodern image-captions.

In addition to being a haunting and stimulating text, *Harris Burdick* is also decidedly a work of postmodernism, a genre that requires active imaginations because neat conclusions are not readily available. As argued earlier, *Harris Burdick* is a supernatural mystery that operates beyond rational boundaries. In her essay "The Mysteries of Postmodern Epistemology: Stratemeyer, Stine, and Contemporary Mystery for Children," Karen Coats argues, "Postmodernism ... challenges the supremacy of the rational, opening new questions regarding the limits of our reason in the face of the irrational" (193). In a postmodern text that refuses to sequentially "tell the story," the generic boundaries of *Harris Burdick* are porous and layered at the same time. According to Coats, in modern fiction, "normality is founded on the exclusion of the abnormal" (193) but in postmodern supernatural mystery, this exclusion is never complete. In order to address the hauntological, we must acknowledge the presence of the abnormal instead of dismissing it as irrational. Simply, the abnormal exists in tandem with the normal; for example, in "Archie Smith, Boy Wonder," ghost orbs can hover over the familiar bed. By accepting this postmodern reality, *Harris Burdick* rejects the familiar metanarratives found in rational mystery, but often uses familiar fragments (Nel 185). In the past, picture books often represented the moral and cultural codes of traditional "societal expectations" (O'Neil 41). However, "postmodern picture books ... offer even greater support to young readers" in a fast-paced multimodal culture (O'Neil 41). Postmodern children's literature does not throw out the structure. Instead, it throws out the construction of pre-ordained moral boundaries and requires the active participation of its audience.

In his innovative work, *The Nimble Reader: Literary Theory and Children's Literature*, Roderick McGillis argues that *Harris Burdick* is postmodern because "it lacks unity of plot; ... no single subject is evident in the pages of the book; the setting appears historical, but this is constructed history, history imaginatively created, not factually presented"; there is a "death of the author" quality to Harris Burdick's absent identity; there is "an opportunity to participate in the creation of the meaning of the images" (154).

This is also the working definition of postmodern literature. It is important to note that postmodern picture books, like *Harris Burdick*, do not eschew meaning or wonder. In his essay "'The Simple Little Picture Book': Private

Theater to Postmodern Experience," Wiam El-Tamami argues that picture books are postmodern "not in the nihilistic sense commonly attributed to it, but in its most joyously freewheeling incarnation" (37). Thus, for El-Tamami and others, *Harris Burdick* is the definitive postmodern picture book: "Each frame is an enigma, a tantalizing invitation to step into the role of Storyteller—a fertile jumping off point for a flight of the imagination" (El-Tamami 39). This is key: *Harris Burdick* subverts the familiar author-reader dynamic by opening the audience's mind to the imaginative possibilities within a narrative. Intended moral lessons disappear, if they ever existed, and the reader is left in charge. Via haunting and spectral landscapes, *The Mysteries of Harris Burdick* re-constructs the traditional moral purpose of a picture book. As the *School Library Journal* notes, "Readers/viewers cross the barrier into the artist's world to share [the artist's] vision. In [*Harris Burdick*], Van Allsburg dares to ignore these boundaries" (152).

Spectral Openings to the Domestic Space

I have chosen to analyze five image-captions from *Harris Burdick*: "Archie Smith, Boy Wonder," "Uninvited Guests," "Mr. Linden's Library," "The Third Floor Bedroom," and "The House on Maple Street." My selected image-captions depict characters ranging from children to one conspicuously middle-aged man. Each illustrates how *Harris Burdick* encourages moral meaning making within its reader, child and/or adult, by offering spectral openings into the traditional domestic narratives. It is the reader who imagines each moral, though he or she is provided a few familiar fragments. Each of the five images-captions illustrates an unbounded domestic space within the mysterious, disjointed genre of postmodern literature. The home, so often the safe space in children's literature, helps us see how the spectral enters the everyday. It asks us to consider how the house is a haunted space. Here, hauntology helps me, as acknowledging the spectral in *Harris Burdick* "reveal[s] something of the enigma of everyday life, the way it can no longer be taken as straightforward" (Del Pilar Blanco and Pereen, *Popular Ghosts* xiii). These spectral, supernatural openings allow an imagined narrative that help make moral meaning. I also chose these image-captions because they intrigued my child and adult imagination. I find them delightfully mysterious and uncanny, their settings both familiar and unsettling.

Unsecured House

The Mysteries of Harris Burdick depicts many unusual locales: a forest glen, a Roman Catholic Church, a Venetian canal. However, the most prominent and recurring setting is the domestic space or home. *Harris Burdick* intrigues its reader by displaying a truly uncanny idea for child and adult alike: the home is not secure. For Sigmund Freud, the uncanny is felt when we are unsettled by the once familiar, i.e., a person, place, or thing. Feeling a sense of uncanniness points to when "something happens in our lives that seems to confirm ... old, discarded [primitive, animistic] beliefs" (154)—something like a supernatural opening to your prosaic, middle class basement or a vine growing out of your nighttime novel. Roderick McGillis suggests that Freud's uncanny is a useful tool when analyzing *Harris Burdick*: "Van Allsburg's world is alive with suggestions of spirits and other forces or even beings ready to erupt into our normal reality at any time" (146). In *Harris Burdick,* these "spirits and other beings" erupt from windows, wallpaper, doorways, and even books. The aforementioned items are familiar, but they are rendered uncanny when "the boundary between fantasy and reality is blurred" (Freud 150–51). Then, they open to new, imaginative worlds.

The home is also a familiar cultural setting in television shows, photographs and films. Homes are often used to create the feeling of security—and also used to unsettle that security. For example, *Harris Burdick*'s, "The House on Maple Street," suggests the horror movie series, *Nightmare on Elm Street,* a franchise where sleep is not secured against supernatural entities. That *Harris Burdick,* as a postmodern picture book, reminds me of *Nightmare on Elm Street* is evidence of its ability to "evoke memories of other related cultural objects" (Spitz, *Inside Picture Books* 14). The cinematic comparison is not without merit, for "picture books can be approached like scripts" (Spitz, *Inside Picture Books* 15).[7] A script begs for performance but no two performances, even by the same actor, are the same. Performance is always changing and unsecured to the script. Van Allsburg's title-image-captions are also unmoored, but they lack the narrative cohesion found in scripts; they do not engage in what Lawrence Sipe terms "synergy," or when "the text and the illustration sequence [is] incomplete without the other" (98). In *Harris Burdick,* Sipe's "text and the illustration sequence" is incomplete unless the reader provides his or her input. Reading *The Mysteries of Harris Burdick* provides "the opportunity to engage in an unending process of meaning-making as every rereading brings about new ways of looking at words and pictures" (Sipe 107). There is no single way to interpret its morals. Like a script, the unbounded homes in *Harris Burdick* open new ways to perform and make meaning.

In the Westernized world, we collectively recognize certain domestic components, i.e., the bedroom and the basement. Children in particular expect a certain security within these spaces. The house should not blast off into space like a rocket, as it does in "The House on Maple Street." It should be a safely bounded space; to find it otherwise suggests that the home's moral and concrete foundations are radically unmoored. In *Keywords for Children's*

Literature, Mavis Reimer defines "Home" in this way: "The idea that the house is, or should be, the center of family life is at the foundation of the contemporary systems of consumer capitalism that are taken to be normative in many of the societies of the developed world. Seen in this light, the intense interest in home in children's literature situates this literature within the dominant ideologies of its societies" (107).

The domestic spaces in *Harris Burdick* exhibit mid–20th century consumer-driven touches[8]: a baseball bat and yo-yo instead of a gaming device; an old-fashioned radio instead of a flat-screen TV; and cuffed pant legs instead of skinny jeans. The *Harris Burdick* images' captions take us back in time—but not *too* far back. With titles like "The House on Maple Street" and "Archie Smith, Boy Wonder," the *adult* reader might be reminded of the 1950s, a weird decade within United States cultural memory. Historian Michael Kammen has written about the "anxious mood of the 1950s" in the United States, a period marked by "a pronounced sense of discontinuity between past and present"—yet another boundary to consider (533). In order to combat postwar anxiety about international, national, state, and local boundaries, there was increased emphasis on the nuclear, heteronormative family within the traditional domestic sphere (Self 4–5). As a postmodern picture book, *Harris Burdick* completely disrupts the traditional, middle-class home by opening its boundaries to all manner of weirdness. There is no closure and no return to the safety of one's home. Instead, the 1950s domestic sphere, with its "dominant ideologies" and prescriptive consumer capitalistic morals, is subverted (Reimer 107). The homes in *Harris Burdick* are open to all manner of spectral entities: ghostly orbs, carpet monsters, flighty wallpaper. In this permissible condition, the reader is able to make her own moral meaning. Instead of conforming to acceptable 1950s morals, the domestic spaces in *Harris Burdick* show the porosity of private life.

Bedroom Unbounded

For Yi-Fu Tuan, a major "landscape of fear" is the porous space. In order to combat the chaos of undefined and thus unsecured parameters, societies across the world recognize three essential boundaries "of the domain, of the house, and of the body" (Tuan 206). First, we crave familiar—and spectral—state and national borders that define us and define others. Second, we need the domestic home, a "bounded space, but it has openings that must be protected" (206). Finally, our bodies require protection because they are permeable and susceptible to all manner of evil: infection, poison, demons. Despite our desire to maintain boundaries, "security is not absolute" (207). Unsanctioned openings are almost always fear inducing—even if that fear is tinged with delight. Within the house, the bedroom is a specific site to elude fears. In *The Brightening Glance,* Ellen Spitz points out how children's bedrooms "matter … [because] they are the setting for significant learning, dreaming, working, and playing" (133). In this familiar homespace, "a child invents and discovers herself" (Spitz, *The Brightening Glance* 137) and that is why *Harris Burdick* uses bedrooms with porous boundaries to further its mysteries and spur the imaginative process. Spitz asks her reader to consider the way it felt to look out one's childhood window and the pleasurable sensation of solitude in "secret spaces" (*The Brightening Glance* 158) where imagination can run free. Here, it is important to consider how a child might imagine the housebound experience differently from an adult. A child might consider the bedroom a safe space to dream because of an assumed adult presence, somewhere, within the house—especially at nighttime. An adult might also see the bedroom as a safe space for child's play, because the child is safely within the house's boundaries. In *Harris Burdick,* the bedroom's porosity implies that these assumed boundaries are negotiable and shifting for both audiences.

In my *Harris Burdick* selections, there are three bedrooms depicted: "Archie Smith, Boy Wonder," "Mr. Linden's Library," and "The Third-Floor Bedroom." In these familiar spaces, an opening or window appears and reveals "secret spaces" where imaginative processes and moral meaning making can occur. First, Archie Smith sleeps by an open window; there is no screen but there is a rolled-up blind. The caption informs us: "A tiny voice asked, "Is he the one?" (Van Allsburg). Archie has been chosen for something, but his giftedness is unknown to him. His room is unremarkable, save for the round bedposts that mimic the glowing orbs floating through the window. There are implied parental protectors, and he is carefully tucked into bed. From the open window, there is a dark space forested with pine trees and silhouetted by the moonlight. The entire scene is peaceful and safe. Even the orbs' presence is more illuminating than invasive; these lights could lead Archie from his everyday existence into something fantastic, but the orbs are soft and slow. They approach with a creeping quality matched by the vine growth in the second bedroom scene, "Mr. Linden's Library." In this image-caption, there is no open window but its metaphorical counterpart: an open book. The nameless girl, carefully tucked in bed like Archie, has been to Mr. Linden's library. In this image, the boundary is not a window or door, but a book. However, this book has a vegetative growth within it, something not evident to the sleeping girl when she first opened the book. The caption reads, "He had warned her about the book. / Now it was too late" (Van Allsburg). Here, an unknown boundary is trespassed and a *Harris Burdick* reader must construct moral meaning by considering what should be done versus what could be done. With each image-caption, there are a variety of conclusions for the observer to consider and the possibilities for moral meaning-making alter with the reader's age.

In the final image-caption, "The Third Floor Bedroom," there is a freshly painted, wide-open windowsill with gauzy curtains blowing in the breeze. The caption reads, "It all began when someone left / the window open" (Van Allsburg). The window looks down on a forested space, similar to Archie's bedroom view, with no human structures in view. In the room, there is a chest of drawers painted a shiny light color, and there is a radiator. The chest resembles Archie Smith's furniture, but this is not his bedroom as there is patterned wallpaper. This wallpaper is the supernatural entryway. Its pattern is vaguely ivy, with birds ascending upwards along the vegetation. However, there appears to be something magical happening, as one bird is missing from the pattern. This creates an irregularity in the picture as the eye is drawn to the absence. The audience also sees another bird preparing to lift-off from the wallpaper and fly out the window. The image is lovely and uncanny. It depicts something so familiar, so everyday, but rendered supernatural. The ghostly movement of the curtains also catches the eye. The reader can almost "feel" the breeze and "hear" the flap of the tiny wings. It is a sensory-laden image, where the subject *is* the viewer. We are looking at the scene and noticing the slight strangeness in the shot. Like the sleeping girl and Archie Smith, something wondrous is happening in "The Third Floor Bedroom" as its familiar fabric transforms into something fantastic.

The dream world is a common motif in Chris Van Allsburg's work. Many of his books depict sleeping and dreaming of adventures that, in reality, occurred (Neumeyer 2). Archie slumbers in fetal position, perhaps offering his opening image-caption as a quasi-birth to the mysteries of Harris Burdick. If he is a well-behaved child, Archie would stay in bed until the sun or his parents awake him—whichever comes first. That is the familiar experience, for both the child and adult reader. But my imagination wants him to be roused by the orbs, to rub the sleep from his eyes and experience an adventure. Or perhaps I am already within Archie's adventure, and his dream world has come true? All we "see" is the deceptively simple image, accompanied by a short caption. Is this "tiny voice" good or bad? Should Archie heed the call to be "the one"? The audience is asked to manufacture a moral identity for Archie that might consider his specialness, his capacity for adventure—or maybe his desire to remain safe and well behaved. In this moral creation, the audience imagines their own moral making process from a multitude of personally constructed possibilities. Perhaps there has always been a desire to run away, to misbehave, to escape into the night. Perhaps there are individual factors that have dictated one's behavior. Perhaps the *Harris Burdick* reader uses Archie as a proxy to take a long-desired adventure. All of these possibilities depend on the reader's subjective construction of a moral.

In "Mr. Linden's Library," the pronouns tell us that we are looking at a sleeping *girl*. Her pose reminds me of Archie Smith, but she has a lit bedside lamp illuminating her. She obviously fell asleep while reading, a common enough occurrence in *my* childhood bedroom. Her left arm is flung down; it probably gripped the top of her book before sleep claimed her. She wears a tank top, and her bed looks soft and clean. She has two pillows to prop her up. Her face is relaxed and tension-free, and I ascertain that her dreams are undisturbed—even as her bed transforms into a garden. Will she awaken to a forest? Or does this image-caption reveal her intimate dream world? The girl has already crossed one boundary, in her decision to open the book at all. Now, she has crossed another boundary between awake and asleep. However, there are more questions than answers: who is Mr. Linden? Why is it "too late"? What will happen now? And what does the book contain? What is it about? It appears to contain a certain storybook motif, the capitalized first letter "H." Is this a meta-fairytale? Is she transforming into something other? In spite of the girl's restful pose, the caption's reproachful tone suggests that she has passed a point of no return and its tone suggests reproach. What *should* the girl do? How has she transgressed? I wonder if this is a commentary on female learning, and the reader is meant to construct a moral that considers traditional gender norms. The girl has presumably disobeyed the request of her male elder, Mr. Linden, and made a conscious choice to read. Historically, literacy was how women "fostered personal independence" (Eisenmann). Perhaps the nameless girl is reading something considered "beyond" her ability. Perhaps she is self-educating about traditional masculine subject matter. Perhaps she is using her "safe space" to learn about issues forbidden to her gender. Here, we see that sleep is not a safe refuge; the fantastic can reach right out and caress or discipline you. The nameless girl has perhaps pushed beyond secure boundaries.

Foundations Unmoored

In *Landscapes of Fear*, Yi-Fu Tuan writes, "every human construction—whether mental or material—is a component in a landscape of fear because it exists to contain chaos" (6). Our homes, our bedrooms, our basements are constructed to maintain a certain sense of security. In "Uninvited Guests" we see a small basement door opening where it should not: beneath the ground. This caption reads, "His heart was pounding. / He was sure he had seen the doorknob turn" (Van Allsburg). Here, I imagine the figure as male, with age unknown. The visible shoe looks like an oxford, the pants are cuffed to suggest 1950s apparel, and an old-fashioned radio is stored underneath the staircase

(I'm reminded of another unnamed character from *Harris Burdick*, battling something "Under the Rug," and so I imagine this pant belonging to a balding man, my mind imagining a cohesive narrative between image-captions). Again, we "see" order: neat bundles of items tied with a tidy bow; a rug stowed in the corner, cans and bottles stored safely away; one lonely ice-skate hung high, lacking its partner; and a box of miscellaneous items: Christmas lights, a roll of something, another container. An important slant of light illuminates this image's spectral boundary: a small closed door, probably three-feet high and presumably known about, given the basement's tidiness. It looks fairytale-esque, like the entrance to a fairy world or the passage to a confined damsel-in-distress. It does not "fit" in with the modern, mid-century aesthetic of the basement; even the material around the door looks ancient and stone-like. As the caption informs us, the small doorknob is allegedly turning. Who or what will emerge, and when? Is this the source of the thing from "Under the Rug" or is it something different? Notice my use of "thing" for it certainly won't be a human (at least not of familiar proportions) whom exits. The cuffed pant figure should open the door and confront the strange boundary. He or she should discover, of his or her own accord, what exists beyond the door—and discover what wants to get in. But what is it? And is it dangerous? Should the cuffed pant figure lie in wait? All of these questions come from the image. We are asked to imagine what exists beyond the familiar boundaries of one's basement. This was an area that did not immediately open up to my childhood play space, but existed in a separate area. I find this image to be Edgar Allan Poe–esque, suggesting that despite modern order, the chaos of the spectral unknown is just one doorknob turn away. This supernatural boundary not only opens beyond the house walls, but it opens beneath the earth. Multiple boundaries are traversed, allowing for the reader to consider many different avenues for moral construction.

    In "The House on Maple Street" we actually witness the house unmoored explosively from its foundation.[9] The caption reads: "It was a perfect lift-off." This image ends the book, a simple gabled house with one light on in what is presumably the attic. Like Archie Smith and the sleeping girl, we have a nighttime setting. It appears the next-door neighbor's house has their windowsills completely open; is this summertime? or will the fantastic seep into a new home soon? Again, my narrative-focused mind looks for consistency. Has all of *Harris Burdick*'s magic occurred in the same house? Do Archie and the sleeping girl and the cuffed pants man and the flying wallpaper all exist within the same House on Maple Street? Other images from *Harris Burdick* exist outside the familiar confines of a house, but I am intrigued by how the continuities of the homespace are rendered, indeed exploded, into the uncanny. Like the house, the reader's mind is freed by these mysterious, deceptively simple drawings that suggest the strange lurks right under the reader's nose. I read these selected images as an exploration of the imaginative development of a child *and* a critique of the enforced social norms that came out of post–World War II domestic narratives.[10] When faced with the liftoff of a neighborhood house, one should run, scream, call for help. Instead, we look on in awe, our imaginations running wild at all the possibilities for this house and for our imaginative processes. And then, we reach for a writing instrument and compose a story.

Transformation

Finally, many of these images, with their porous boundaries, are about transformation. In "Archie Smith, Boy Wonder" and "Mr. Linden's Library," we observe the transformation from day to night, from awake to asleep. We also see the world changing for Archie and the unnamed girl. The movement from day to night also suggests a new beginning, the start of the dream world and the resetting of one's batteries. Sleep is also important for "a growing child [who] enters school and encounters a new environment of noisy youngsters, strange adults, and confusing topography" (Tuan 15). *Harris Burdick*'s postmodern discontinuity and pedagogical usefulness might reflect this new "landscape of fear," for the children depicted are school-aged. In *Landscapes of Fear*, Yi-Fu Tuan writes, "To grow up, the child must leave the security of home and parents for the bewildering and frightening world beyond" (20). Several of *Harris Burdick*'s illustrations show this leaving, but in a slow, processorial fashion; some of the depicted children have already left the security of home while others are only *now*, in the moment of the image-caption, being shown the spectral exit. Tuan discusses the concept, found in many cultures across time, that the child is "unformed nature" (34) in need of boundaries and subjected to a fear "boot camp" by parents: don't go out after dark or you'll see ghosts; if you misbehave you will be abandoned. However, this is often evidence of adult fears and the desire for children "to submit, adapt and live" (Tuan 34). What happens when the child progresses from childhood to the ultimate moment of moral meaning making, adolescence? Occupying a liminal space between childhood and adulthood, the adolescent is spectral: "adolescents exist uneasily between childhood and maturity.... [They] also uncomfortably unsettle location, dismantling the difference between public and private space" (Thurschwell 240). The private bedroom, basement, and house space transforms into a public space by its inclusion in the *Harris Burdick* image-captions; each space is accessible to the public reading audience who makes moral meaning alongside the image-caption subjects.

Conclusion

In *The Uses of Enchantment*, Bruno Bettelheim argues that the folk fairy tale is "existential" because it "confronts the child squarely with the basic human predicaments" (8). In this confrontation, the child must consider moral meaning making in human experience. Let me argue, once more, that *Harris Burdick* is a postmodern, fairytale picture book set among unbounded domestic spaces. Yet, the children in each image-caption are not given the narrative opportunity to make a moral decision; that honor is bestowed upon the reader. By presenting the reader with spectral openings to the familiar domestic space, *The Mysteries of Harris Burdick* requires its audience to make moral meaning: how *should* the image-caption resolve? As a young reader myself, I embraced the mysteriousness of these image-captions. I accepted the mysterious narrative put forth by Van Allsburg, but I wanted to *make* meaning for the first time as a reader. The supernatural entrances haunted me, and I wrote stories to make moral meaning for Archie Smith, the nameless girl, the cuffed pant individual, the living wallpaper, and the explosive house. This is apparently what readers are supposed to do. In an 1987 interview Van Allsburg described *The Mysteries of Harris Burdick* as "basically a thematic apperception test" (Kiefer 667), or a psychological exam where the construction of a narrative from unrelated images reveals much about individual "circumstances, experiences, and preoccupations" (Colman). Looking at the narratives created by Van Allsburg's "test" reveals much about how we make moral sense of the world. As a result, *Harris Burdick* lingers, ghost-like, because of its absent author, its missing stories, and its lost linear narrative. We assimilate the familiar fragments into morals that negotiate supernatural elements in tandem with our own experiences. It is a fantastic way to experience the unknown in the everyday—and face the fact that no one, not even the author, has all the answers.

Notes

1. In a Nov. 2011 YouTube interview, Van Allsburg views the *Harris Burdick* image-captions as "a way to persuade young people that they were authors and they did not know it. All they needed was the right little spark" ("Chris Van Allsburg Talks...").
2. 2011's *The Chronicles of Harris Burdick* contained an Introduction by Lemony Snicket, himself a fictional entity and the pseudonym for author Daniel Handler.
3. *Harris Burdick* refers to the original 1984 publication.
4. For scholarship on *Harris Burdick*, see El-Tamami 38–39; Gavin 216–17; Neumeyer 6 and McGillis.
5. For information on spectral manifestations, see Davies 18–19, 133–36, 201–04.
6. See O'Neil 44–50 for one pedagogical approach to *Harris Burdick*.
7. See Byrne for information on one theatrical version.
8. When Van Allsburg received the images in the mid-1980s, Harris Burdick allegedly brought the image-captions "thirty years ago" (Van Allsburg).
9. For additional analysis on "The House on Maple Street," see McGillis 68–69.
10. See Self for more on the post–World War II nuclear family 4–7.

Works Cited

Bettelheim, Bruno. *The Uses of Enchantment: The Meaning and Importance of Fairy Tales.* New York: Knopf, 1976. Print.
Byrne, Terry. "They are hoping for a storybook ending." *Boston Globe* 22 June 2008. ProQuest. Web. 3 Nov. 2015.
"Chris Van Allsburg Talks about *The Mysteries of Harris Burdick.*" *YouTube.* YouTube, 3 Nov. 2011. Web. 1 Dec. 2015.
Coats, Karen. "The Mysteries of Postmodern Epistemology: Stratemeyer, Stine, and Contemporary Mystery for Children." *Mystery in Children's Literature: From the Rational to the Supernatural*, ed. Adrienne E. Gavin and Christopher Routledge. New York: Palgrave, 2001. 184–201. Print.
Colman, Andrew M. "Thematic Apperception Test (TAT)." *A Dictionary of Psychology*, 4th ed. 2015. Oxford Reference. Web. 15 Nov. 2015.
Davies, Owen. *The Haunted: A Social History of Ghosts.* London: Palgrave, 2007. Print.
Del Pilar Blanco, Maria, and Esther Pereen. Introduction. *Popular Ghosts: The Haunted Spaces of Everyday Culture.* New York: Continuum, 2010. ix-xxiv. Print.
_____. Introduction. *The Spectralities Reader: Ghosts and Haunting in Contemporary Cultural Theory.* New York: Bloomsburg, 2013. Print.
Derrida, Jacques. *Specters of Marx.* New York: Routledge, 2006. Print.
Eisenmann, Linda. *Historical Dictionary of Women's Education in the United States.* Westport, CT: Greenwood, 1998. eBook Collection. Web. 26 Jan. 2016.
El-Tamami, Wiam. "'The Simple Little Picture Book': Private Theater to Postmodern Experience." *Alif: Journal of Comparative Poetics* 27 (2007): 25–43. Web. 3 Nov. 2015.
Freud, Sigmund. *The Uncanny.* Trans. David McClintock. New York: Penguin, 2003. Print.
Gavin, Adrienne E. "Enigma's Variation: the Puzzling Mysteries of Avi, Ellen Raskin, Diana Wynne Jones, and Chris Van Allsburg." *Mystery in Children's Literature: From the Rational to the Supernatural*, ed. Adrienne E. Gavin and Christopher Routledge. New York: Palgrave, 2001. 210–18. Print.
Gavin, Adrienne E., and Christopher Routledge. Introduction. *Mystery in Children's Literature: From the Rational to the Supernatural.* New York: Palgrave, 2001. 1–13. Print.
Kammen, Michael. *Mystic Chords of Memory: The Transformation of Tradition in American Culture.* New York: Vintage, 1991. Print.
Kiefer, Barbara. "Chris Van Allsburg in Three Dimensions." *Language Arts* 64.6 (1987): 664–73. Web. 3 Nov. 2015.
McGillis, Roderick. *The Nimble Reader: Literary Theory and Children's Literature.* New York: Twayne, 1996. Print.
"Moral, n." *OED Online.* Oxford University Press, Dec. 2015. Web. 15 Dec. 2015.
"Morality, n." *OED Online.* Oxford University Press, Dec. 2015. Web. 15 Dec. 2015.
Nel, Phillip. "Postmodernism." *Keywords for Children's Literature*, ed. Phillip Nel and Lissa Paul. New York: New York University Press, 2011. 181–86. Web. 24 Nov. 2015.
Neumeyer, Peter F. "How Picture Books Mean: The Case of Chris Van Allsburg." *Children's Literature Association Quarterly* 15.1 (1990): 2–8. Web. 3 Nov. 2015.
O'Neil, Kathleen. "Once Upon Today: Teaching for Social Justice with Postmodern Picturebooks." *Children's Literature in Education* 41 (2010): 40–51. Web. 3 Nov. 2015.
Reimer, Mavis. "Home." *Keywords for Children's Literature*, ed. Phillip Nel and Lissa Paul. New York: New York University Press, 2011. 106–09. Web. 24 Nov. 2015.
Self, Robert O. *All in the Family: The Realignment of American Democracy Since the 1960s.* New York: Hill and Wang, 2012. Print.
Sipe, Lawrence R. "How Picture Books Work: A Semiotically Framed Theory of Text-Picture Relationships." *Children's Literature in Education* 29.2 (1998): 97–108. Web. 3 Nov. 2015.
Spitz, Ellen Handler. *The Brightening Glance: Imagination and Childhood.* New York: Pantheon, 2006. Print.
_____. *Inside Picture Books.* New Haven: Yale University Press, 1999. Print.
Thurschwell, Pamela. "The Ghost Worlds of Modern Adolescence." *Popular Ghosts: The*

Haunted Spaces of Everyday Culture, ed. Maria Del Pilar Blanco and Esther Pereen. New York: Continuum, 2010. 239–49. Print.

Tuan, Yi-Fu. *Landscapes of Fear*, 2d ed. Minneapolis: Minnesota University Press, 2013. Print.

Van Allsburg, Chris. *The Mysteries of Harris Burdick*. Boston: Houghton Mifflin, 1984. Print.

Crossing the Threshold
Ghosts and Haunted Houses as Moral Messengers
BRENDA S. GARDENOUR WALTER

On a chilly October night, a gnarled tree skeleton creaks in the wind in front of a spooky old house on a hill. Inside, a filmy ghost floats through forlorn halls, waiting for a child to enter. Thus begins many a children's picture book about ghosts and haunted spaces. These books are often released around Halloween and meant to be good scary fun. Just beneath the surface of their seemingly silly and simple narratives, however, children's books about haunted houses are embedded with serious discourses about the seen and unseen worlds. In opening the book, the child steps across the threshold of the text and enters a supernatural space akin to Huizinga's "magic circle." The book, like the spooky house between its covers, is haunted by wispy spirits, many of which serve didactic purposes as they waft across the pages. For example, the ghost in the book can convey moral messages, such as the value of respecting others, even if those "Others" at first seem frightening. The spirit might likewise teach the importance of seeing the world from multiple and often-conflicting perspectives. At its very best, the child's journey into the haunted house-book is a journey into the self, one that brings the child face to face with the issues of life, death, embodiment and—ultimately—the ghost-soul that haunts his or her own body-house. Picture books about haunted houses, then, are not simply spooky tales, but alive with possibilities for meaningful and often emotional discussions about complex human issues.

Picture books are "always about feelings, whether they are ostensibly about feelings or not" (Yanof 1). This is particularly true of picture books that explore haunted houses, an experience that, for many small children, can be emotionally intense. Focalization, the perspective from which the story is told, has the power to either diminish or intensify the emotional responses of the child as he or she navigates the dialectic relationship between visual picture and spoken narration (Nodelman 2; Nikolajeva and Scott 118–19). For example, one category of haunted house picture books features zero-focalization, in which the story is narrated from a third-person perspective and voiced by the authoritative and often adult reader. In the adventures of the Berenstain Bears in *The Haunted House* (2010), *The Haunted Lighthouse* (2001), and *The Ghost of the Forest* (1988), as well as the more complex narrative in Eve Bunting's *In the Haunted House* (1990), the child experiences scary events from a visual and textual distance and in the reassuring company of an adult. The frightening spirit in all of these texts is ultimately revealed to be a friendly face in disguise and no ghost at all. These narratives allow both the reader and the child to enjoy the scariness of the story while being assured that spooks and hauntings are part of imaginative play and nothing to be truly afraid of.

While zero-focalized narratives argue that ghosts and supernatural entities exist only as pretend characters within the pages of the book, multiple-focalized narratives—which are told from at least two perspectives and sometimes feature diegetic discourses—allow for the potential existence of ghosts and haunted spaces in the world beyond the book. In many of these narratives, ghosts and their haunted abodes are presented as very real, albeit adorable and harmless. Both *Ghosts in the House* by Kohara Kazuno (2010) and *Ten Timid Ghosts* by Jennifer O'Connell (2000) feature witches who move into haunted houses and attempt to subdue their ghostly inhabitants. In the first story, a kindly young witch domesticates the ghosts with their consent, transforming them into bed sheets and curtains; in the second, a mean old witch scares the ghosts out of their home until the displaced spirits join forces to take it back. Both books include the perspective of the cute ghosts, conveyed through images and text; because they are emotive participants and not merely objects to be feared, the ghosts become vehicles for teaching compassion, kindness, and respect. Emmanuelle Eeckhout's *There's No Such Thing as Ghosts* (2008) uses sweet spirits in a haunted house as a medium for playing with ideas of belief and skepticism. The main character is a little boy with a ghost catching net who enters into a haunted house in search of spooks. Throughout this truly diegetic text, the boy repeatedly exclaims that he doesn't see any ghosts at all; the pictures, however, tell a very different tale, as the reader and the child see ghosts following the boy through the house on every page. One can almost hear the child yelling at the little boy in the book, "Look behind you! The ghost is right there!" Like *Ten Timid Ghosts* and *Ghosts in the House*, Eeckhout's book examines ghostly phenomenon and haunted spaces from a safe distance; reader and child never enter the house or engage with the spirits from a first person perspective. All of these books allow for the existence of ghosts and therefore have the potential to stimulate discussions of the soul, the body, and life after death in a not-so-scary and even quite humorous way. While ghosts might exist in the world beyond the book, the child is assured that they are not mean or scary but friendly and deserving of compassion and acceptance.

Picture books about haunted houses that feature single focalization, or first person narrative, engage most directly with issues of embodiment, death, the soul, and the existence of invisible entities. In these mostly-pictorial texts, the child enters into gothic haunted spaces alone and is left to explore their dark recesses, excited and terrified of what he or she might find. In Ruth Brown's *A Dark, Dark Tale* (1992) and David A. Carter's *In a Dark, Dark Wood: A Old Tale with a New Twist* (2002), the child is drawn slowly through scary forests and haunted houses, moving further and further into the unknown. While Brown's book ends with the discovery of a cute little mouse, startled by the child viewer-listener going bump in the night, Carter's book ends with a ghost who jumps off of the page. Two books by Bill Martin, Jr., offer more frightening and even existential scares. In *Ghost Story* (1970), the child enters a haunted house to discover a dark spirit who then chases him or her out of the house and into the forest. In *The Haunted House* (1970), the child is lead through a gothic manse and up to an attic containing a mirror that reveals the child him or herself to be the ghost. These books are made all the more frightening because they are illustrated from a first-person perspective, which brings the child viewer into direct contact with the haunted house and its resident ghost. The sensation of being in haunted spaces such as these can be overwhelming, requiring the child to moderate the pace of the story. In the spaces in between the pages, the child might ask fraught questions about complex issues such as the location of the soul in the human body, what happens to the body and soul after death, and whether the child him or herself will become a ghost, wandering alone in the dark, long after life has passed. In first-person haunted house narratives, the ghost exists not only in the book and in the house, but also within the child.

The Ghost in the Book: "Spooks? There are no such things"

Written by Stan, Jan, and Mike Berenstain, *The Berenstain Bears in the Haunted House* (2010), *The Berenstain Bears and the Haunted Lighthouse* (2001), and *The Berenstain Bears and the Ghost of the Forest* (1988) tell tales of haunted spaces that turn out not to be haunted at all. Each of these books features zero-focalization in which an omniscient third-person narrator, voiced by a trusted adult, reveals all of the secrets behind the story's purported "haunting" to the child listener (Yannicopoulou, 76). This feeling of omniscient distance is furthered by illustrations that place the viewer in a position to see all of the events in their entirety as they unfold. Accompanied by the voice of a trusted adult and at a safe visual remove, the child experiences the spooky story with the continual reassurance that ghosts and haunted houses are not real. For example, in *The Berenstain Bears and the Haunted House*, Brother and Sister Bear go searching for their kitten Gracie in the old haunted house on Spook Hill. As the child watches Brother and Sister wander through the illustrated manse, he or she is invited to open paper-flap doors and curtains to see what lurks behind them. This active participation might at first seem potentially frightening; however, the size of the child's hand in relation to the small doors and curtains mitigates much of the risk. Likewise, each lifted flap confirms that the house isn't haunted by ghosts or monsters, but by smiling frogs with glowing yellow eyes, a scary creature that turns out to be Brother's reflection in the mirror, mice at a table, a family of squirrels eating dinner, raccoons taking a bath, and even a raven reading, what else, *The Raven* by Edgar Allen Bear. Deep within the house, Brother and Sister Bear find kitten Gracie in the lap of the home's owner, Mrs. Grissus, who is "very nice" even if she does "live in a haunted house." Of course, the house isn't really haunted at all; instead of scary ghosts and spooks, the house is inhabited by cute woodland creatures engaged in middle-class domestic activities such as cooking, dining, bathing, and reading. Similarly, *The Berenstain Bears in the Haunted Lighthouse* features a spooky space devoid of spirits. An avid history buff, Papa Bear takes the family on vacation to the old Rocky Shore Lighthouse which is rumored to be haunted by the ghost of the old lighthouse keeper, Captain Salt. Despite several seemingly scary events, such as glowing footprints and ghostly footfalls, skeptical Brother and Sister investigate the building and discover the angry ghost of Captain Salt—who turns out to be a lonely old man who is very much alive. He explains to the Bear family that when the lighthouse was shut down, he did not have anyplace else to go, so he stayed on and pretended to haunt the place in order to protect his enormous collection of nautical artifacts. The children help Captain Salt transform the once "haunted" old lighthouse into the Rocky Shore Nautical Museum, where he lives and works as curator, tour guide, and storyteller. Both *The Haunted House* and *The Haunted Lighthouse* prove to children that haunted spaces are not haunted at all, but comfortable homes and historical structures worth investigating and preserving for their own sakes.

The Berenstain Bears and the Ghost of the Forest argues unequivocally that ghosts and spooks do not exist. In this story, Brother, Sister, and Cousin Fred are off to spend a night in the forest with their Bear Scout troop. After being told that he is not invited, Papa Bear tells the children that he wouldn't go with them anyway because the forest is haunted by "a parade" of spooks led by the "boss of them all, the Ghost of the Wood." Mama Bear tells the children that spooks are "nonsense" and that Papa is "just trying to give" them "a scare." When the children meet Scout Leader Jane, they tell her about the Ghost of the Wood, and she assures them that spooks aren't real, "there are no such things!" The belief that ghosts aren't real is affirmed throughout the story; safe with the omniscient narrator, the child viewer sees Papa Bear make his ghost costume from a sheet, watches Scout Leader Jane construct her spook costume, and through visual cues recognizes Mama Bear behind her spooky outfit as well. The result is a not-very-scary yet quite funny story with a safe ending. "It's a double ghost lesson ... there are no such things and there never have been," announces Jane at the story's conclusion, "but just as sure as night follows day, it's fun to be scared of them anyway!" In the Berenstain Bears series, potentially scary subjects are engaged with at a narrative and visual remove. Children listener-viewers are reassured by the omniscient narrator and comforting images that ghosts, haunted houses, and the supernatural are not real, but created in the human imagination.

Unlike the Berenstain Bears books, which tell spooky tales from a distance, Eve Bunting's *In the Haunted House* brings the child viewer closer to spirits and monsters while still maintaining visual boundaries that convey a sense of safety. The text begins with the ominous line "This is the house where the scary ones hide. Open the door and step softly inside." In the accompanying image, two Seuss-like feet with whimsical sneakers, one small and red and the other large and blue, step over the threshold, making clear that the child viewer is only observing the narrative and is not experiencing the haunted house in the first person. As the two feet make their way up stars and move from room to room, they encounter all manner of frightening creatures, from ghosts and vampires to a mummy, "as dead as can be. So why does his dead eye keep looking at me?" The scary potential of these images is mitigated not only by the cuteness of the monsters, but also by the use of floating and decentered vantage points that give the child viewer a sense of freedom and mobility. For example, the book's opening images are drawn from a floor-level perspective, while the sleeping mummy is viewed from ceiling height. Several images include visual clues that the haunted house with all of its ghosts and monsters might not be as scary is it seems; for instance, a recently used can of red paint is seen peeking out from behind a box marked "Do Not Open" that appears to have blood on it. The child's visual journey through the haunted house is accompanied by the adult's reading of a playfully spooky rhyming poem containing snippets of dialogue that a frightened child listener might find reassuring. "Give me your hand, you're as brave as can be. I know you're not frightened, but stay close to me." Whether this assurance is spoken by the character with the big foot or the little foot is unclear until the book's conclusion, in which a terrified father and gleeful young daughter emerge from the haunted house and "into the day that does sparkle with sun. Halloween houses are so much fun." Despite the long line of children waiting to go inside, the daughter wants to go through the haunted house again. The final images frame the book, showing not merely their feet as they cross the threshold, but their whole bodies, including the father's pensive look and the daughter's delighted face as she marvels at the ghosts who, the secret revealed, smile almost lovingly back at her.

Eve Bunting's *In the Haunted House* is perennially popular with children who love the spooky story and its funny ending, in which the child is brave and the adult is scared of silly monsters. One woman on Goodreads.com writes that while reading the book to her granddaughter, "she acted like she might have been scared," but by changing her tone in reading the poem, the granddaughter not only "finished the book" but "even giggled through some of the pages." Adult readers love Bunting's book not only because of its sense of humor, but also because—much like the Berenstain Bears books—the child can experience all of the fun of being frightened and exploring a haunted space with the reassurance that ghosts and haunted houses aren't real. "It celebrates that perfect feeling of loving to be scared, but knowing that you are really safe" (Goodreads). In all of these books, the feeling of safety is reinforced through the use of third person perspective, which provides a sense of distance, in both the narration and the imagery. They likewise arrive at the same comfortable resolution—that haunted houses and ghosts are created by living people to scare other living people for good fun. There are no ghosts or haunted houses. If ghosts *do* exist, it is only within the pages of the book and the human imagination, and nowhere else. This repeated insistence that ghosts don't exist, while soothing to a potentially frightened child, does not invite any meaningful discussion about death, the soul, and the afterlife. Instead, these issues are sidestepped, saved for another day, or simply spirited away.

The Ghost in the House: "Ghosts are people, too"

Rather than outright dismiss the existence of ghosts and haunted spaces, books such as *Ghosts in the House* by Kohara Kazuno (2010), *Ten Timid Ghosts* by Jennifer O'Connell (2000), and *There's No Such Thing as Ghosts* (2008) by Emmanuelle Eeckhout allow for the existence of the supernatural—not simply for a Halloween scare—but in order to convey a series of liberal moral messages about alterity, acceptance, and respect. In *Ghosts in the House*, an adorable little girl and her cat buy a house. As she crosses the threshold, she is confronted by an enormous ghost swooping down the stairs, its eyes looking directly into hers. At first the little girl appears frightened; despite this, she enters the house and unpacks her bags, revealing that she is not "just a girl," but a witch who knows "how to catch ghosts." Wearing her pointy hat, she and her black cat mount her broom and fly room to room, collecting ghosts and placing them in a laundry bin. "How lovely," she says, "I hope there are some more." Her words and smiling face make clear that she is unafraid of the ghosts and bears them no animosity. To reinforce that her intentions and actions are not to be construed as violent, the ghosts are drawn with faces that convey surprise and delight, with many of them smiling sweetly as they are placed in the bin, washed in the machine, hung to dry in the fresh air, and returned to the home as curtains, bed sheets, tablecloths, and other domestic items. The book's final image depicts the witch and her cat snuggled in beneath the last two smiling ghosts, who have become cuddly blankets. "And they all lived happily ever after." A deceptively simple tale, *Ghosts in the House* conveys several moral messages. In addition to featuring a smart, strong, and independent girl who relies on her creativity and intelligence to solve problems, the book argues that many different creatures can share a single space if they are willing to work together for the common good. Interestingly, black cats, witches, ghosts, and haunted houses are often "Othered" as objects of fear; here, they are smart, friendly, kind, domesticated, and therefore safe, which teaches children that even though "Others" might look different or scary, they often want the very same things other people do—security, respect, and love.

Like *Ghosts in the House*, *Ten Timid Ghosts* (2000) by Jennifer O'Connell tells the story of a witch who buys a haunted house and learns about respect and cooperation—but from a very different perspective. In this case, the witch is not a sweet little girl but a wicked middle-aged witch, green and warty, who brings an entire moving van of items up to a haunted house while its current inhabitants, ten shy ghosts, peer fearfully out of the windows. As she walks toward the house, she carries a box marked with the word "DANGER" as well as a skull and crossbones, the age-old signifier for poison. The refrain makes her intentions clear: "Ten timid ghosts in a haunted house, a witch moved in and wanted them out." Unlike the kindly little witch in *Ghosts in the House* who wants to share the house with its spirited residents, this witch means to evict the harmless ghosts from their home completely. Using props from the box marked DANGER, the witch scares the ghosts out of the house one by one. A goofy rubber skeleton, a bat on spring, a stuffed cat, a spider on a string, a silly monster outfit, and a toy mouse are enough to rid the house of six of the ghosts; in each of these scenes, the child can find visual clues that the witch is making these toys move in very conventional ways and not by magic. Some of the props used by the witch are a bit scarier, such as a screeching owl puppet, a ghoulish mask, and a vampire costume; in these vignettes, both visual and textual clues are embedded in the images to reinforce that these scary things are still just tricks. The owl puppet, for example, has an exaggerated tag marked "owl puppet." In the scene were the witch is dressed like a ghoul, the child can see a bright white empty box marked "ghoul costume," while the vampire scene features a jar marked "powder," a bottle of ketchup, face paint, and a piece of construction paper from which fangs have clearly been cut. Even children who cannot read will spot these items, recognize their role in the tale, and ask the adult what they say, which defrays the spookiness of the story even further. By the time the witch uses the tenth prop, a poorly constructed mummy costume made of toilet paper, the ghosts and the child viewer have figured out the witch's game. All ten ghosts, now hiding in the forest near the house, gather together and decide that, having been treated poorly, it is time to take back their home: "One mean old witch in a haunted house, ten brave ghosts WANTED HER OUT." Together, the ghosts rush into the house and scream "BOO!" The witch loses her hat and wig and runs from the house, while the ghosts return to domestic bliss, dancing together and handing out Halloween candy to trick or treaters who aren't afraid of the timid ghosts or their haunted house one bit.

On the surface, *Ten Timid Ghosts* is about a selfish bully taking advantage of those who are innately kind and shy. The depiction of the witch as mean and unfair allows children to identify with the timid and frightened ghosts, which are typically viewed as things to be afraid of and not entities deserving of compassion. Unlike *Ghosts in the House*, in which the spirits merely smile their assent, the ghosts in *Ten Timid Ghosts* not only communicate through facial expressions, but also ultimately find their voice, saying "This isn't fair, we live in there!" as they watch the wicked witch enjoy their home from the "deep dark wood." Throughout the tale, the child viewer sees the injustice from the perspective of the ghosts and rallies behind them as they retake their house. It isn't in the nature of these timid ghosts to scare anyone; in fact, as individuals they are passive and easily frightened away. In the face of injustice, however, the ghosts join together, realize their strength, and right the wrong that has been done to them. The moral message here is quite clear. Everyone, no matter how small or big, weak or strong, has a voice; those voices, when unified, can create positive change in the world by standing up for the vulnerable and the oppressed—even those individuals are potentially-spooky ghosts. In this book, the child learns to advocate for "thers," to show them compassion, and in so doing to see the world from multiple perspectives. For example, the living might see the ghost's spooky old house as haunted, but for them it is a home like any other, a place to dance, sleep, and read. Just because a house is different doesn't mean that it has to be scary. A similar theme is echoed in *Hush Baby Ghostling* (2009), a picture book by Andrea Beaty and Pascal Lemaitre, in which an adorable baby ghost is afraid of human children and daytime, preferring instead monsters, nighttime, and moonlight. His ghost mother comforts him, singing, "Nestle safe beside me in our haunted home, and dream a dream of darkness where the wild monsters roam." Through such tales, a child might learn that the very "Others" he or she is afraid of might see the child's home and lifestyle as strange and terrifying. Just as the child intends the ghost no harm, so the ghost intends the child no harm; in between, there is room for compassion, compromise, respect, and understanding.

Like *Ghosts in the House* and *Ten Timid Ghosts*, Emmanuelle Eeckhout's *There's No Such Thing as Ghosts!* (2008) uses a journey through a haunted house to teach tolerance and respect for multiple perspectives, in this case for skepticism and belief in the supernatural. In this story, a little boy moves to a new neighborhood and his mother warns him to stay away from the "strange" old house on the corner because "people say it's haunted." He does not believe her, because "there's no such things as ghosts," but he grabs his butterfly net and sets out to explore the house because, if ghosts *do* exist, he's "going to catch one." The haunted house, drawn in silhouette, at first appears menacing as it seems to reach forward and swallow the brave little boy. The accompanying text, "I opened the door and stepped inside," also sounds ominous. As the little boy crosses the threshold, however, he is greeted not by a scary creatures but by myriad gleeful ghostlings holding a banner that says, "Bienvenue!" Despite their obvious enthusiasm and delight at having company, the boy does not see them, but instead moves from room to room in search of his quarry. Ghosts float everywhere, some of them shyly peeking out at him, others following him closely; he even passes a ghost cooking soup and a whole line of anxiously squirming ghosts queued up to go the bathroom, but still does not see them. "This house isn't haunted," he states flatly. The book concludes with the little boy leaving the house, his mission to catch a ghost unfulfilled, but his belief that ghosts don't exist confirmed. The ghosts, however, are sad when he leaves them, their voices having gone unheard, their faces unseen, and their joy unknown.

In *There's No Such Thing as Ghosts*, the obvious discrepancies between the words, spoken from the perspective of the skeptical little boy, and the pictures, which show ghosts heaped in every room of the house, encourages the child to counter the narrative on every page. The conflict between "verbal and visual" in this hetero-diegetic text establishes "an inherently dialogic relationship" between word and image, reader-viewer and book, adult and child, all of which "transforms textual space into a place of conflict, conversation, and," in some cases, "resolution" (Yannicopoulou 66). As the little boy continues to deny the existence of ghosts, the child might laugh at him for not seeing the silly spirits all around him. This "multi-modal discourse" works not only to create a lively reading experience, but also to convey complex moral messages about belief and disbelief (Painter 2). The child sees the ghosts, and so believes in them, at least as they exist in the book. The existence of these very unfrightening ghosts, however, might act as a springboard for further questions about ghosts beyond the book. Are ghosts real? Some people believe they are, and some people do not. Can they be seen? Some people have seen them and some people have not. Is it always necessary to see things in order to believe in them? In families of faith, this might lead to a discussion about god or gods, and how some individuals believe with their hearts rather than just their minds. The perspective of skeptics and atheists might also be addressed. The little boy in the haunted house only believes in what he can see; the child viewer sees the ghosts and believes in them. There is no simple solution or definitive answer. The moral message here is to honor multiple viewpoints, to be faithful to your heart, and to be open minded, lest you miss out on the opportunity to meet new friends who are very different than you are—even if they are ghosts in a book.

The Ghost in Me: "I was there"

In most children's picture books, great care is taken both to temper the potentially frightening experience of encountering ghostly beings in haunted houses and to avoid overly-fraught questions about ghosts as disembodied human souls. Some texts, such as the Berenstain Bears books and Eve Bunting's *In the Haunted House*, use zero-focalization and visual cues to assure young children that neither ghosts nor haunted spaces exist outside of the human imagination. Other picture books, such as *The Haunted House, Ten Timid Ghosts*, and *There's No Such Thing as Ghosts* allow for the potential existence of spooks and haunted spaces beyond the pages of the book, but suggest that ghosts are future friends and that both they and their haunted homes deserve respect. In all of these picture books, the child crosses the threshold of the haunted house at a narrative remove, safe in the company of an authoritative adult reader. The spooky journey into the house's shadowy rooms and creaking hallways and back out into the sparkling night or "light of day" comes to a "comfortable conclusion," one that sidesteps deeper philosophical issues associated with the supernatural and with ghosts. Not all children's picture books, however, take such a safe approach. Ruth Brown's *A Dark, Dark Tale* (1992) and David A. Carter's *In a Dark, Dark Wood: An Old Tale with a New Twist* (2002), for example, feature pictures drawn from a first person perspective, which transforms the child from a passive viewer into an active participant in the narrative. *A Dark, Dark Tale* begins by placing the child alone on a bleak and rainy moor, populated only by a screech owl and rabbits. Turning the page, the child is led into a forest complete with badgers, bats, and mushrooms, as well as myriad eyes glowing in the shadows. Deeper into the darkness, the child encounters a gothic castle, and on its cobwebbed front steps meets a small black cat, which beckons the child to enter and leads him or her through darkened rooms and hallways, all of which feature hidden faces that, once noticed, appear to stare directly at the viewer. At last, the cat brings the child into a playroom and to a cabinet, in which sits a "dark, dark box" that contains a cute little mouse, tucked into bed and terrified of the child who is creeping around in the dark. In opening the box, the child identifies with the thing that goes bump in the night, the very cause of the mouse's fear. Simultaneously, the child identifies with the scared mouse—its wide eyes peering out from covers pulled up to its chin— an image that might be an accurate reflection of the child him or herself at that very moment, tucked into bed and experiencing the scary story. Just as the adult soothes the frightened child, so too might the child feel inclined to comfort the scared little mouse.

A Dark, Dark Tale is an intense journey for the young reader who does not yet know what lies in the dark, dark box in the creepy old house; the discovery of the little mouse discharges much of the tension, allowing the child to enjoy the spooky atmosphere of the story on subsequent readings without worrying that a ghost might jump out and frighten him or her. While the narrative of David A. Carter's *In a Dark, Dark Wood: An Old Tale with a New Twist* is nearly identical to that in *A Dark, Dark Tale*, it gives no such assurance of safety to its readers. Carter's book, like Brown's, begins by placing the child-viewer alone in a dark forest of gnarled trees with swirling mist; with each page, the child is led into a haunted house and through its elongated hallways and crypt-like openings to encounter statues of robed figures, weird paintings, stone gargoyles, and other tropes culled from classic horror films. The odd low angles from which the rooms are drawn, as well as glowing mist-tendrils that curl across each page, disorient the viewer, making him or her feel not only small but also as if something impossible to see is lurking just behind his or her back. The experience of this haunted space is made all the more frightening because there is no friendly cat companion to serve as a guide. Ultimately, the child arrives at the enormous old cupboard, which contains alchemical equipment, a mysterious creature bottled in a jar, and the dreaded box in the dark, dark corner. The black shadow of a wavering hand, perhaps that of the child, reaches out to open the box. Upon turning the page, the child does not discover a cute mouse to discharge the tension; instead, an enormous pop-up ghost leaps from the box into the world beyond the book, reaching out to touch the reader-viewer with glowing green arms. Unlike Ruth Brown, who provides her reader with a scary but safe journey through an old house that is, in the end, not haunted at all, David Carter confronts his reader with a haunted house and a very real, multidimensional ghost who can be touched and touches others, who is seen and *sees* the viewer, face to face.

David Carter presents his young readers with a tangible spirit, both spooky and fun, that exists both in the book and in the physical world beyond the book. While curious children might begin to wonder about ghosts in their closets and under their beds who might leap out and frighten them, the book does not encourage deep existential discussions about the relationship between the human body and soul, or the spirit world that exists beyond the veil of death. Two remarkable books by Bill Martin, Jr., do just that, shifting the focus from the ghost as "Other" in the books' haunted house to the ghost that lives in the child's haunted body. Martin's *A Ghost Story* (1970), like many other haunted house books both before and after it, begins by placing the child in a dark forest, all alone and in first-person perspective, and guiding them into a spooky house, through its dark corridors, and to a creaky cupboard, which in this tale hides a "dark, dark bottle" containing a black "ghosty ghost." Once discovered, the ghost pushes the cork from the bottle, ascends the cellar stairs, floats through the house, and glides out into the forest. Free from the house's constraints, the ghost catches up with the child-reader who first entered the house and discovered the bottle. As the ghost's eyes meet those of a truly terrified child both in and beyond the book, he slips into "*your* dark, dark pocket." The book's final illustration is of the black ghost floating in an amorphous and shadowy space—perhaps in the pocket, the body, or the mind of the child him or herself—with the billowing text, "He's got *you*!" The use of second-person in the text, when read aloud, confirms for the child listener that the ghost is in his or her own pocket, that the ghost now inhabits his or her physical being as a haunted house-body. Unlike other ghosts, this one is unbound from the book; as a moral messenger, he might facilitate a discussion of ghosts as human souls and the fate of those souls, including that of the child, after death.

The child's identification with the ghostly "Other" and conception of his or her body as a haunted house is writ large in Martin's *The Haunted House* (1970), in which an unidentified "I" emerges from the woods and into creepy old house on a "dark and stormy night." Crossing the threshold, the child-viewer explores the manse in its entirety, room by room. The complex ink and water color images of these spaces contain hidden faces and shapes. Some of these shapes are drawn intentionally, while others appear through the pareidolia effect, a "hardwired" feature of the human brain that creates familiar images, such as faces, from discrete visual elements (Sagan 45). All of this gives the impression that the house is full of secrets and entities, just beyond the viewer's line of sight. Despite this plenum, the text reinforces that the haunted house is empty except for the viewer, tiptoeing from room to room. In each space, from the kitchen to the bedroom to the basement, the words "No one was there" are graven into the images at odd angles, waiting to be found. The last room is the creepy and cobwebbed attic; as the child turns the page, he or she is confronted with a cute little monster ghost who floats in a darkened empty space, staring into a mirror and back out at the viewer, with text that reads, "I was there." Throughout the book, child-narrator has been alone in the house; in the attic, the "I" is revealed to *be* the ghost, which the child sees as he or she gazes into the mirror. The mirror creates "a sense of first-person perspective comparable to a self-portrait in a painting," affirming that the ghost and the child are one, haunting the house alone in the darkness (Nikolajeva 119). The ghost's wide eyes, open and vulnerable, connect with those of the child, reflecting the spirit within the child's own body.

Bill Martin, Jr.'s *A Ghost Story* and *The Haunted House* are simple narratives about spooky subjects with powerful existential potential. In these books, the haunted spaces are truly haunted, in the first case by a scary ghost, in the second case by an open and plaintive spirit. In opening the haunted book and crossing the threshold into the haunted house, the child is entering into their own haunted body to discover the spirit-soul wafting within. Once the body-house is dilapidated and abandoned, what happens to the soul within? Does it haunt another structure, or does it journey to another place? What if, after death, there is only darkness, and the individual spirit is forgotten? Unlike other stories about haunted houses that either dismiss the existence of ghosts completely or use them as signifiers for alterity, Bill Martin's books open up a space for potentially fraught conversations about the experience of human embodiment and the existence (or not) of ghosts as human souls who persist beyond the veil of death.

Works Cited

Beaty, Andrea, and Pascal Lemaitre. *Hush Baby Ghostling*. New York: Simon & Schuster McElderberry Books, 2009. Print.
Berenstain, Stan, and Jan. *The Berenstain Bears and the Ghost of the Forest*. New York: Random House, 1988. Print.
_____. *The Berenstain Bears and the Haunted Lighthouse*. New York: Harper Collins, 2013. Print.
Berenstain, Jan, and Mike. *The Berenstain Bears and the Haunted House*. New York: Harper-Festival Books, 2010. Print.
Brown, Ruth. *A Dark, Dark Tale*. New York: Puffin Books, 1992. Print.
Carter, David A. *In a Dark, Dark Wood: An Old Tale with a New Twist*. New York: Little Simon & Schuster, 2002. Print.
Eeckhout, Emmanuelle. *There's No Such Thing as Ghosts!* San Diego: Kane Miller, 2008. Print.
Goodreads.com. Reviews of Eve Bunting, *In the Haunted House*. 15 Dec. 2015. http://www.goodreads.com/book/show/458958.In_the_Haunted_House. Web.
Kohara, Kazuno. *Ghosts in the House*. San Francisco: Square Fish-MacMillan, 2010. Print.
Martin, Bill, Jr. *A Ghost Story*. New York: Holt, Rinehart, and Winston, 1970. Print.
_____. *The Haunted House*. New York: Holt, Rinehart, and Winston, 1970. Print.
Nicolajeva, Maria, and Carole Scott, *How Picture Books Work*. London: Routledge, 2013. Print.
Nodelman, Perry. "The Eye and I: Identification and First-Person Narratives in Picture Books," *Children's Literature* 19 (1991), 1–30. Print.

_____. *Words about Pictures: The Narrative Art of Children's Picture Books*. Athens: University of Georgia Press, 1990. Print.
O'Connell, Jennifer. *Ten Timid Ghosts*. Chicago: Cartwheel Scholastic, 2000. Print.
Painter, Claire, J. R. Martin, and Len Unsworth. *Reading Visual Narratives: Image Analysis of Children's Picture Books*. Sheffield: Equinox, 2013.
Sagan, Carl. *The Demon-Haunted World: Science as a Candle in the Dark*. New York: Ballantine, 1997. Print.
Yannicopoulou, Angela. "Focalization in Children's Picture Books." *Telling Children's Stories: Narrative Theory and Children' Literature*, ed. Mike Cadden. Omaha: University of Nebraska Press, 2010. Print.
Yanof, Judith. "Books and Feelings: The Power of the Picture Book and the Inner Life of the Child—A Joint Conference by the Boston Psychoanalytic Society and Institute and PEN New England's Children's Book Caucus." Presented at the Boston Psychoanalytic Society and Institute. Boston, 19 Oct. 2002. http://robieharris.com/?page_id=145. Web.

About the Contributors

Simon **Bacon** is an independent scholar based in Poznan, Poland. He is working on a monograph, *Becoming Vampire*, and coediting *Growing Up with the Undead*.

Corwin R. **Baden** is completing Ph.D. coursework in English at Old Dominion University in Norfolk, Virginia. His research explores the alterity of Chinese miners in Ballarat, Australia, during the 1850s gold rush, which is also the basis for his novel, *So Much Depends*.

Rebecca A. **Brown** teaches college writing courses at North Seattle College. She is the coeditor of *Monsters and Monstrosity from the Fin de Siècle to the Millennium*. Her publications focus on monsters in picture books, evil children in horror cinema and ghosts in YA-fantasy novels.

Mariaelena **DiBenigno** is a Ph.D. candidate in American studies at the College of William & Mary in Williamsburg, Virginia. Her dissertation examines how certain narratives haunt public history sites.

Kelly F. **Franklin** is a full-time English instructor at Southwestern Community College in Creston, Iowa. She writes about young adult literature, popular culture, performance, queer theories and zombies.

Brenda S. **Gardenour Walter** is an associate professor of history at the St. Louis College of Pharmacy, St. Louis, Missouri. Her research examines the role of Aristotelian discourse, learned medicine, and scholastic theology in the construction of alterity and the continued influence of medieval otherness in supernatural horror.

Gerald Raymond **Gordon** is an associate professor in the Global English Department at Baika Women's University, Ibaraki, Osaka, Japan, where he teaches composition and cultural studies. He is also active as a poet, writer and improviser in music and visual arts.

Carla **Kungl** is an associate professor of English at Shippensburg University, Shippensburg, Pennsylvania, with interests in cultural studies, literature of the Victorian era and the fin de siècle, detective and other popular fiction and technical writing.

About the Contributors

Lisa **LeBlanc** is an associate professor of English at Anna Maria College in Paxton, Massachusetts. Her research interests include the intersection of literature and psychology.

Carla B. **Morrissey** is a librarian at the Mondor-Eagen Library at Anna Maria College in Paxton, Massachusetts. She is interested in the psychosocial variables related to the persistence and achievement of economically and educationally disadvantaged college students.

Melissa **Mullins** is finishing her dissertation for a Ph.D. at the University of Lausanne. Her research interests deal with the adaptation of French and German fairy tales into the 19th-century British state in burlesques, burlettas, and extravagances.

Leslie **Ormandy** teaches composition and English at a rural Oregon community college, and occasionally teaches courses on vampires in literature. Her research interests are monsters as they reflect modern culture in children's literature.

Lloyd Isaac **Vayo** is a lecturer in cultural studies and comparative literature at the University of Minnesota–Twin Cities. He has written extensively on 9/11 and terrorism, popular music and literature.

Holly A. **Wheeler** is a professor of literature and writing at Monroe Community College in Rochester, New York, where she teaches courses in children's literature, detective fiction, American literature and advanced writing. Her research interests include dystopian children's fiction, female super heroes and action figures.

Index

Abominable Snowman 16
acceptance 8–11, 66, 74–75, 110, 115–116, 122, 195–196, 206, 212, 228, 231
adaptation 53, 143–144, 147–148, 152, 154, 156, 174, 189, 242
ADHD 51, 62
agency 10, 34, 38, 45, 51, 123–124, 127, 137, 145, 210
agenda 1, 65–66, 70, 145, 196, 204
alterity 179, 196, 206, 231, 238, 241
anthropomorphism 65
Anti-Oedipus 96, 100–101, 108
anti-Semitism 113–114, 119
Aquinas, Thomas 198–199
archetypes 33, 40, 46, 113–114, 119, 126, 128, 188
Ardam, Jacquelyn 22
Arthur (Arthurian legend) 34, 38
Asma, Stephen 25
Assimilation 1, 3, 66, 71–72, 94, 98–99, 103, 113–114, 118–119, 127, 134, 136, 144, 148, 162, 177, 179
Auerbach, Nina 123
augmentation 83
authority 4, 11, 41, 90, 94, 117, 130–132, 186, 196, 200, 202, 205

Bader, Barbara 164
Bakemono Zukushi 94
Baku 93
Basile, Giambatisto 145, 147, 153
Beauty and the Beast 60–61
Becker, Helaine 182, 189–190
bedrooms 218–220
Berenstain Bears 227–231, 235
Bettelheim, Bruno 33, 48, 55, 57–58, 213, 127–128, 138–139, 187, 193, 213, 223
Biddick, Kathleen 33, 39, 43
binary opposition 27, 133, 196, 198–199, 201, 204–205, 213
Block, Ernst 58–59
Blue Oni 96–97, 99–101–102, 106–108; *see also* Oni; Red Oni

Bodmer, George 19, 23
boundaries 11, 158, 159, 164, 165, 167, 169–172, 179–180, 181, 188, 191, 210, 214–215, 217–218, 221–222, 230
Bradley, Barbara, and Jennifer Jones 18, 29n3
Buddhism 95 108
bully 40, 69, 74, 126, 134–135, 233
Bunnicula: A Rabbits Tale of Mystery 115–116

Caldecott, Randolph 189
Caldecott Medal (Award) 75, 176–178, 186
capitalism 100
Carson, Rachel (*Silent Spring*) 46
Castle of Otranto 175
character development 3–4, 11, 12n1
Christianity 144, 149, 184
Coach Gill 129
Coats, Karen 28, 214, 242
Cohen, Jeffrey Jerome 2, 12, 15, 26–27, 43, 48n3, 88, 112–113, 149, 173n1, 210
Cold War 161–163, 165–166, 171
colonialism 8–9, 69, 112–113, 149
colonize 32, 34, 177
Comics Code Authority 186
compassion *see* empathy
Conservative Christianity 11, 195
consumerism 37, 38
Cosmology 93, 95, 196, 198, 201, 204–205
Count Orlock 119
Crain, Patricia 27
critical thinking 129, 133–134, 140, 164
Cross (Christian) 39, 179–180, 182–183
Cruikshank, George 147
Cyrus the Sea Serpent 158, 166–169

Darling, Lois, and Louis 158, 161, 162–166
David A. Carter 236–237
death 12, 34, 37, 42, 50, 85, 87, 89, 90, 95, 101, 133, 175–176, 179, 188, 191, 201, 206, 214, 226, 228, 231, 237–238
DeBord, Guy 182
Deleuze, Gilles 96, 100–101

243

244 Index

demons 21, 95–96, 99, 111, 149, 199–200, 206, 217
Derrida, Jacques 211, 215
desecration 181, 192
desire 21, 51, 57, 67, 87, 100–101, 104, 106, 108, 116, 148, 150, 166, 169, 182, 185, 192, 211, 217, 219, 222
deterritorialization 96, 101, 107–108
Dickens, Charles (Scrooge) 33–34
diegetic discourse 227
diet 116–117, 127
difference 102, 104–107, 105, 112, 116, 118–119, 123; see also "other"
dismemberment 35, 76
Disney, Walt 176
diversity 159
"Do Monsters Dream?" 25
Dr. Seuss 23, 32–33, 35–36, 38–44, 46, 48n4
Dr. Tallow 130
domestic space 181–182, 190, 210, 215–217, 223
Dracula 7, 10, 66, 110–117, 119, 185–188, 190
Dracula (book/film) 110
dreams 55–56, 93, 120, 220
Dreamworks 178
Duzer, Walk 176, 178

eco-criticism 8, 42
ecology 33, 38–40, 45–46, 47–48, 65
educate 65, 68; see also lesson; teach
embodiment 2, 226, 228, 238
Emmanuelle Eeckhout 227, 231, 234
empathy 10, 67, 71, 99, 161, 164, 167, 192, 195, 206
empowerment 160
enculturation see assimilation
equality 121, 195
ethnocentrism 67
eucatastrophic 177
Evangelical Christianity see Christianity
Eve Bunting 227, 230–231
exorcism 201–202
externalization 52–53, 62

fairytales 213
Falwell, Jerry 184
fear 8, 16, 21, 24–24, 27, 38, 40, 50, 58, 70, 73–75, 85, 94, 105, 111, 114, 146, 162, 173, 179, 185, 188–189, 191–192, 197, 202, 206, 214, 217, 220, 222, 232, 236
fee (fairy) 142–145
feminism 35, 127, 131–132 133, 136–137
Fisher King 34, 41
focalization 195–195, 205–206, 226–228, 235
Force, Charlotte Rose de la 145
Foucault, Michael 52
Frankenstein 65–66, 75, 173, 185,-187, 188, 190
Frau Gothel 144, 146, 148, 152–153

Freud, Sigmund 48, 55–58, 61, 100, 216
Fritz Freleng 38, 48ch2n4
Fulgham, Robert 64

Game of Thrones 35
Gannon, Susan R. 146–147
gender 8, 12, 35, 70, 78, 111, 133, 136–138, 152, 167, 186, 220
Gendron, Darren J. 24
ghosts 3, 11–12, 33, 35, 43, 82, 95, 122, 182, 184, 188–190, 192, 195, 197, 205–206, 211, 215, 222, 226–238
Ghosts in the House 189
ghouls 89, 180, 182, 186
Goldilocks 70–72
golem 178–183
Gothic 36, 44, 111, 116, 120, 122, 175, 177, 182–183, 186, 189, 197, 228, 235
green see ecology
Green Knight 38
Green Man 46
Grover 72–73
Gruesome and Bloodsocks 117
Guattari, Felix 96, 100–101, 102, 106–108

Halberstan, Judith 111
Halloween 120, 175–170, 183–185, 187–192, 197, 205, 226, 231
Hamada, Hirosuke 96, 98
Hampire 7
Hansel and Gretel 58, 149, 152
haunted houses 12, 175–177, 179, 186–188, 190
hauntology-211 215
"Hell Houses" 184
Henirich, Kramer 149
Heuscher, Julius 55
Historicism 8
Holiday, Jane 117
Household Stories 147
Hunt, Peter 148
Hunter, Lynn 21
hybrid 26, 93, 99, 159, 169, 174ch4n1
ID (Freud) 26, 187–188

identity 33, 44, 52, 61, 73–74, 98–100, 102, 106, 108, 110–111, 136, 138, 214, 219
ideology 64, 182, 196, 204
illustration 4–7, 10–12
imagination 25–28, 33, 35, 48ch2n3, 58, 78, 86, 88, 93–94, 112, 115, 122, 137, 158, 162–163, 166, 175, 196, 200, 205, 209–210, 213–215, 222, 230–231, 235
immigrant/immigration 68, 73, 112, 114, 117, 120
inclusion 69, 71, 74, 123, 196–197, 222
Indian Ocean 165
individuation 32–33, 41–42, 48
indoctrination 1, 4, 11, 25
instruction 9, 65
internalization 81, 88

Index 245

intertextual 7, 12, 34, 155
inversion 199–200
isolation 82, 114, 143
iteration 16, 80, 82–84, 165, 188

Jampire 10–11, 138–139
Japan 93–94
Japanese monsters 93, 94
Jung, Carl 33, 61, 127

kappa 92
Kohara, Kazuno 189

Lacanian 9, 23, 28
L'Engle, Madeleine 176
Lerkim 35–36, 39–41, 45, 47
lesson (teaching a) 46, 65, 78–79, 107, 130, 164, 211, 213, 230; *see also* educate; teach
Lewis, C.S. 176, 180, 184
Lewis, Patrick 22
life after death 206, 228
liminality 35
Lindsey, Hal 202
A Little Book of Monsters 21
Little Red Riding Hood 55, 173
Loch Ness Monster 164–165
The Lorax: book 9, 32–35, 38, 43–44; character 33–38, 40–41, 47
Luthi, Max 148
Lynch, P.J. 151
Lyons, Sherri Lynne 159–159

M Is for Monster: A Fantastic Creatures Alphabet 22
magic circle 197, 226
Magnus, Olaf 158–159, 168
Malleus Maleficarum 149
Martin, Bill, Jr. 228, 237–238
masculinity 122, 131, 133, 136, 138, 167
McGee, Ted 20
medieval 25, 32–35, 38–39, 42, 45–46, 93, 159–160, 165, 171–172, 184, 198–199
memory 55, 89–90, 112, 119, 121–123, 217
Missrule (Lord of, Time of) 185
The Monster Alphabet 15
The Monster at the End of the Book 72–74
monster experts 93
Mummy (book) 40, 127, 133, 135, 140; as creature 233
Mysteries of Udolpho 175

Napoli, Donna Jo 156
New World Order 202
NewAge boy 114, 133, 202, 204
Nig, Joseph 158
The Night Before Halloween (Book) 188
non-threat 22, 24, 72, 75
Nordelman, Perry 5–6, 80, 141, 163, 170
Nosferatu: A Symphony of Horror (film) 119
nuclear family 196, 201, 204

occult 146, 176, 183, 191, 197, 201
O'Connell, Jennifer 227, 231–232
Oedipal 56–58, 101
Ogata, Amy 162
ogress 11, 142–143, 147
Old Age Boy 134–135
Once-ler 32–41, 43–47
Once Upon a Time: On the Nature of Fairy Tales 148
Oni 10, 94–97, 100–103, 106; *see also* Blue Oni; Hamada; Red Oni
"Other" *as* outsider 8, 25, 38, 65, 67, 71–72, 74–75, 76n1, 96, 98–102, 143, 165, 167, 173, 195, 237; *see also* difference
ouroboros 37

patriarchy 117, 123–124
patriotism 196, 204
Patrosinella 145–146
Peet, Bill 158, 166
Pentamerone 147
Percival 40, 41,-42
Persinette 145
Phoneme 17, 19
pleasure principle 56
pop-up book 78, 80, 91, 100
post-colonialism 8, 23, 42, 69
post-modernism 12, 214–215
pseudo-encropresis (fecal soiling) 54, 62
psychoanalysis 57, 100, 183

race 9, 38, 43, 69, 111
racism 68, 75
radical inversion 199
Rapunzel: A Fairy Tale Adventure (book) 152
reality principle 56
Red Oni *96–99, 101–108*; *see also* Blue Oni; Oni; Red Oni
Red Oni Cried (book) 96, 100–101, 108; *see also* Blue Oni; Oni
religion 11, 51, 175, 177–180, 184, 187 191–192, 206
religious freedom *see* religion
resolution 127, 213, 231, 234
respect 53, 69, 98–99, 105, 128–129, 156, 161, 171, 180, 193, 195, 202, 203, 227, 231–232, 234–235
Rime of the Ancient Mariner 36, 37
Rossi, Francesca 151
Rough Rider 40
Ruth Brown 65

Santat, Dan 75
Sarbin, Theordore R. 62–63
Satan 114, 179, 183, 197–207
Satanic Panic 202
Satanic Rites of Dracula (film) 114
Satanic Ritual Abuse (book) 197, 205
Satanic Ritual Abuse (SRA psychology) 203–204
Satan's Underground (book) 203

246   Index

schizoanalysis 101
schizophrenia 100, 101 104, 106–109
Schultz, Friedrich 145
Sea Serpent 3, 8, 11, 158–174
The Sea Serpents Around Us (book) 130
security-oriented society 102
semiotics 6, 10, 13, 38, 224
Sendak, Maurice 8, 61, 63–64, 68–69, 172
singularity 99–100, 106
Sipe, Laurence 7, 12–13, 29, 81, 92, 216, 224
Sir Gawin and the Green Knight 38
skepticism 80, 227, 234
Sneaky Poo 54
social construct 2, 207
social norms 1, 94, 102–103, 108, 178, 222
socialization 3, 18, 128, 137, 159, 173
Society of Spectacle (book) 182
socio-politics 11, 55, 58
sorceress 11, 142–143, 145–149, 151, 153–155, 157, 206
soul 12, 38, 47, 95, 205, 226, 228, 231, 237–238
space, sacred 180–186, 188, 193
spectrality 210–211
spirituality 36, 95, 175–176, 181–183, 197, 201, 206, 208
Spradlins, Michael 15, 20
SRA *see* Satanic Ritual Abuse
stepmother 56–57, 59, 127, 143
stereotypes 70, 98, 99, 121, 123, 137, 150, 155, 166, 168–169
Stine, R. L 24
Stoker, Bram 10, 111–112, 124
Stone, John 72
stranger danger 76, 78, 88, 90, 115, 204
Stratford, Lauren 203
Structuralist 8, 25, 27, 63
Super Secret Monster Patrol (S.S.M.P., book) 123, 127, 130
superego 48, 56, 188
supertextual 9, 78, 81, 91
surrogate 11, 142–147, 149, 154–156
synergy 6–7, 12, 81, 217

Tea Party 196
teach 1, 3–4, 9, 12, 15, 18–19, 23–25, 29–30, 45–45, 51, 60, 64, 66, 68, 70, 74–77, 87, 90, 92, 94, 102, 127–133, 139, 166, 181, 192, 205, 211–212, 214, 224, 226–227, 232, 234; *see also* educate; lesson
Ten Timid Ghosts (Book) 189
territorialization 96, 98, 102–103
terror 44, 74, 78–79, 82–83, 94, 97, 104, 119, 180, 197, 202, 242

threat 42, 48, 55, 58, 66–70, 78–79–82, 83–85, 87–89, 90, 94, 103, 113–114, 116, 137, 159, 161–162, 168, 173, 177, 181, 183, 185, 191, 204; *see also* non-threat
tolerance 180, 183, 234
Tolkien, J.R.R. 33
trauma 39, 41, 56, 74, 79, 89, 90–91, 201
Tuan, Yi-Fu-214 217, 220, 222

uncanny 140, 216, 219, 221, 224
United Stated Department of Education 16

values 3,-4, 8, 11, 71, 98–99, 102, 108, 128,-129, 140, 166, 181–182, 192, 195–197
vampire 1, 3, 7, 10, 110–122, 138, 177, 186, 230, 232–233, 242
Vampires (Colin Hawkins and Jackie Hawkins) 118
violence 55, 57, 74, 85, 150, 159, 162, 170, 179, 186
Vlad the Drac 116–123

werewolves 27, 121–122, 187
White, Michael 52–54
Wicca 179, 183, 192–193
Willems, Mo 66, 699, 70–72
Williams, David 23, 27
Windling, Terry 144
wish projection 59
witch 3, 11, 27, 39, 46, 58–59, 61, 120, 127, 142–143, 145, 147, 148–155, 157, 176, 180, 184, 189–190, 193–195, 197, 199–200, 202, 205–206, 227, 232–233
witchcraft *see* witch
witchcraft treatises 200
Wolfman 187
Wormell, Chris 158, 169

xenophobia 73–76

Yaden, David 17–18, 21, 26
Yanov, Judith 79, 92
youth (Seuss's *Lorax*) 33, 36, 40–44

Zauberin 143–144, 146–147; *see also* witch; sorceress
Zell 156
Zen Buddhism 108
zero-focalization 228, 235
Zhihui, Fang 19
Zipes, Jack 58, 127, 144–145, 148
zombie 17, 29–30, 184, 187–188, 241

www.ingramcontent.com/pod-product-compliance
Lightning Source LLC
Chambersburg PA
CBHW051218300426
44116CB00006B/619